Henry Bronson

Papers of the New Haven Colony

Historical Society. Vol. 1

Henry Bronson

Papers of the New Haven Colony
Historical Society. Vol. 1

ISBN/EAN: 9783744734103

Printed in Europe, USA, Canada, Australia, Japan

Cover: Foto ©ninafisch / pixelio.de

More available books at **www.hansebooks.com**

PAPERS

OF THE

NEW HAVEN COLONY

HISTORICAL SOCIETY.

VOL. I.

NEW HAVEN:

PRINTED FOR THE SOCIETY.

1865.

At a meeting of the New Haven Colony Historical Society held Monday Evening, January 16, 1865, HENRY BRONSON, JAMES M. WOODWARD and HORACE DAY, were appointed a committee to superintend the publication of the papers read before the Society.

THOMAS J. STAFFORD, PRINTER.

CONTENTS.

RECORD OF THE ORGANIZATION

OF THE

NEW HAVEN COLONY HISTORICAL SOCIETY.

———•••———

At a meeting of the Court of Common Council of the city of New Haven, held at the City Hall, Monday evening, October 6th, 1862, the following memorial was presented:

"The subscribers, citizens of New Haven, respectfully represent, that in none of the towns within the limits of the ancient New Haven Colony does there exist any organization for the collection and preservation of books, maps, newspapers, pamphlets or other documents, or relics illustrating its past or its current history.

"Associations of this nature are common in other cities, and often subserve important public ends by the facilities they present for the determination of questions connected with boundaries, water courses, highways, municipal domain, &c., with the public health, with the increase of population, and with other subjects of importance to the general welfare. They further tend to cultivate a laudable spirit of attachment to the places of our birth or residence.

"An Association for such objects, open to all who may wish to unite with it, is proposed by a number of our citizens, on condition

1

that a room suitable for its purposes can be obtained in the new City Hall.

"The design of the Association is to vest in the city the ultimate ownership of such books, papers, &c., as they may collect; and they respectfully request the coöperation of the City and Town Authorities in the furtherance of this useful public project, by appropriating a suitable room in the City Hall for the use of the Association, when duly formed.

Thomas R. Trowbridge,	George H. Watrous,	James M. Woodward,
W. S. Charnley,	E. T. Foote,	Morris Tyler,
Chas. Atwater, Jr.,	Horace Day,	William Downes,
P. S. Galpin,	T. B. Townsend,	Chas. W. Allen,
J. S. Griffing,	E. K Foster,	A. McAlister,
Frederick Croswell,	J. T. Collis,	E. S. Quintard,
H. M. Welch,	G. H. Scranton,	Henry E. Pardee.
Lucius G. Peck,	Francis Wayland,	

"On motion of Councilman Watrous, the foregoing Memorial was referred to the Mayor and Aldermen, to confer with the Board of Selectmen of the Town, with power to grant the prayer of the petitioners, if, upon such conference, it should be deemed advisable."

Attested by WILLIAM DOWNES, *City Clerk*, in the Common Council Records, Vol. VIII., p. 307.

SATURDAY EVENING, October 11th, 1862.

"At a meeting of the Mayor and Aldermen of the City, and the Selectmen of the Town, held at the Mayor's office, to consider the petition of Thomas R. Trowbridge and others for the use of a room in the City Hall for the New Haven Historical Association, it was voted to grant the use of the room and vault on the third floor of the building, the same being over the Collector's office, for such use and purpose, so long as said City and Town have no occasion to occupy the same; it being understood that the City and Town shall be at no expense in fitting up said rooms."

Attested by Mayor H. M. WELCH, as one of the Committee, in Vol. I., p. 13, of the Records of the Mayor and Aldermen.

TUESDAY EVENING, October 21st, 1862.

At an informal meeting of signers to the foregoing memorial, held at No. 11, Leffingwell Building, Frederick Croswell, Esq., was appointed Chairman, and Horace Day, Esq., Secretary. On motion of James M. Woodward, Esq., the Chairman and Secretary were appointed a Committee to take such measures as may seem necessary, preliminary to a public meeting for the organization of a New Haven Colony Historical Society.

In accordance with such appointment, the Committee made arrangements for a meeting of gentlemen known to be interested in the formation of a Historical Society, to be held Monday Evening, October 27th, 1862.

MONDAY EVENING, October 27th, 1862.

The following named gentlemen met, by invitation, at the house of Wm. A. Reynolds, Esq., No. 20 Elm street. (The house stands on the home-lot and is built on the cellar of the dwelling of John Davenport, the first minister of New Haven.)

Wm. A. Reynolds,	E. Edwards Beardsley,	Pierrepont B. Foster,
Chas. Atwater, Jr.,	Henry Bronson,	Charles R. Ingersoll,
Leonard Bacon,	Frederick Croswell,	Samuel Punderson,
John W. Barber,	Horace Day,	Leonard I. Sanford.
Timothy Bishop,		

Mr. Reynolds was requested to preside. After a free interchange of views on the subject which had called them together, a Committee, consisting of Henry White, Esq., Leonard Bacon, D. D., Horace Day, Esq., Frederick Croswell, Esq., and Henry Bronson, M. D., were appointed to propose a plan for the organization of a Historical Society, and to call a public meeting of citizens, to whom such plan should be submitted for approval.

FRIDAY AFTERNOON, November 7th, 1862.

The Committee above named met at the office of Henry White, Esq., and having agreed upon Articles of Association, proper to be presented to the consideration of their fellow-citizens, issued through the several daily newspapers of the City the following call for a public meeting :

"NEW HAVEN HISTORICAL SOCIETY.

" At a meeting of gentlemen assembled at the house of Wm. A. Reynolds, Esq., the undersigned were appointed a Committee to prepare a plan for the organization of a Historical Society for the ancient Colony of New Haven, and to call a public meeting of citizens interested in the preservation of our local records and traditions to whom such plan should be submitted.

" In accordance with this appointment, the Committee give notice that such public meeting will be held this (Friday) evening, at $7\frac{1}{2}$ o'clock, at the office of the Mayor, to which all who are interested in the formation of the proposed Association are respectfully invited."

(Signed)   HENRY WHITE,
                  LEONARD BACON,
                  HORACE DAY,
                  FREDERICK CROSWELL,
                  HENRY BRONSON.

New Haven, Nov. 14th, 1862.

FRIDAY EVENING, Nov. 14th, 1862.

At a meeting of citizens called at the office of the Mayor, for the formation of a Historical Society, there were present

Harmanus M. Welch, Mayor,	Charles L. Chaplain,	Luzon B. Morris,
James F. Babcock,	William S. Charnley,	Frederick W. Northrop,
Leonard Bacon,	Horace Day,	William S. Porter,
E. Edwards Beardsley,	William Downes,	Samuel Punderson,
Sylvanus Butler,	Elial T. Foote,	William A. Reynolds,
Samuel C. Blackman,	William Goodwin,	William E. Sanford,
Fisk Parsons Brewer,	John C. Hollister,	Alfred Walker,
Henry Bronson,	Charles R. Ingersoll,	George H. Watrous,
Elisha Lord Cleaveland,	Henry C. Kingsley,	Henry White.

The meeting was called to order by Henry White, Esq. Mayor Welch was appointed Chairman, and Horace Day, Esq., Secretary. Mr. White stated the object for which the meeting had been called, and that the plan proposed by the Committee for the organization of a Historical Society was in the hands of the Secretary. It was ordered to be read, and was then taken up, article by article, and after amendments and additions, was adopted, as follows:

CONSTITUTION.

ARTICLE 1. This association shall be known as the New Haven Colony Historical Society.

ARTICLE 2. The object of the Society shall be to collect and preserve such books, pamphlets, newspapers, broadsides, maps, plans, charts, paintings, engravings, lithographs, and other pictorial representations; manuscripts, autograph letters, curiosities and antiquities of every kind as may be connected with or may illustrate the local history of the towns included within the ancient New Haven Colony; to preserve such traditions as now exist only in the memories of aged persons; to encourage historical and antiquarian investigation and to disseminate historical information.

ARTICLE 3. A President, Vice President, Secretary, Treasurer and an Advisory Committee of not less than ten members, shall be annually chosen on the last Monday of November.

ARTICLE 4. These officers shall together constitute a Board of Directors, who shall have charge of the collections made by the Society, shall provide regulations for their safety and proper use, and shall prepare business for the regular meetings of the Society.

ARTICLE 5. Any person may become a life member of the Society by the payment of twenty-five dollars; or an annual member by the payment of one dollar.

ARTICLE 6. The Mayor of the City of New Haven, the President of Yale College, and the Town Clerk of New Haven, shall be ex-officio members of the Advisory Committee; and the Aldermen of the City, and the Selectmen of the Town of New Haven, shall be ex-officio members of the Society.

ARTICLE 7. The Society shall hold its meetings on the last Monday evening of each alternate month, and at such other times as the Directors may appoint.

ARTICLE 8. The Collections made by the Society shall never be broken up by sale nor by division among its members, nor shall they ever be removed from New Haven; nor shall any article be exchanged or disposed of except by the unanimous vote of the Directors or by the consent of the donors.

ARTICLE 9. This Constitution, with the exception of the eighth Article, (which is of the nature of a contract,) may be altered or amended by a two-third vote of the members present at any annual meeting; *provided*, that notice of such amendment shall have been given at some meeting at least one month previous.

MONDAY EVENING, December 29th, 1862.

The following By-Laws, proposed by a Committee consisting of Rev. Dr. Beardsley, Henry White, Esq., and Charles R. Ingersoll, Esq., and recommended by the Directors, were unanimously adopted:

MEMBERS AND OFFICERS.

I. Life-members, wherever resident, and annual members residing within the limits of the ancient Colony, or the present County of New Haven, shall alone be entitled to vote in the meetings of the Society; and the term of all annual memberships shall expire with the Annual Meeting next after subscriptions are paid.

II. Honorary members may be chosen by ballot at a regular meeting of the Society, at which not less than ten members are present, upon nomination of the Directors; *provided*, such nominations shall have been made at a previous regular meeting. They shall consist of persons residing out of the Colony and County of New Haven, who may be distinguished for important public service to the cause of historic investigation and general literature.

III. The President shall preside at all meetings of the Society and of the Directors; shall call, by himself or the Secretary, special meetings, when required by five members, and shall deliver or make provision for an address at the Annual Meeting.

IV. The Secretary shall have custody of the files, records and seal of the Society, and shall keep an accurate journal of its proceedings, and also of the proceedings of the Directors.

V. The first elected member of the Advisory Committee shall conduct the correspondence of the Society.

VI. The Treasurer shall receive all fees for membership, and all other moneys due, and all donations or bequests of money made to the Society; shall pay upon the order of the President such accounts as may be approved by the Directors or the Society, and shall, at the Annual Meeting, render a minute statement of his receipts and disbursements, and of the property and debts of the Society, which statement shall be examined and audited by a Committee appointed at such meeting for that purpose.

VII. The Directors may appoint a Librarian and Curator, who

shall, under their supervision, arrange, protect and catalogue all books, pamphlets, manuscripts and other articles deposited in the rooms of the Society; and shall, before every Annual Meeting, make a full report to the Board of the condition of the library and collections.

VIII. The Directors shall provide for the reading of one or more papers upon historical subjects at each regular meeting of the Society; or for the delivery of a historical lecture—the manuscripts of which, with the consent of the authors, shall be owned and preserved by the Society.

IX. Committees on the various departments of the action of the Society may be appointed by the Directors to report, as the Board from time to time may prescribe.

MEETINGS.

X. The Directors shall meet on the last Monday evening of each alternate month, and at such other times as the President may specify; and five shall constitute a quorum.

XI. Notice of the Annual Meeting of the Society shall be given in one or more public prints; and in all meetings duly called and notified, ten members shall be a quorum for the transaction of any business.

XII The order of proceedings at the meetings of the Society shall be as follows:

1. To read the minutes of the preceding meeting.
2. To report donations.
3. To read letters received in correspondence.
4 To attend to unfinished business.
5. To receive written communications or lectures.
6. To receive verbal communications.
7. To transact miscellaneous business.

DONATIONS AND DEPOSITS.

XIII. All donations to the Society and deposits with the same, shall be entered in a book kept for that purpose, and reported to the next regular meeting of the Society, and proper written acknowledgments shall be made therefor.

XIV. Any alteration of these By-Laws may be made at a regular meeting of the Society, such alterations having been proposed at a previous meeting or by the Directors.

At a meeting of the Society, held March 30th, 1863, on motion of Hon. William W. Boardman, the officers were requested to take measures for obtaining a Charter for the Society, from the Legislature of the State. Henry White, Esq., and Charles R. Ingersoll, Esq., were appointed a Committee for this purpose, who subsequently presented the following Charter, as having been granted by the Legislature. It was accepted by a unanimous vote of the Society, at its Annual Meeting, November 30th, 1863.

CHARTER.

GENERAL ASSEMBLY OF THE STATE OF CONNECTICUT,
May Session, 1863.

Upon the petition of Henry White and others, showing that they, with sundry other persons, have formed a Society called The New Haven Colony Historical Society, for the collection, preservation, and publication of historical and genealogical matter relating to the early settlement and subsequent history, especially of New Haven and its vicinity, and incidentally of other portions of the United States; which object is deemed to be of public interest and utility; and praying for an act of incorporation for these purposes:—

Resolved by this Assembly, That Henry White, E. Edwards Beardsley, Leonard Bacon, Henry Bronson, William A. Reynolds, Thomas R. Trowbridge, Samuel Punderson, Frederick Croswell, Horace Day, Elial T. Foote, Henry C. Kingsley, Charles L. English, Elisha L. Cleaveland, Charles R. Ingersoll, and their associates, the present members of said Society, and their successors, be, and they hereby are constituted, a body corporate by the name of "The New Haven Colony Historical Society," and by that name shall have perpetual succession, shall be capable of suing and being sued, pleading and being impleaded, and also of purchasing, receiving, holding and conveying any estate, real or personal ; may have a common seal, and the same may change at pleasure ; may establish such rules and by-laws, not contrary to the charter or the laws of this State, as they may from time to time deem necessary or convenient, relating to the qualifications and admission of members, the times and places of meetings, the election of officers, and all other matters connected with the objects, membership, and government, of said corporation : *provided however*, that said corporation shall not hold, at any one time, real estate, the annual income of which shall exceed five thousand dollars.

And be it further resolved, That the President of Yale College, the Mayor of the City of New Haven, and the Town Clerk of the Town of New Haven, shall be, ex-officio, members of said corporation.

And be it further resolved, That said corporation shall meet once in each year for the election of a President, Secretary, Treasurer, and such other officers as may be designated, from time to time, by the rules and by-laws of said corporation : *provided however*, that in case of a failure to hold an annual meeting, or elect its officers, said corporation shall not thereby be dissolved ; but the officers of said corporation may and shall continue to exercise the powers and duties of their several offices, until others shall be duly appointed in their stead.

And be it further resolved, That the first meeting of said corporation shall be held in the City Hall, in New Haven, at such time as shall be designated by Horace Day, notice thereof being previously given in one or more newspapers printed in said New Haven: *provided however*, that this act shall be subject to be revoked or altered, at the pleasure of the General Assembly.

Approved, June 17th, 1863.

OFFICERS

OF

THE NEW HAVEN COLONY HISTORICAL SOCIETY,

ELECTED NOVEMBER 28th, A. D. 1864.

PRESIDENT,

HENRY WHITE.

VICE-PRESIDENT,

E. EDWARDS BEARDSLEY.

SECRETARY,

HORACE DAY.

TREASURER,

NATHAN PECK.

DIRECTORS.

LEONARD BACON,	WILLIAM A. REYNOLDS,
HENRY BRONSON,	SAMUEL PUNDERSON,
THOMAS R. TROWBRIDGE,	HENRY C. KINGSLEY,
ELIAL T. FOOTE,	ELISHA L. CLEAVELAND,
CHARLES L. ENGLISH,	JOHN W. BARBER,
CHARLES R. INGERSOLL,	HENRY DUTTON,
JAMES M. WOODWARD,	NATHANIEL A. BACON.

Curator and Librarian—JOHN T. COLLIS.

OFFICERS OF THE SOCIETY FROM ITS ORGANIZATION.

President,		*Secretary,*	
HENRY WHITE,	1862.	HORACE DAY,	1862.

		Treasurer,	
Vice President,		WILLIAM S. CHARNLEY,	1862–1863.
E. EDWARDS BEARDSLEY,	1862.	NATHAN PECK,	1863.

DIRECTORS.

LEONARD BACON,	1862.	SAMUEL PUNDERSON,	1862.
*FREDERICK CROSWELL,	1862–1863.	ELISHA L. CLEAVELAND,	1862.
HENRY BRONSON,	1862.	CHARLES R. INGERSOLL,	1862.
ELIAL T. FOOTE,	1862.	EDWARD H. LEFFINGWELL,	1863–1864.
WILLIAM A. REYNOLDS,	1862.	JOHN W. BARBER,	1864.
HENRY C. KINGSLEY,	1862.	JAMES M. WOODWARD,	1864.
THOMAS R. TROWBRIDGE,	1862.	HENRY DUTTON,	1864.
CHARLES L. ENGLISH,	1862.	NATHANIEL A. BACON,	1864.

Curator and Librarian—JOHN T. COLLIS, 1863.

* Deceased.

LIST OF MEMBERS

OF THE

NEW HAVEN COLONY HISTORICAL SOCIETY,

FROM ITS ORGANIZATION TO MAY, 1865.

——————◆◆◆——————

LIFE MEMBERS.

Henry White,....................	1862	John A. Davenport,‡..........	1862
Thomas R. Trowbridge,..........	"	Roger S. Baldwin,§.............	"
Charles L. English,.............	"	James M. Townsend,...........	"
Henry Bronson,.................	"	Henry Hotchkiss,...............	"
Leverett Candee,*..............	"	Erastus C. Scranton,...........	"
Eli Whitney,...................	"	Cornelius S. Bushnell,..........	"
James Brewster,................	"	Mary L. Hillhouse,.............	"
Joseph E. Sheffield,...........	"	James E. English,.............	"
Nathan Peck,..................	"	Lucius Hotchkiss,..............	"
Wm. W. Boardman,.............	"	Ezra C. Read,................	1863
Henry Trowbridge,.............	"	Richard S. Fellowes,..........	"
Hervey Sanford,...............	"	Nathan Beers Ives.............	"
Augustus R. Street,...........	"	William B. Goodyear,..........	1864
Pelatiah Perit,†..............	"		

——————

ANNUAL MEMBERS.

Luzon B. Morris............	From 1862	Leonard Bacon............	From 1862
Harmanus M. Welch,...........	"	James Mont. Woodward,........	"
Elial T. Foote,.................	"	William A. Reynolds,..........	"
James F. Babcock,.............	"	William Goodwin,.............	"
William Slater Charnley,........	"	Samuel C. Blackman,‖..........	"

—————————————————————————————————

* Deceased, 1865. † Ibid., 1864. ‡ Ibid., 1864. § Ibid., 1863. ‖ Ibid., 1864.

C. G. Bentel............	1862	Henry B. Harison............	1862
William E. Sanford,	"	Frederick W. J. Sizer,	"
Richard M. Clarke,	"	Henry B. Smith,	"
Charles R. Ingersoll,	"	William Fitch,	"
Wilson H. Clark,	"	Henry Peck,	"
Horace Day,	"	Philemon Hoadley §,	"
E. Edwards Beardsley,	"	Elihu Yale,	"
John W. Barber,	"	Chauncey Goodrich,	"
William S. Porter,	"	Sidney A. Thomas,‖	"
William Downes,	"	Theodore D. Woolsey,	"
Alfred Walker,	"	Henry E. Pardee,	"
Charles Atwater, Jr.,	"	George P. Fisher,	"
Elisha L. Cleaveland,	"	John B Robertson,	"
Frederick Croswell,*	"	John T. Collis,	"
Leonard J. Sanford,	"	Israel Harrison,	"
Minott A. Osborn,	"	Andrew L. Kidston,	"
William B. Baldwin,	"	Benjamin Silliman, Jr.,	"
Edwin A. Tucker,	"	Lemuel S. Punderson,	"
W. H. H. Blackman,	"	Howard Sherman,	"
George B. Bassett,	"	Charles N. Johnson,	"
James Gallagher,	"	George C. Dickerman,	"
Colin M. Ingersoll,	"	David L. Ogden,¶	"
Augustus Lines,	"	David W. Buckingham,	"
Henry S. Johnson,	"	Daniel Trowbridge,	"
Amos Townsend,	"	Susan Trowbridge,	"
Henry C. Kingsley,	"	Worthington Hooker,	"
Isaac Thomson,	"	Sherman W. Kuevals,**	"
Raymond A. White,	"	Daniel C. Gilman,	"
Walter Osborn,	"	William T. Eustis, Jr.,	"
Levi B. Bradley,	"	William C. Fowler,	"
Henry D White,	"	Alfred S. Monson,	"
Francis Wayland, Jr.,	"	William Johnson,	"
Austin A. Hill,	"	Stephen D. Pardee,	"
John S. Graves,	"	Leonard Bradley,	"
Ralph I. Ingersoll,	"	Noah Porter,	"
Ezekiel H. Trowbridge,	"	Edward E. Salisbury,	"
Gustavus R. Elliot,	"	Philos Blake,	"
Alexander McAlister,	"	Charles Thompson,	"
Samuel Punderson,	"	James M. Mason,	"
Phillip S. Galpin,	"	William W. Prescott,	"
Pierrepont B. Foster,	"	Charles Fabrique,	"
Benjamin Noyes,	"	William W. Rodman,	"
John B. Carrington,	"	John Ritter,	"
Charles Peterson,	"	Nathan H. Sanford,	"
Jonathan Knight,†	"	Samuel W. S. Dutton,	"
Tilton E. Doolittle,	"	Edward E. Atwater,	"
Charles S. A. Davis,	"	Henry T. Blake,	"
Marcus Merriman,‡	"	Gardner Morse,	"
Wilbur F. Day,	"	Benjamin Silliman,††	"
Nathaniel A. Bacon,	"	H. Odenkirchen,	"
George H. Watrous,	"	Andrew W. DeForest,	"
Sidney M. Stone,	"	Nathan Smith,	"
Henry Dutton,	"	Charles Hooker,‡‡	"
E. Hayes Trowbridge,	"	Samuel Hayes,	"
James M. Whiton,	"	S. J. Hayes,	"

---

* Deceased, 1863.   † *Ibid.*, 1864.   ‡ *Ibid.*, 1864.   § *Ibid.*, 1863.   ‖ *Ibid.*, 1865.
¶ *Ibid.*, 1863.   ** *Ibid.*, 1863.   †† *Ibid.*, 1864.   ‡‡ *Ibid.*, 1863.

Eleazer T. Fitch,..................1862	Frederick P. Gorham,............1862
Martha D. W. Reynolds,......... "	James Winship,.................. "
Harry Prescott,................. "	Henry O. Hotchkiss,............1863
Edwin Harwood,................ "	Thomas H. Totten,............. "
William L. Kingsley,........... "	John M. Garfield,............. "
Thomas H. Pease,.............. "	Wyllys Peck,.................. "
Samuel Noyes,................. "	Fisk P. Brewer,............... "
Lucius Gilbert,................ "	Edward C. Beecher,........... "
Spencer T. Parmelee,.......... "	Arthur D. Osborne,........... "
Amos F. Barnes,... .... "	Caleb Mix,................... "
Edward H. Townsend,.......... "	S. Bryan Jerome,............. "
Charles A. Lindley,........... "	E. Whitney Blake,............ "
Edward H. Leffingwell,........ "	Fordyce Beals,............... "
John P. Atwater,.............. "	Beriah Bradley,.............. "
Samuel P. Bowles,............. "	Nathaniel Jocelyn,............1864
John H. Benham,.............. "	William C. DeForest,.......... "
W. R. H. Trowbridge,.......... "	Eli S. Quintard,.............. "
Edwin Marble,................ "	Charles Peck,................ "
Lucien W. Sperry,............. "	Daniel G. Phipps,............ "
Charles H. Bunce,............. "	Charles W. Allen,............ "
David J. Peck,.. .... "	Henry O. Beach.............. "
Henry B. Oatman,....... ..... "	Milton S. Leonard,........... "
Nathaniel F. Thompson,........ "	William R. Shelton,.......... "
Benjamin F. Mansfield,........ "	Jonathan W. Pond,........... "
E. Huggins Bishop,............ "	Gideon O. Hotchkiss,......... "
William B. DeForest,.......... "	Noyes C. Mix,............... "
Patrick Morrissy,............. "	Atwater Treat,............... "
Thomas N. DeBowes,.......... "	Edward Downes,............. "
William B. Bristol,..... ...... "	Robert Blair,................ "
Louis H. Bristol,............. "	Horace C. Peck,............. "
Simeon E. Baldwin,........... "	Charles Nicoll,.............. "
Elam Hull, Jr.,............... "	Henry Champion,............ "
Ruel P. Cowles,.............. "	Samuel Mallett,............. "
Elias Pierpont,............... "	Ralph D. Smith............. "
Henry Trowbridge, 2d,........ "	Daniel W. Lathrop,.......... "
John E. Earle,............... "	Henry Wadsworth,........... "
Morris Tyler,... .... "	Ira Merwin,................. "
S. Dryden Phelps,............ "	Levi Ives,................ "
David A. Tyler............... "	James N. Palmer,............ "
Norton J. Buel,*........ :..... "	David T. Hotchkiss,.......... "
Joseph Sheldon,.............. "	Charles Robinson,........... "
Amos Gilbert,................ "	James W. Goodrich,.......... "
George H. Scranton,.......... "	E. Peck................... "
John S. Beach,............... "	George Gill,................ "
Edward I. Sanford,........... "	Willis M. Anthony,.......... "
Samuel Rowland,............. "	Alfred Daggett,............. "
Sidney M. Stone,............. "	Hiram Stevens,............. "
Robert H. Osborn,............ "	

* Deceased, 1864.

THE NEW HAVEN COLONY.

By HENRY WHITE, Esq.,

PRESIDENT OF THE SOCIETY.

The ancient Colony of New Haven is the special, although not the only field of labor of this Historical Society. In consequence of the early absorption of the Colony into Connecticut, and the obliteration of much of its boundary line, there is an indistinctness in the conceptions even of many intelligent persons, in relation to its peculiar characteristics as a colony, as well as to its geographical limits. It may be that some who live on its soil, and are *colony born* and lineal descendants of its ancient worthies, are ignorant that there ever existed such an independent government. For the purpose of removing some of this indistinctness of conception, it is proposed in this paper to give a brief account of the origin of the Colony, its organization, and the arrangement and limits of its territory.

In all these respects, the New Haven Colony differed somewhat from the other three New England colonies with which it was confederated. It was the youngest sister of this first Anglo-American family of States. In its origin it had no organized connection with any chartered company or commercial association in England, nor with any earlier colony in America.

In its construction it was not coeval with the settlement of its territory; and its constituent parts were not the products of the growth and development of the primary settlement, but were, for the most part, separate organized bodies called plantations, which by their combination constituted the Colony. In the arrangement of its territory it was not compact; but was composed of three disconnected tracts, separated from each other by intervening portions of another colony, or by a wide body of water. The similarity of their plantation organizations, and the identity of their views of the most desirable pattern for government in church and state, rendered the fusion of these scattered settlements into one colony, under the pressure of outward danger, easy and for a time perfect. Until just before its dissolution, there were no symptoms of any want of strength or vigor in its government. It compelled as entire obedience to all its laws at home, and moved as promptly and efficiently in all its external relations, as any of its sister colonies. But the secession of some of these plantations, which, under the management of their neighbor of Connecticut, preceded and made inevitable the dissolution of the Colony, was probably effected more easily by reason of these peculiarities in its formation and territory. Three of these plantations, New Haven, Milford and Guilford, were undoubtedly the result of a united simultaneous effort in England, for the common objects of a united emigration and of a contiguous settlement. The agricultural portion of these emigrants came mostly from the three English counties of Yorkshire, Hertfordshire and Kent. It is not an improbable conjecture that before they left England they were arranged by these affinities into three companies—the Yorkshire men, for the most part, uniting with the London merchants and tradesmen who settled New Haven—the Hertfordshire men forming the bulk of the company which settled Milford—and the Kentish men going in a body to Guilford. The careful reader of the early records of the colony will find many things which favor this hypothesis.

The Colony of New Haven, or the New Haven Jurisdiction, as it was more frequently called, was composed of six distinct plantations, combined in one jurisdiction or government, namely, New Haven, Milford, Guilford, Stamford, Southold (L. I.) and Branford. Five of these plantations were settled before the body politic, called the colony, was formed. A brief sketch of the formation of each of these six plantations will throw light upon the character of the colony which was formed by their combination.

The main body of the settlers arrived in the harbor of New Haven in April, 1638, and remained about fifteen months without a formal civil or ecclesiastical organization. They had recognized and solemnly affirmed certain general principles which were to govern their political and ecclesiastical institutions, and they entered into covenant with each other, that their organizations when formed should conform to these principles. The Guilford company joined them in the spring of 1639. During this long interval, the chrysalis period of their life as a church and state, they accomplished the selection and purchase from the Indian tribes of the territory which they needed for their habitation. In these transactions each company acted separately, although sojourning together. The Indian deed of New Haven, at first called Quinnipiac, was made to Theophilus Eaton, John Davenport, and others, November 24, 1638, and a second deed of a tract on the north of the first purchase, was made to the same persons December 11, 1638. The Indian deed of Milford, at first called Wepowauge, was made to William Fowler, Edmond Tapp, Zechariah Whitman, and others, February 12, 1639. The Indian deed of Guilford, at first called Menunkatuck, was made to Henry Whitefield, Robert Kitchell, William Leete, and others, September 29, 1639.

The title to the territory being acquired, the next step was to organize these three companies as political and ecclesiastical bodies. The New Haven company was the first to move. The preliminary meeting was held in June, 1639. The organization of the church, according to a tradition preserved in Trumbull's History of Connecticut, was completed August 22, 1639. The organized action of the civil community commenced October 25, 1639. In all these proceedings of the New Haven company, the members of the Milford and Guilford companies took no part, although they were then residing in New Haven.

The Guilford company removed to their purchase in August, 1639, and the Milford company to theirs in November, 1639, and each company, immediately on entering on the occupation of its territory, commenced its distinct and independent organized action. Thus at the close of the year 1639, three independent civil and ecclesiastical communities had begun to live and grow on the north shore of Long Island Sound—alike in the fundamental, political and religious principles on which their organizations rested, and alike in the methods by which they were expecting to strengthen and build upon these foundations.

The fourth plantation of the combination was Stamford, at first called Rippowams. It commenced its life as an organized community in the spring of 1641. Its territory was purchased from the Indian claimants by the planters of the New Haven plantation, in July, 1640; and in October, 1640, was sold by them to a company composed principally of dissatisfied members of the Wethersfield church, who removed to Stamford early in 1641. At first they were a constituent part of the New Haven plantation. Such planters as were qualified, were admitted as freemen of the New Haven plantation, and voted in New Haven whenever they were able to be present at the elections. The magistrates and other civil officers of Stamford were chosen at the elections in New Haven, or appointed by the courts there. The church at Stamford was, however, entirely distinct from the church in New Haven.

Greenwich was an appendage to Stamford. Its territory was purchased from the Indians by Robert Feake and Captain Patrick, in 1640, with the intent, as was claimed by the people of New Haven, of annexing it to New Haven. But the first planters, under the guidance of Capt. Patrick, endeavored, in 1642, to put themselves under the jurisdiction of the adjacent Dutch government of New Amsterdam. In 1650 the territory was ceded by the Dutch to the New Haven Colony. Its inhabitants at first refused submission; but in 1656 they acknowledged the authority of the New Haven Jurisdiction, and became a part of the plantation of Stamford.

The fifth plantation was Southold, on Long Island, at first

called Yennicock. This place came into notice as a civil community in April, 1642. Its territory was purchased from the Indian tribes in the summer of 1640, by the New Haven plantation, and was settled by a company from Hingham, in the county of Norfolk, in Old England. Like Stamford, it was for a time a constituent part of the New Haven plantation. The inconvenience of attending the general courts in New Haven from Southold, was no greater than from Stamford. The title to its territory was not formally conveyed to the planters of Southold until the 25th of June, 1649.

These five plantations, New Haven, Milford, Guilford, Stamford and Southold, were the original, component parts of the New Haven Colony. Branford, at first called Totokett, the sixth plantation of the combination, was not organized as a civil community until 1644, the year after the Colony commenced its political existence. The territory of Branford was for the most part included in the second purchase made by the New Haven planters from the Indians, in December, 1638. There was an abortive attempt in 1640 to establish a settlement there, by Rev. Samuel Eaton, a brother of Theophilus Eaton. After its failure, the territory of Totokett was again sold by the New Haven planters to William Swaine and others, from Wethersfield, who, in consequence of the continued difficulties in the church there, had determined to seek a new home. They were joined in 1644 by the church of Southampton, on Long Island, under the guidance of Rev. Abraham Pierson. Upon the union with Connecticut, this church, with its pastor, removed again, to Newark, in New Jersey, for the same reasons which had led to their former removal to Branford. They wished to be free to carry out their cherished plan of a pure church and a godly government, in the ways they judged best adapted to that end—and one of their ways, not the least in importance in their judgment, was, to restrict all political power to members of the church. Connecticut would receive no such plant among her vines. It was in truth an exotic in our fallen world; and when transplanted again, found the soil of New Jersey not a whit more favorable to its growth and development than that of Connecticut.

2

From this account of the origin of the six plantations which composed the Colony of New Haven, it appears that no one of them can be considered as properly an off-shoot or growth from the New Haven plantation. The territory of the last three was indeed purchased by the New Haven plantation, and no doubt for the express purpose of promoting the settlement of planters of like principles with themselves in church and state; but in every instance the planters who formed the settlements were not, in any appreciable number, colonists from the New Haven company. They were bodies of men already associated, to some extent, before they came into the neighborhood of New Haven. Only one colony, strictly so called, was attempted by the New Haven people. This enterprise was in 1641, at Delaware Bay. Land was purchased from the Indians on both sides of the Delaware river, and a settlement commenced on the east side, at a place now called Salem, in the southern part of the State of New Jersey. A number of families removed thither from New Haven. A few months, however, after they landed, they were dispersed and compelled to abandon the settlement by a combined force of the Dutch and Swedes, both of whom claimed the territory. The parent plantation at New Haven was too distant to give them timely support, and the two colonies of the Dutch and Swedes, although jealous of each other, were more jealous of these enterprising English settlers. This first disaster occurred in 1642. About two years afterward, a second attempt was made. A vessel was sent from New Haven with another colony, destined for the same place; but on its way thither, incautiously entering the port of New Amsterdam, for the purpose of completing its outfit, it was seized by the Dutch government of that colony as soon as its destination was discovered, and was compelled to return to New Haven, with considerable loss of property. Ten years after this, in 1654, a movement was again made in New Haven to fit out another expedition to the same place, with a third colony, and leave was given to the Deputy Governor and one of the military officers of the place to go with them; but the report of a considerable addition to the numbers and strength of the Swedish colony on the Delaware, discouraged the adventurers, and the scheme was then finally abandoned. The first colony, in 1641, did not remain long enough to be organized as a distinct plantation, or even to acquire a distinctive name. Its only appellation was, "The settlement at Delaware," or "at Delaware Bay."

The combination of the six plantations into the New Haven Colony or Jurisdiction occurred in the same year with the Confederation of the four New England Colonies of Plymouth, Massachusetts, Connecticut and New Haven, and was brought about by the pressure of the same danger from without. The report of combinations among the Indian tribes for the purpose of destroying the English settlements had occasioned great alarm, which was increased by the suspicion that the French were instigating these movements. To meet this danger, the Confederation of the four colonies was formed May 19, 1643. The combination of the plantations around New Haven commenced about April, 1643, and was completed in October of the same year.

The first allusion on our record to such an union is on the 6th of April, 1643, when Mr. Eaton and Mr. Gregson were appointed by the General Court of the New Haven Plantation, commissioners for the Jurisdiction of New Haven, to go to Massachusetts to treat about the Confederation. The word jurisdiction in this record describes what was expected rather than what was accomplished. The New Haven plantation, with its dependencies of Stamford and Southold, might, with some propriety, assume this name; but it is altogether probable that there was already an understanding among the leading men in the independent plantations adjacent to New Haven that this union was to take place. Without such an understanding, the New Haven plantation could not have expected to be admitted even as a contracting party in the Confederation, much less to have had an equal voice with Massachusetts, Connecticut and Plymouth in the great questions of making war, raising armies, and negotiating treaties, which were expected to form no inconsiderable part of the business of the alliance. In July, 1643, Guilford became formally a member of the New Haven Jurisdiction, and about the same time, probably a little earlier, Stamford and

Southold ceased to be constituent parts of the New Haven plantation, and took the position of distinct plantations and members of the Jurisdiction. But the completion of the combination was delayed until October by a difficulty with Milford, which had not built its little State squarely on the foundation which the other plantations deemed so essential, and which was supposed to have been secured by their preliminary covenants. Milford had conferred the privilege of voting and holding office on a few who were not in church fellowship. A compromise was however effected, by which the freemen already admitted in Milford, in deviation from this fundamental rule, were to continue to vote in all meetings within that plantation on matters relating solely to that plantation, but were excluded from voting on matters pertaining to the Jurisdiction, and from holding any public trust for the Jurisdiction ; and no one was thereafter to be admitted a freeman except in conformity with the fundamental rule.

On the 27th of October, 1643, the constitution of the New Haven Colony was formally settled and adopted by the five plantations then existing. A few months later, in 1644, Branford, which was then first organized as a plantation, was added to the number, and completed the Colony. The inchoate state of the Colony in May, 1643, when the articles of confederation of the four colonies were signed, is recognized in the language used in the caption of those articles to describe the contracting parties. The colony of Massachusetts was styled "Plantations under the government of Massachusetts," and so Connecticut and Plymouth were respectively described; while New Haven is called the Government of New Haven, with the Plantations in combination with it. But after October, 1643, the New Haven Colony could have been appropriately described in the same terms as the others, viz., as Plantations under the government of the New Haven Jurisdiction.

As thus completed the New Haven Colony remained an independent and efficient body politic, not behind its sister colonies in influence and importance, or in the worth and ability of its public men, until its forced dissolution on the 13th of December, 1664.

The exact limits of the Colony cannot now be easily determined, in consequence of the changes which have occurred from time to time in the boundary lines of the towns in our State. An approximation can however be made.

The territory of the Colony was composed of a central and principal portion, and of two outlying tracts on the east, and on the west, nearly equi-distant from the central portion, and separated from it, the one on the east, by the waters of Long Island Sound, and the one on the west, by an intervening portion of the colony of Connecticut.

The central and largest portion comprised the principal part of the present county of New Haven, but did not extend as far northward. The following towns of the county of New Haven were not within the limits of the colony :—Southbury, Middlebury, Waterbury, Wolcott and Meriden. A portion of the following towns of the county were outside of the limits of the colony : Oxford, Naugatuck, Prospect and Cheshire. The south west part of Durham, now in the county of Middlesex, was included in the colony of New Haven.

The present townships of New Haven County, which were within the bounds of the New Haven Colony, may be arranged in three tiers—the southern on the shore of the Sound, the central and the northern. Beginning at the west side of the county and proceeding eastward, the southern tier includes Milford, Orange, New Haven, East Haven, Branford, Guilford and Madison.

The central tier includes Derby, Seymour, Woodbridge, Bethany, Hamden, North Haven and North Branford.

The northern tier includes part of Oxford, part of Naugatuck, part of Prospect, the largest part of Cheshire, the whole of Wallingford and a small part of Durham.

The western outlying territory comprises the present townships of Greenwich, Stamford, Darien, and the west part of New Canaan.

The eastern outlying territory on Long Island comprises the present townships of Southold and Riverhead, except the islands of Plum Island, the Gulls and Fishers Island, which now belong to the town of Southold, but were not included in the Colony.

Such, in its origin, in its organization and in its territory, was the old Colony of New Haven; whose work in helping to lay broad and deep the foundations of our free and beloved country we honor, and the memorials of whose departed worthies we gather and with pious care preserve.

READ DECEMBER 29, 1862.

CIVIL GOVERNMENT IN THE NEW HAVEN COLONY.

By Rev. LEONARD BACON, D. D.

READ JANUARY 26, 1863.

————◆◆◆————

WE commonly date the commencement of the New Haven Colony in the month of April, 1638,—the 15th day of that month (in the old style) being identified as the first Christian Sabbath kept here by a worshiping assembly. The company of emigrants who kept that Sabbath on a little knoll close by the creek, in what is now George street, had sailed from Boston on the 30th of March, the most of them having arrived at that port in two ships, (one of them the Hector,) probably chartered by themselves, on the 26th of June, 1637. They had emigrated from England not as individuals and families looking for new homes, but in a body, and with the purpose of establishing a community by themselves. England had become an uncomfortable residence for men of their opinions on the religious, ecclesiastical, and political questions of the times; and impelled by the same motives which brought over to this country more than twenty thousand English emigrants in the twelve years from 1628 to 1640, they had undertaken to do their part towards making a new and better England on this side of the Atlantic. Not acting under any commission or charter from the English crown, or from any other human authority, they considered themselves at liberty to institute for themselves, by mutual agreement and compact, such government as should be in their judgment best suited to the ends for which they had emigrated from their native country.

Our President, in the valuable paper which he read to us a month ago, gave us all the information that can now be had concerning the arrangements under which the founding of this new Colony was attempted. That paper suggests the correction of an error into which the historians have naturally fallen.* In a meeting of the free planters, on the 4th of June, 1639, for the purpose of founding the civil and ecclesiastical institutions of their Colony, reference was made, (as the record incidentally shows,) to a provisional arrangement under which they had previously acted. The words of the record are, " Whereas there was a covenant solemnly made by the whole assembly of free planters of this plantation, the first day of extraordinary humiliation which we had after we came together," &c. Afterwards, it is said, " this covenant was called a plantation covenant, to distinguish it from a church covenant, which could not at that time be made, a church not being then gathered." It has been inadvertently assumed that the phrase " after we came together " has the same meaning as if it had been " after we came to this place." The agreement or formal contract, whatever it was called, under which they enlisted in their enterprise, must have been made before they sailed from London. Having neither charter nor commission from any superior authority, and acting simply as a voluntary association or copartnership, they must have had articles of agreement—something in the nature of a constitution and by-laws for the transaction of their business as a company. Their mutual contract, binding them to what they knew would be a costly and hazardous undertaking, must have had some provision for obtaining the necessary capital, and must have defined the rights and powers both of the company and of the several stockholders or adventurers. It must have defined the method in which the business of the partnership should be conducted, who should be trustees or managers, and what should be the form and manner of their responsibility to the company. If their compact contemplated originally the possibility of their planting themselves on territory not covered by the chartered government of Massachu-

* Trumbull, I., 97.

setts, it must have included some plan for at least a provisional government of their Colony in that contingency. Business men of large experience, like Eaton, Gregson, Goodyear, and others, would hardly have engaged in an enterprise requiring a capital of £36,000—certainly they would not have hazarded in it all their dearest earthly hopes—without some well-considered and definite contract among the partners.

The "plantation covenant" mentioned in the record to which I have referred, seems to have been a religious agreement additional to their original compact as a business copartnership. It may have been made after the company, with the reinforcements which it gathered in Massachusetts, had actually "come together" for their migration to this place. In such circumstances, they would of course find a scriptural precedent for a "day of extraordinary humiliation" before their embarkation. The example of Ezra was before them—the same example which John Robinson and the pilgrims of Leyden had imitated before the embarkation on the Speedwell at Delft-Haven, when Robinson preached from the words, (Ezra viii. 21,) "Then I proclaimed a fast there at the river of Ahava, that we might afflict ourselves before our God, to seek of him a right way for us, and for our little ones, and for all our substance." It is a curious coincidence, and perhaps not absolutely undesigned, that as Ezra (viii. 31) and his company "departed from the river of Ahava on the twelfth day of the first month, to go unto Jerusalem;" so the farewell letter to the government of Massachusetts, subscribed by Davenport and Eaton, in behalf of their associates, is dated "the 12th day of the first month." Among the solemnities of their "day of extraordinary humiliation," wherever it may have been kept, was an act of religious covenanting. That act was in some sort a substitute for the formal covenant by which a Congregational church is constituted, and which every member takes upon himself at his admission to full communion. For reasons which to them seemed conclusive, but which are unknown to us, a church could not be constituted at that time. In some instances a company of emigrants became a church, in the Congregational way, before leaving England, and came across the Atlantic with their ec-

clesiastical institutions already organized.* This was done by
the company who settled the town of Windsor:—they formed
their church at Plymouth, in England, the place of their ren-
dezvous and embarkation, on a day set apart for fasting and
prayer, (which they doubtless would have described as "the
first day of extraordinary humiliation which we had after we
came together;") and as a church, with pastor and teacher, they
came first to Dorchester, in Massachusetts, in 1630, and five
years afterwards removed to Windsor. But for some reason
"the free planters" of Eaton's company judged it impracticable for them to constitute a church "the first day of extraordinary humiliation which they had after they came together,"
(whether in England or in Massachusetts;) and therefore, as
Christian men, they formed, with religious solemnities, a sacred
compact, which "was called a plantation covenant to distinguish it from a church covenant which could not at that time
be made."

The purport of the plantation covenant—though not a formal copy of it—is distinctly given in the record. It is in these
words: "That as in matters that concern the gathering and
ordering of a church, so likewise in all public offices which
concern civil order, as choice of magistrates and officers, making
and repealing of laws, dividing of allotments of inheritance,
and all things of like nature, we would all of us be ordered by
those rules which the Scripture holds forth to us." Obviously,
this is more like a provisional church covenant, than it is like
a provisional arrangement for the civil government of their
Colony. It is nothing else than a religious bond, by which
they promised each other, with solemn vows to God, that in
the work before them of founding a church and a state, they
would be guided by the rules of duty given in what they unanimously recognized as the word of God. As Christian men,
holding in the memorable words of Stillingfleet, that "the
Bible alone is the religion of Protestants," they were to be
governed by the Bible, both "in matters that concern the gathering and ordering of a church," and "likewise in all public
offices [duties] which concern civil order." They made a sol-

---

* Contributions to Ecclesiastical History of Conn. 511.

emn covenant with each other and with God, that in choosing
their magistrates and officers, in making and repealing laws for
the government of their civil commonwealth, and in the parti-
tion and tenure of real estate, (which I understand to be the
meaning of the phrase "dividing allotments of inheritance,
and all things of like nature,") they would, individually, ["all
of us,"] be governed—not merely by religious motives and im-
pulses—but by such "rules" as were given to them in the
Bible, which was their religion. How far they understood,
and in what respects they misunderstood the Bible as a rule of
duty, it would be aside from my present purpose to inquire.
But I may say that when they covenanted to govern themselves in all their work of founding a Christian church and a
Christian state by those rules of duty which they should find
in the Scriptures of the Old and New Testaments, they only
professed distinctly and explicitly what all Christian men profess implicitly. Our age is doubtless much more enlightened
than theirs; but even in this age the man who would profess
that his religion is purely ecclesiastical, and has no control over
his conduct as a member of society and an elector in a self-gov-
erned commonwealth, would be regarded in all churches of all
denominations as a very scurvy Christian at the best.

The provisional government, then, under which the Colony
continued for more than a year after the landing in April,
1638, was not constituted by the "plantation covenant," but
must have been arranged in the original agreement, or articles
of copartnership under which the "free planters" associated in
England. So far as I am informed, only two documents are
now in existence from which we can make any inference concerning that provisional government. The first is the farewell
letter, already referred to, which was addressed to the government of Massachusetts eighteen days before the company set
sail from Boston for "the parts about Quillypieck," and which
being evidently, though not formally, written in the name of
the company, is subscribed by John Davenport and Theophilus Eaton, as if they had authority to speak for the rest.* The

---

* Savage's Winthrop, I., App. G, p. 484.

other is the deed—or rather two deeds—by which the Indians of this place and its vicinity ceded their ownership of the soil, (whatever it may have been.) One of those deeds is entitled, "Articles of agreement between Theophilus Eaton and John Davenport and others, English planters at Quinopiocke, on the one party," and a certain "Indian Sachem of Quinopiocke" and his counselors (whose names are of little consequence to us) "on the other party." The other is in like manner entitled "Articles of agreement betwixt Theophilus Eaton, John Davenport, and sundry other English planters at Quinnypiork, on the one part," and a native chief on the other part.* It seems then that the power of speaking in behalf of "the free planters" as a company, and of purchasing land for them and entering into stipulations and contracts with the natives, was chiefly in the hands of those two men. In all respects Eaton was the natural and proper leader of the enterprise, considered as a commercial adventure or as a political experiment. His eminence as a London merchant, his public service as representative of King Charles I., at the court of Denmark, and his former relation to the Massachusetts Colony as one of the Assistants or Directors before the charter of the corporation was brought over from England to this country, made him, in all commercial and civil respects, the most conspicuous man in the company. His share in the capital of the company was three times greater than that of any other partner, being £3,000, or one-twelfth of the whole. Davenport was one of the nine whose shares in the capital of the company were each £1,000; and his superiority of learning and talents, as well as his conspicuousness as vicar of a metropolitan parish, and as a leader of the Puritan party in the Church of England, made him as naturally and fitly the ecclesiastical leader of the enterprise. The power of acting for the company, and probably of directing their affairs, seems to have been chiefly in the hands of these two men—though limited, no doubt, by the articles of agreement, and limited, of course, by the necessity of constant consultation with their associates. We cannot presume that the general meeting of the free plant-

---

* Col. Rec., I., 1-7.

ers, on the fourth of June, 1639, was the first meeting of the kind.

But whatever that provisional government was, the free planters seem to have been in no haste to get rid it. It was not till the 25th of October, 1639, when the planters had occupied their purchased territory more than eighteen months, that the new civil government was completely instituted and formally installed. The meeting of June 4th, (commonly spoken of as the meeting in Mr. Newman's barn,) was "a meeting to consult about settling civil government according to God, and about the nomination of persons that might be found by consent of all fittest for the foundation work of a church." As we read the record of that meeting, so carefully and clearly written, whatever may be our disposition to find fault, we cannot but admire the distinctness, the deliberateness, and the unanimity of the proceedings. The result may be summed up thus: First, the free planters, without a dissenting vote, though not without discussion, adopted what was afterwards called the Fundamental Agreement,—"namely, that church members only shall be free burgesses,—and they only shall choose among themselves magistrates and officers to have the power of transacting all public civil affairs of this plantation, of making and repealing laws, dividing inheritances, deciding of differences that may arise, and doing all things and businesses of like nature." Secondly, twelve men (or, as their names are given on the record, eleven) were chosen to designate from among themselves, or from among others whom they should publicly nominate as candidates for that trust, the seven founders of the church and of the state. The act of those seven in founding the church, was to make them free burgesses in the commonwealth; and they were to choose other free burgesses "out of the like estate of church fellowship."

On the 25th of October "those seven only who were in the foundation of the church, namely, Mr. Theoph. Eaton, Mr. John Davenport, Mr. Robt. Newman, Mr. Math. Gilbert, Tho. Fugill, John Punderson, and Jeremy Dixon," assembled to institute the new and permanent government of the civil commonwealth. The title "Court" is given to that assembly of seven—the Septemvirs or Septemviri, as they would have been called at Rome. "The Court being settled according to the fundamental agreement," "after solemn prayer unto God, did proceed as followeth.*

"First, all former power or trust for managing any public affairs in this plantation, into whose hands soever formerly committed, was now abrogated and from hence forward utterly to cease.

"Secondly, all those that have been received into the fellowship of this church since the first gathering of it, or who, being members of other approved churches, offered themselves, were admitted as members of this court." Three members of this church and six of other approved churches were thus admitted, making the entire number of free burgesses sixteen.

A "charge," in the nature of an oath of fidelity, was given to the new burgesses and accepted by them; and in that charge or oath of allegiance to "the civil government here settled," there was no implication of allegiance due to the King of England, or to any other government under heaven.

After these preliminary transactions, "the court proceeded to the choice of a Magistrate and four Deputies to assist in the public affairs of the plantation." The election, however, was not made till Mr. Davenport had first expounded two texts of Scripture, "wherein a magistrate according to God's mind is described." Deut. i. 13. "Take ye wise men, and understanding, and known among your tribes, and I will make them rulers over you." Exod. xviii. 21. "Moreover thou shalt provide out of all the people able men, such as fear God, men of truth, hating covetousness, and place such over them," &c. In conformity with these principles, "Mr. Theoph. Eaton, a member of this church, a man well known and approved by the court as fitly qualified for that office according to the said description, was by full consent chosen Magistrate for the term of one whole year." The elected Magistrate was inducted into office by a solemn charge founded on the charge which Moses gave to those whom he appointed rulers in Israel. Deut. i. 16,

---

* Col. Rec., 20.

17. Then " Mr. Robert Newman, Mr. Matthew Gilbert, Mr. Nathaniel Turner, and Tho. Fugill, were chosen Deputies to assist the Magistrate in all courts called by him for the occasions of the plantation for the same term of one whole year ;" and by the formality of a similar charge they in their turn were inducted into office.

At the same time " Tho. Fugill was chosen Public Notary," his duty being " to keep a faithful record of all passages and conclusions of the court," and of anything else which the court might require to be recorded.   In like manner, " Robert Seely was chosen Marshall," and it was made his duty " to warn courts according to the direction of the magistrate, to serve and execute warrants, to attend the court at all times and to be ready and diligent in his person or by his deputy to execute the sentences of the court, and in all other occasions to attend the service of the plantation in all things apertaining to his office."

" It was further agreed " that there should be a yearly election of all officers " at a General Court to be held for this plantation the last week in October."

Thus the organization of their government was completed. But where were their laws? Were the laws of England in force here—whether acts of parliament or common law? No. They had not come three thousand miles away from England to be governed by what were then, or by what were soon likely to be, the laws of that country. What then? Were they to establish here the Roman or civil law, which was the basis of all the jurisprudence of continental Europe? No. Should they leave their clearings, their buildings, their various labors connected with the beginning of civilization here, to frame a code for themselves. No, they were far too wise for that, Should they simply direct the Magistrate and Deputies to administer justice at their own discretion? No, that would be to establish a despotism. What then? An entire body of laws was summed up in the simple enactment " that the word of God shall be the only rule to be attended unto in ordering the affairs of government in this plantation." With this enactment the record of that first session of " the court," October

25th, 1639, is closed. All other systems of jurisprudence—the canon law, the civil law, and even the common and statute law of England—were expressly excluded from this Colony. Instead of the English maxim that Christianity is "part and parcel" of the law of the land, it was established that here the rules of civil justice given in the Holy Scriptures should be the only law. In another record not long afterwards, the fundamental agreement, made and published by full and general consent when the plantation began and government was settled," is said to have been "that the judicial law of God given by Moses and expounded in other parts of Scripture, so far as it is a hedge and a fence to the moral law, and neither ceremonial nor typical, nor had any reference to Canaan, hath an everlasting equity in it and should be the rule of their proceedings."

It is hardly necessary to say that in these proceedings the founders of the colony made a virtual declaration of independence. The record implies no profession of allegiance to the king of England whose subjects they had been, no pretense of exercising authority in his name, and no allusion to the protection which they might expect from their sovereign; but instead of all this we find a distinct abjuration of all the laws to which they had been subjected in their native country. A new government with a new system of jurisprudence was to be established here.

The "plantation," as they called it, of New Haven had at first no higher officer than the single "Magistrate" who was chosen to his office for one year, and who was assisted by four "Deputies." At the second election, October 29, 1740, "Mr. Eaton [was] chosen Magistrate again;" and "Mr. Robert Newman, Mr. Gregson, Mr. Gilbert, and Captain Turner [were] chosen Deputies." At the third election, October 27, 1641, two Magistrates were chosen, Mr. Eaton and Mr. Goodyear; and at the same time Mr. Gregson, Mr. Robert Newman, Mr. Gilbert, and Mr. Wakeman, were chosen "Deputies *for this plantation.*" At the fourth election, October 26, 1642, Mr. Eaton and Mr. Goodyear were chosen "Magistrates *for this town* this ensuing year;" and "Mr. Malbon, Mr. Gregson,

Mr. Gilbert, and Mr. Wakeman [were] chosen Deputies for this ensuing year, *to assist in the courts by way of advice, but not to have any power by way of sentence.*" Just as another year was closing, October 23, 1643, a combination was effected between New Haven with its outlying plantations, and the independent towns of Guilford and Milford; and three days afterward there was a "General Court of Elections held at New Haven for this Jurisdiction." Then, for the first time, Mr. Eaton was chosen Governor; and Mr. Gregson, Deputy-Governor. Magistrates were also chosen additional to the Governor and Deputy-Governor, one for New Haven, two for Milford, and one for Stamford. In the same Court of "Elections" "Deputies for the Court of Combination" were chosen, namely, Captain Turner and Mr. Lamberton,—"the Court of Combination" being a congress of Commissioners from the four United Colonies of Massachusetts, Plymouth, Connecticut, and New Haven. The union of the four colonies for mutual defense and support had just been instituted; and, for the sake of coming into that federal union on equal terms with the older colonies, the "New Haven Jurisdiction" was constituted, and the previously independent colonies of Milford, and Guilford united with New Haven and its plantations in what was thenceforth commonly called the New Haven Colony.

On the day following that first General Court of Elections for the Jurisdiction, namely, on the 27th of October, 1643, there was "a General Court held at New Haven for the Jurisdiction." The Court consisted of the Governor, Deputy-Governor, and three other Magistrates, with Deputies from New Haven, Milford, Guilford, and Stamford; and its first business was to make a form of government, or, as we should say, a Constitution for the Colony. Doubtless all that was essential in that Constitution, or "Fundamental Agreement," as it is called in the record, had been settled beforehand in the negotiations and arrangements which resulted in the union of Milford and Guilford with New Haven, and under which the General Court for the Jurisdiction had assembled. But the modern distinction between a convention or constituent

Assembly meeting to form a constitution and a Legislature acting under the constitution, had not then been invented; and therefore the fundamental agreement appears on the record as settled and established by the General Court. A revised copy, enlarged by the addition of some details and explanations, and modified by some unimportant changes, is found in the printed laws of the New Haven Colony.

The system of government established by the "Fundamental Agreement," even with the details which were introduced into the revised and printed copy, is very simple, and yet is in most points strikingly similar to the more complicated constitution under which we are governed to-day. Without pretending to be democratic, it establishes a pure republic, with no hereditary privileges, and with no distinctions of honor or power for birth or blood. A brief but careful summary of the "Fundamental Agreement" will complete the design of this paper. Taking the revised copy, we have the several articles of the constitution arranged distinctly in the following order.

I. SUFFRAGE AND ELIGIBILITY TO OFFICE.

The theory is held by some that the right of voting in political elections is among the universal and inalienable rights of human nature. But, as a matter of fact, there is probably no democracy in the world which does not assign some limit to the right of suffrage, the principle of the limitation being always that political power should be entrusted to those most likely to use it for the common welfare. For example, under the present constitution of this State, there are several limitations on the right of suffrage. Not only are women excluded, and children, and every young man under twenty-one years of age, however well educated, or however qualified for military service, but also every man who cannot read in the English language, and every man who has been convicted of a serious crime, and every man who is not technically white.

In the Fundamental Agreement, which was the written constitution of the New Haven Colony, admission to the right of suffrage was dependent on two conditions. First, the man (for women had never been thought of in such a connection) must be a "planter," one who had personally engaged in the enterprise of planting the colony. Thus all transient persons or temporary residents were excluded—all the indented or hired servants whom the planters had brought with them—all who had no permanent interest in the community. Secondly, the man must be, at the time of his admission, a " member of some one or other of the approved Churches of New England." It was presumed that such persons would vote conscientiously and intelligently, and would carefully guard those religious and ecclesiastical institutions for which the "planters" of the colony had migrated into this wilderness.

Men thus qualified, having been once admitted to the right of suffrage, were thenceforward " free burgesses;" nor does it appear that, by any ecclesiastical process, they could be divested of their political power. Still less could they in that way be divested, as in England, of civil rights, for while it was ordained that only the " free burgesses" should have any vote in elections, or should be eligible to any office, it was expressly provided that " all others admitted to be planters have right to their proper inheritance, and do and shall enjoy all other civil liberties and privileges, according to all laws, orders, or grants, which are, or hereafter shall be made for this Colony." The authors of the Fundamental Agreement had not left their native country without having had occasion to consider seriously what disabilities, both civil and political, were, by the common law of England, consequent upon an ecclesiastical sentence of excommunication from the Church of England.

II. ELECTIONS.

The general election for the Colony was held annually at New Haven, on the last Wednesday in May,—though at first, for a few years, the election was on the last Wednesday in October. On the appointed day for the election, all the "free burgesses," or "freemen of the jurisdiction," were to " attend that service," either in person or by proxy, without any summons ; and, "according to their best light from the word of

God," they were to "vote in the election of Governor, Deputy-Governor, Magistrates, Commissioners for the United Colonies, Treasurer, Secretary, Marshall, or any other officer then chosen for the Jurisdiction." Voting by proxy at the general election, was provided for by the regulation "that when any of them [the 'free burgesses'] cannot conveniently come, they may send their votes, either written or in some other way, sealed up in the presence of the rest of the freemen in the plantation where they dwell, or the greater part of them." Some further regulations were made for the sending of votes in exceptional cases, "that so the liberty of the freemen may be preserved, they may have means to attend their duty, and their votes may be directed according to their particular light." One of the regulations was that in voting for and against a candidate for office, "an Indian corn" might be put in for an affirmative vote, and "a bean" for a negative vote.

III. THE GENERAL COURT FOR THE JURISDICTION.

The General Court for the Jurisdiction was to consist of the Governor, Deputy-Governor, all the Magistrates, and two Deputies for each recognized plantation or town. The Deputies were to be chosen " either yearly, or against the approach of any such General Court;" and they were strictly representatives, "as having the power and voices of all the said freemen derived to them." All the members of the Court were to sit in one House; but it was provided that "nothing shall be concluded, and pass as an act of the General Court, (unless in cases expressly excepted,) but by the consent and vote of the major part of the Magistrates, together with the consent and vote of the greater part of the Deputies."

At least one session of the General Court was to be held annually, and always at New Haven, unless the major part of the court see cause for a time to alter the place. That regular session was to be on the last Wednesday in May, " first to carry on the elections, and after to consider and order all such other affairs of the Jurisdiction as fall within their cognizance, trust and power." Special sessions might be held at the call of the Governor, or, in his absence, of the Deputy-Governor, or, in their absence, of any two Magistrates.

The powers and duties of the General Court, were,

1. "To provide for the maintenance of the purity of religion, and suppress the contrary, according to their best light and directions from the word of God."

2. "To declare, publish, and establish, for the plantations within their jurisdiction, the laws " " for holiness and righteousness" which God hath " made and given us in the Scriptures, which in matters moral, or of moral equity, may not be altered by human power or authority," and also " to make and repeal orders for smaller matters not particularly determined in the Scriptures, according to the more general rules of righteousness, and while they stand in force, to require due execution of them."

3. " To require an oath from all the Magistrates, Deputies, or Assistants, &c., in every court of judicature, for the faithful discharge of the trust committed to them ;"—also " to call them to account for the breach of any laws established, or for other misdemeanors in their places, and to censure them as the quality of the offense may require.'"

4. " To impose an oath of fidelity and due subjection to the just laws standing in force, upon all the freemen, planters, and inhabitants fit to take an oath, with due penalty for obstinate refusal."

5. To provide for the military defense of the Colony, "whether against Indians or other enemies ;" and, under the Articles of Confederation, " to order all affairs of war and peace, levying of men, &c."

6. To regulate trade "with Indians and others," " and to settle and levy rates, contributions, and impositions upon all sorts of persons, lands and goods, within this Jurisdiction, as the public service and occasions of church or commonwealth may from time to time require."

7. To act as a court of appeals in civil and criminal causes, from all inferior tribunals.

IV. THE COURT OF MAGISTRATES.

All the Magistrates (of whom it was intended that there should be one or more in every town) were to "meet and sit at New Haven, at least twice a year," namely, on the Monday before the Court of Elections in May, and on the third Wednesday in October. This Court of Magistrates was a judicial court, " to hear, examine and determine all weighty and capital causes, civil and criminal, above those limited to Plantation Courts, and to receive and try all appeals duly brought to them from Plantation Courts," and also to call all persons to account " for breach of any laws or orders established, or for other misdemeanors, and to censure them as the quality of the offense may require." Less than four were not to be a quorum; and in case of an equal division among the members of the court, the vote of the Governor, or, in his absence, of the Deputy-Governor, was to be the casting vote.

V. THE PLANTATION COURTS.

"For the ease of the inhabitants," there were to be " Plantation Courts to hear and determine inferior causes." These courts were of two sorts.

1. In every plantation, or town, where there was a Magistrate, one or more, the " freemen " were to choose at least two Deputies, and might choose three or four at their discretion. These Deputies, by the way, are not the same with the Deputies or Representatives in the General Court, but were only to represent the " freemen " in the Plantation Court, and to assist the Magistrate or Magistrates there. "Any civil cause, betwixt party and party, in value not exceeding twenty pounds," might be tried and determined in that court; "and any criminal cause, when the punishment by Scripture light exceeds not stocking and whipping, and if the fine be pecuniary, when the fine exceeds not five pounds."

2. By calling in two other Magistrates from neighboring plantations, the Plantation Court might become competent to try " any civil cause, though of the highest value, and any

criminal cause, provided it be not capital, extending to the life of the offender.

From the Plantation Courts, of both sorts, appeals and complaints might be brought to the Court of Magistrates.

Such, without any material change, was the constitution of civil government in the New Haven Colony, from 1643, when the several plantations were united under a common jurisdiction, to 1664, when the people submitted, reluctantly, to the charter government of Connecticut.

HISTORY OF THE CUTLER LOT,

CORNER OF CHAPEL AND CHURCH STREETS, NEW HAVEN.

By HENRY WHITE, Esq.,

PRESIDENT OF THE SOCIETY.

READ DECEMBER 29, 1862.

THE history of the Cutler Corner has been selected as the subject of this paper, because it affords both a convenient vehicle for introducing some notices of our earliest institutions, and an illustration of the great amount of local history and biography which lies wrapped up in our early records, waiting for the patient hand and loving eye which shall unroll and read it in a connected and intelligible story.

There is no reason to suppose that this corner is richer in such materials than many other lots within the nine squares of our city. But it has at this time a prominence arising from its central position and aspiring building which will justify the selection. It is the lot along whose two fronts the greatest number of feet is daily treading, and on which towers the loftiest private building yet erected in our city.

This history will consist chiefly of notices of its successive owners, following a brief description of the lot and an account of the buildings which have stood on it prior to 1776.

The Cutler lot is so named from Richard Cutler, its proprietor for the longest period, who held it forty-six years. As owned by him, it was much larger than the present small corner lot bearing his name. It was identical with the original lot located

on this corner in the first division of lots made in 1639, with
the exception of a small notch on the southwest corner, about
sixty-six feet square, which had been sold to Trinity Church
before Richard Cutler became the owner.   The original lot, as
laid out in 1639, had a front on Church street of about one
hundred and thirty-nine feet, and on Chapel street of about
two hundred and thirty-five feet.   It extended therefore from
the corner, southward on Church street to the north line of
Boardman's Building, and eastward on Chapel street to the west
line of Mitchell's building.

SUCCESSION OF OWNERS.			TITLE.
William Jeanes,............	9 years,	1639 to 1648.	Allotment.
John Meggs,..................	10 years,	1648 to 1658.	Deed.
Town,.....		1658 to 1658.	Cession.
Jervis Boykin,................	2 years,	1658 to 1660.	Grant.
Isabel Boykin,................	13 years,	1660 to 1673.	Will.
Nathaniel Boykin,.....	32 years,	1673 to 1705.	Will.
James Denison,..............	3 years,	1705 to 1708.	Will.
Samuel Mix, Sen.,.............	22 years,	1708 to 1730.	Deed.
Samuel Mix, Jun.,.............	27 years,	1730 to 1757.	Will.
Children of Samuel Mix, ...	2 years,	1757 to 1759.	Inheritance.
Rebecca Abigail Mix, wife of			
Richard Woodhull,..........	5 years,	1759 to 1764.	Division.
Richard Cutler,..............	46 years,	1764 to 1810.	Deed.

BUILDINGS.

Wm. Jeanes, the first owner, built a dwelling house on the
lot and lived in it.   This building probably fronted on Church
street, and was occupied by John Meggs, the next owner, and
by the Boykin family, who succeeded Meggs.   After the purchase of the lot by Samuel Mix, who succeeded the Boykin
family in 1708, this building was probably taken down, for no
mention is made of any building on the lot until after it was
purchased by Richard Cutler, in 1764. He erected two dwelling
houses—one on the corner, in which he lived, and which
remained until it was destroyed by fire within the last three
years; the other on the east end of the lot, fronting on Chapel
street, which he sold in 1782 to Dr. Hez. Beardslee, from Hartford, who occupied it, and after his death it was sold, in 1792, to
Dr. Obadiah Hotchkiss, who lived in it until his decease.

In 1752, Samuel Mix sold to the Episcopal Church a small

piece of land, between sixty and seventy feet wide in front, on which was erected, in 1752, their first house of worship. It was taken from the southwest corner of the original lot, and was occupied for this use until 1818, when the lot was sold to John Scott, and by him to Asahel Tuttle, and the building was pulled down.

SOME ACCOUNT OF THE OWNERS.

WILLIAM JEANES.

William Jeanes, the first owner, was one of the first settlers, possessing a moderate estate, and one of the signers of the Fundamental Agreement.

The Fundamental Agreement, as it is called in our records, was the constitution of civil government for the town, adopted by the first settlers at their meeting in Mr. Newman's barn in June, 1639; and in accordance with which, in the October following, the organization of the community was completed by the enactment of laws and the election of officers.

The intervening months between June and October were probably busily occupied in gathering the harvests, and in surveying and dividing the land among the planters. This Fundamental Agreement was the constitution, as we should now call it, under which the settlers of New Haven conducted their affairs as a separate and independent community for three years, until 1643. It was then enlarged in its provisions so as to adapt it to the Colony or Jurisdiction of New Haven, which was then organized by the combination, with the settlement of New Haven, of the adjoining independent communities of Milford and Guilford. These had been previously organized on foundations very similar to those of New Haven.

The term Governor was not used as a name of office until after this combination. For three years, Theophilus Eaton, either alone or in conjunction with Stephen Goodyear, was annually elected in October, Magistrate, not Governor. In the spring of 1643, and annually afterwards in every spring, he was elected Governor of the Jurisdiction until his death.

The names of all the planters present at the meeting in Mr. Newman's barn, and assenting to its proceedings, were appended to this fundamental agreement by the Secretary. Others who were accidentally absent from the meeting, subscribed it afterwards with their own hands. We have by this means the autograph signatures of thirty-five of the first settlers—among which is that of William Jeanes.

William Jeanes, although he came with the first settlers, was not admitted as a freeman until May, 1648. Before that time he was a free planter—then he became a free burgher and member of the general court—or, as it was afterwards more commonly called, a freeman.

The name of freeman or free burgher was borrowed from the nomenclature of the trading corporations or guilds and subordinate municipalities of the old world, where at first these terms denoted merely the nature of the tenure and service by which the land and buildings in the city or borough were held of the feudal lord. But for some time before the settlement of this country, the political privileges which the cities and boroughs had won by force, or purchased by money from the feudal aristocracy, began to give an important political significance to these terms; and to be a free burgher in a city or borough, gave not only the right to hold land and to exercise one's trade or calling within its limits, but also a voice in the government and legislation of the country. The tradesman or mechanic, who was a free burgher in a borough, had his representative in Parliament, as truly as the county family, whose ancestors had come in with the Conqueror, and whose names were found in Domesday book.

Most of the early settlements in this country were connected more or less closely with trading corporations in England, and were planted under their auspices. But the first government of New Haven, although it borrowed the names of its officers and members from corporations of this class, had no connection with any of them; nor does it appear to have been organized as a corporation until the meeting in June, 1639. The first settlers, or adventurers, as they were sometimes called, had some articles of association, by which certain powers of managing the joint property of the association were delegated to specified individuals, but the details of this arrangement have not been preserved. It was probably entered into before they left England, as in their negotiations with the Massachusetts people for a place to settle, they spoke of those who were still in England for whom they were acting, and who expected to form one community with them. The objects of this preliminary association were to explore and occupy a site in the new world which should furnish a home and a country for themselves and their posterity. They had expected to find it within the limits of Massachusetts, where their association would still hold them as one community, until they could organize a government. Discovering, however, on their arrival at Boston, that they would be obliged to locate in townships separated from each other by towns already settled, and would thus lose their individuality as a community, they concluded to seek a location beyond the limits of any colony then existing. They therefore sought to find a new and fair haven, where the merchant and trader, as well as the husbandman, would find scope and facilities for their respective pursuits; and having found it in this spot, they asked no leave of the Plymouth or Virginia companies, or of the Lord Say and Seal, or of the Lord Brooke, or of any but of the Lord their God, and of the Indian tribes whom God had led here before them, and who had by his gift the only prior right which they cared to acquire. At this famous meeting in Mr. Newman's barn, whatever powers and trusts, under their old articles of association, had been vested in any persons, were expressly surrendered and abrogated; and by the adoption of this fundamental agreement the political state sprang at once into being, out of the members of the old association, by the free action of all, after a deliberation and discussion, the like of which is not found in history.

One feature of this political community is worthy of notice. No one was debarred from the highest political privileges and honors which the State had in its gift, by reason of his poverty or of his humble calling. Here was an association composed of men of a great variety of grades as to property and rank in the old world, men of large means, and men of no means except their hands or heads or growing families. In such an association, those who furnished the capital, and gave their personal labor and skill to its management, must necessarily have had the major vote in its plans and measures, and could easily have retained the legal right to the control. But by this fundamental agreement, Theophilus Eaton, who had invested £3,000, and Stephen Goodyear and George Lamberton, who had invested each £1,000, were placed on a level as to privileges and legal power of control, with William Peck, the husbandman, who had put in only £12, and who was much straitened by having only half of a small lot for his house lot, and with John Brocket, the carpenter, who had put in but £15, and with Master Ezekiel Cheevers, who had put in but £20. Whomsoever else they sought to bar out, it was not the poor laborer, or poor mechanic, or poor schoolmaster, because they were poor and humble.

The free burghers or free men of this new State, among whom William Jeanes was admitted in 1648, were such of the free planters, as by the provisions of the fundamental agreement were intrusted with the right of voting in the enactment of laws and in the election of officers, and with the power of holding office. The most important qualification was, as is well known, membership in the church.

Beginning with seven who were first selected, not as pillars, but in the more appropriate language of the record, "for the foundation work," nine were added at their first meeting in October, 1639. Three more freemen were added during the remainder of the year, 1639, and by the end of the year 1645 the number was increased to 70.

William Jeanes, by becoming a freeman in 1648, did not thereby cease to be a free planter. The free planters, as distinguished from the freemen, were all those who were members of the preliminary association of which mention has been made, and who by virtue of this membership were entitled to a share in the lands which were purchased and made valuable by the joint property, efforts and industry of the association. Their number at first was about 120, and the amount of capital invested was about £36,000, subscribed in sums varying from £10 to £3,000. Most of them had joined the company in England, probably in London, and had come over together in the ship

Hector; others who had already settled in Massachusetts, but who were valued for their skill as mechanics, or their experience as soldiers, were induced to join the company while they tarried in Massachusetts. Others had joined the company in England and had contributed to its funds but were detained at home for various reasons, and never became domiciled here.

After the government was organized, no one was allowed to purchase lands of the planters, or of the Indians, unless he was already a free planter, or unless he furnished satisfactory evidence that he would become a desirable acquisition to the settlement, and was thereupon admitted to be a free planter. The necessity which hence arose that every sale of lands should be reported to the court for the purpose of approval or disapproval, led early to the plan of having a book in which all conveyances of land should be entered—a system of registration which has proved of signal advantage to the community. The original object of the record here, was not so much to guard the purchaser against fraud as the public against an undesirable inhabitant.

The original free planters, as well as all those who were afterward admitted as such by virtue of their purchase of lands and approval by the court, were required to subscribe their assent to the fundamental agreement, and also, with other classes, to take the oath of fidelity to the government. They and their children were the stock from which the body of freemen or free burghers or members of the court were from time to time replenished. The descendants of these free planters and of those who had purchased rights of them, formed in later years the quasi-corporate body of proprietors of common and undivided lands, to whom belonged the fee of all undivided lands within the township, and who from time to time within the first 120 years held meetings and divided among themselves by lot large tracts successively of their fair inheritance until the estate has become so reduced that a committee of five proprietors, authorized by the legislature to act for the whole, are deemed sufficient to take care of and manage what little remains to be cared for.

The free planters and their families did not, however, consti-

tute the whole body of inhabitants.   There were also temporary
residents, not free planters, whose number was small.   Some
of these resided here for the purpose of trade.   The advantages for trade and commerce which the situation of the town
and the enterprise and capital of its first settlers gave to New
Haven over most of the other settlements in New England, at-
tracted merchants from other colonies, both English and Dutch.
The residence of such merchants and tradesmen was favored, although they were not allowed to hold lands or to participate in
any political rights, and were required to take the oath of fidelity to the government so long as they continued residents.
They were at first exempted from taxation.   After a few years,
however, when the expenses of the colonial and town governments had become large and were increasing, and the burden
of taxes on the owners of land had become heavy, the thought
naturally occurred to them that a government which cost
so much to maintain, was worth something to all who enjoyed its protection.   This idea was after a little time ma-
tured and embodied in the following ordinance, passed in
1645.   "For that some of considerable estates and trading do
live in the town, and have hitherto enjoyed comfortable fruit
of civil administrations and charges, themselves, in the mean
time, having small or no rates, it is ordered that henceforward
all such shall be rated, from time to time, as this court shall
judge meet."   In immediate application of the law it was ordered at the same court that for the present Mrs. Stolion
should pay after the rate of 20 shillings a year to the treasurer,
Mr. Godfrey 20 shillings and Mr. Leach 40 shillings a year.
These were at that time the most prominent of the resident traders.   This was not a heavy tax, as compared with that which
many of the free planters had to pay.   Gov. Eaton's yearly
tax was about £10-10, Gov. Goodyear's £10, Captain Lamberton's £4, Robert Newman's £2-10, and there were 50 others of the
free planters whose yearly tax ranged from £3 to about £1.

In this class of temporary residents may be properly included
those who came as stewards or agents of those members of the
association who for various reasons had not come over to this
country.   These stewards were men of good character, most of

whom eventually became themselves free planters. Richard Mansfield, the ancestor of all the Mansfields of this vicinity, was one of this class. He was steward of Mr. Marshall. Another portion of the temporary residents were the additional laborers required at times by the enterprises of manufacturing or navigation which were undertaken for the sake of promoting the growth of the town. The iron works in East Haven and at Stony Creek, and the building of vessels from time to time, required more labor than could be furnished by the planters or their families. These transient laborers were a constant source of trouble. For the most part they had no sympathy with either the religious or political views of the planters. They came only for the wages they received, and were endured only because their labor was indispensable. Many of them were ignorant and vicious, and all the preaching which they were obliged weekly to attend, and the admonitions of the magistrate before whom they were in almost as constant attendance, failed to transform them into the likeness of their employers. Few became permanent inhabitants. The more common termination of their residence, if they lingered beyond the time for which they were hired, was a whipping and sending out of the colony.

With these transient laborers must not be confounded those who were technically called servants, who were bound to labor on farms or otherwise for a term of years. These servants usually formed a part of the families of their masters and were more accessible to their influence. When they were turbulent and mischievous they were punished by the master, not arbitrarily, but with the advice and under the direction of the court. Many of them became permanent and useful inhabitants after their term of service expired. There was a law forbidding the sale of these servants out of the confederate colonies of New England, without a special license from the government of the colony to which they belonged.

To return to William Jeanes, the first owner of the Cutler lot. He was employed in 1651 as a teacher of the common school for the town, at a salary of £10 a year from the town, the rest of his compensation to be made up by the parents; and

such was his ability that in 1652 he received a call to Wethersfield to teach the school there, which call he obtained leave
of the town to accept, but returned to New Haven the following year.   About the year 1655 he removed to Northampton,
in Massachusetts, where he was a school teacher and recorder
of lands or town clerk for 20 years.   In that new settlement
he frequently conducted religious worship on the sabbath.
This service was frequently rendered by school masters in the
absence or illness of a settled pastor.   Our Ezekiel Cheevers,
of academic notoriety, sometimes performed this duty in New
Haven, and the magistrate took care that his ministrations were
properly appreciated—for among sundry gross miscarriages
which brought a severe whipping, under the advice of the
court, upon one of those servants to whom we have alluded,
was "scoffing at the word of God which was preached by
Mr. Cheevers."

It is reported of Mr. Jeanes that at the first settlement of
Northfield, Mass., a town on the Connecticut river above
Northampton, he preached to the people their first sermon
under an oak tree; but, this settlement having been soon
broken up by the Indians, he returned to Northampton, where
he died, in 1690.   He had a wife and several children while he
lived in New Haven, and several more children after his removal to Massachusetts.   None of them returned to New
Haven, and the name was not known among us for many
years.   His descendants are numerous in Massachusetts, spell-
ing their name without the first e, which their ancestor used in
his signature on our records.

JOHN MEIGS.

The second owner was John Meggs, who acquired his title
to the lot by purchase and conveyance from William Jeanes,
the first owner.   The conveyance is on record, and readeth on
this wise: "Wm. Jeanes passeth over to John Meggs his
house and house lot, lying at the corner over against Mr.
Gregson's, betwixt the house lot of John Budd and the highway."   John Meggs or Meigs was the son of Vincent Meigs;
and is said to have come from Weymouth or Rehoboth, in

Massachusetts, to New Haven. He was not one of the first settlers. He took the oath of fidelity here in 1644, and in the same year was admitted a freeman.

He was a tanner and currier by trade, and being active in business gathered property; but he fell under the displeasure of the town for the quality of his leather and of the shoes made from it, "in a single pair of which," the court say, "several evils appear, such as contempt of court, continued unrighteousness, (he having been before the court for the same trouble once before,) and other similar evils, and how many shoes he had made and sold of such faulty materials and so loaded with evils, the court say they know not." Dissatified with so much strictness about leather, and with the fines which attended his want of care in the matter, he seems to have surrendered or sold this lot to the town, who were probably willing to facilitate his departure, and about the year 1658 he removed with his father to Guilford. There, when the troubles with Connecticut arose, he took an active part on the side of the Connecticut usurpation, as was to be expected from one who had enjoyed his experience of the New Haven government.

He accepted the appointment of constable for Guilford from the Connecticut authorities, in defiance of the New Haven jurisdiction. In 1662 he was an inhabitant of Killingworth, where he died in 1672, leaving a large estate. He had a wife while living in New Haven, and he left one son and four daughters. The son was an ancestor of Colonel Return Jonathan Meigs of Connecticut, one of the heroes of the Revolution, whose expedition to Long Island was one of the most brilliant achievements of that war. The son of Colonel Meigs, of the same name, was in later times Governor of Ohio, and Postmaster General of the United States.

The pleasant story of the origin of the name Return Jonathan, from the earnest outcry of the maiden fearing that by her want of decision she had lost her lover, must, I fear, be given up, as the Christian name of Return, without the Jonathan appended, is found belonging to the grandfather of the first Return Jonathan, as well as to others of the family. The

name in its origin had probably more to do with a return to
the love of God than to an earthly love.

GERVASE BOYKIN.

The third owner was Gervase Boykin, who acquired his
title in 1658, by grant from the town, after the surrender of
John Meigs. Gervase or Jarvis Boykin was one of the first
settlers, and was present and assenting at the forming of the
fundamental agreement. He was a carpenter by trade and
came from Charington, in the county of Kent, in England, to
Charlestown in Massachusetts, in 1635, and was probably solicited, while there, to join the New Haven enterprise, from their
need of his skill. His estate at first was small, but he was useful and trustworthy in his calling. In building the first meeting house, and in the repairs which were made on it from time
to time, his advice was always sought. There was full occupation for one of his trade for some years, for New Haven had
at first a larger number of good substantial houses than any
other town, in proportion to the number of its inhabitants. In
order to encourage the erection of dwelling houses, they were
exempted from taxation during the first ten years of the settlement of the town.

In the latter part of his life he had accumulated some
property, and he was employed as an agent for managing
property by several who had removed from New Haven.

He had a gift for public service which the town used, making
him one of the Selectmen or Townsmen, as they were at first
called, at the first election ever held in the town for that office,
which was in 1651, and he served again in 1657 and 1658.

In the military line he went through the grades of corporal
and sergeant, relatively as honorable, and giving as much influence and importance then, as the rank of major and lieuten-
ant-colonel of the militia does now. He died in 1660, leaving
a comfortable estate to his wife Isabel.

His family, at his first coming, consisted only of himself and
wife; at his death he left three children, viz.: Nathaniel,
Bethiah, who married James Denison, and Sarah, who married
Samuel Edwards of Northampton, Mass.

This Cutler lot was not his first home lot. He removed to it and lived on it two or three years only before his death.

ISABEL BOYKIN.

The fourth owner was Isabel Boykin, the widow of Jervis Boykin, who in 1660 acquired title to the lot, and probably by the will of her husband, although the will is not now extant. She survived her husband thirteen years, during which time she lived upon the lot, and dying in 1673, left it by her will to her son Nathaniel. Her name and that of her husband (Isabel and Gervase) have more of a Norman sound than was common among the first settlers. His name was, however, soon flattened down to Jarvis.

NATHANIEL BOYKIN.

The fifth owner was Nathaniel Boykin, son of Gervase and Isabel Boykin. He was born before 1640, as he took the oath of fidelity in 1660. He died in 1705, without wife or children. He is called a husbandman, which designation is equivalent to that of farmer at the present day, and he probably lived on this lot. With his death the name of Boykin disappears from our records.

JAMES DENISON.

The sixth owner was James Denison, who, in 1705, acquired title to the lot by the will of his brother-in-law, Nathaniel Boykin. He also was a farmer, and first appears in New Haven in 1662, when he was twenty-one years old, on the occasion of his marriage with Bethiah Boykin, daughter of Gervase Boykin. There were families of the name of Denison in the neighborhood of Boston, and also at Stonington, in Connecticut. From what place he came has not been ascertained. Soon after his marriage he purchased a share in the South-end neck, a large tract of good land in East Haven, on the shore of the Sound. He became a resident and wealthy land owner in that village in 1683, ranking on the assessment list among the largest of the proprietors. He died in 1719, at the age of seventy-eight, having had eight children,

five of whom lived to adult age. He probably never lived on
the Cutler lot.   From his youngest son, James, were descended,
in the third generation, four brothers, citizens of New Haven,
Austin Denison, Abel Denison, Charles Denison and Henry
Denison, whose worth of character and success and usefulness in their various occupations, as merchant, shipmaster,
lawyer and banker, have made the name of Denison honored
and beloved in this community.

SAMUEL MIX.

The seventh owner was Samuel Mix, who, in 1708, acquired
the lot by purchase and conveyance from James Denison.
Samuel Mix was a younger son of Thomas Mix and Rebecca
(Turner) Mix.   Thomas Mix, though not among the first
comers, was here early, and though in his youth wayward and
requiring some regulation, he became ultimately a substantial
and wealthy inhabitant.   At his death, in 1692, he divided his
large estate among ten children, all of whom became heads of
families, and the sons persons of repute.   Samuel was a farmer, or, more properly, a landholder, and left his estate to his
children, larger than he received it.   He married Rebecca,
daughter of George Pardee, July 26th, 1699, and died in
1730, having had three children, Samuel, George and Stephen.
Stephen died young.   Samuel and George survived their father,
and divided his estate.   George Mix settled in North Haven,
having received most of his portion in land in that village.
Samuel remained in New Haven.   Samuel Mix, the father,
never lived on this lot.   It was during his ownership, or that
of his predecessor, James Denison, that the original dwelling
house was removed.

For many years after 1772 there was but one house on the
south side of Chapel street, along the whole line from Church
street to State street, and that one was very near to State
street.   On the north side of Chapel street, between the same
limits, there were but two, or, at the most, three houses.
Chapel street was then comparatively of little importance.
The stream of travel inland, from the water and from State
street, instead of surging through Chapel street to Church

street, as now, then glided easily along George street to the south end of Church street, and through Church to the Meeting House on the Green, and thence to the few farmers who lived north and west of the central square or market place. Few ventured through the lonely lane that seemed to have been left open from State street to the southeast corner of the central square, more from a regard to the symmetry of the town plot than for any important use. It could hardly then be said to have been of common convenience and necessity. Indeed the adventurous man who first built for his own residence a house on this part of the street was commemorated, by having his name associated with it, in common parlance, and even in the public records, where we find the street called, " The lane leading to Zuriel Kimberly's house."

Samuel Mix.

The eighth owner was Samuel Mix, Junior, son of the former Samuel Mix, who acquired title to this lot in 1730, by the will of his father. Samuel Mix, the son, was an inn-keeper, whose house of entertainment was on the corner of Elm and College streets, near the site of the Divinity College. He never lived on the Cutler lot. He sold to Trinity Church the southwest corner of the lot, where they erected their first house of worship. He was born in 1700—was married January 1, 1728, to Mrs. Abigail Cutler, and died in 1757. Of eight children only two daughters survived him and inherited his estate. He increased by the profits of his business the large estate in lands received from his father, so that these two daughters were esteemed heiresses, and did in truth make their husbands wealthy. One married Richard Woodhull, and the other, in 1766, became the second wife of Jonathan Fitch, son of Gov. Thomas Fitch of Norwalk, and for many years steward of Yale College. The widow of Samuel Mix married William Greenough, a man of some importance, who gave his name to his wife's house and lot, on the corner of Elm and College streets, which for a long time was called the Greenough house.

REBECCA ABIGAIL WOODHULL.

The ninth owner was Rebecca Abigail Mix, daughter of Samuel Mix, who soon after her father's death married Richard Woodhull, May 2, 1762. For two years she was tenant in common with her mother and sister, of this lot. By a division of the estate made in 1759, she became sole owner of the Cutler lot.

Richard Woodhull, her husband, was descended from Richard Woodhull of Brookhaven, Long Island, one of the first settlers of that town, then under the jurisdiction of Connecticut. The Richard Woodhull of New Haven was a younger brother of Gen. Nathanial Woodhull, a revolutionary officer of some note and usefulness, who died of wounds received in a disastrous battle on Long Island. Richard graduated at Yale College in 1752, was tutor four years, until 1761, then settled in New Haven, and was admitted to the bar in November, 1762, and practiced law here. His residence was on the corner of Elm and Church street, now occupied by Austin & Gilbert, and which for many years was called the Woodhull corner. He died in 1779, leaving only one child, a daughter, who became the wife of John Brainard, former sheriff of the county.

RICHARD CUTLER.

The tenth owner was Richard Cutler, who acquired title to the lot by purchase and deed from Mrs. Woodhull, in 1764, soon after her marriage. Richard Cutler was from Fairfield—was born in 1736, came to New Haven about 1760, married Hannah Howell, daughter of Deacon Thomas Howell and Mary (White) Howell. He was a goldsmith—an active man of business, accumulated a fair estate, built the house on the corner, which was lately destroyed by fire—made it his residence and died there in 1810, aged 73. His descendants of his own name and of other names are still found in New Haven. Before his death he had sold, in 1782, to Dr. Hezekiah Beardslee, a physician from Hartford, fifty-three feet in front of the east part of the lot, which afterwards became the property and residence of Dr. Obadiah Hotchkiss. After the death of Richard

Cutler, in 1810, the remainder of the Cutler lot was divided into seven lots and distributed among his children. To follow the history of these seven portions would be passing from the domain of the historian into that of the conveyancer, whose duties require him to range over the last fifty years of our records to gather its treasures for the private use of his clients. One fact, however, connected with the modern ownership of this lot may be mentioned here, which is interesting because so uncommon in these days of change—two of these seven portions, one of which is the corner itself, have belonged to the same family for more than a century—being still for the most part the property of the descendants of Richard Cutler.

HISTORY OF TRINITY CHURCH, NEW HAVEN,

By FREDERICK CROSWELL, Esq.*

READ MARCH 30, 1863.

———— ••• ————

In the year 1781, before the close of the Revolutionary War, a book was published in London, with the following title: "A General History of Connecticut, from its first settlement under George Fenwick, Esq., to its Latest Period of Amity with Great Britain," &c., "By a Gentleman of the Province." Its authorship has, by common consent, been attributed to the Rev. Samuel A. Peters, a native of Hebron, in Connecticut, a clergyman of the Church of England, and a zealous loyalist. He fled from Hebron and went to England in the year 1774, to escape the annoyances and persecutions to which he had subjected himself, by the too free expression of his unpopular political sentiments. (*Political Magazine, Vol. II.*, page 6, &c., &c.) He, however, never acknowledged the work to be his. As a history, it has never been regarded as reliable—but its sarcastic style and satirical spirit, together with the malicious

---

* Judge Croswell died July 11, 1863, aged 50 years.

At a meeting of the Directors of the Historical Society, held August 31st, 1863, the following resolution, presented by Thomas R. Trowbridge, Esq., was unanimously adopted:

"Frederick Croswell, Esq., one of the projectors, and an officer of this Society, having deceased since the last meeting of this Board, his associates unanimously direct the Secretary to enter on the Records of the Society, this expression of their respect for the purity of his private and the unsullied probity of his public character, for his wide sympathy with the unfortunate and unhappy, and for the active interest he ever felt in whatever was connected with the past history, the present improvement, and the future prosperity of New Haven."

raillery with which it abounds, have combined to give it a wider reputation than it would ever have attained, had it been limited to the statement of simple truths. An edition was republished in New Haven some thirty years since, notwithstanding which it has become very rare, which fact constitutes its chief value.

The main object of the author probably was to avenge himself for some of the indignities that had been inflicted upon him in Connecticut, by holding up those at whose hands he had suffered to the ridicule of the people, and especially of the tories of England. If such was his purpose, it appears to have been successfully achieved. The " Political Magazine," a very ardent tory publication of that day, made copious extracts from it—one of which, as it seems to be an appropriate introduction to the subject of this paper—is here quoted. The mode of its presentation, it will be perceived, is very similar to that adopted by the newspapers in our own day, in calling attention to "sensation paragraphs" and "astounding developments"—to wit :

A CURIOUS DISCOVERY OF CONNECTICUT VIRTUE AND HONESTY, BY MR. HARRISON, LATE COLLECTOR OF THE CUSTOMS AT NEW HAVEN, IN THAT COLONY.

"The true character of Davenport and Eaton, the leaders of the first settlers of New Haven, may be learnt from the following fact:—An English gentleman, by the name of Grigson, coming on his travels to New Haven, about the year 1644, was greatly pleased with its pleasant situation ; and after purchasing a large settlement, sent to London for his wife and family. But before their arrival, he found a charming situation, without the blessing of religious and civil liberty, would not render him and his family happy ; he resolved, therefore, to quit the country and return to England, as soon as his family should arrive, and accordingly advertised his property for sale ; when lo ! agreeable to one of the Blue Laws, no one would buy, because he had not, and could not, obtain liberty of the Selectmen to sell it. The patriotic virtue of the Selectmen thus becoming an unsurmountable bar to the sale of his New Haven estate, Mr. Grigson made his will, and bequeathed part of his lands toward the support of an Episcopal clergyman, who should reside in that town, and the residue to his own heirs. Having deposited his will in the hands of a friend, he set sail with his family for England, but died on his passage. This friend proved the will, but died also soon after. The record was dexterously concealed by glueing two leaves together ; and after some years, the Selectmen sold the whole estate to pay taxes, though the rent of Mr. Grigson's house alone in one year would pay the taxes for ten.

Some persons, hardy enough to exclaim against this glaring injustice, were soon silenced, and expelled the town. In 1750 an Episcopal clergyman was settled in New Haven; and, having been informed of Mr. Grigson's will, applied to the town clerk for a copy, who told him there was no such will on record, and withal refused him the liberty of searching. In 1768, Peter Harrison, Esq., from Nottinghamshire, in England, the King's collector at the port of New Haven, claimed his right of searching the public records; and, being a stranger, and not supposed to have any knowledge of Grigson's will, obtained his demand. The alphabet contained Grigson's name, and referred to a page which was not to be found in the book. Mr. Harrison at first supposed it to have been torn out; but, on a closer examination, discovered one leaf much thicker than the others. He put a corner of the thick leaf into his mouth, and soon found it was composed of two leaves, which with much difficulty having separated, he found Grigson's will! To make sure work, he took a copy of it himself, and then called the clerk to draw and attest another, which was done. Thus furnished, Mr. Harrison instantly applied to the Selectmen, and demanded a surrender of the land which belonged to the church, but which they as promptly refused; whereupon Mr. Harrison took out writs of ejectment against the possessors. As might be expected, Mr. Harrison from a good man, became, in ten days, the worst man in the world; but, being a generous and brave Englishman, he valued not their clamors and curses, though they terrified the gentlemen of the law. Harrison was obliged to be his own lawyer, and boldly declared he expected to lose his cause in New England; but after that he would appeal and try it, at his own expense, in old England, where justice reigned. The good people knowing Harrison did not get his bread by their votes, and that they could not baffle him, resigned the lands to the church on that gentleman's own terms; which in a very few years will support a clergyman in a very genteel manner. The honest Selectmen yet possess the other lands, though report says Mr. Grigson has an heir of his own name, residing near Holborn, in London, who inherits the virtues of his ancestor, and ought to inherit his estate."

No member of this Society, probably, needs to be assured that this absurd story, so discreditable to the good faith and honesty of our ancestors, is utterly false and without foundation. No formal attempt has ever been made to vindicate the character of the public authorities of New Haven from the preposterous charges of this veracious "historian." For, taken in connection with the other extravagancies of the volume, they have ever been regarded here, where the proofs of their falsity are at hand, as too monstrously absurd to require either notice or denial. But as a certain learned Irish gentleman thought Gulliver's Travels true in the main, although containing "*some* things which he could not prevail upon himself to believe," so this book numbers several believers in whole or in

part, and is probably the source of most of the erroneous prejudices that prevail amongst the ignorant and vulgar concerning
the early history of the Colony, and the manners and morals
of the people of Connecticut—and there are many, neither ignorant nor vulgar, who have been impressed by this particular
story, with the idea that the public officials of New Haven did,
at some time or other, and in some way or other, attempt to
defraud the Episcopal Church of property to which it was justly entitled.   But the most rigid examination of the public
records affords the clearest proof of the entire groundlessness
of the injurious imputation.

Thomas Gregson was one of the earliest settlers of New Haven, and one of the most prominent men in the Colony, where
he was elected to several important offices.   Although he was
not one of the "seven pillars" of the New Haven Church, he
was a zealous member of it, and an ardent believer in Davenport's doctrines.   Episcopacy, of course, had no attractions for
him, and he probably would have looked upon the advent of a
"surpliced priest" in the Colony

> " with as favorable eyes,
> As Gabriel on the devil in Paradise."

He, with Captain Turner, and several other of the principal
men in the Colony, embarked on board Captain Lamberton's
vessel, which sailed on its ill-starred voyage in the month of
January, 1646.   Neither ship, passengers nor crew were ever
afterwards seen or heard from; but an apparition of a ship,
which was supposed to be the same, was seen in the air by
many persons in New Haven, in the month of June following.
On the 2d day of November, 1647, an inventory of his estate
was exhibited to the Court of Probate and recorded, (see *Probate Records, Vol. I., Part I.*, pp. 12, 13, 14,) but nothing further was done in the way of the settlement of his estate until
several years afterwards.   He left no will, but died intestate,—
and was the only man by the name of Gregson that ever lived
in the Colony.   He had several daughters, but left only one
son surviving him, and he went to England and died there.
In the final settlement and distribution of Thomas Gregson's

estate, which did not take place until April 3, 1715, there was set, with other property, to " The heirs of Richard, the oldest and only son of the deceased, 1 acres ¾ and 24 rods of the Home lot, north part," (*Probate Records, Vol. IV.*, pp. 397-8,) and this is the land, the greater part of which was afterwards owned by Trinity Church, and known as the Glebe.

On the 520th page of the 10th volume of the New Haven Land Records, is the record of a conveyance from William Grigson, of the City of London, Gent., to the Rev. Jonathan Arnold, of the land described above, in trust, " for the purpose of building and erecting a church thereupon, for the worship and service of Almighty God, according to the practice of the Church of England, and a parsonage or dwelling house for the incumbent of the said intended church for the time being, and also for a church yard to be taken thereout for the poor, and the residue thereof to be esteemed and used as Glebe Land by the minister of the said intended church for the time being forever." It is dated March 6, 1736, and is recorded in the neat calligraphy of Samuel Bishop, Clerk, and like all the public records of New Haven, is, and has always been, open for the inspection of all. There is a complete transcript of this deed appended to these pages, for the accommodation of those who may desire to read it entire. (Appendix B.) •

Considered as a conveyance, this deed was of little if any value. The grantor was not only not in possession of the land described in the deed at the time of its execution, but other parties had been in possession of it for many years—besides which, the instrument was deficient in the acknowledgment of the grantor, which was necessary to render it valid.* The title under which Trinity Church afterwards held the Glebe Land was derived from an entirely different source—and no claim was ever made to that valuable property by the Church under this deed—which, nevertheless, is interesting as an historical document. From it we learn the genealogical fact that the grantor was the grandson and heir of Richard Grigson, who was the son of Thomas Grigson, of New Haven— and that he was also a zealous member of the Church of Eng-

---

* See Statutes of Connecticut, Revision of 1808, p. 653 and foot notes.

land, and was desirous of promoting the interests of that Church
in Connecticut. It furthermore sets forth the interesting historical fact that the Rev. Jonathan Arnold was then in London
soliciting subscriptions for the purpose of building a Church
and Parsonage in New Haven, and that he was a missionary
of the Society for the Propagation of the Gospel in Foreign
Parts.

Mr. Arnold, the grantor and trustee named in the deed in
question, was a graduate of Yale College of the Class of 1723,
and succeeded the Rev. Samuel Johnson as minister of the
Congregational Church in West Haven. He conformed to the
Episcopal Church in 1734, and was ordained in England in
1736, and was appointed a missionary of the Propagation Society for West Haven, Derby and Waterbury. He is said to
have subsequently sailed again for England, and to have been
lost on the voyage thither. Doubts, however, are entertained
as to the truth of this tradition.

At this time the members of the Church of England were
very few in New Haven. According to the best information
that can be obtained, there was then but one churchman in the
town, and he was a man in the humble walks of life. (*Churchman's Magazine, Vol. I.*, p. 261.)

It cannot therefore be a matter of surprise if the people of
New Haven should have regarded with suspicion and dislike
any attempt on the part of Mr. Arnold to introduce amongst
them a form of religion against which they entertained the
most inveterate prejudices, which they had not only inherited,
but which had been carefully fostered and intensified by their
education. Nor could they reasonably have been expected to
view with indifference any effort to divert the fairest portion
of the possessions of one of the original founders of the Colony, to purposes so foreign to his intentions and their own con-
victions, as those contemplated by William Grigson's deed.
Yet there is nothing in the public records of New Haven to
show either that Mr. Arnold ever attempted to obtain possession of the property described in the deed, or that any means
were ever taken to prevent him from doing so, and until a recent period it has been generally believed that no such events
ever occurred.

Disputed titles to land often lead to disorders and bloodshed, especially in newly settled countries, and few things are more difficult to be quietly accomplished than the dispossession of the actual occupant of land, howsoever slight his legal title to it may be.

In Chapin's review of Hall's " Puritans," &c., it is stated that very soon after the distribution of Thomas Gregson's estate in 1716, the part set to the heirs of Richard Grigson was taken possession of by Daniel Thompson and Joseph Whiting, who occupied it for many years. And furthermore, that when William Grigson executed the deed, "Mr. Arnold was also authorized and empowered to settle the whole matter, and furnished with the requisite proof and papers. After Mr. A's return to America, Whiting contrived to obtain clandestine possession of Mr. Arnold's papers, which were never returned, and he was not allowed to search the records for other proof in regard to it. He applied to the public authorities for redress, but could procure no aid." The authority for these statements is not given. Allowing them to be correct, it appears that Mr. Arnold was prevented from getting possession of the property in question by the cupidity and dishonesty of Joseph Whiting, who was one of the descendants of Thomas Gregson, and had been in possession of it for many years, and for whose misconduct the public authorities were not responsible. If it is true that Mr. Arnold was not allowed to search the records by those in whose custody they were, nothing can be said in justification of the fact. But in order to entitle it to credit, it should be established by the clearest proof.

An extract has been recently published from a letter written to the Secretary of the Propagation Society from Fairfield, dated March 29, 1739, in which Mr. Arnold's case is stated as follows: " William Grigson, of London, Esq., made a donation of a piece of land in New Haven to him, as trustee for the Church of England, to build a church on, and when he went to take possession, and make improvement of said land by ploughing the same, he was opposed by a great number of people being resolute that no church should be built there, who in a riotous and tumultuous manner, being (as we have good reason to believe) put upon it by some in authority, and of the chief men in the town, beat his cattle and abused his servants, threatening both his and their lives to that degree, that he was obliged to quit the field. And though he made presentments against sundry of them for breach of the peace to the civil authority, yet they refused to take cognizance of it, and so he could obtain no relief." This is signed by Samuel Seabury, (the father of the Bishop,) Ebenezer Punderson, Jonathan Arnold, Samuel Johnson, J. Wetmore, Henry Caner and John Beach, who, it is believed, were the only Episcopal clergymen then in the Colony. (*See Documentary History of the Episcopal Church in the United States, Vol. I.,* p. 169.)

The testimony of such witnesses is certainly not to be called in question. And considering that the land was already in the possession of other parties, and that Mr. Arnold's title was of a very doubtful character at best, it can readily be believed that any attempt on his part to take possession of the property would be resisted by those who were in actual possession, and claimed it as their own—and that he would be considered and treated by them as a trespasser. The contest appears to have been between private individuals, in which the public authorities were not necessarily involved. Similar occurrences are not unusual even at the present day. This question cannot be satisfactorily determined, however, without a thorough examination of the whole correspondence of the Society on the subject, and that cannot be immediately obtained. But measures have been taken for procuring it, which, if successful, will afford further opportunities for investigation and the establishment of the truth.

The exact time of the organization of the Parish of Trinity Church has not been ascertained. But the Churchmen of New Haven had become sufficiently numerous, in 1752, to contemplate at that time the building of a house of worship. On the 28th day of July of that year, Samuel Mix executed a deed, conveying, for the consideration of £200 old tenor, to Enos Alling and Isaac Doolittle, "for the building of a house of public worship, agreeable and according to the establishment of the Church of England," a certain piece of land containing twenty square rods—being four rods wide, fronting westerly on what is now called Church street, and being five rods deep. (*New Haven Land Records, Vol. XX.*, p. 210.) (Appendix D.)

Thus far a remarkable fatality seems to have attended the conveyances of land for the benefit of the Episcopal Church. This deed, like that of William Grigson, was not acknowledged by the grantor, who died shortly after its execution. But upon the petition of the grantees to the General Assembly, at the October session of 1756, that body confirmed their title to the land by a Resolve, "That the petitioners have liberty to record said deed in the Records of the town of New Haven, and the same being so recorded, shall and may be used and improved as the deed of said Mix for the passing the estate in said lands as fully and effectually to all intents and purposes as if the same had been acknowledged by the said Mix." (*New Haven Land Records, Vol. XX.*, pp. 210 and 211.) The land conveyed by this deed is that upon which the first house of worship of Trinity Church was built. It was completed in 1753. Stiles mentions it in his "Itinerary," and states its dimensions as being 58 by 38 feet, according to the measurement made by him in 1760. (*Vol. I.*, p. 21.) From the same source it appears that the Churchmen then residing in New Haven had increased to the number of twenty-four families, comprising eighty-seven souls. (P. 7.) The land upon which it stood has recently been purchased by Hon. James E. English.

In Mr. Chapin's centennial discourse, it is stated that a Church (parish?) was formed in New Haven in 1755. (P. 11.) This statement is probably correct, and is made on the authority of Dwight's Statistical Account of New Haven, (p. 43,) although no evidence of the fact appears in any official record.

The first minister of the Episcopal Church in New Haven was the Rev. Ebenezer Punderson. This gentleman graduated in Yale College in the year 1726. He was settled over the Second Congregational Church in Groton as pastor from January, 1728, to February, 1734, when he conformed to the Church of England, and became an itinerant Missionary in Connecticut of the Propagation Society. He was afterwards, (in 1753,) at his own request, appointed a Misssionary to the

Church in New Haven. He removed to Rye in 1762. Dr. Dwight says that he died there at an advanced age—(p. 45)—and Mr. Chapin repeats the same statement, on his authority, (p. 13.) That Mr. Punderson did not die at a very "advanced age," is evident from the inscription upon a monumental stone erected to his memory in Rye, a copy of which has been kindly furnished by one of his collateral descendants, and which shows that he died "Sept. 22d, 1764, at 60 years of age."

Mr. Punderson was succeeded in New Haven by Rev. Solomon Palmer, in 1763, who remained until 1766. He removed to Litchfield, where he soon after died. (*Dwight's Statistics,* p. 45.) He graduated at Yale College in 1729, and was settled over a Congregational Church in Cornwall until 1754—at that time he conformed to the Episcopal Church and went to England for Orders. He probably died at Litchfield in 1770. (*See Chapin,* p. 13.)

The first recorded evidence of the existence of the parish of Trinity Church, as an organized society, is contained in the *New Haven Land Records, Volume XXVII.,* p. 369, where is recorded the deed of Enos Alling to " Timothy Bonticou and Isaac Doolittle, *Church Wardens,* and Christopher Kilby and Stephen Mansfield, *Vestrymen* of Trinity Church, in New Haven, and ye rest of ye members of ye sd Episcopal Church." This instrument conveys to the grantees and their successors a certain piece or parcel of land, containing one acre and a half, more or less, situated and lying at a place called Grigson's corner, on the Town plat in said New Haven—bounded northerly on the Market Place or highway—easterly on highway or Town street—southerly by land in possession of Samuel Cook, and westwardly by land in possession of Ralph Isaacs, together with the dwelling house, barn and other buildings thereon."* This is the deed under which Trinity Church acquired a lawful title to the Glebe Land, and it is dated Oct. 31, 1765. It is not necessary to explain here how Enos Alling became possessed of this property. A reference to the public records of the town will show that he obtained his title by legitimate pur-

---

* Appendix E.

chase from those who had lawfully derived theirs from the heirs of Thomas Grigson, the original proprietor.* A quit-claim deed, properly executed and *acknowledged*, was obtained from William Grigson, of Exeter, England, (the great-grandson of Richard,) dated Oct. 26, 1768, which extinguished any possible title that the heirs of Richard Grigson may have had to the property in question, and confirmed that of Trinity Church, which, however, without it was sufficiently perfect. (*New Haven Land Records, Vol. XLV., p. 519.*)†

Up to this period no light is thrown upon the history of Trinity Church from its own records, of which there are none in existence previous to the commencement of the ministry of Rev. Bela Hubbard, in 1767. The facts concerning the contemplated building of the first Church, the organization of the Parish, and the purchase of the Glebe, have been mostly derived from the records of the town, while the scanty memorials of the two earliest Missionaries of New Haven have been supplied from such sources as have been attainable, and which have been carefully designated. The Parochial Register and the Parish Records will constitute the authority upon which the succeeding statements concerning the history of the Church will be made.

A brief notice of the "Society for the Propagation of the Gospel in Foreign Parts," which has been so frequently alluded to, and which has exercised so important an agency in the foundation of the Episcopal Church in this country, cannot be considered out of place here. It is probably the oldest Protestant Missionary Society in the world. It was incorporated in the year 1701, during the reign of William III. Through its means the Gospel has been carried to various and remote parts of the world, wherever British arms and British commerce have established a knowledge of the English tongue. By it the Episcopal Church was planted and carefully nourished in America until it was able to take care of itself, and to repay its obligations, in part, by sending forth missionaries in the same cause to other regions destitute as our own then were. This

---

* Appendix F.   † Appendix C.

truly venerable society is flourishing at the present day with undiminished vigor, and its efforts are attended with a degree of success unsurpassed by that of any similar institution.

The Rev. Bela Hubbard commenced his labors as a missionary of the Society to New Haven in the year 1767, at which time the Church had been built and the Parish organized. In the Register kept by him is written upon the first page, by his own hand, "Trinity Church, New Haven, Notitia Parochialis, A. D. 1767. Bela Hubbard, Missionary." There is little of general interest in this volume, its contents consisting mainly of the records of marriages, baptisms and funerals, from which he made his periodical reports to the Society. The Parish of Christ Church, in West Haven, enjoyed a stated portion of his services,—but it appears from his "Notitia" that his field of labor was very extensive, and was not confined to the limits of either parish. Here are recorded services performed in Amity, Bethany, Branford, East Haven, Fairfield, Farmington, Foxon, Guilford, Hamden, Killingworth, Milford, New Haven, North Guilford, Stratford, Saybrook, Stratfield, Woodbury and West Haven.

The first record of the choice of officers of the Parish is contained in this volume, and is in the following words :

"At a meeting of Vestry of Trinity Church, New Haven, on Easter Monday April 16th, 1770,

Chosen Mr. ISAAC DOOLITTLE, } *Ch. Wardens.*
and Capt. STEPHEN MANSFIELD, }

Mr. ENOS ALLING, *Clerk.*

Capt. CHRISTOPHER KILBY, }
Capt. ABIATHAN CAMP, } *Vestrymen.*
Mr. JOHN MILES, }

JAMES POWERS, *Sexton.*

The same book contains records of the annual election of Wardens, Vestrymen, &c., on Easter Monday of each succeeding year until 1777, but has no account of their proceedings, or those of the Parish. The officers once elected were seldom changed. Rotation in office has been little practised in the Parish, and consequently much discord has been avoided, and harmony and good will have generally prevailed among its members and in its councils.

Under the date of August 28th, 1772, is the record of the baptism of "Moses Paul," an adult Indian of the Mohegan tribe, in the Jail House, a little before his execution for the murder of —— Cook, of Waterbury." (*See Dwight's Statistics*, p. 36.)

Another entry records the burial of Peter Harrison, Esq., Collector of His Majesty's Customs of the Port of New Haven, May 7, 1775. Mr. Harrison was the gentleman through whose heroic exertions, according to the " historian " before quoted, Trinity Church obtained possession of the estate devised to it by Thomas Gregson, in his fabulous will.

The first record of the Parish as a Society is dated Easter Monday, March 31, 1777, and is commenced in these words:

"The Parishioners of Trinity Church convened at the usual place and chose Enos Alling, Esq., and Mr. Isaac Doolittle, Church Wardens for the year ensuing; Messrs. Charles Prindle, Benjamin Sanford, Daniel Bonticou, Ebenezer Chittenden and Samuel Nesbit, Vestrymen."

The annual meetings of the Parish have always been held on Easter Monday in each year. The " usual place" of holding them was the Church. At these meetings Rev. Mr. Hubbard was almost invariably present during the whole period of his rectorship—and after the election of Wardens and Vestrymen, he appointed a Clerk. The clerks of his appointment, however, appear to have had nothing to do with the records of the Parish. Their principal duty was to lead the responses of the congregation during public worship, and to designate the psalms and hymns to be sung. The office has now become extinct, it is believed, in all the parishes in New England.

The Wardens and Vestrymen generally held a meeting very soon after the parish meeting, at the residence of some one of their number, for the purpose of organization, when they made choice of a " Clerk of the Vestry " from their own members. His duty was to keep the records of the Parish meetings, and of the Vestry meetings, which in those days were not very frequent.

At a meeting of the Wardens and Vestry, held Sept. 11, 1777, a committee was appointed to dispose of the school money belonging to the Church, and to engage a woman to teach such a number of small children belonging to the Parish as may be sent to her for so long a time as the money shall last." In those days the school money was divided among the various ecclesiastical societies, in proportion to their numbers, and the children belonging to them were instructed in paro-. chial schools. In view of the character of the instruction dispensed in our public schools under the present system, it is hoped that the suggestion will not be considered obtrusive, that a return to the old plan might be attended with very beneficial results.

At a meeting of the Wardens and Vestry, March 3d, 1777, "they agreed," in the words of the record, "to purchase a proper book for the purpose of recording all the votes and doings of the Vestry this year and hereafter ; and to leave a sufficient number of leaves at the beginning to transcribe the old one," &c. A book was accordingly purchased, in which all the records of the Parish and Vestry meetings have been kept from Easter Monday, 1777, until Dec. 12, 1853. Although several leaves were left "at the beginning of the book," the old one was never transcribed, and it is supposed to be irrecoverably lost.

Enos Alling died Sept. 11, 1779. He had been re-elected Warden at the annual meeting of the Parish in that year,— had been appointed Parish Clerk by Mr. Hubbard, and had also been elected Treasurer by the Wardens and Vestry. At a meeting of the surviving Warden and the Vestry, held on the 14th of October, in the same year, Ebenezer Chittenden was chosen Warden [from their own number] to supply the vacancy caused by the death of Mr. Alling.

It is the occasion of much regret that so little has been preserved concerning the personal history of Enos Alling, whose zeal in the cause of the Episcopal Church obtained for him, among his contemporaries, the honorary title of "Bishop" Alling, by which name he is better remembered, and is more frequently mentioned, even now, than by his baptismal one. He left no lineal descendants, which may perhaps account for the absence of more perfect memorials of him than can now be ob-

tained.* He graduated at Yale College in 1746, in the same
class with President Stiles, and afterwards became engaged
successfully in commercial pursuits. He was a member of the
Society for the Propagation of the Gospel, in the operations of
which he was deeply interested. He enjoyed the reputation,
during his life, of being a man of honor and integrity, and died
at the age of 61 years.

At the time of Mr. Alling's decease, Mr. Hubbard was residing in his house. In the month of October following, he removed to the dwelling that had formerly belonged to Abiathar
Camp, which stood on the ground now occupied by the Chapel
Street Church, where he resided for several years.

At the annual Parish meeting, March 27, 1780, it was voted
" that each member, whether Wardens or Vestrymen, who shall
neglect to attend an evening meeting, when properly adjourned, shall pay one shilling in hard money for the benefit of the
parish poor, unless he can shew a reason that is satisfactory."
This incentive to punctuality did not prove to be efficient, for
at the next adjourned meeting of April 12th, there was no business done, " for want of members," as the record significantly
sets forth.

An organ had been purchased and set up in the Church in
the year 1784, and at a Vestry meeting held Dec. 29, in that
year, it was voted " that those persons who have been benefactors to the Church, by contributing for an organ, should, as a
tribute of gratitude for their liberality, have their names, with
the respective sums of their subscriptions, recorded in this
book." " The following, therefore, is the subscription at length:
Whereas, there having been former subscriptions signed by
sundry persons in town, it is agreed by the Church Wardens
and Vestry of said Church, that they be not holden to any but
the present. We whose names are subscribed do engage to pay

---

* Enos Alling's widow was the daughter of Capt. Samuel Miles. Some time after the death of Mr. Alling, she became the wife of Hon. Jared Ingersoll. She
died Dec. 3, 1786, in the 54th year of her age, the wife of Captain Joseph Bradley, to whom she had been married the previous April.—*Conn. Journal for Dec.
6, 1786.*

unto the Rev. B. Hubbard, Mr. Richard Tritton, Col. Joseph Drake, Mr. Elias Shipman, Mr. Isaac Beers and Mr. William Powell, the committee appointed to collect the money and purchase the s^d organ, the several sums affixed to our names. New Haven, 12th Jan. 1784."

At the annual Parish meeting, Easter Monday, March 28, 1785, it was " *Voted*, That the Wardens and Vestry are the Society's Committee according to law"—and as such they have been held and regarded ever since—their powers and functions being the same as those of such committees of the other ecclesiastical societies. It was also voted, "That there be no further burials under the body of the Church, except those families some members of which have already been buried there, by which is understood the heads of those families and their children—only excepting any person leaving a legacy of thirty pounds, and particularly desiring that liberty."

At a Parish meeting held Oct. 5, 1785, it was voted, "That Rev. Mr. Hubbard is allowed the deficiency of salary he received from England, until Easter next, as Missionary." Although the language of this vote is not very clear, the probability is that Mr. Hubbard about this time ceased to be the Missionary of the Propagation Society.* There is a memorandum in his "register," under date of May 9, 1785, in these words: "Wrote to the Secretary of the Society in England, Dr. Morice." There is no intimation as to the subject of his communication, but it doubtless had reference to his resignation of his mission. The meaning of the vote seems to be that Mr. Hubbard should receive from the Parish for salary, at the following Easter, an amount equal to what he would have received from the Society, had he continued in its service.

At the same meeting it was voted, "That the sum of ten pounds be paid unto the Right Rev. Samuel Seabury, Bishop of this State."

As this is the first mention that is made of Bishop Seabury in the Records, it seems to be an appropriate place for the in-

---

* A salary of £60 was voted to Mr. Hubbard at the annual meeting of 1784, at which time he probably became the Rector.

troduction of a very brief notice of some of the leading inci-
dents of his life. He was a native of Groton, in this State,
and was a graduate of Yale College of the Class of 1748. He
was consecrated Bishop of Connecticut on the 14th day of November, 1784, at Aberdeen, in Scotland, by the *Primus* and
two other of the non-juring Bishops of the Scottish Episcopal
Church, under circumstances that are generally too well known
to require repetition. On the day subsequent to his consecration, a *Concordat* was signed by the consecrating Bishops and
the new Bishop of Connecticut. In the fifth article of this instrument, it is declared that "as the celebration of the holy
eucharist, or the administration of the body and blood of
Christ, is the principal bond of union among Christians,
as well as the most solemn act of worship in the Christian
Church, the Bishops aforesaid agree in desiring that there may
be as little variation here as possible"—and it was agreed between them that Bishop Seabury should, "by gentle methods
of argument and persuasion, endeavor to introduce by degrees
into practice" the communion office of the Scottish Church, if
upon examination he should find it "agreeable to the genuine
standards of antiquity." The Bishop of Connecticut was faithful to his covenant. He was a member of the General Convention of the American Episcopal Church, held in 1789, at
which the Book of Common Prayer now in use was set forth
and established. In this book the order for the administration
of the Lord's Supper differs from that in the Liturgy of the
Church of England by certain additions, by which it is made
to conform more closely to the Scottish form, and particularly
to the "genuine standards of antiquity"—which will be apparent to those who may be sufficiently interested to examine
it, and compare it with the most ancient liturgies that have
been preserved. This important reform is attributed to the influence which was exerted upon that occasion by Bishop Seabury.

At the regular annual meeting in 1787, Moses Bates was appointed organist, and was allowed to occupy the house in which
he then lived without being required to pay rent, as a compensation for his services.

At a Vestry meeting, Sept. 17th, in the same year, £10 lawful money was directed by vote to be paid to Bishop Seabury ; but the vote contained the proviso that this donation should not be considered as a precedent for any future claims upon the Church by the Bishop.

At a special Parish meeting, Jan. 14, 1788, Doct. Samuel Nesbitt was appointed a delegate from the Parish to the Convention of the representatives of the other churches in the Diocese, to be held in Waterbury on the 13th of the following February, to devise ways and means for obtaining the salary of Bishop Seabury, and he was furnished with a certified copy of the tax list of the Society.

At the annual meeting in 1788, it is recorded that Dr. Nesbitt made a report of the doings of the Convention at Waterbury, which he had attended as delegate. There is no record of the report, but its substance is sufficiently apparent from the vote that was passed in reference to it, by which the doings of the Convention were approved, and that agreeably to the recommendation of the Convention, the Parish should raise a sum equal to a half penny on the pound, on the amount of the tax list, for the support of the Bishop, which sum was to be raised by quarterly collections in the Church, and that if a sufficient amount should not be obtained by that method, the deficiency should be made up from the Treasury.

Dr. Nesbitt was again appointed to represent the Parish in the Diocesan Convention to be held at Wallingford, on the 7th of May following, "to ratify or amend the doings of the former Convention at Waterbury."

A vote was passed authorizing Mr. Hubbard to officiate in West Haven "four or more Sundays," and authorizing the Vestry to fix the sum to be paid into the treasury by the Church in West Haven for Mr. Hubbard's services.

At the Vestry meeting March 31, 1788, Moses Bates was re-appointed organist, with the additional office of *Sexton*, and for his services was to have his house rent free, as before.

At the same meeting it was also voted " that for the conveniency of describing the lots and boundaries of the church lands, that the street beginning in Chapel street, between the

houses of Robert Fairchild and Abel Buel, be called and
known by the name of Gregson street, and that the street beginning in Church street, running between the house of Levi
Hubbard and the house at present leased to Moses Bates,
westerly until it meets Grigson street, be called and known by
the name of School Alley." Also, "that a new lane, twelve
feet in width, be laid out between Grigson street and Church
street, from Chapel street to School Alley." Whether or not
this last vote was ever carried into effect, does not appear.

There is an entry in Mr. Hubbard's "Notitia," in the following words: "July 8, 1788. Buried Mary Chatterton, aged 19,
who was killed with lightning at the house of Mr. Stephen
Ball, July 8, in yᵉ evening." This is believed to be the only
instance of death caused by lightning that has ever occurred
in New Haven.

At a special Parish meeting Nov. 17, 1788, Dr. Nesbitt,
who had then received Holy Orders, resigned the office of
Senior Warden, to which he had been elected at the previous
annual meeting.

At the same meeting a proposition was received from Messrs.
Wm. McCrackan and Josiah Burr to build an addition of
twenty feet to the rear of the Church, and to make such alterations in the position of the pulpit, reading-desk and chancel,
as the proposed addition might make proper, and to have the
whole finished in two years, without expense to the Church,
provided the Parish would secure to them and their heirs the
possession of all the new pews in the space created by the proposed addition and alterations, to be built and placed under
the direction of a committee to be appointed by the Parish for
the purpose. This offer was accepted by the Parish, and a
committee was appointed "to negotiate an exchange with
Richard Cutler for land on the east end of the Church (lot) belonging to him, for so much of land on the north side of said
Church (lot) as may be necessary for extending the rear of the
Church twenty feet."

At a special Parish meeting called by Rev. Mr. Hubbard, at
the request of the Vestry, Feb. 9, 1789, to take into consideration the propriety of building a Vestry Room, the proposition

was rejected unanimously. " The general opinion was (in the words of the record) that the finances of the Church would not at that time admit of it."

At the annual meeting April 13, 1789, Jonathan Ingersoll, Esq., was appointed a delegate to the Convention of the Diocese, to be held in Middletown, to deliberate upon the propriety of sending a delegate at large from this Diocese to the proposed " General Convention to be held at Annapolis, said to be for the uniform discipline of the American Episcopal Churches and other purposes."

A special Parish meeting was held Oct. 1, 1789, "for the purpose of taking into consideration a draft (probably of a form) for the consecration of our Church by our Diocesan Bishop." At an adjourned meeting, held on the 5th of the same month, it was "agreed to suspend the consideration of the deed of dedication recommended by Rev. Mr. Hubbard," because the General Convention was then in session in Philadelphia, and their doings might require some alterations to be made in the instrument. A further adjournment was made to the 14th, and finally to the 22d of the same month. As there is no record at the last named date, nor at any subsequent period, of the consecration of the Church, the presumption is, that for some reason now unknown, the solemn act was never performed.

As an evidence of the great scarcity of money at this time, at a Vestry meeting held on the 15th of February, 1790, the collector of the rates or ecclesiastical tax was authorized to take other property in the place of money in payment.

The Church appears to have been a good deal embarrassed by debt for some years, and at the annual meeting in 1790 it was voted that a subscription should be opened by the Wardens and Vestry for raising the sum of £150 to be applied to the extinguishment of the demands against the Parish. Besides it had been found necessary, or at least convenient, for the purpose of saving expense, to employ the Rector but three-quarters of the time, at a reduced salary. A proposal was made to him, by the Wardens and Vestry, in 1791, to serve the Parish three-fourths of the time for £100. Mr. Hubbard accepted the proposition on condition that he should be at liberty to leave the Parish at his pleasure.

At the annual meeting in 1792, the same provision was made for Mr. Hubbard as in the year before. Col. Drake and Mr. Isaac Beers were appointed a committee to confer with similar committees of the other societies in relation to the subject of the erection of a fence around the burying ground. Upon their report to the special meeting convened for the purpose of hearing and acting upon it, a tax of 1½d. on the pound was laid to procure means for the expense, and the same committee were appointed to superintend the building of the fence on the part of the Parish, and to spend the balance of the money, if there should be any, in setting out trees in the burying ground.

It was about this time that measures were begun for laying out a new cemetery, which project was afterwards completed in a manner most creditable to all the parties concerned in it, and which it is only necessary to allude to here. At the same meeting it was voted "that the committee confer with the committees of the other societies concerning some convenient place for another burying ground, and ascertain the price for which the same may be purchased, and make a report of the same to the Society."

At the annual meeting April 1st, 1793, Mr. Christian Hanson and Mr. Asa Austin were, by vote, "requested to attend in the galleries on Sundays, to prevent the disturbances of the boys." And a similar vote was passed at every succeeding annual meeting, as long as the old church continued to be used as a place of worship. A traditional anecdote has been preserved, which may be appropriately introduced here, as showing the necessity for this action on the part of the Parish, and as exhibiting a whimsical method of imparting sound doctrine, and of illustrating a distinction with a difference. One Sunday, during service, a great disturbance was made in the gallery, by the irreverent conduct of one of that class of mischievous boys for which Church street has been for many years distinguished, and which is far from being extinct in that locality at the present day. A gentleman among the worshipers, who was pos-

sessed of a really devotional spirit, but had at the same time a
very choleric temper, submitted to the annoyance until his patience was quite exhausted, when he seized the boy by the col-
lar and rushed with him into the porch.   There, shaking the
culprit almost to dislocation, he roared in a voice of thunder,
" You —— little rascal, how dare you behave so in a *Church?*
You thought you was in a Presbyterian meeting-house, didn't
you—hey?"

Some time during this year a bell was procured and hung in
the belfry.   It was probably cast by Isaac Doolittle, but this is
a surmise merely, as there is nothing on the records to show
where it was obtained.   Among the proceedings of the Vestry,
at a meeting on the 26th of Sept., 1793, is the following
record :

> " It being reported that, without any order or direction of the Wardens and
> Vestry of said Church, the bell has been rung on the two preceding Saturday
> nights, by some person unknown, therefore,
> " *Voted,* That in our opinion the ringing of the bell at the above mentioned
> time was very improper and irregular, and that we do not countenance the same ;
> and that no person in future be permitted to ring the said bell on Saturday or
> any other nights, unless ordered by the Society at large."

At the annual meeting April 20, 1794, the Wardens were
authorized to have the Church painted, and to borrow a sum
not exceeding £50 to pay for it.   And at a Vestry meeting in
the same year, "Mr. Salter, an organist from England," was
engaged to play the organ for six months, to be paid at the
rate of twenty guineas per annum.   Mr. Salter remained for
many years in the situation to which he was at this time appointed.   There are yet members of the Parish living who remember the exquisite performances with which he used to delight them.   He lived to quite an advanced age, and became
wholly blind before he died.   By the exercise of his talents he
supported his family in a respectable manner ; and it is no dis-
paragement to his successors to say that none of them have
surpassed him in skillful execution and tasteful performance
upon an instrument which is better adapted than any other to
the purposes of public worship.

At the annual meeting in 1795, a committee was raised to

enquire into the expediency and probable cost of building a
gallery in the Church, but as the estimated cost was over £100,
the consideration of the subject was postponed, for the reason
that the town had been put to great expense in consequence of
the sickness that had prevailed the previous year.

In 1796, Mr. Hubbard was again employed for the whole
year at a salary of £140, from which it is inferred that the
finances of the Parish were in an improved condition. At a
Vestry meeting, April 30, 1796, in the words of the record,
" 'twas also agreed at this meeting that the First Society have
liberty to make use of the church bell for all purposes they
need until theirs can be run over anew." It is not probable
that the First Society availed itself of this courteous offer, as
the proffered privilege would be about as valuable as that of
borrowing a neighbor's knocker. But it is agreeable to find
such an evidence of good will from the one society to the other on record, and it was unquestionably fully appreciated by
the party in behalf of which it was exhibited.

In 1797, Mr. Hubbard's salary was raised to £155. He was
to have the privilege of officiating at West Haven seven Sundays in the course of the year, but in case he did so, the parish
there was required to pay Trinity Church $50 for his services ;
and this arrangement was renewed annually until 1802.

A vote was passed at the annual meeting in 1797, "that ten
dollars be paid out of the Society's treasury towards the public wells and pumps in this city.

Bishop Seabury had died suddenly in New London on the
25th of February, 1796, and the Rev. Abraham Jarvis had
been elected to succeed him. At a special Parish meeting,
Oct. 2, 1797, Capt. Joseph Bradley and Col. Joseph Drake
were " chosen delegates to attend at the consecration of the
Bishop elect in New Haven." In the volume containing Mr.
Hubbard's " Notitia," is the certificate of the consecration of
Bishop Jarvis in Trinity Church, dated Oct. 18, 1797, and
signed by the consecrators, Bishops White, Provost and Bass.

At a Parish meeting, Nov. 27, 1797, it was voted, " That
there be a contribution every Sabbath after church at night for
the benefit of the poor of the Parish. The contributions to

continue through the winter." The custom begun at this time has been continued in Trinity Church to this day ; but the collections in late years have been made monthly during the winter, instead of weekly, as then.

At a Vestry meeting, Dec. 23, 1797, certain persons, being poor members of the Parish, were designated as suitable recipients of the money collected in pursuance of the last mentioned vote; and a committee was appointed " to confer with the committee of the other ecclesiastical societies about assisting a certain class of poor inhabitants, not members of either society."

In the course of this year, (1797,) after various conferences, estimates and votes on the subject, a contract was made for building side galleries in the Church, and the Wardens and Vestry authorized to borrow six hundred dollars on the credit of the Parish to meet the expense.

At a Parish meeting, Oct. 22d, Messrs. Joseph Bradley, Richard Cutler and John Barker were " appointed agents to make application to the General Assembly for the formation of the Parish into a School Society according to law."

In the volume of "Notitia" is a record of the death of Isaac Doolittle, Feb. 13th, 1800, Æ 78. Mr. Doolittle was an enterprising citizen of New Haven. He was a native of Wallingford, but came here to reside at a very early age. The Church, of which he was so long a member, was the object of his warm, zealous and earnest attachment. His contribution of the means necessary for building the first house of worship were more liberal than those of any of his cotemporaries. He was one of the earliest wardens whose name appears upon record. His business pursuits were various. He was a manufacturer of brass clocks, of the kind that used to stand in a solemn looking case, in a dark corner, greeting each visitor in the same language that Doctor Blimbers addressed to little Paul Dombey. There are some few still remaining with his name upon their faces, one of which it is hoped may yet be found in the possession of this Society, as an interesting relic of the past. He was also engaged in the business of casting bells. His foundry was on the south side of Chapel street, above York, in the place where the house stands that was erected by the late John W. Fitch. During the Revolutionary war, he, in company with Jeremiah Atwater and Elijah Thompson, made large quantities of gunpowder at their mills in Westville. This business was continued there until the beginning of the present century.

At a Vestry meeting, Dec. 9, 1801, it is recorded that "a letter from Mr. Ashbel Baldwin was laid before us requesting a payment of 25_{100}^{50}$ by the 1st January, 1801, as our proportion of a tax laid by the General Convention for the use of the Academy at Cheshire. The Vestry requested Mr. Hubbard to write to Mr. Baldwin to forward the vote of the Convention, that the Church here may be satisfied of the object contemplated by the money." And further, January 31, 1801, that "The vote of the Episcopal Convention was laid before them about raising out of this Parish the sum of 25_{100}^{50}$ for the benefit of the Academy at Cheshire. *Voted*, That a subscription be set on foot immediately for the above purpose, and that Stephen Atwater carry round the subscription."

In a short memoir of Bishop Seabury, it is said that "he fully appreciated the value of sound learning as the handmaid of religion, and was the projector of a Church college in Connecticut, of which Cheshire Academy was the first fruit." This institution is deserving of something more than a mere episodical notice in a paper like this. It has exercised a very important influence in the history of the Church, especially in this Diocese. It has been a nursery for the ministry, and many of the ablest and most useful Episcopal clergymen of Connecticut in the past generation were educated there. One of its former principals or rectors is now a resident of New Haven, the respected pastor of a flourishing church, and a prominent officer of this Society. Let us cherish the hope that at no distant day he will find sufficient leisure to favor us with a history of that valuable institution.

In 1803 Mr. Hubbard's salary was fixed at $520 for the year. He was to have the liberty of preaching in West Haven seven Sundays in the year, for which the parish there was to pay to Trinity Church the sum of $60. A similar arrangement was made each succeeding year until 1806.

At the annual meeting in 1804, "a committee was appointed to consider the propriety of enlarging the Church, repairing or taking down the steeple and building a cupola, and any other repairs necessary to be made in the Church." Nothing further appears to have been done this year in the matter.

In 1806 Mr. Hubbard's salary was fixed at $650, and his services engaged for the whole year.

At a Vestry meeting, Oct. 20, there was a vote authorizing the erection of a stove in the Church, under the direction of the Wardens and Vestry, provided it should be done free of expense to the Society.

In the course of 1807 the old steeple was taken down and a cupola built in its stead, and the Church generally put in repair and painted. Mr. Hubbard's salary for this year was fixed at $700.

In 1808 Dr. Hubbard's salary was reduced to $650, which sum was appropriated for that purpose annually thereafter, during his life.

In the course of this year, at the request of Dr. Hubbard, the Parish engaged the services of the Rev. Salmon Wheaton as an assistant minister to the rector. His engagement ended about Oct. 20th, 1810, and he was paid for his services at the rate of $200 a year. Overtures were then made to the Rev. S. F. Jarvis to supply the place that Mr. Wheaton had filled, for the term of six months, at the same salary that had been paid to the former. It is recorded that, at a special parish meeting held Dec. 8, 1810, it was stated to the meeting that it was well ascertained that the sum proposed to be offered to Mr. Jarvis would not be considered by him as adequate to a support, it was therefore " *Voted*, That the Society do nothing on the subject."

It was at the annual meeting in this year (1810) that the subject of building a new church was first discussed, " and Elias Shipman, John H. Jacocks and John Hunt, Jr., were appointed a committee " to set a subscription on foot to ascertain the minds of the members of the Society."

The Rector yet remained without an assistant. A special Parish meeting was convened June 9, 1811, when the Wardens and Vestry, as the Society's Committee, were authorized to extend a call to the Rev. Henry Whitlock, of Norwalk, to be the assistant minister of the Parish, with a salary of $800 a year. The call was accepted, and Mr. Whitlock commenced his duties shortly afterwards.

In the "register" is recorded the death of Ebenezer Chittenden, May 11, 1812, at the age of 86. Mr. Chittenden had been one of the earliest wardens of the Church, having been first chosen in 1779, to supply the vacancy caused by the death of Enos Alling. He was also appointed Parish Clerk by Mr. Hubbard, in 1791, which office he continued to hold until the time of his death, and which expired with him.

This year (1812) was also made memorable in the annals of Trinity Church, by the decease of its Rector. The faithful missionary, the pious priest, the watchful pastor, after a life spent in the service of his Master, was called to his reward on the 6th day of December, 1812, in the seventy-third year of his age, and the forty-fifth of his ministry, as Missionary to and Rector of the Church. His memory is yet green among the children and children's children of those who knew and loved him, and enjoyed his ministrations, and his name is never mentioned by them but with affection and veneration.

When this task was first undertaken, it was with the expectation that the narrative of events illustrating the history of Trinity Church would be extended to a more recent period. But the materials have been so much more abundant than was anticipated, that notwithstanding the care that has been taken to exclude all irrelevant matter, and to condense the facts into the smallest compass consistent with intelligibility, the limits that were at first prescribed for the purpose have been already transcended. It has been thought advisable, therefore, to proceed no further at present, but to resume the subject upon some future occasion, should it be considered desirable.

In whatever has been herein written, every endeavor has been made to render justice to all parties concerned. And although a jealous regard for the reputation of the original set-

tlers of New Haven and of their descendants is freely con-
fessed, it has not been attempted, consciously, either to justify or palliate any willful misconduct of theirs, or to withhold,
disguise or distort the truth. The Puritan founders of the
Colony were men who sincerely believed in their own principles, and made many and great sacrifices in support of them,
and they endeavored to act consistently with them. It is
true that they shared in the common inheritance of human corruption, and sometimes the old Adam would show that
he was not quite dead within them. So far as the conflicts of
their descendants with the Episcopal Church are concerned,
the worst that can be said of them is that they conducted
themselves very much as other men of equally earnest convic-
tions and violent prejudices would have done, under similar
circumstances.

The late Rev. Dr. Croswell, in 1856, began the preparation of
a collection of facts, which was intended for future publication, if circumstances should warrant it, under the title of
"Annals of my Parish." The narrative commenced with the
incumbency of Dr. Hubbard, and can be continued to the
latest period of the life of the author, from the papers that he
prepared and arranged with reference to the subject. Very
little use, however, has been made of these annals in this sketch,
as they could not well be made available for the purpose; but
most of the facts contained herein have been derived directly
from the original sources.

Henry White, Esq., has kindly furnished several memoranda, which have saved me much time and trouble, by indicating
the particular volumes of the public records in which are to be
found the various deeds and conveyances of property in which
Trinity Church has been concerned.

The Rev. Dr. Beardsley and the Rev. Wm. L. Kingsley
have also loaned various valuable documents, which have been
of great service in the preparation of this outline, especially of
that part of it which relates to the earliest days of the Church
in New Haven.

APPENDIX.

A.

A LIST OF THE WARDENS, VESTRY, AND OTHER OFFICERS OF TRINITY CHURCH, FROM 1765 TO 1812.

WARDENS.

Timothy Bonticou, 1765; Capt. Stephen Mansfield, 1770 to 1774; Isaac Doolittle, 1765, and 1770 to 1777, and 1783 to 1785; Abiathar Camp, 1775, 1776; Enos Alling, 1777 to 1779; Joseph Browne, 1778 to 1787; Ebenezer Chittenden, 1779 to 1782; Samuel Nesbit, 1786 to 1788; William McCrackan, 1788 to 1809; Joseph Bradley, 1791 to 1798, and 1800 to 1809; Jonathan Ingersoll, 1799, and 1810 to 1812; William Walter, 1810 to 1812.

VESTRYMEN.

Stephen Mansfield, 1765; Christopher Kilby, 1765, and 1770 to 1772, and 1774; Abiathar Camp, 1770 to 1772, and 1774; John Miles, 1770 to 1772, and 1774 to 1775, and 1781 to 1784; Dr. Daniel Bonticou, 1774, 1775, 1777, 1778; Ambrose Ward, 1774 to 1776, and 1778 to 1780; Charles Prindle, 1775 to 1782; Ebenezer Chittenden, 1774, 1775, and 1777 to 1779; Thomas Davis, 1775; Benjamin Sanford, 1775 to 1783; Dr. Samuel Nesbit, 1777 to 1782; Elias Shipman, 1778 to 1782, and 1793 to 1812; Capt. Thomas Rice, 1780 to 1784; Richard Cutler, 1780 to 1782, and 1785; William McCrackan, 1780, and 1782 to 1787; Joseph Bradley, 1781, 1782, and 1791 to 1793; Anthony Perit, 1781, 1782; Elijah Forbes, 1781 to 1783; Isaac Beers, 1782, and 1792 to 1810; Russell Clark, 1784, 1785; Zina Denison, 1784, and 1786, 1787; Joseph Drake, 1786 to 1790; Josiah Burr, 1788 to 1791; William Powell, 1788, 1789; Samuel Humiston, 1788; Jonathan Ingersoll, 1789 to 1798, and 1800 to 1809; John Heyliger, 1790; Jared Mansfield, 1790 to 1794; John Nicoll, 1794 to 1796; John Barker, 1795 to 1812; Frederick Hunt, 1797 to 1809; Timothy Phelps, 1799; Nathan Smith, 1805 to 1812; Chas. Denison, 1808 to 1812; John H. Jacocks, 1808 to 1812; Elijah Thompson, 1809; Samuel Hughes, 1809 to 1812; John Hunt, Jr., 1810 to 1812; Ward Atwater, 1810 to 1812; Andrew Kidston, 1810 to 1812; William McCrackan, Jr., 1810 to 1812; Alexander Langmuir, 1811; Solomon Collis, 1812.

DELEGATES TO DIOCESAN CONVENTION.

Dr. Samuel Nesbit, 1787, 1788; Jonathan Ingersoll, 1789 to 1793; William McCrackan, 1794; Joseph Bradley, 1795 to 1797; Thomas Green, 1799, 1800, and 1802; John Barker, 1798 and 1801; Stephen Atwater, 1803 to 1805; Joseph Drake, 1806; Charles Denison, 1807; John H. Jacocks, 1808 to 1810; Nathan mith, 1812.

CLERKS OF THE VESTRY.

Daniel Bonticou, 1777, 1778; Elias Shipman, 1779; Samuel Nesbit, 1779 to 1782; John Miles, Jr., 1783; Jared Mansfield, 1784. 1786, 1787, 1791 to 1794; Thaddeus Perit, 1785; William Powell, 1788 to 1789; John Barker, 1795 to 1809.

PARISH CLERKS APPOINTED BY REV. DR. HUBBARD.

Enos Alling, 1778, 1779; Joseph Brown, (sub-clerk,) 1778, and 1780 to 1785; Levi Hubbard, 1784; Isaac Beers, 1785; Jared Mansfield, 1786; Joseph Browne, 1787 to 1789; Ebenezer Chittenden, 1791 to 1800, and 1809 to 1812; William Kilby, (sub-clerk,) probably 1800 to 1812.

ORGANISTS.

Moses Bates, 1787, 1788; Daniel Salter, 1794 to 1797, and 1799, 1800, 1803 to 1812; John Ives, Jr., 1798, 1801.

B.

COPY OF WILLIAM GRIGSON'S DEED TO JONATHAN ARNOLD.

From the New Haven Land Records, Vol X., p. 520.

This indenture, made the twenty-sixth day of March, in the ninth year of the reign of our Sovereign Lord, George the second, by the Grace of God, of Great Britain, France and Ireland, King, Defender of the Faith, &c., and in the year of our Lord one thousand seven hundred thirty and six, between William Grigson, of the City of London, Gent: son and heir of William Grigson, late of the same place, Gent: deceased, who was the only surviving son and heir of Richard Grigson, formerly of New Haven, in New England, but lately of the City of Bristol, deceased, which said Richard Grigson was the only son and heir of Thomas Grigson, late of New Haven aforesaid, deceased, of the one part, and the Reverend Jonathan Arnold, of New Haven aforesaid, in the Colony of Connecticut, in New England aforesaid, Clerk, of the other part. Whereas, the said William Grigson is seized in fee simple to the use of him and his heirs amongst other lands of and in one acre and three-quarters of an acre of land or thereabouts, be the same more or less, situated and being in the town and county aforesaid, abutting on the common land or land not taken up or appropriated on the North, on the common highway leading from the common land to the water side on the East, to land now in possession of John Thompson on the South, to the estate of one Mr.

Atwater, lately deceased, on the West; and whereas the said William Grigson, out of his piety towards God, and out of his zeal for the protestant religion and the Church of England, as by law established, hath of his own free will resolved to give and grant the same premises to the said Jonathan Arnold and his heirs in trust, nevertheless, for the building and erecting a Church thereupon for the worship and service of Almighty God according to the practice of the Church of England, and a parsonage or dwelling house for the incumbent of the said intended Church for the time being, and also for a Church Yard to be taken thereout for the burial of the poor, and the residue thereof to be esteemed and used as Glebe Land by the minister of the said intended Church for the time being for ever; and whereas the said Jonathan Arnold being a minister of the Church of England, a missionary from the Honorable Society in England for propagating the Gospel in Foreign Parts, and a gentleman who is at great charge, trouble and expense in soliciting a subscription for and towards the building and erecting the said intended Church and parsonage house aforesaid, he, the said William Grigson, hath therefore made choice of the said Jonathan Arnold, his heirs and assigns, to be trustees for the end and purpose aforesaid, and is desirous as far as in him lies that the said Jonathan Arnold, and such son or sons as shall be educated and qualified for the same, may be presented after the decease of the said Jonathan Arnold, and for the want of such son or sons so qualified, then such person or persons as shall be nominated and sent over from time to time as missionaries from the Honorable Society aforesaid. Now this indenture witnesseth that the said William Grigson, upon the consideration aforesaid, and of five shillings of lawful money to him in hand paid by the said Jonathan Arnold before the executing hereof, the receipt whereof is hereby acknowledged, hath given, granted, released and confirmed, and doth by these presents give, grant, release and confirm unto the said Jonathan Arnold, in his actual possession, now being by virtue of a bargain and sale to him thereof, made by the said William Grigson for one whole year, by indenture dated the day before the date hereof, and by force of the statute for transferring uses into possession, and his heirs and assigns, all that the aforesaid one acre and three-quarters of an acre of land, be the same more or less, in New Haven aforesaid, with all and singular the rights, members and appurtenances thereof, and the reversion and reversions, remainder and remainders, rents and profits thereof. To have and to hold the said one acre and three-quarters of an acre of land, and all other the premises hereby granted, or intended to be, with appurtenances, unto the said Jonathan Arnold, his heirs and assigns, for ever to the uses, intents and purposes hereinbefore recited and mentioned concerning the same, and to no other uses, interest or purposes whatsoever. In witness whereof, the parties aforesaid to these present indentures have hereunto interchangeably set their hands and seals the day and year first above written.   WM. [Seal] GRIGSON.

Sealed and delivered, being first duly stampt, in presence of
  HENRY CANER,
  WM. LATHROP.

The above is a true copy of the original deed, September 6th, 1738.

                                  p. SAML. BISHOP, *Clerk.*

C.

COPY OF WM. GREGSON'S DEED TO TIMOTHY BONTICOU, &c.

Land Records, Vol. XLV., p. 519.

To all people to whom these presents shall come—GREETING:

Know ye that I, Willm Gregson, of the City of Exeter, in the Kingdom of Great Britain, Gentleman, in consideration of five shillings money received to my full satisfaction of Timothy Bonticou and Isaac Doolittle, Church Wardens, and Christopher Kilby and Stephen Mansfield, Vestrymen of Trinity Church, in New Haven, in the County of New Haven, in the Colony of Connecticut, and the rest of the members of the s^d Episcopal Church, do remise, release, and forever quit claim unto them, the said Timothy Bonticou, Isaac Doolittle, and the rest of the professors of the Church of England, and members of the said Trinity Church for the time being, and to their successors, all my right, title, interest, claim, challenge and demand whatsoever in and unto a certain piece or parcel of land, containing in quantity one acre and half, be the same more or less, situate, lying and being at a certain place call'd Gregson's corner, in the Town plot in said New Haven, bounded Northwardly on the Market place or highway, Easterly on highway or Town street, Southerly by lands in possession of Samuel Cook, and Westerly on land in possession of Ralph Isaacs, together with the dwelling house, barn and other buildings thereon. To have and to hold the said remised and released premises, with all and singular the appurtenances unto them, the said releasees and their successors and assigns forever, to their own proper use, support and maintenance of the said Church. And I, the said Willm Gregson, do for myself, my heirs, Ex^rs and Adm^rs, by these presents, covenant to and with the said releasees, their successors and assigns, that I shall not, nor will, nor shall my heirs or assigns, or any of them, ever have, challenge or claim any right, title or interest in or to the same, or any part thereof, and therefrom shall and will be ever barred and secluded by these presents. In witness whereof, I have hereunto set my hand and seal, this 26th day of October, A. D. 1768.

WILLIAM GREGSON. [Seal.]

Sealed and delivered in presence of   (Ex.)

SIM GANDY.
JOHN DANE.

City of Exeter, on the day and date above written, personally appeared Willm Gregson, signer and sealer of the foregoing instrument and ackn^d the same to be his free act and deed.

Before me, PHILIP DACIE, Mayor, and one of His Majesty's Justices of the Peace for the City and County.

Received for Record Sept. 4, 1782.

D.

COPY OF SAMUEL MIX'S DEED TO ENOS ALLING AND ISAAC DOOLITTLE.

To all people to whom these presents shall come—GREETING:

Know ye y^t I, Saml Mix, of New Haven, in ye county of New Haven, in ye Colony of Connecticut, in New England, for the consideration of Two Hundred pounds money, old ten^r, rec^d to my full satisfaction of Enos Alling and Isaac Doolittle, of s^d Town, County and Colony above s^d, do give, grant, bargain, sell and confirm unto ye s^d Enos Alling and Isaac Doolittle, for the building of house for public worship, agreeable and according to the establishment of ye Church of England, one certain piece of land, being the south west corner of my lot, which lot lies at the south-east corner of the Market place, opposite to the corner known by the name of Gixson's corner, which piece of land is to contain in quantity twenty square rods of land, bounded as follows: East and North by the above mentioned Saml Mix his lot, West by a highway, and Southerly by John White's home lot, which land is to lie four rods by the highway west, and is to run five rods deep from the s^d highway, parralel to the above mentioned John White his lot, &c. To have and to hold s^d above granted and bargained premises, with the appurtenances thereof, unto them, ye s^d Enos Alling and Isaac Doolittle, their heirs and assigns for ever, for the use aforesaid, and also I, the s^d Saml Mix, do for myself, my heirs, Ex^{rs} and Adm^{rs}, covenant with the s^d Enos Alling and Isaac Doolittle, their heirs and assigns, that at and until the ensealing of these presents I am well seized of the premises as a good, indefeasible estate in fee simple, and have good right to bargain and sell the same in manner and form as is above written, and that the same is free of all incumbrances whatsoever, and furthermore I, the said Saml Mix do by these presents bind myself, my heirs, for ever to warrant and defend the above granted and bargained premises to them, the s^d Enos Alling and Isaac Doolittle, their heirs and assigns, against all claims and demands whatsoever. In witness whereof, I have hereunto set my hand and seal, this 28th day of July, in the 26 year of His Majesties reign, A. D. 1752.

SAMUEL MIX. [Seal.]

Signed, sealed and del^{vd} in presence of
  MOSES MANSFIELD,
  ELISHA WHITTLESEY.
New Haven Land Records, Vol. XX., p. 210.

E.

COPY OF ENOS ALLING'S DEED TO TRINITY CHURCH.

To all people to whom these presents shall come—GREETING:

Know ye that I, Enos Alling, of New Haven, Town and County and Colony of Connecticut, for the consideration of two hundred and seventy-one pounds five shillings lawful money, rec^d to my full satisfaction of Timothy Bonticou and Isaac Doolittle, Church Wardens, and Christopher Kilby and Stephen Mansfield, Vestrymen of Trinity Church, in s^d New Haven, and ye rest of ye members of ye s^d Episcopal Church, do give, grant, bargain, sell and confirm unto ye s^d Timothy Bonticou, Isaac Doolittle, and ye rest of ye Professors of ye Church of England and members of s^d Trinity Church, for ye time being and to their successors, a certain piece or parcel of land, containing one acre and a half, more or less, situate and lying at a place called Gregson's corner, in ye town plat, in s^d New Haven, bounded Northerly on the Market Place or highway, Easterly on highway or Town street, Southerly by land in possession of Saml Cook, and Westwardly by land in possession of Ralph Isaacs, together with ye dwelling house, barn, and other buildings thereon. To have and to hold ye s^d bargained and granted premises, with all and singular the appurtenances unto them, ye s^d grantees, and their successors and assigns, forever to their own proper use, for the support and maintenance of s^d Church, and I, ye s^d Enos Alling, do for myself and my heirs, Ex^{rs} and Adm^{rs}, covenant with ye s^d grantees, their successors and assigns, that I shall not nor will, nor shall my heirs or assigns, or any of them, ever have, challenge or claim any right, title or interest in or to ye same, or any part thereof, but thereof and therefrom shall and will be ever barred and secluded by these presents. In witness whereof, I have hereof set my hand and seal, this 31st day of October, 1765.

ENOS ALLING. [Seal.]

Signed, sealed and delivered in presence of
　　JERE^h TOWNSEND, JR.,
　　ROBERT BROWN.
New Haven Land Records, Vol. XXVII., p. 369.

F.

THE TITLE OF TRINITY CHURCH TO THE GLEBE LAND, TRACED AND DEFINED IN THE FOLLOWING ABSTRACT.

Copied from a document furnished me by Henry White, Esq.

The title of Trinity Church to the Glebe Lot, so called, is derived through two deeds.

Vol.	P.		
27	369	1st. A quit claim deed from Enos Alling, dated	Oct. 31, 1765.
45	319	2d. A quit claim deed from Wm. Gregson, dated	Oct. 26, 1768.

Enos Alling's Title.

27	368	Warranty deed from Sarah Humpherville, Adm^x of Benj. Humpherville,	Sept. 12, 1765.
27	369	Quit claim deed of dower from Sarah Humpherville,	Sept. 12, 1765.

Benj. Humberfield's Title.

17	131	Warranty deed from Timothy Alling,	1752.
21	79	"　　"　　" Asa Morris,	1758.
21	144	"　　"　　"　　"　　"	

Vol.	P.	

Timothy Alling's Title.

Vol.	P.		
16	260	Warranty deed from Abraham Thompson,.................	1751.
16	261	" " " " "	1748.

Abraham Thompson's Title.

13	84	Warranty deed from David Atwater,...............	1748.

David Atwater's Title.

12	91	Warranty deed from Jonathan Atwater,...............	1743.

Jonathan Atwater's Title.

11	520	Warranty deed from John Thompson,................	1742.

John Thompson's Title.

Quit claim deed from David Thompson,................1743.
Daniel Thompson was the great grandson of Thomas Gregson, the first owner, and, with his father, had been in possession more than 40 years, claiming exclusive ownership.

Asa Morris' Title.

21	210	Warranty deed from James Thompson,............	1757.
21	91	" " " Israel Dorman.	

James Thompson's Title.

Warranty deed from Daniel Thompson,................1756.

Israel Dorman's Title.

21	90	Warranty deed from Wm. Denslee,...............	1758.

Wm. Denslee's Title.

20	425	Warranty deed from James Thomas,...............	1757.

HISTORY OF LONG WHARF IN NEW HAVEN.

By THOMAS R. TROWBRIDGE, Esq.

READ MAY 25, 1863.

———◆◆◆———

FROM the earliest history of our town, the Wharf has been one of its institutions, and one of no secondary importance. New Haven having been founded by commercial men, their attention was early given to whatever would facilitate business. Wharf accommodations were of paramount importance; hence, early legislation to promote the building of wharves was seen to be indispensable. At first several small private wharves were contemplated, but it was soon evident that combined efforts in this as in all great undertakings were essential to success; consequently the inhabitants individually, and I may say unitedly, combined their efforts in the construction of one *great* wharf, that should accommodate the town as it then existed, and as it might thereafter need.

Long Wharf was therefore laid out on a grand scale, *too great,* as it has always proved, for the profit of its owners, but not too extensive for the prosperity of the colony or town. As a pecuniary speculation it was a great failure, or rather a constant succession of failures; but stimulated by the need of a wharf for the business of the place, public spirited men were successively engaged in the enterprise, and after many failures in the expected revenues to be derived therefrom, the work made progress. But it was not until 1811, that it approached its completion, and it is only recently that it may be said to have been finished as originally contemplated.

In all the long period that has elapsed since the first " *conscription*," as it may be called, when " every male inhabitant of the town between the ages of sixteen and sixty years " was to give four days work towards building a wharf, the interest of the town in the success of wharves may be considered as being of the greatest importance. The inhabitants of the town, as well as the State of Connecticut, have uniformly and without exception always granted all the *legislative* aid needed, and probably no enterprise has so constantly been regarded with undiminished favor as the well being of *Long Wharf*. It has always needed the fostering care of the town, for as a source of profit to its owners it has *never* equaled their just expectations. Exposed to the " winds and waves," the owners have often seen their expected revenues swept away, yet the work has been sustained, and I hazard nothing in saying that as a commercial city, New Haven owes its chief importance to the great Wharf. Unlike most other seaports, our harbor is very shallow, and but for this wharf vessels would have avoided the place, as from the distance to be lightered, and the few hours that would permit even *boats* to approach the shore, the delay attending landing goods by lighters would have been very tedious, so that transacting shipping business would have been well nigh impossible. Now vessels drawing fifteen or sixteen feet of water can readily approach the wharf, and discharge their cargoes with a despatch unusual in other places.

The cost of building the wharf it is impossible to ascertain. Thousands upon thousands of dollars have been lost in the enterprise. Since the abandonment of the work by all former companies, the present owners have expended upwards of eighty thousand dollars in the undertaking.

In the year 1801, the crisis which had been feared, (and in fact foreseen,) came. So much money had been already sunk that many of the owners declined investing more, while those that were not deterred by the already heavy losses, were equally inclined, and DETERMINED to go on with the work.

These, with a few other public spirited citizens, took hold anew, advancing $14,000, which, in 1810, they had expended, with $7,000 additional, yet the work was not nearly completed. Thereupon other public spirited men, not wharf merchants alone, but men of all professions and occupations in other parts of the town, came forward to its assistance, and advanced $36,000 more, until, in 1812, the wharf was extended nearly to its present termination, the final termination, however, not being reached until 1855. The landing places at the earliest settlement of the Colony were on the creek west of Meadow and George streets. It is well known that the founders of our Colony landed far up the stream, near the junction of College and George streets. That was called the *upper* landing. A much more important one on this stream was near, or at the place where Whiting street crosses the creek. Indeed, there was quite a large *Bay*, if I may so express it, extending up to this point. The writer has heard his father say that when he was a boy the place was pointed out to him by one of the old men of the town, where he had seen a vessel from Bristol in old England discharge her ballast on to a small wharf, at the place where Mr. LeGrand Cannon's garden now is, at the junction of Whiting street and the creek.

The earliest records that I find relating to wharves in our town, refer to the necessity for them for the landing of goods from the old country, from the *Barbadoes* and from Boston.

"On the 5th August, 1644, Mr. Malbon, Mr. Lamberton and Mr. Evance, having *seriously* considered the *great damage* which this towne doth suffer many ways, by reason of the flatts which hinders vessels and boates from coming neare the towne when the tyde is anything low, did propound to the Court, that if they will grant them Four days worke for *every man* in the towne fro sixteen to sixty years old towards the digging of a channell and let them have the benefit of a *Wharfe*, and Ware house, (which they will build) upon such terms as shall be agreed betwixt themselves, and a committee, whom they desired the Court then to chuse to treat with them about it, they will dig a channell which shall bring boates (at least) to the end of the street beside Will Preston's house, at any time of the tyde, except they meet with some invincible difficulty which may hinder their digging the channell so deep."

This proposal designed to make the landing places on the west bank of *the creek* which ran between Fleet and State streets on

7

the west, and Union street on the east. Will Preston's house was on the corner of State and Chapel streets.*

To this proposition the Court ordered, "that they shall have the help propounded by them, viz.: four days' work of every male in the town from sixteen years old to sixty, those that cannot worke to hyre others to work in their stead, and those that can to work in their own persons." A committee of eight were appointed, "with the advice of the Governor and magistrates to treate with the said undertakers, and agree upon such tearmes as may be equal and for the public good, setting down in writing what is done and expected on either part."

This project seemed in truth to have been a commercial necessity which called for such a conscription.

On the 22d of October, 1645, "Mr. Lamberton propounded that he might have a piece of ground near his house to sett a a ware house by the creek, and for a *wharf* also, and he will give the towne soe much as it is worth." This wharf was to be near Cherry and State streets. Mr. Lamberton was lost in the *great ship* in 1646, and of course had not completed his wharf.

On the 30th of October, 1648, "Mr. Evance propounded to the Court that *he* might have liberty to make a wharfe about the point against Phillip Leakes, and a bridge over the creeks mouth there, so as they might come to unload a boat at half' tyde."

This wharf was also to be built on the same creek, near the lower ends of Union and Fleet streets. "It was also propounded that a sluice might be made at the creek's mouth to keep up the water, that it might wear a channell, and a wharf built there to unload goods upon, *dry* at any time of tyde." This sluice was to be made from Fleet to Union street, where East Water street now crosses these streets,—the place where " Sabin's dyke " was subsequently made.

On the 14th of May, 1649, "The committee formerly chosen to consider about making the wharves and a bridge over the

---

* Since this paper was written, Ralph I. Ingersoll, Esq., informed the writer that about sixty-five years since the widow of General Wooster was visiting at Governor Ingersoll's, and upon her going home just at dusk, his mother sent him to see that Mrs. Wooster, being an old lady of about eighty years of age, reached home in safety. In passing where Chapel street railroad bridge now is, Mrs. Wooster informed him that *she had seen* a vessel in the creek at that place, and wished him to remember that fact.

mouth of the creek were desired to issue it, and it was referred to them to order some course to be taken for clearing the flatts of some logs, and pyles, and stones which the Court was informed lye up and down, whereby vessels that come in ar in danger of being hurt."

It was soon perceived that the place for wharves was *in the harbor*, to accommodate *vessels*, as well as boats and lighters, for in 1663, November 23d, Mr. Samuel Bache had a grant (for a warehouse) "about fifty or sixty feet and as far down into the flats as he should see cause to build 'a wharf or dock.'" This was at the water side at the lower end of Fleet street. This place eventually came into the possession of Mr. Jonathan Atwater, and may be considered as the first wharf built in the harbor, and this with the succeeding grant to Mr. Thomas Trowbridge may be regarded as the commencement of Long Wharf.

In January, 1682, "Mr. Thomas Trowbridge requested a grant of land by the water side for a warehouse and *wharf*. The town granted twenty-two feet in width and thirty feet from high water mark upwards, and two or three rods into the flats, the town ordering that it should be free for any of the town to land upon, and not pay for it, provided that it do not hinder Mr. Trowbridge's own occasions." This wharf was located at the foot of Fleet street, eastward and adjoining *Master* Bache's grant, and all subsequent grants for wharves commence from this and Master Bache's grant.

On the 25th of December, 1710, "The townsmen returned report to the town that they had set out to Mr. Jonathan Atwater, according to Bache's grant, sixteen feet at the east side of the house called Bache's warehouse, and thirteen and a half feet on the west side, running parallel into the flats, according to the town grant made to Mr. Bache, which is fifty feet in breadth."

On the 30th of April, 1717 "Mr. Jonathan Atwater, Mr. John Woodward, Capt. Joseph Whiting, Sergeant Munson, Mr. John Mix, and Mr. Joseph Mix, made application for a grant for a wharf at the foot of the street that goeth down to the water by Mr. Prout's."

Mr. Prout resided in a spacious brick mansion built by his father-in-law, Mr. Henry Rutherford, whose widow afterwards

married Governor Leete of Guilford. This house is said to
have been the first brick house built in the town, and stood
where Mr. Massena Clarke's store now stands, and will be
remembered by some now present as the ",Brick Fort," so
called, from the fact of its having been occupied during the
late war with Great Britain as barracks for soldiers, and from
its antiquated appearance and very small windows, which
resembled "port holes." Mr. Rutherford had his warehouse
directly opposite, which some years ago was occupied by Mr.
James Townsend as a "barber's shop." It is still standing and
is one of the oldest buildings, and probably the very oldest in
New Haven. The frame is substantial, and it will doubtless
stand for many years to come. The application that was
made for this Wharf by Mr. Atwater and others was "for
eight rods wide, and in length to the channel, beginning
at and including Mr. Trowbridge's and Mr. Atwater's grants."
It was made on the 13th of May, 1717, and is described as
"commencing at the southeast corner of Mr. Trowbridge's
warehouse, a line extending south thirty-seven degrees east, to
the channel, but the Wharf is to be sufficiently high to keep
things dry at high water."

December 27th, 1731, it was "Voted, that so many of the
proprietors of the town as incline so to do, shall have free
liberty to give what money they please, so far as shall be needed
towards the building of the wharf, to the extent of three,
four, or five hundred pounds." And I conclude from these
donations, and from the former grants which seem to be
embraced within this later grant, that the Wharf had now
become a fixed fact, and had taken the name of Union Wharf.

In 1736, however, but little had been done towards building
the wharf, for I find that Mr. Atwater sold nine-tenths of the
grant to Isaac Gorham, Francis Browne, Hannah Hall, Wm.
Greenough, Joseph Miles, Samuel Cooke, Samuel Miles, and
John Bradley, Jr., for £10.

These new proprietors commenced their work with energy,
and now it appears for the first time to have been called Long
Wharf, to distinguish it from the small wharves in the creek,
and from the smaller wharves, that may have been built on

the shores. So much was expended within the succeeding two years that on the 11th of November, 1738, the Wharf extended into the harbor about *twenty-six rods*. At this time Mr. William Greenough, "the ship carpenter," sold one undivided twentieth part, being one half of his interest, for £26 10s. current money, (or at the rate of £530 for the whole wharf.) Mr. Greenough's ship yard was at the foot of Meadow street, where he built several vessels. He was a prominent man in the town. His home lot was where our late highly esteemed fellow citizen, Capt. Gilbert Totten, had his residence. Greenough's Point, one of the old local land-marks, was at the junction of the harbor with the bay previously alluded to back of Meadow street. His ship yard was located there on account of the depth of water at that point. It is within the remembrance of the writer, that sloops of considerable size, say of sixty or eighty tons, were laid on the shore directly at the foot of Meadow street for the purpose of caulking and graving. Tradition informs us that Captain Kidd sailed up that bay, and buried his treasures in the bank of the stream near Silver street. Within the present century persons have been engaged in digging for these coveted treasures in the bank at the junction of Silver and Hill streets. At the time that Trowbridge's Dyke was built, the only way to get on to the land opposite Greenough's Point was over the bridge on what is now Congress Avenue. That fact shows the importance of this *inlet* from the harbor, a branch of which also extended south-easterly nearly to Howard Avenue. I will here mention that notwithstanding the greater depth of the water in the *West Creek*, the stores seem to have been built mostly on Fleet and State streets, consequently the landing places were mostly located on the *East Creek* in front of these stores. I think the exposure to severe southerly storms was greater in the bay west of Greenough's Point, than farther eastwardly.

Although the popular name of the wharf was Long Wharf, being then about five hundred feet in length, yet its proper name was Union Wharf, for the first regular record that I find on the "books" of the company, is under date of the first Tuesday in February, 1744–5, when a meeting of the propri-

ctors of the Union Wharf was called at the house of Mr.
James Peck, Jr., (at the head of the wharf,) formerly Mr.
Atwater's. "Voted, that the committee agree with and employ
some suitable person either by the month or otherwise, as
they shall think best, to provide proper materials and to build
and carry on said Wharf with the utmost expedition." The
work was now hurried forward with great energy, for in
1746-7 it had become a great work, and "a committee consisting of Mr. John White, Wm. Greenough, Colonel David
Wooster, Captain Joseph Trowbridge, and Samuel Miles were
appointed to consider what sums shall be taken for the wharfage of ye Union Wharf." It had become important to regulate that matter, for the Wharf was progressing so rapidly that
in 1748, the proprietors were made glad by the income for
that year, being £181 14s. 1d., (accurate men in accounts in
those days.) The whole of this income was expended in repairs and the extension of the Wharf. In 1749 the Wharf was
let for the year to Mr. Chauncey Whittelsey for £81 old tenor,
"and if the receipts do not amount to said sum and pay for
care and trouble then said sum was to be abated." Evidently
Mr. Whittelsey was satisfied with his bargain, and required
no abatement, for in 1750, it was put up at public vendue and
again let to Mr. Whittelsey for £105. No dividends were
made, but all the net income was expended in carrying forward the great enterprise. Its value consequently in a pecuniary view was uncertain, for in 1752 Mr. Gorham offered to
the other proprietors one-half of a right, being one-twentieth
part of the whole, for £20, "but they did not incline to buy it."

At a meeting in 1752, it was voted "that all the income
be laid out in repairing the Wharf, together with all the
monies and debts that now belong to the Wharf." In 1753
the income was $160 17s. 11d., of which had been expended for
repairs during the year, £91 10s., allowed wharfinger for his
trouble £30; leaving the net income but £39 7s. 11d. This
seemed but a poor return for all the cost and trouble, and it
was voted "that the Treasurer be desired and he is hereby
desired and directed, to deliver the notes for the monies now
due for wharfage, &c., speedily, into the care of Mr. Jared

Ingersoll, that they may be put in suit and the monies recovered. From this time, 1753, the enterprise seemed to flag. Great trouble and expenditure (with no dividends) discouraged many of the proprietors, as was expressed in a petition by some of the more spirited and hopeful of them, to the General Assembly of the State in 1760. " The owners had become numerous, and no systematic efforts seemed to be adopted, some lost faith in the success of the enterprise, some had died, and their interest going to heirs, some were careless about the Wharf." These petitioners felt desirous that the Wharf should be supported, and on their representation a charter was granted May 22d, 1760, under the name of the "Union Wharf Company."

The proprietors assembled February 9th, 1761, at the house of Mr. Daniel Lyman, but hearing that a number of vessels belonging to New Haven were taken and carried into Martinique, adjourned without doing any business. This was during the war between Great Britain and France, while we were colonists of the mother country.

On the 21st of August, 1762, Joseph Trowbridge, Enos Alling, Thomas Howell, Jacob and Solomon Pinto, Michael and Eli Todd, represented that they had expended for repairs, since 1760, £212 11s. 8d., and "that they were willing to further repair the Wharf and keep it in repair, provided they may be entitled to the avails of wharfage, 'till they are also paid for past and future advances." This proposition was satisfactory to the company.

March 12th, 1770, "several gentlemen proposed to subscribe considerable sums towards building a ' Pier,' on the Union Wharf grant, by the side of the channel, thereby " *Voted* to set about it as soon as materials, and proper persons to do the work could be had," and on the 23d of March, it was " *Voted* to provide the materials and build a wharf, beginning at the channel." This was "*the Pier*," eighty feet square, built for the use of large vessels, where they might lie in safety. It was substantially built, though not filled up in the middle for many years. As an example of the favor which was extended by the inhabitants of the town towards this grand

enterprise, then in great need of assistance, I mention a few
of the subscriptions that were made in 1771 towards the completion of this pier. Everything, almost, (except money,)
was subscribed. We must remember that this was just before
the Revolution, when *money* was scarce, and *barter* was the
order of the day. Of these subscriptions Mr. Jesse Leavenworth gave 100 bushels of salt, on demand ; David Gilbert £1
in shoes ; Daniel Old 40s. "in his way ;" Capt. Joseph Trowbridge 2 anchors of brandy " when he returns," (he was probably going to sea;) Capt. Wells 110 gallons of molasses ; Mr.
Austin 22s. in a castor hat ; Mr. Ezekiel Hayes £2 " in black-
smithing work," (a good payment, as the stone work was to be
doweled ;) Capt. Daniel Forbes a barrel of molasses ; Mr.
Thomas Howell £15 in West India goods ; Edward Meloy
£10 in rum ; Isaac and Elias Beers £6 in English goods, on
demand ; Jonathan Osborne £2 in labor ; Isaac Whitney 15
bushels salt, on demand ; Robert Fairchild £1 in labor ; Adam
Babcock £10 in shoes ; Abiather Camp 40 bushels salt, and
20s. in cash, (marked paid ;) Jabez Colt 30s. in axes or work ;
James Blakeslee 30s. in pressing of hay ; David Atwater, Jr.,
£4 10s. in rum, on demand ; Joseph Adams £1 "in my way ;"
Wm. McCracken £2 in English goods, on demand ; Enos
Alling 100 bushels salt ; Stephen Alling 4 hogsheads ; John
McCleave £5 in West India goods, and £3 in a boat, (marked
paid ;) Wm. Lyon 10s. in brazier's work ; Jacob Thompson 4
pairs shoes, (marked paid ;) Joseph Bradley £3 in freight to
New York ; Samuel Howell £5 in beef. The farmers in the
vicinity gave liberally of loads of timber ; Mr. Davis, a schoon-
er load of stone ; Stephen Peck 30s. in work, and promised 30s.
more, (marked paid.)

These are but a part of sixty recorded donations. It is
probably one of the most extraordinary subscriptions on
record, as a public spirited offering from a community interested in the welfare of a great public enterprise. Mr. Michael
Todd was also a liberal contributor.

The labor on this " Pier " was very great, for it was building
on soft mud ; the proprietors, however, persevered, and finally
the pier was completed, but it had well nigh discouraged the

people, the expense and trouble being so great and the means so limited. At this time the wharf extended as far as Mr. Ezra Hotchkiss' store, near the intersection of Canal Basin Wharf with Long Wharf. In 1772 the proprietors were desirous of connecting the pier with the wharf, nearly one-third of a mile apart. They petitioned the General Assembly for liberty to set up *a lottery* to raise £1,500 lawful money to be laid out on Union Wharf.

The General Assembly, friendly as it always had been, made the grant for the purpose of extending the wharf to the pier, allowing one or more lotteries, to raise £1,000, and no more; and providing "That the managers, Enos Alling, Thomas Howell, Adam Babcock, David Wooster, Nathan Beers, Jonathan Fitch, Benjamin Douglass, and Michael Todd, were to be sworn to a faithful discharge of their trust, and if the tickets cannot be sold, the managers shall return to the adventurers the money paid for the tickets." I do not think that this plan was successful, for I cannot find in the accounts any receipt of proceeds. The Company, however, voted in 1774, "to build a strong bridge of chestnut timber, from the end of the present Wharf to the new piece designed to be built, the bridge to be twenty feet long." This is the famous "First draw," as it was called within the recollection of those who a few years ago were boys, when this swimming place was so much frequented.

This place was a sort of "*neutral ground,*" where, laying aside the usual "noli me tangere" look, the "*down* town boys and *up* town boys" would socially intermingle. The students, however, generally went down for the purpose of bathing to the "first and second rails" on the shore. I suppose that they were not *very good* swimmers, as it was necessary to be adepts in the art, to venture in the deep water at the wharf. This separation of students from *town boys* was beneficial, as many "fights" were thus prevented.

From the appearance of things about this time, I conclude that the prospects were looking rather unfavorable for the Wharf, for on the 22d of February, 1774, a committee was appointed to inspect and audit the accounts of the Wharf since

1760, the time of the formation of the new company. We must bear in mind that no dividends had yet been paid, and money was running low, and, like prudent people, they were looking to see where it all was.

In 1782 things were looking badly for the Wharf. What little revenue was received was expended on repairs, and on the 8th of July, Mr. James Rice made an offer to collect the wharfage for the current year, *gratis*. Mr. Joseph Howell made the same offer for the next year, Mr. Michael Todd for the third year, and Capt. Joseph Munson for the fourth year.

In this year it was " *Voted*, that any of the inhabitants that will give fifty shillings to repair the 'Pier,' shall be proprietors of the Wharf, and the proprietors will thankfully accept the donations that have been made, *or shall be*, for repairing the Wharf."

In 1784, the General Assembly again extended its aid, by passing an act "that no vessel shall in future be cleared out of the harbor of New Haven, by the naval officer, until he shall receive a certificate in writing from the wharfinger, that the customary wharfage is paid, or that none is due. This was a new evidence of the interest felt by the people of the State in the welfare of the Wharf in New Haven.

The commerce of the town had suffered during the revolutionary war to such extent, that the income for 1785 was let at public vendue for £102 lawful money.

In 1789, a petition was presented to the Congress of the United States representing the importance for trade and commerce, that the Pier in New Haven Harbor should be maintained and kept in good order, and proposing to *give it* to the United States, provided that they would keep it in repair, and that vessels belonging to this port may use it *free*, and no additional taxes be laid on them for the use that they make of the Pier. The negotiation, however, was unsuccessful. In later years, the Government was glad to avail itself of this Pier to erect a light house thereon.

In 1790, all private measures towards raising money to complete the wharf seemed exhausted. Accordingly the proprietors again went to the General Assembly for authority to set up a new lottery to raise £3,000. The grant was obtained without opposition, but New York having prohibited the sale of foreign tickets in that State, the proprietors petitioned for permission to sell their tickets in the *City* of New York, representing "that the lottery was to raise money to repair and extend the wharf, which was of vast importance to the trade and commerce of New York, as well as of New Haven." They also represented that our people were adventurers daily in New York lotteries, but it was of no avail, "Dutch obstinacy prevailed over the lamb-like meekness of the Yankees," and the petition was denied. The lottery speculation was not successful, for in 1799 the managers had realized but £98 2s., of which sum £39 11s. was paid to Col. Drake for money he had expended on the wharf in repairs, and the balance was ordered to be laid out in additional repairs.

I cannot find that up to this time (in 1799) any dividends had ever been paid to the owners of the wharf. Every dollar of its earnings had been expended towards repairing the wharf and in its extension.

It was now only too evident that the final crisis, long foreseen, was at hand. These public spirited men had expended large sums on an immense work, for which the times were not auspicious. The long war of the Revolution had ruined the foreign and domestic trade, the work they had undertaken was of vast expense, time after time the sea had swept away its income, and all its revenues had been required to keep in repair what had already been built. The propritors saw that their exertions were about to fail, still for two years more they hoped and struggled on, but struggled in vain.

On the 16th day of February, 1802, the crisis arrived, and the old company that had existed in fact almost from the first settlement of the town, saw that they could go no farther, and that under a *new organization* their long cherished plans must be completed. Time after time the inhabitants had shown their interest in the great enterprise by contributing largely and freely, but there was a limit to these applications, although they had always been generously met. To show the interest

that this entire community felt in the work, which they justly
regarded as of immense importance to the prosperity of the
town, the following list is given. I mention but a part of the
host of contributors on record:

Ralph Isaacs, ...£12 00s. 00d.				
Isaac Beers,..............	9 16			
Elias Beers,..............	9 10			
Daniel Lyman,...........	10			
Wm. Douglas,............	10			
Jesse Leavenworth,.......	16 10			
Enos Alling,.............	60			
Jabez Colt, ...	4 12	6		
Col. Nathan Whiting,.....	6			
Jonathan Ingersoll,.......	2 10			
David Austin, Esq.,.......	10			
Anthony Perit,...........	6			
Adam Babcock, ...	16			
Richard Cutler,..........	20			
Samuel Howell, ...	5			
Benjamin Brown,.........	2 10			
Nathan Beers,...........	15			
Jacob Thompson,.........	3 19			
Caleb Trowbridge,........	15			
Daniel Trowbridge,.......	7 10			
John Hall, Wallingford, ...	2 10			
Eliakim Hall, " ...	2 10			

Thomas Howell,........£40 00s. 00d.			
Daniel Forbes, ...	3 18		
Col. Leverett Hubbard,..	12		
Abiather Camp, ...	10 10		
Gad Wells, ...	21		
Elias Shipman,.........	10		
Benedict Arnold,.......	10		
Jared Ingersoll,.........	8		
Edward Meloy, ...	19		
Samuel Miles, ...	10		
John White,...	5		
Jonathan Atwater,......	5		
Joseph Trowbridge,.....	10		
Jonathan Atwater, Jr.,..	5		
Frances Browne,........	8 13	6	
Benjamin English,......	2 10		
David Atwater, Jr.,.....	13		
Hezekiah Sabin, ...	12 10		
Samuel Chew,..........	10 11		
Thomas Rice, ...	12		
Abraham Bradley, 2d, ..	4		
Ebenezer Peck,........	3		

The list embraces but a small number of those who contributed to the work. The vast majority of these contributors
generously relinquished all rights in the wharf which they might
have acquired by donations.

This new organization was accordingly made by another
company being formed of contractors to extend and complete
the work, which they agreed to do. They further agreed to
furnish fourteen thousand dollars towards maintaining and
extending the wharf. The new company, however, embraced
many of the original owners, in fact all who were willing to
advance more money, (as several of them did.) The two companies—the old company and the "*Contractors*," as they called
themselves,—acting together harmoniously, the contractors
taking a lien upon the property of the old company until reim-
bursed for their expenditures. The work *now* went forward
with great energy. At this time the wharf was made of tim-

ber and bridges from the *first bridge* to Capt. Forbes' store or second draw, making its whole length about two thousand feet. The work was done under the superintendence of Mr. Samuel Punderson, who was also the contractor for the principal part of it. His energy and skill greatly contributed to the early completion of that part extending to the second bridge, and to the very extensive repairs to the *old* wharf and pier, which required thorough rebuilding. Mr. Punderson entered into the spirit of his work as one of the old "*town born*" should have done.

The wharf, by this additional element infused into the enterprise, was now thoroughly repaired and put in *first rate* condition. Money was expended freely; and business, again stimulated by good wharf accomodations, was prosperous. An assessment was laid to the amount of $7,000 additional capital, to be furnished by these contractors, to be expended on extending and repairing the wharf, the amount first agreed upon being found entirely inadequate to do what was contemplated by the old company.

In the period between 1802 and 1810, the enterprise was deemed so important that these contractors raised $36,000 more, and in 1810 were incorporated by the name of " Contractors to rebuild and support Union Wharf and Pier in New Haven," the old company preserving their original name of " Union Wharf Company," both companies acting harmoniously in all cases for the general welfare of the wharf, and for the interests of the town.

The extension of the wharf to the "Pier" was now determined on, and the old proprietors were at length to see the completion of their long cherished plans. A contract was made on the 28th of July, 1810, to build the wharf solid from the second bridge to the pier, a distance of 1,350 feet, and the whole wharf to be raised above high tides.

Of this company of contractors in 1802, of whom there were thirty-three, not one is now living. Of the company of sixty-five contractors that were incorporated in 1810, only five are now living, viz: Mr. Truman Woodward,* Mr. Ezra Hotchkiss,

---

* Since deceased.

Mr. Elias Hotchkiss, Mr. Henry Huggins, and Mr. Timothy Bishop. Of these, Mr. Bishop and Mr. Elias Hotchkiss are the only original share holders at present owning shares in the Wharf, Mr. Bishop being the venerable President of the Company. He is also one of its Directors, and has been such for a period of fifty-two years, and for the whole time a devoted friend to the wharf. Mr. Elias Hotchkiss is also a Director of the Company. The old Company still maintains its organization and transacts its regular annual business, &c.

The length of the wharf is 3,480 feet, and is the longest wharf in the United States. A gentleman traveling last year in the State of Iowa, while stopping at a hotel in one of the interior towns of that State, casually heard some one speaking of New Haven and of its institutions. He mentioned Long Wharf, saying, "it is the longest wharf in the *world*, that it exceeded five miles in length and was built by a negro; that many had attempted to build it, but being constructed on soft mud, it could not be made to stand and was abandoned; that this negro then contracted to build it, merely to show what a *black man* was capable of doing, and that he succeeded." I do not know where the man obtained his information; probably, from his *conceit* of New Haven, he was a descendant of the "*town born*." But it is a fact that nearly 1,500 feet of this wharf was built in 1810 and 1811 by a colored man named William Lanson.

Mr. Lanson, for he was thus known in his *better days*, deserves a passing notice for his enterprise in connection with this contract. He quarried the stone at East Rock, built a wharf to load them from into scows, and thus carried them to the wharf. He was respected as a man of energy and skill, and was a useful citizen. Becoming involved in his latter days, he fell into bad repute, but even then was a man receiving considerable respect for his previous worth. He was capable of *great things*.

The history of Long Wharf is certainly very remarkable. At the present day it would be considered a great undertaking to construct such a wharf, but at the time of its commencement and for many years subsequently, with the limited means of its projectors, it was one of the great enterprises of the age. The subscriptions made from time to time show the scarcity of money during its progress.

This wharf was the pride and boast of the "*town born*," a walk to the end of it on holidays being very customary both with men and boys. Great sport it was for the boys to go on the wharf, on the arrival of vessels from the West Indies, when oranges and cocoanuts were gratuitously distributed, when long rows of hogsheads of sugar and molasses yielded their sweets freely to the boys. What "*town boy*" who was not acquainted with the names of all the vessels and of the captains and sailors! Who has not heard of "Captain Brown," such an idolizer of the "*town born*," and who had such an aversion to all "interlopers," who, when on one of his numerous voyages at sea, his vessel in imminent peril of sinking, and it becoming necessary to throw the cargo overboard to lighten the ship, to save the lives of the crew and for the safety of the vessel, directed the goods belonging to the "*interlopers*" to be thrown over, and to save those belonging to the "*town born?*" Who has not heard of "Wharf Law," by which, when any offense was committed on the wharf that required attention, and for which "up town" would have caused the incarceration of the offender, the wharf merchants, in contempt of such imprisonment, took the law into their own hands, and meeted out due punishment on the spot, and let the culprit go? If deserving of more severe discipline than the more ordinary one of corporal punishment, they condemned him to "run the gauntlet" as far as the stores extended, and this with a promise to leave town, generally ended the matter and answered the purpose. The wharf had a law of its own, judge and jury, but no lawyers, for the men were such that confidence was felt that they would do right, and every indulgence was shown to its merchants.

In the year 1779 the stores on the wharf were burned by the British troops. In 1820 nearly all the stores on the wharf were consumed in the great conflagration which destroyed over a quarter of a million of dollars worth of property.

To have lived in the days when "Merchant Princes" congregated on the wharf in business, was a time well worth living in. In *old times*, on rainy days, called "*rat days*," from the immense quantity of these animals that were drowned out of their holes by the *high tides* that generally swept over the wharf, it was a common thing for the merchants to assemble at the *Tavern* at the head of the wharf for a *good time*, where, discussing the state of the West India trade, the state of the country, and affairs generally, with their "*bowl of punch*" or "*half and half*" of the genuine "Grenada or Antigua," of their own importation, they would pledge to the success of the "Army of the Revolution." It was on a day of this description, when nearly all were assembled, that the astounding news was received of the treachery of their old friend and fellow West India merchant, Benedict Arnold. They could not believe that one who in 1775 was with the foremost to march in defense of his country, could ever betray it; but when the evidence was past controverting, they consoled themselves with the reflection that *Arnold* was not a "*Long Wharf* merchant;*" had he been located on that venerable wharf, he would never have been a traitor.

Long Wharf has produced such men as Elias Shipman, Henry Daggett, Ward Atwater, Thomas and Henry Ward, Solomon Collis, Benjamin Prescott, James Henry, Roger Sherman, Samuel A. Foot, Jehiel Forbes, Wm. J. Forbes, Lockwood DeForest, Russell Hotchkiss, Henry Trowbridge, Timothy Bishop, Andrew Kidston, Elnathan Atwater, Joseph N. Clark, Richard M. Clarke, Ezra Hotchkiss, Elias Hotchkiss, Enos A. Prescott, Justus Hotchkiss, Laban Smith, Walter Budington, Justus Harrison, Elijah Austin, not to mention hosts of others, *men of mark*. And in this connection the name of Roger Sherman, son of the signer of the Declaration of Independence and a framer of the Constitution, should receive more than a passing remark. Mr. Sherman was connected with Long Wharf, as one of its truest friends, for more than half a century. In its darkest and most perilous days he was ready with his counsel and his open purse, was a sound and able adviser, and no man ever did more for its prosperity than Mr. Sherman. An officer of the company from 1810 to 1847, he was always

its strong friend; long prior to that period he was a chief pro-
moter of the enterprise, and lived to see the completion of the
work for which he had done so much. My friends will pardon
me if I also mention the name of my honored father, as one
who was ever devoted to the interest and welfare of the Wharf.

I trust that it will not be considered out of place if I here
pay a passing tribute to the memory of some of the New Haven shipmasters of the olden time. Among hosts of those noble men were Capts. Daniel Greene, Wm. Howell, Caleb Brit-
nall, Caleb Trowbridge, Joseph Trowbridge, Capt. Brown,
("the town born,") Capt. Phipps, James Goodrich, John T.
Trowbridge, Gad Peck, Thos. Painter, Thomas Ward, Henry
Ward, Henry Denison, Daniel Truman, John Davis, Nathaniel
F. Clarke, Roswell Trowbridge, James Hunt, Elias Trowbridge,
Frederick Hunt, Elnathan Atwater, Alva Granniss, William
Sheffield, Wm. Moulthrop, Simeon Hoadley, Joseph Thomp-
son, Gilbert Totten, Richard M. Clarke, Samuel Jas. Clarke,
Ichabod Smith, Samuel Chew, John Hood, John Bradley,
John B. Hotchkiss. This list could be extended to include
hundreds of worthy men.

Commodore Hull, prior to commanding the glorious old Iron-
sides, had commanded a West Indiaman from this port, and multitudes of others could have been found here in New Haven
well worthy to uphold the honor of the " Stars and Stripes."

The world has never produced a more intelligent set of merchant captains than those who have commanded New Haven
vessels; men not only capable, thorough bred seaman, but
men able to transact the whole business of their voyages, selling their cargoes abroad and purchasing return cargoes. Some
of the most lucrative East India voyages, combined with seal-
ing voyages in the Pacific, were made from this port by our
New Haven captains. The profits on some of these voyages
were almost fabulous, and at the present day, in many of our
houses, any quantity of *China ware* may be found, that was
brought home by our townsmen from their China voyages.

The West India voyages also were often very remunerative.
On this subject I propose hereafter to write another paper.

8

Custom House Square, at the head of the Wharf, was originally built upon, very closely. There were three entrances to Long Wharf from Fleet street. In 1818 this Square was opened by the removal of the buildings, through the combined aid of the General Government, the Town, and the Wharf. It was originally the intention to extend Union street to the wharf, and arrangements were made for this purpose, but in some way through a misunderstanding, it was not accomplished.

In 1822 an addition was made to the wharf, by the extension, a distance of one hundred and five feet down the channel, of a wharf thirty feet wide.

In 1826 the Farmington Canal Company received permission from the Wharf Company to connect their Basin Wharf to Long Wharf. In 1848 the New York and New Haven Railroad Company had permission to cross the wharf by their railroad. In 1852 the Railroad Company had permission to fill up the Canal Basin, for work-shops, car houses, &c., &c.

Within the last ten years additions and improvements have been made to the Wharf at an expense exceeding $10,000. In its structure will be found parts of the Island of Malta, stones from the Rock of Gibralter, ballast from Sicily, gravel from the harbor of Dublin, stones from Bristol in England, rocks from the Gulf of Para, and from the Islands of St. Domingo, Porto Rico, Gaudaloupe, Martinico, Trinidad, Antigua, St. Vincents, St. Lucia, St. Barts, St. Eustatia, St. Kitts, St. Croix, in fact from almost every island in the West Indies. An excavation for a building often exposes some of these contributions from foreign countries, and wherever New Haven vessels have prosecuted their voyages, almost every port visited has contributed materials that have been used in the construction of this wharf; and probably, by excavating, a greater collection of foreign minerals could be made from this wharf than from any other spot in the United States.

This brings down the history of Long Wharf to the present time. I feel that so much detail must have tired the patience of the Society, and that I have not done justice to this great enterprise, which has been in existence nearly as long as our town, an enterprise that was projected and conducted by the best men of New Haven, and one that has been of vast importance in promoting the growth of our city as a commercial place. I trust that at some future time some one more able than myself to do justice to the Wharf, may prepare a better history. I am certain, however, that no one will ever be found who has a more profound respect and esteem for its founders, and for Long Wharf itself, than the writer.

I necessarily reserve the history of the "Wharf Merchants," and of the "West India Trade," for a future evening.

THE PARSONAGE OF THE "BLUE MEETING HOUSE,"

THE SITE OF THE PRESENT ST. THOMAS CHURCH.

By E. E. BEARDSLEY, D. D.

READ SEPTEMBER 28, 1863.

———◆◆◆———

DIEDRICH KNICKERBOCKER begins his wonderful history of New York with a description of the world, its form and features, its cosmogony or creation, and the theories of sundry sages and philosophers concerning its texture and planetary movements. In like manner, I open my subject this evening, "THE PARSONAGE OF THE BLUE MEETING HOUSE," with a description of New Haven, its lands and lots, its primitive rules and regulations, and its early outward appearance and internal improvements.

If we step back into the history of the past two hundred and twenty-five years, we find a colony of adventurous planters preparing to enter upon the possession of the territory now occupied by the site of this goodly city. It was a rude region then, where the Indian roamed and had his hunting grounds.

> "No spire, no mast, no mansion rose;
> Smokes, here and there, from out the screen,
> Denoted still an Indian scene."*

Five years before, the settlement of Connecticut had been commenced on the banks of the river which gives name to the State, and following the trail of the Pequot warriors, the white men had explored the coast, with its inlets and bays, from the mouth of the Thames to Unqnowa, beyond the mouth of

---

* Hillhouse—"Sachem's Wood."

the Housatonic. Their glowing account of the beauty and fertility of the lands, and perhaps the suggestion of Capt. Stoughton, that they were too good for Dutchmen to seize and possess, arrested the attention of John Davenport and his associates, then recently arrived at Boston, and waiting, to use his own words, for "the eye of God's Providence" to "guide us to a place convenient for our families and for our friends." Many inducements were offered them to remain in Massachusetts, and blend their influence and their wealth with the earlier emigrants, but these inducements were quite unavailing, for along with the desire to secure a goodly heritage, seems to have been the determination to plant a distinct colony that might frame its own laws and owe no allegiance to a General Governor. An exploring party, therefore, composed of Eaton and a few of his friends, in the autumn of 1637, selected Quinnipiack, the Indian name of this place, as the seat of the new Colony, and early in the spring of the succeeding year, the whole company sailed from Boston, and, in due time, anchored their ships in Quinnipiack harbor. Religious exercises very appropriately followed their disembarkment, and a plantation covenant followed their settlement,—

" For they, in Newman's barn, laid down
Scripture foundations for the town."

The New Haven Colonists respected the rights of the Indians, and purchased their lands of Momaugin, sole Sachem of Quinnipiack, his council and company, for a consideration. Protection and friendship were mutually pledged, and there is no record that any conflict afterwards sprung up between the settlers and the natives about the right of occupancy or possession. Prof. Kingsley, a fair historian, who probed the motives and the acts of these London adventurers, says: "The treatment of the savages of Pennsylvania by William Penn, was not a whit more equitable or kind, than that showed the native inhabitants of this spot. The distinguishing policy of Penn, in his intercourse with the Indians, consisted in this, that he allowed no lands to be purchased of them except on account of the government;—the very course pursued here."

It is a fact worthy to be noted, that the Indians of Quinnipiack were a fading tribe when the English sought to purchase their lands. Powerful enemies—especially the Pequots
and the Mohawks—had reduced their numbers, so that of
" men or youth grown to stature fit for service," less than fifty
are counted in the original deed signed by the chief sachem
and his council. Their weakness, therefore, must have made
them in a measure submissive. They were not equal to an
open conflict with their new neighbors, if they had a cause,
and they could not take them by surprise,

" Since our good sires, in their old hall,
Met armed for combat, prayer and all !"

The lands purchased of the Indians were disposed of by lot.
Every planter, after paying his portion of the expenses arising
from laying out and settling the plantation, drew a lot or lots
of land in proportion to his estate, or rather to the amount
which he had expended in the general purchase, and to the
number of heads in his family.

To JASPER CRANE was so allotted the land—an acre and a
half—now covered by the buildings extending on Elm street,
from the first house in Sheffield's block to Orange street, and
on Orange street to the lot held by the trustees of the Hopkins Grammar School. His neighbor on the east was John
Davenport, and on the south a lot appears to have been assigned at first to Owen Rowe, a tradesman in London, who forfeited
his proprietorship here by not joining the Colonists. He chose
to remain in England, where he became a Colonel in the great
civil war, and one of the Regicides who affixed their seals to
the warrant for executing the King. His sorrow for that deed
after the Restoration, and his joy with all his countrymen at
the incoming of Charles II., together with his willingness to
accept the mercy of the sovereign, saved him from the inflic-
tion of the Royal sentence, and he died in the Tower of London on Christmas day, 1661.* The occupancy of his town lot

---

* See note in Savage's edition of Winthrop's History of New England, Vol. I.,
p. 475.

in New Haven is marked by a peculiar record.   At a General
Court, held the 1st of September, 1640, it was ordered that
" when Mr. Rowe's lot shall be fenced in, our Pastor shall have
a way or passage left eight foot broad betwixt it and Mr.
Crane's lot, that he may go out of his own garden to the Meeting House."   That private path entered Church street on the
north side of the building in which we are assembled, and over
it, or over the public one leading by the front of his mansion,
Davenport serenely walked, little dreaming that two centuries
onward an enduring sanctuary would rise, casting its shadows
upon these paths, and within whose portals doctrines and worship
would be maintained identical with those which he had himself
accepted and taught, when Vicar of St. Stephen's Church, in
Coleman street.   If the child had not been born and named
before it was known where its residence would be, there had
been some historic propriety in taking the name of the first
Christian martyr as the designation of St. Thomas Church.

Jasper Crane built a house and resided for a time on the
eastern part of his lot.   On the 7th of January, 1650, he
" passed over to Christopher Todd his home lot and housing
upon it, and all the accommodations belonging to him here at
the town ; Christopher Todd accepted it."   He was from the
first concerned in the settlement at East Haven, to which place
he removed; thence to Branford, and finally to Newark, N. J.,
where he died at an advanced age in 1681.   He was a prominent man in the councils of the New Haven Colony, and one
of its magistrates and deputies to the General Court, both
before and after the union with Connecticut.   Being a sur-
veyor, he laid out much of the town plot, located grants, and
settled division lines and disputed titles.   Two grants of land
were made him in East Haven, one " in the fresh meadow, towards Totoket," and the other of upland.   He built a house
there on the east side of the green, where he lived and traded a
couple of years, and there his son Jasper was born.   According to Dodd,* he was an overseer and agent in the Iron Works,
(the well-known bog-ore furnace,) which had the encouragement of the town, and was probably the first establishment of

---

* " East Haven Register," p. 27.

the kind within the present limits of Connecticut.   Not pleased, perhaps, with his location and business as a merchant, he sold his home lot, his farm of sixteen acres, to Matthew Moulthrop. Sept. 7, 1652, and established himself in Totoket or Branford, removing thither with his family, and joining the settlers from Wethersfield and Southampton, L. I.   He was a guiding light in the deliberations of that town, and its first deputy to the General Court having jurisdiction in this Colony.   After the union of New Haven and Connecticut, he still represented its interests; but the people of Branford becoming dissatisfied with the union, particularly with the feature allowing the right of suffrage to such as were not members of the Church, projected a new settlement, and sent agents to examine certain lands in New Jersey, near the mouth of the Passaic river. Their report was so favorable that Mr. Pierson, the minister at Branford, with a part of his congregation, resolved to begin immediately the settlement at Newark.   Though Jasper Crane was one of the twenty-three persons who signed the first compact in 1665 to remove, yet he lingered behind and continued to direct the affairs of Branford, heading the list of signers to a church covenant formed for those who remained.   But in 1668 he disposed of his property and joined his associates at Newark, carrying with him the same energy, enterprise, prudence and piety which had marked his whole course here from the planting of the Colony.   He was a deputy and magistrate at Newark, and one of the purchasers of the Kingsland farm, now known as Belville.   His children were JOHN, born before the father emigrated to this country; HANNAH, who married Thomas Huntington; DELIVERANCE, baptized at New Haven, 1642; AZARIAH and JASPER.   Azariah became a deacon in the Presbyterian church, at Newark, and married Mary, daughter of Robert Treat, then a resident of the place.   Mr. Treat subsequently returned to Connecticut and was made Lieutenant Governor in 1676.   Nearly all the Cranes of New Jersey—a worthy and respectable family—can trace their pedigree to Jasper, the elder.   Whether he has any descendants in this region, I know not, but he will never be forgotten, so long as Crane's bar, receiving its name from him, continues to be washed by the tides in our harbor.

CHRISTOPHER TODD, the next owner of the Parsonage lot, was one of the original planters, whose autograph signature is upon the records of the Colony. He was a farmer and a miller. The town erected a grist mill where Whitney's Gun Factory now stands, which he rented and afterwards purchased. He lived in the house on the eastern part of his Elm street lot and possessed lands remote from his residence. He had three sons and three daughters, JOHN, SAMUEL, MARY, GRACE, MICHAEL and MERCY. He died in 1686, leaving a will, in which he named all his surviving children. Grace Todd, his daughter, a child of thirteen, appears upon the records of the General Court as an offender " for concealing from her master and mistress" some indelicate liberty which an Indian had taken with her, and for this, and because she "afterwards spoke of it to boys and girls in a jesting way," she was sentenced to be " whipped." She was married five years later to Richard Mattocks, who deserted her, and her father in his will provided for her support, speaking of her as one who was incompetent to take care of herself or of any estate. The residence of Christopher fell, in the division of the estate under the will, to his eldest son, John, who married for his first wife Sarah, daughter of Matthew Gilbert, one of the seven pillars of the New Haven Church. She lived but a short time and died childless. He married again and had sons and daughters. The eldest of his sons (John) married Hannah ———, and died before his father, (with whom he appears to have lived,) leaving three children, John, Joseph and Thankful. To these children, " for divers good causes and considerations thereunto moving him—but more especially for the love, good will and natural affection, which he had and did bear to them," the grandfather gave, Feb. 22, 172¾, to " be equally divided between them, the house, barn and homestead where his son John lived and [which he] died possessed of." The widowed mother of these children married Caleb Tuttle, and in 1733 she and her second husband became owners of two-thirds of the property by deed from her sons John and Joseph Todd. Thankful Todd, who married David Punderson, held the remainder. No subsequent conveyances were made until 1748, and thus the property continued in the right of the Todd family and its connections for nearly a century, (ninety-eight years.) The Todds are numerous and respectable in this vicinity and in towns included within the limits of the ancient Colony of New Haven. What proportion of those who bear the name in other parts of the country has sprung from CHRISTOPHER, cannot well be traced. It is certain the Church and State have alike been honored by their talents and their services.

In the last days of the year 1741, *thirty-eight men*, who, to quote their own phrase, "had by long and sorrowful experience found the preaching and conduct of Rev. Mr. Noyes in a great measure unprofitable," addressed a memorial to the First Ecclesiastical Society of New Haven, asking permission to withdraw in charity and establish a Separate Society. Among these signers were Caleb Tuttle, David Punderson and Joseph Burroughs. The prayer of the memorial was not granted,— but divers causes, and especially the "Great awakening" throughout the churches in New England, helped on by Whitfield and preachers of his class, emboldened the disaffected members to proceed, and availing themselves of the Act of Toleration, they united in an association and directed their efforts to provide immediately a house of worship. Having been denied the privilege of placing it on the public square, they purchased of Mr. Burroughs the lot on the southeast corner of Elm and Church streets, now occupied by St. John block, and prepared to build. "The alienation and hostility," says Dr. Dutton,* "which had grown up between the two churches, and the excitement which agitated the community, when it was known that the new meeting house was to be raised, have no parallel in these times. The First Society sent a Committee to remonstrate against the raising of the house, declaring it very hurtful to their Society and a *public nuisance*, and desiring those engaged in it forthwith to desist." Other steps, even that of appealing to the General Assembly, were taken to hinder its erection. A remonstrance read while the builders were in the act of raising a part of the frame, diverted

---

* History of the North Church in New Haven, p. 49.

their attention to such a degree that it fell with a tremendous crash; whereupon, the Old Lights, as the adherents of Mr. Noyes were termed, cried out that Providence was evidently against the enterprise. The long sticks of timber were stealthily cut in the night season, but being replaced by others, over which a guard was set, the building was finally raised and completed. Various artifices were resorted to and great pains used to keep up the interest in the new organization and gather members. In 1753 the Committee for the time being "had power thereafter to call a meeting by sending a *drum* about the First Society in New Haven, to make proclamation at the corners, at the least of the middle square, that the members of the Tolerated Society were desired to meet." This, as we now view things in the Church militant, does not appear to have been exactly respectful to the Old Lights, nor a very genteel method of warning a Society's meeting. The preaching of the New Light ministers, too, was so much more attractive than the dry, trenchant logic of Mr. Noyes, that the worshipers, though paying taxes to the First Society till 1757,* rapidly increased,

----

* Some of the remarks made when the reading of the paper was finished, were reported in the New Haven Daily Register as follows:

The members were obliged to pay taxes for the support of the First Society until 1757, when they were set off by an act of the Legislature. The manner in which this was brought about was explained in a conversation at the end of the reading. It seems that a sharp contest was kept up for many years between the old and new lights. The Legislature, being of the "old light" persuasion, steadily refused to relieve the "new lights" of the burden of sustaining the first Church. Finally, on the occasion of a Society meeting at the first Church, the "new lights" rallied in their strength and outnumbered their opponents. They proceeded to execute a *coup d'etat* which settled the case for all time. They voted to accept the "Blue Meeting House" as the Church, voted a salary to their minister, &c.—in fact voted themselves in, and the rest out. Next year they rallied again, and voted that as the minister of the first Church (who had, of course, refused to go to the "New Light" meeting house) had steadily neglected to attend public worship, he was not entitled to a salary, and they stopped it! This brought matters to a crisis, and though Mr. Noyes succeeded afterwards in collecting his salary by a suit at law, the "old lights" found they had got an elephant on their hands, and gladly consented to a division of the parish and a remission of the taxes to escape worse troubles. This is believed to have been the origin, in New England, of poll parishes—*i. e.*, two or more societies having a common geographical existence. So bitter did the controversy between these two churches become, that, about a hundred years ago, a deacon of the "new

and the meeting house was afterwards enlarged for their accommodation. It was not owing to any peculiar cast of theology that it was called the "Blue Meeting House," but in 1761 considerable coloring seems to have been needed, for the Society voted that "the Meeting House wanted *coloring*, and the pulpit to be finished and *colored*, and the breastwork of the galleries and pillars to be *colored*," and probably *blue* was the tint then given to the exterior and preserved in a measure till the edifice was removed.* After a checkered history of light and shade, the Society was at length dissolved and merged into what is now the "North Church," and its property sold. The bell which rung the zealous worshipers together at the hour of prayer, hangs in the tower of the Episcopal Church at Cheshire, and when suspended in the old church there, at a different elevation, it was said to have been heard in more towns than any other bell in the county.

The movement to erect a Meeting House was followed by another to secure a parsonage. In 1748, the Society employed Mr. John Curtiss to preach for them, and Caleb Tuttle and David Punderson, with their wives, conveyed to him one half acre and seventeen rods of the western part of their lot, running one hundred feet on Elm street. The Society had stipulated for this ground and built on it the house for a minister. After two years Mr. Curtiss left and the parsonage was returned and conveyed to David Austin and John Woodin. They, calling it in the instrument of conveyance, "one certain messuage and tenement," deeded it in 1751 to Rev. Mr. Samuel Bird, who had been chosen Pastor of the Separate Society,—it being the Society's gift to him on condition that he paid for what had been laid out upon it after Mr. Curtiss' departure, amounting to a thousand pounds, old tenor. Mr. Bird resided

---

light" church, having invited his father, who was a deacon in the "old light" church, to attend the funeral of his child, the "old light" deacon refused in a written note, declaring that he would not enter into a "new light" church to attend the funeral of his son's child.

* Lampblack is said to have been mixed with the paint to make it durable, and thus the blue tinge was produced.

Dr. SAMUEL PUNDERSON, on the authority of the late E. C. HERRICK, Esq.

here until his death, and willed his homestead to his children, Samuel, Thomas, Sybil, Margaret and Mabel Sarah. By subsequent conveyances and descents, it became the property of Rodolphus E. Northrop, son of Dr. Joel Northrop, who married Mabel Sarah Bird. Mr. Northrop narrowed the dimensions of the original parsonage grounds by selling the garden in the rear to Titus Street,—eight feet on the eastern side to Abraham Bradley, and reserving for himself twelve feet on the western, which he added to a strip that he had previously purchased. The lot, therefore, on which the Parsonage of the Blue Meeting House stood, was reduced to eighty feet front by one hundred and fifty feet deep, and this was bought in January, 1849, by St. Thomas Parish, for $4,300—having been in possession of the Bird family just as long as it was held by the Todd family, that is, ninety-eight years. I trust the present ownership is fixed for more than another century.

Before I proceed farther, a word should be said about the eastern part of the original lot. It was sold in 1751 to Lieut. Nathan Whiting, afterwards Col. Whiting, in the army of the old French war. He died in 1771, and before a score of years had elapsed, his heirs sold it to Pierpont Edwards, after Orange street had been opened. The names of several owners appear between that time and the present,—but they need not be traced here. If the history should ever be pursued, it will probably be mentioned, that when the chimney of the old mansion was removed to make room for the house in which I now reside, a pot of gold was discovered secreted therein, supposed to have been too carefully "laid up " by Colonel Whiting ! ! The number enriched by it was never publicly announced and the story lacks confirmation.

The Rev. Samuel Bird came to New Haven from Dunstable, in the province of New Hampshire, where he was invited to become a pastor of the church and to "settle himself, July 6, 1747." He was the son of Benjamin Bird, Esq., by his wife Joanna, was born at Dorchester, Mass., March 17, 172$\frac{3}{4}$, and entered Harvard College in 1740. About two months before his class graduated (May 12, 1744) he was expelled from college for his course in advocating the New Light Theology—then spreading with its attendant excitements through the land. He was fined twelve shillings for seventeen days' absence from College, without leave, in the autumn of 1743—and the con- jecture is that these days were spent in mingling with the followers of Whitfield and promoting their cause. His enthusi- asm led him to oppose the regularly settled clergy, and in his prayers and intercourse with people he used language derogatory to the piety of Jonathan Bowman, at that time the minister of his native place, and one of the overseers of the College. Being of an arbitrary disposition and in- dignant at the young enthusiast for not showing him more respect both as a minister and an officer of the Institution, Bowman brought the matter before the Faculty and sought his punishment. Much excitement ensued, partaking of the spirit of the times and high words and some insults passed between the parties. The College authorities, feeling the abuse heaped upon them by the New Lights, favored the complaint of the overseer,—a thing which would hardly be done now in a similar case, and the result was the ex- pulsion of Bird for his religious enthusiasm and the evils which grew out of it.* He married MABEL, daughter of Hon. Thomas Jenner of Charlestown, Mass., who died early, leav- ing one child—a son. He married for his second wife, SARAH, daughter of John Prout, Esq. of New Haven, by whom he had twelve children, five of whom only survived him, two sons and three daughters. His eldest son, SAMUEL, graduated at Yale College, in 1776, and the father directed in his will that his education and what he had done for him was not to be charged to him in the distribution of his estate—these being his "acknowledgment that he was his eldest son." He also in his will "authorized his executors to sell his negro girl (Lille Pink) if they judged best, with the full consent of his wife, the money to be put to use or as should be judged best for the benefit of his heirs."

Mr. Bird was a man for the times and for his people. It does not become me to enter into the religious history of that

---

* MS. Letter from John Langdon Sibley, 1863.

critical period; but the part which he bore in the controversy, carried on for nearly a score of years between the First
and Separate Societies, shows him to have been possessed of
energy, influence and intellectual strength. "His form and
manner," we are told, "were commanding, his voice powerful,
his elocution handsome and impressive, his sentiments evan-
gelical." At the age of forty-four, in the vigor of his man-
hood, he requested a dismission from his charge, giving as the
reason, "the habitual state of his blood and the frequent returns
of nervous disorders which the prosecution of the work of the
ministry tended to increase." His request was granted in
January, 1768, with a recognition of his "great and eminent services," and a gratuity of "ten pounds over and above
his salary" for the preceding year. He continued to occupy
the Parsonage, which was now his private property, and
turned his study into a store and carried on a general mercantile business. He was an intense patriot in the war of the
revolution, and when the British came to New Haven, he
fled to Hamden, taking with him his family, and the cow
that furnished them milk. The barn where his heavier
goods were stored was entered by the enemy, and so also was his
house, and wanton destruction followed. In the inventory of
his real estate, there is put down the allowance for losses sustained from the British, entitling him to one hundred and
thirty-one acres of land in the Connecticut Reserve. He
received of his customers and redeemed for the poorer people
largely of the Continental currency, and of course lost largely.
He bought or inherited through his wife lands enough to
have made him very wealthy, if they had then possessed a
fraction of their present value. He died in 1784, at the age
of sixty, from inoculation for the small-pox, and was buried
at midnight. Dr. Stiles in his Literary Diary, notes his
death, with this brief eulogy: "He was a man of religion."

Samuel Bird, the eldest son, married a daughter of Capt.
David Phipps of New Haven, and moved to Birdville, Georgia.
After her death he married a lady in that State.

Thomas, the other son, married for his first wife, Nancy Still-
well, lived to be upwards of forty, and left at his death two or
three children.

Daniel S., the youngest of his two sons by his first wife, and the only *Bird* in this region that has flown from the nest in the Parsonage of the Blue Meeting House, resides at present in New Hartford, and has frequently been a Lay-delegate from the parish there to the convention of the Protestant Episcopal Church in the diocese of Connecticut.

Mabel Sarah, the eldest daughter, was married to Dr. Joel Northrop of New Milford, May 15, 1777. He graduated at Yale College in the same class with her brother Samuel, studied medicine and practised his profession in this city and vicinity, besides having a store and carrying on the drug business. He built the stone house just out of the city on the Derby turnpike, which now stands a deserted ruin. Dr. Northrop died February 9, 1807, and his widow survived him just twenty-eight years. Their children were a daughter and six sons. The daughter was married to Elihu Ives, of this city, and lived but a few months.

One of his sons was lost at sea, and another died in the dew of his youth.

John Prout, his eldest, born in 1778, married Lydia Camp, of Litchfield, by whom he had several children. He died six years ago in Berlin, Wisconsin. One of his daughters, a handsome girl, married against her father's will, John Ridge, the Indian Chief of the Cherokee nation, and several years afterwards, he was killed in bed at the side of his wife by his own people, from supposed complicity with the course pursued by the General Government in regard to their removal and the payment for their lands. Ridge was a member of the Foreign Mission School, at Cornwall, in this State.

Amos, the third son of Dr. Northrop, graduated at Yale College, in 1804; went to Charleston, South Carolina, where he studied law, married a Miss Bellinger, and died in 1812, leaving two sons and a daughter. One of the sons adopted the profession of his father, and the other, a graduate of West Point, was a captain in the United States army, and resigned upon the outbreak of the present civil war.

Samuel Bird, another son of Dr. Northrop, was also a graduate of Yale and a captain in the United States navy.

He married a lady of Charleston, where he had his residence, but died childless in 1826.

Rodolphus E., the sixth and last who held any title to the Parsonage property, resided in this city, and was a carpenter and carver by trade. He died in 1860.

Deacon Levi Ives married, for his second wife, *Margaret*, the daughter of Rev. Samuel Bird, named in his will, by whom he had three children, two sons and a daughter.

It is curious to note how families die out in a place or lose their male representatives. John Prout, the father of Mrs. Bird, was for many years Treasurer of Yale College, one of its earliest graduates, and, as the inscription upon his tomb-stone reads, a "gentleman of established character for probity, and for seriousness." He died in 1776, and left no male issue,—his son John having died in his youth in 1732, four years after his graduation from College. And so the name of a family, prominent and influential in the first century of the Colony's history, is lost in the next, except that it continues to designate a narrow alley between Fleet and Meadow streets, sometimes called Peggy's Elbow.

The Parsonage of the Blue Meeting House is still standing and habitable. No edifice that has been occupied continuously for a hundred years can fail to have varied associations, and 'this, surely, if it could speak, would have some strange tales to relate. In one of its chambers, Whitfield lodged as he passed in his later years over the great stage road between Boston and Philadelphia ; for the early espousal of his cause, which cost Bird his college honors, ripened into a warm personal friendship, interrupted only by death. Within this house, we may suppose, were concocted the principal schemes to keep alive the spirit of the Separate Society and encourage its doubly-taxed members to wait patiently for a day of deliverance. If nothing was done without conference with the minister, we may believe that its threshold was frequently crossed by grave Deacons and earnest Committees, seeking the light of *his* wisdom to guide them in any new perplexities. We may believe, also, that the Parson was sometimes in joy at the success of his party and the advancement of his Church, that, to use the words of quaint George Herbert, "he sometimes refreshed himself, as knowing that nature will not bear everlasting droopings, and that pleasantness of disposition is a great key to do good ; not only because all men shun the company of perpetual severity, but also for that, when they are in company, instructions seasoned with pleasantness, both enter sooner, and root deeper." In this mansion, we know, the road to heaven and the road to earthly gains were both studied, for here, high Christian hopes were fostered, and mercantile plans diligently prosecuted. Here, many things were *weighed*, from the ponderous theology of Mr. Noyes down to a chest of tea and a pound of sugar.

I have said that the Parsonage of the Blue Meeting House is still standing and habitable. When the lot, with its build-ings, was purchased by St. Thomas Parish, steps were taken at once to erect upon it a convenient Chapel for temporary use. The old mansion, which, in its better days, had sheltered so many *Birds*, was sold for one hundred dollars, and removed to Ashmun street, near the entrance into York Square, where it was refitted and repaired without changing its essential features. It is now occupied by sundry families of Hibernian descent—thus furnishing another verification of the Scripture proverb, " He that buildeth the house hath more honor than the house."

THE GOVERNOR GILBERT LOT,

ON THE NORTHEAST CORNER OF CHURCH AND CHAPEL STREETS.

By E. L. CLEAVELAND, D. D.

READ MAY 30, 1864.

———— ◆◆◆ ————

AFTER the organization of civil government by the colonists of New Haven, and the laying out of the town plot in nine squares, the first step was to assign, by allotment, to each proprietor of the association, and to each head of a family, a house-lot on, or adjacent to the nine squares, together with out-lands lying beyond the nine squares, and within two miles of the center. The amount of land assigned to each was determined partly by the property invested in the enterprise, and partly by the size of the family. But the grouping of the various neighborhoods seems to have been regulated by no regard to this, nor to social position, nor official rank; but rather, so far as can be discovered, on some principle of elective affinity, following the law of earlier associations in the old world. It was quite natural that those who came from York-shire, and had been acquaintances and friends there, having known and become attached to each other by the endearing experience of common sufferings for a common faith, should have preferred to form one neighborhood in their New Haven home. The same was doubtless true of those who came from Hertfordshire. The Londoners, more numerous still, would form other neighborhoods. These groups, called quarters, seem to have formed sub-communities, with certain officers and committees to take care of their out-lands; and sometimes the inhabitants held meetings among themselves in relation to their common interests. These quarters were generally distinguished by the names of leading individuals residing within their respective limits,—such as the Governor's quarter—Mr. Davenport's quarter—Mr. Newman's quarter—and sometimes, in case of death or removal, the name of some other prominent surviving individual was substituted. While the people from Hertfordshire settled on the northeast corner of George and York streets, and the Yorkshire colonists settled the northeast corner of Chapel and York streets, the quarters of the London emigrants were in the more central parts of the town, or what are now, at least, more central. The squares bounded by Church, Chapel, State and Elm, and also by State, George, Church and Chapel, were chiefly occupied by Londoners, and perhaps the more wealthy of the colonists.

The first named of these two squares, was the Davenport quarter, and was divided into ten distinct allotments. One of these, the lot of Matthew Gilbert, forms the subject of the present paper. This lot was on the southwest corner of the square. It extended on Chapel street as far as the lot originally assigned to John Chapman, now the site of Henry N. Whittlesey's store. On Church street it reached to the north line of the lot now occupied by the Third Congregational Church.

The lot extending from the north line of Mr. Gilbert's original assignment, to the north line of the lot on which the City Hall now stands, was assigned to Mr. Owen Rowe. Mr. Rowe was one of the wealthiest men connected with this colonial enterprise; being rated at £1,000. But he probably never came over here to receive his share of the land. In 1639, Mr. Crane, the rear of whose lot on Elm street joined the rear of this lot on Church street, and who probably had occupied the latter, was ordered by the town to pay Mr. Rowe's rates. And it was voted, that if the original proprietor did not come the next year, the land should be at the public disposal. In September, 1640, the town gave Mr. Davenport a passage way, eight feet wide, across the north side of this lot, thus enabling him to go directly from his own garden to the meeting house. In April, 1643, the town, by vote, assigned one third of the Rowe allotment to Matthew Gilbert, to whose premises it was contiguous,—one-third, or the north part, to Mr. Davenport, and the other third, or middle portion, to Thomas Munson, on condition that he would build a suitable house on it, and devote himself to making wheels and ploughs for the good of the colony. He, however, failing to comply with these conditions, *this* third of the Rowe lot was set off to Mr. Davenport. The third, assigned to Matthew Gilbert, extended to Court street, and enlarged his original allotment to about two acres. Matthew Gilbert was one of the foremost men in the settlement. He is supposed to have come from London, but of his birth, parentage, or previous history, nothing is now known. From the confidence reposed in him, and the services required of him, it may be presumed that he was in the prime of life and the maturity of his powers, when he emigrated with this colony. He was one of the two who, in 1639, were chosen the earliest deacons of the first church in this city, which office he held until 1658, when he voluntarily resigned. He was one of the seven pillars selected to bear up both Church and State. From an early period, and for a long term of years, he was, in civil affairs, second only to Governor Eaton. On his broad shoulders were laid the burdens of magistracy ; and in those days the office was no sinecure. He was first deputy magistrate, and after Milford and Guilford were comprehended in the Jurisdiction, he was Deputy Governor ; a change of name only, not of office. To this honorable position he was reëlected by the colonists.

No name, except that of Governor Eaton, appears more frequently in the records, in connection with important public business, and high and difficult trusts, than that of Matthew Gilbert. It is impossible to resist the conviction that he was a man, in whose integrity, piety, strong common sense, and large capacity for public affairs, his fellow-citizens reposed entire confidence, and with perfect safety—a confidence that was never abused, and never shaken. His property was rated

at £600. Mr. Gilbert died in 1680; and from him are descended the numerous families of Gilberts in this town and
vicinity.   The mysterious letters " M. G.," chiseled on the
rude grave stone near the Centre Church, which the fertile
imagination of Dr. Stiles translated into William Goffe, (supposing the M. to be an inverted W.,) and which somewhat
violent theory has caused multitudes to dilate over those
rough memorials, with admiration for the renowned regicide,
there is now little reason to doubt, were the modest epitaph of
the first Deputy Governor of New Haven Colony.   And it is
a striking evidence, either of the poverty of the times, or of
the slight importance attached to mere monumental inscriptions, or of both, that a man, who for forty years had filled so
large a space in the public eye, and whose hand, like that of a
wise master-builder, had wrought so skillfully and ably on the
foundations of the infant Church and State, should have left
nothing to mark his final resting place but unshapely blocks of
stone, with the simple initials of his name.   But what cared
these men for such things, since " *their* record was on high,"
and " their names were written in the Lamb's book of life?"
Expecting themselves to be monumental " pillars in the temple
of God, to go no more out," they were the less concerned that
their memories should be perpetuated on earth by pretentious
marble.   Yet all the more incumbent is it upon us to see to it
that some appropriate column or tablet, breaking the silence of
two centuries, deciphering the obscure initials of the rude
head stone, shall henceforth hold up to the love and admiration of posterity the honored name of Matthew Gilbert.

The ownership of the first proprietor of the lot now in
question, commenced in 1639, and terminated with his death
in 1680, a period of forty-one years.   For more than ten
years before this, he was the only one of the original proprietors living on this square.   Many changes had transpired.
Mr. Davenport had removed to Boston; Governor Eaton had
been dead many years,—nearly all the leading colonists who
came with Governor Gilbert from England, and with whom he
had been so happily associated in laying the foundations, had
now passed away.   He was one of the few original pioneers

who were spared to see the goodly vine which he had assisted to transplant and nourish in this new world, growing strong and healthy, putting forth new branches and spreading itself through the land, until it had become interlocked with other vines, springing from other but kindred roots, and forming with them a consolidated union, civil and ecclesiastical.

Governor Gilbert left two sons, Matthew and Samuel, between whom the home lot was divided, Samuel taking the south side on Chapel street, and Matthew taking the north side, fronting on Church street, being the Gilbert portion of the Rowe lot. On this northern part Governor Gilbert, before his death, had erected a dwelling house for his son Matthew.

Samuel Gilbert died in 1721, and was succeeded by his son Samuel Gilbert, 2d. His father, however, before his death, had sold to John Gilbert, his nephew, a small piece on the northwest corner of the original Gilbert allotment, to be used as a "Sabbath day house." This Sabbath day lot, (two rods square,) passed by will and deed from Samuel Gilbert, Senior, to his nephew, John Gilbert, from him to Aaron and Joseph, sons of John, and from them, in 1770, to John Danielson.

After the death of Matthew Gilbert, son of the Governor, the date of which I do not know, his part of the old homestead, on the north side, was sold by his widow and children to William Lyon, a tailor by trade. This was the first William Lyon who came to New Haven. His wife was Experience Hayward or Howard. They had two children, William and Experience. This second William Lyon was the father of Colonel William Lyon, the well known President of New Haven Bank.

William Lyon, the tailor and purchaser of the Gilbert place, died before the year 1743. His purchase must have been as early as 1735. His house stood near the site of Mr. Henry O. Hotchkiss' house.

After the death of William Lyon in 1743, his widow and children remained in the house on Church street. In 1749, they sold it to their aunt Silence Hayward, but probably continued to live there. In 1752, Silence Hayward sold the north half of the lot extending to Court street to Yale Bishop, the

husband of Sibyl Gilbert.   In 1754, she sold the south half to
John Brainerd of Perth Amboy.   And in 1758, John Brainerd, then of Newark, sold his lot to Timothy Alling.   John
Brainerd's interest in this lot was natural and legitimate.   In
1752, he had married Experience, only daughter of William
and Experience Lyon ; and he was therefore buying back his
wife's former ownership in the estate.   And this fact connects
the subject of the present paper with one of the most memorable names in the religious history of the country, and one of
the most interesting enterprises in the rise and progress of
modern Christian missions.   John Brainerd was a younger
brother of David Brainerd, that burning and shining light,
whose short, brilliant career guided so many of the aborigines
of this land from paganism to Christ,—whose glorious example
quickened our churches to a more positive missionary spirit,—
in later times kindled the ardent soul of Henry Martin with
the like holy zeal for the salvation of the heathen,—and in all
times will stimulate kindred spirits to noblest deeds of piety
and benevolence.   John Brainerd was the seventh child of
Hon. Hezekiah Brainerd and Dorathy Mason, his wife.   He
was born at Haddam, February 28th, 1720, and graduated at
Yale College in the class of 1746.   If he entered College at
the beginning of the Freshman year, he must have suffered the
sharp trial of witnessing the proceedings which resulted in the
expulsion of his brother David.   But although he must have
felt it to be an unrighteous thing to punish with such relentless severity a fault for which humble and ample confession
was promptly offered, yet he continued with his class until
regularly graduated.   The interest pertaining to John Brainerd, arises not much, if at all, from his being the brother of
David, but rather from the fact that he was a man of the same
type of character, the same deep toned piety, the same missionary spirit, and especially to the fact that he entered into his
brother's labors among the Indians, and devoted his life to
their spiritual welfare.   He was not thought equal to David
in intellectual ability, but in regard to personal piety, he stood
as high as his brother.

Directly after leaving college, he entered on the theological studies preparatory to the Christian ministry, and was soon authorized to preach. Simultaneously with this, he was requested by the correspondents of the society for promoting Christian knowledge in foreign parts, to take his brother David's place, who was obliged to journey to New England for the benefit of his health, then rapidly failing. In April, 1747, he repaired to the Indian settlements in New Jersey, where David, since 1743, had prosecuted his labors. His brother never returned, but closed his saintly life at Northampton in the autumn of that year. In consequence of this event, John Brainerd, having been ordained in February, 1748, took sole charge of the field where David had labored with such remarkable success. His ministry was attended with the same kind of results, though not to the same degree, as his brother's. He remained continuously at his work until 1755, when, owing to various disturbing causes, one of which was the French war, the settlement was broken up, and he withdrew from it for a season. Soon after, receiving a call to settle in Newark, he moved there with his family, and continued until June, 1756. The managers of the missionary society, however, supposing they had then a prospect of securing the lands on which the Indians were then living, desired him to resume his mission. To this he consented; and giving up his Newark call, moved with his family to Brunswick, as being the most convenient point from which they could reach the Indians as then situated. Here he remained until September, 1757, more than a year, when the project of gaining the land falling through, he was again dismissed from the service. The church at Newark still remaining without a pastor, they renewed their call, which he accepted, and entered immediately on the duties of the pastorate. In less than two years he was again solicited in behalf of the Indians, for whom land had at length been secured by governmental treaty. At the solicitation of the Governor of the Colony, and by advice of the Presbytery, he resigned his charge in Newark, and resumed his labors once more among his beloved Indians. About this time he seems to have entered the army for a brief period, probably as a temporary chaplain. The Indians, too, of his congregation, during every year

of the war, had enlisted into the King's service far beyond
their proportion—and in every campaign more or less of them
had died. In 1757 they lost nearly twenty of their men, taken
prisoners at Fort William Henry. These causes had greatly
reduced their numbers at the mission, and checked their work.
He continued in this mission, laboring much also as a home
missionary among feeble churches, and white communities destitute of the means of grace, performing occasional services for
the College at Princeton, of which he was twenty-six years a
trustee, until he finally withdrew from New Jersey and removed to Deerfield, in Massachusetts, in 1777, where he
preached for the remainder of his life. His death took place
March 18th, 1781, at the age of sixty-one, and his remains re-
pose beneath the floor of the Congregational Church in Deerfield. In 1757, Mr. Brainerd lost his wife—an affliction of
which he speaks in the strongest terms of grief. Within a few
months afterwards, two of his three children were taken from
him, leaving only his daughter Mary, who became the wife of
Dr. Ross, of New Jersey. Mr. Brainerd married for his second
wife, Mrs. Experience Price, who died without issue in 1793.

It is a pleasant thought that in the humble dwelling of William Lyon, standing on this honored site, consecrated to Christ
by Pilgrim piety, the spirit of modern missions breathed its
earliest and purest aspirations from the loving hearts of John
and Experience Brainerd. Here they walked with God—here
they planned and prayed for the conversion of the heathen—
here they sometimes met, on their visits home, circles of Christian friends, and reported the wonderful things God had
wrought through their instrumentality among the Indians. It
is no exaggeration to say, that from this spot a holy influence has
radiated, in beams of light and love, throughout the wide world
of missionary enterprise, and that it will continue to be felt
until the earth shall be filled with the knowledge of the Lord,
as the waters fill the sea.

Returning to the succession of ownership, we find that in
1761 Timothy Alling had sold the north part of the lot now
covered by the Tontine block to Joshua Chandler, and the
south part to Medad Lyman. In 1765, Joshua Chandler's title

passed over to Naphtili (Hartmeyer,) and in 1779 Charles Chauncey became its owner, and from his heirs, I believe, it was purchased by the association known as the Tontine.

Medad Lyman, who bought the south part of Timothy Alling's lot, joining the north line of the present church lot, sold out, in 1773, to Jonathan Fitch. Fitch sold it in 1785 to Joseph Pynchon. In 1789 it was bought by William Joseph Whiting, whose wife was a Lyman. Mr. W. died early, leaving a family of young children, which his widow heroically brought up on narrow means, without soliciting aid of any one. To do this, however, she was obliged to sell her house, and remove to a smaller one in a remote part of the town. She was the mother of George I. Whiting, and grandmother of Dr. Wm. J. Whiting, of this city. She sold the place in 1806 to Nathaniel Rossiter, better known as Sheriff Rossiter. The next owner was Addin Lewis, who was succeeded by Harvey Hoadley—he was followed by H. Lee Scranton, who sold it to the present owner, Henry O. Hotchkiss.

We now come back to the north half of the original Gilbert lot, covered at present by the Third Congregational Church. The succession of proprietorship here runs down from Gov. Gilbert through Samuel 1st, 1679—Samuel 2d, 1721—Samuel 3d, 1744—John Danielson, 1766. At this point, after a century and a quarter of ownership and actual residence, the name and blood of the Gilbert family disappeared. In 1774 John Danielson sold his title to Charles Chauncey, whose name, more than that of any other, is identified with the place, in the recollections of the present generation.

Charles Chauncey was son of Elihu Chauncey, Esq., of Durham, grandson of the Rev. Nathaniel Chauncey, of Durham, great grandson of Rev. Nathaniel Chauncey, of Hatfield, Mass., and great great grandson of President Chauncey, of Harvard College, who was the emigrant ancestor of all the Chaunceys in this country; and he proved himself worthy of this excellent and honorable descent. He was born at Durham, May 30, 1747. In consequence of feeble health in the youthful period of his life, he did not receive a collegiate education. But such were the strength and quickness of his mind, such his zeal and diligence in study, and so rapid and extensive his acquisitions in learning, that this defect in his early training was fully supplied to him. He studied law with James Abraham Hillhouse, Esq., and was admitted to the bar in November, 1768. He at once took a prominent position in his profession, and steadily rose to eminence as an advocate. His wife was Abigail Darling, daughter of Deacon Thomas Darling, of New Haven; and the first home to which he introduced his young bride, was the house he had just bought of John Danielson. It was a small building when Mr. Chauncey purchased it, but it gradually increased by successive additions on every side except the front. Here Charles and Abigail Chauncey,—he twenty-seven, and she twenty-six years of age,—commenced housekeeping; and here they remained almost fifty years, and both of them died in the home where all their children were born. Mr. Chauncey's success at the bar, secured for him, in 1776, the appointment of Attorney for the State of Connecticut; and in 1789 he was elevated to the bench of the Superior Court. Both of these positions, so diverse in character, he filled with marked ability. In 1793 he resigned the judgeship, and retired from the practice of law. Soon after this he opened a private law school, to which he delivered a course of lectures. In this employment he continued for many years; and such was his skill and success in preparing candidates for the bar, that many of the finest young men in the country were drawn to his instructions, and not a few of the most eminent lawyers of the past generation received their legal training from his hand.

In 1777, Yale College gave public testimony of his talents, scholarship and services, by conferring upon him the degree of Master of Arts; and in 1811, Middlebury College honored him with the degree of Doctor of Laws. After retiring from the bench and from the business of the courts, he gave much of his time to reading, study, and superintending the education of his children. His thirst for knowledge was intense; he needed not the spur of ambition, or the pressure of official duty, or the necessity of subsistence, to urge him into the paths of literature and science. He loved study for its own sake. His reading was on the most extensive scale, and his investigations, of the most thorough and exhaustive character, especially in the department of law. Descended from a long line of eminent ministers of the gospel, famous and mighty in their day, he had a peculiar fondness for theological researches, which he prosecuted with such zeal and success, that he became one of the most intelligent theologians of his time. Endowed with a mind so vigorous, active and fertile, so highly cultured by discipline, and so richly stored with well digested and classified learning, we are not surprised that he was held in high respect by educated men; we can understand why President Dwight spent much time in his society, and can believe the tradition that the President sometimes, before committing to the press, read his manuscripts to the Judge for his criticism.

Judge Chauncey made a profession of his faith in Christ, at an early period of his life, and was a member of the First Church in this city. He served at one time as a deacon of this church, I have been credibly informed, though his name does not appear in the published catalogue of officers. He often represented the church in ecclesiastical councils, and was for a long time one of its most prominent members. His familiarity with theology and church polity drew to him many applicants for advice in religious matters, and he was often employed as counsel in ecclesiastical trials.

When the Rev. Moses Stuart succeeded the Rev. Dr. Dana in the pastorate of the First Church, Judge Chauncey did not sympathize in the religious change that followed. He was a friend of Dr. Dana, of Dr. Dana's way of preaching, and of the type of theology of which Dr. Dana was one of the last and ablest representatives. Taking exception to some sentiment advanced by Mr. Stuart in the pulpit, the judge withdrew from attendance on his ministry. This occasioned some inquiry and agitation in the church, but the matter was ultimately dropped, leaving Judge Chauncey in regular standing. He did not resume his attendance, however, even after the settlement of Dr. Taylor, with whom he was on terms of personal friendship; but it appeared that this continued absence was caused by physical infirmity which disabled him from attending through an entire service.

In a eulogy pronounced at his funeral, President Day speaks of Judge Chauncey's religious character in terms of unqualified confidence. He describes his declining years as hallowed by religious faith, and cheered by Christian hope. And he speaks of his closing hours, as blest with the peace of God. From another source, I learn that in his last sickness he sent for the deacons of the church and conversed with them in a kind and Christian spirit concerning his relations to the church, and explained to them, as above stated, the reason which for several years had detained him from the house of God.

Judge Chauncey was sensitive, over sensitive perhaps, to slights or wrongs, whether real or imaginary; yet in his family and among the friends in whom he confided, he was affectionate and genial, and happy in the love of others. His house was the home of all the domestic virtues and graces,—the true, the pure and the beautiful,—where intelligence and refinement shed their clearest and softest light, and where over all, religion spread her sacred mantle. Of this lovely circle Judge Chauncey was the honored head and center—loved and revered by all.

In height he was nearly six feet, stoutly built and corpulent. His features were strong and massive, the brow heavily overhanging his blue eyes, and the whole head and figure expressive of dignity and force. His death occurred April 28, 1823. His wife died Dec. 24, 1818. Their children were Charles, Elihu, Sarah, Abigail and Nathaniel. They were all born on this spot—all carefully trained by the skillful hand of their parents. All the sons were educated at our college. Of the entire number, Nathaniel is the only survivor. Never had parents more reason to be satisfied with the results of their home culture than Judge Chauncey and his excellent wife.

Their oldest son, Charles, was examined and accepted for admission to Yale College at the age of ten, but was kept back a year, and then entered, and graduated at fifteen—one of the youngest graduates of the college. Young as he was, he stood high in his class for scholarship, and higher still for loveliness of character. His appointment at Commencement was a Greek dialogue, in which, I may be excused for saying, that Solomon Williams, son of Wm. Williams, of Lebanon, was his associate,—a youth nearly if not quite as young, who, like himself, had passed an acceptable examination for the Freshman Class, at the early age of ten years,—a bosom friend of Chauncey, whose home while in college was at Judge Chauncey's house, and who had the same faultless amiability, the same exquisite refinement of character, as his young friend. Five years ago, I heard Judge Boardman,* of New Milford; now, I believe, ninety-six years of age, repeat from memory, after the lapse of more than half a century, the first sentence of that Greek dialogue.

Charles Chauncey, Jr., after studying law five years with his father, removed to Philadelphia, where, after considerable delay, he was admitted to that bar,—then thought by Chief Justice Ellsworth and others the ablest in the country,—and commenced that high and ascending career which in the course of a few years placed him among the first of American jurists. A purer, more honorable or loftier character never adorned the legal profession. It was formed after the highest models of gentlemanly grace, and Christian integrity and refinement. The limits of this paper will not allow of any extended notice of his life, nor is it needful. Few have forgotten the burst of sorrow and exalted eulogy, that from the press, the bar and the pulpit, found eloquent utterance at the intelligence of his death. He died Aug. 30, 1849.

Elihu Chauncey graduated four years after Charles, and followed him to Philadelphia, where he entered the legal profession. He was every way worthy of his family and of the noble brother by whose side he steadily rose to honorable distinction. Turning aside from the law, he became first a journalist, at the head of the United States Gazette. Subsequently he became distinguished as one of the ablest of financiers, and achieved brilliant success in the inception and completion of important works of public improvement. He died April 8, 1847, lamented by state and church as only a great and good man can be lamented.

Sarah Chauncey, third child of Judge Chauncey, of New Haven, married, in 1814, William Walton Woolsey, and thus

---

* Since deceased.

became the step-mother of President Woolsey.   She died Feb. 8, 1856.

Abigail Chauncey, the fourth child of Judge Chauncey, died unmarried, June 11, 1814.

Nathaniel Chauncey, the fifth and youngest child, still resides in Philadelphia.   The old homestead continued in the family several years after Judge Chauncey's decease, sometimes occupied by private families, but more generally used as a boarding house.   It was at length purchased by the late Harvey Hoadley, who removed the old mansion, intending to erect a large hotel in its place.   But the sudden and lamented death of that energetic and public spirited citizen, frustrated his plans.   The place was then sold to Henry O. Hotchkiss and William Forbes; and in the Spring of 1855 it was purchased from them by the Third Congregational Society.   The church edifice which now stands upon it, was commenced in July of that year, and completed in August of the year following.

The writer has been often amused at the perplexity of the public, and particularly of the press, as to a convenient popular designation for this church.   Sometimes it is called the "Church Street Church," which, besides its unpleasant alliteration, is objectionable as confounding it with a church of somewhat different creed further down the street.   Sometimes it is called by the name of the pastor, which is not very respectful to the ecclesiastical organization that owns and worships in it. Since the legal title of Third Congregational Church seems to be generally declined, it might relieve the editorial fraternity of their embarrassment, to substitute as more appropriate and euphonious than either of the foregoing, the name of the Chauncey Place Church.

On the corner of Church and Court streets stood at the commencement of this century, and how much earlier I do not know, the house now occupied by Rev. Dr. Bacon.   Here, for a long series of years, was kept the principal tavern of the city.   It stood back three or four rods from Church street, and was precisely the same size as at present.   This tavern was kept by a Mrs. Smith, a widow from the eastern part of the state, whose family were refined and courteous.   She was succeeded in the establishment by her daughter, Miss Nancy

Smith, a lady of great urbanity and excellence. And afterwards another daughter became mistress of the house, viz.: Mrs. Prentice, wife of Col. Prentice, who was an officer in the Revolutionary army. It was subsequently occupied by Gov. Foote, and by a Mr. Lewis, but whether as a tavern or not I am uninformed. About the year 1809 Jacob Ogden commenced tavern-keeping there. It was then known as the Coffee House. Mr. Ogden had formerly been a resident of Hartford, and in wealthy circumstances. A reverse of fortune constrained him to engage in the business of keeping a public house. He is well remembered by the present generation for his genial and even jolly good humor, the cheery welcome, the kindly sympathy, and facetious pleasantry with which he received and entertained his guests,—the generous table he spread, the famous coffee he made, and the excellent care he took of all who came under his roof. He used to say, that having spent his principal at Hartford, he had now come to New Haven to live on the interest. He was accustomed to signify his readiness to serve a friend, by the formidable declaration, "I'll fight for you, I'll fight for you." That this did not always have the desired effect, he discovered, in one instance at least, when two clergymen drove up to his door, and seeing a large number of military in the yard and house, hesitated about stopping. Mr. Ogden came out and urged them to come in. Finding them still undecided, he resorted to his favorite expression, "Ill fight for you, my friends, Ill fight for you." This brought the reverend gentlemen to the point at once, who immediately whipped up, to find a tavern where there was no occasion for any one to "fight for them." A farmer who had sold him some hay, and concealed himself in the load while it was on the scales, thus adding two hundred pounds to the weight, was surprised to find his trick discovered, by Mr. Ogden's gravely claiming him as a part of his purchase. Mr. Ogden continued the coffee house until 1824, when he retired, and soon after the property passed into the hands of the Tontine association, who the next year erected the present hotel block. This large establishment has been kept, first by Drake and Andrews, then by Andrews alone, then by Jones and Allis, then by S. W.

Allis alone, and then by H. Lee Scranton, and then by the present landlord, Israel H. Ross.

It now remains to speak of the changes on the south part of Governor Gilbert's lot on the corner of Church and Chapel streets, covered by the Exchange building, and running down to Henry N. Whittlesey's store. I have already stated that this fell to the share of Samuel Gilbert, son of the Governor. At his death, in 1721, the property descended to his son, Samuel Gilbert, 2d, who died in 1730, leaving it to his son, Samuel 3d, and his daughter Sibyl. Samuel took the western or corner lot, and Sibyl the eastern part fronting entirely on Chapel street. Sibyl Gilbert married Yale Bishop. In 1760, Samuel Gilbert, 3d, sold out his interest in the old homestead to John Beecher, and in 1766, Mr. and Mrs. Bishop sold their portion to Timothy Bonticou, who resold that same year a part of his purchase to John Miles. John Beecher was succeeded in the corner lot by his son, Thaddeus Beecher, well remembered by a few of our elder citizens. Thaddeus Beecher had a store on the corner of Church and Chapel, and a dwelling house adjoining. He is spoken of by those who remember him, in terms of high respect, as a most worthy and substantial citizen. His business was conducted in the most honorable and thorough manner. Every resident of New Haven, who desired to procure the choicest groceries, or liquors of the finest brands, knew that they were to be had, if anywhere, at Thaddeus Beecher's. After his death, the place was sold, January 3d, 1824, to the Eagle Bank. Thaddeus Beecher's house was then moved off from the premises, and transferred to the south side of West Chapel street, between York and Park streets. The kitchen, however, was moved a few rods to the west of its old position, and is now in the rear of the store occupied by Benjamin Beecher.

The Directors of the Eagle Bank laid the foundation of a banking house on or near the site of Thaddeus Beecher's store and had carried up the walls several feet above the ground, when the work was arrested by the failure of the Bank,—a catastrophe that shook the city like an earthquake, and sent distress and dismay into many families. The walls remained

several years as they were left by the blow that struck down
the institution, a monument to the thousands who passed them
from time to time, of the folly that " begins to build, but is
not able to finish." In 1831, December 8th, the creditors and
assignees of the Eagle Bank sold the property to Jehiel
Forbes & Son, who proceeded immediately to erect upon it the
large and imposing structure which now adorns it.

The property occupied by the two brick buildings next to
the Exchange, on the east, was sold by the heirs of Thaddeus
Beecher to Eli B. Austin, in 1823. Here Mr. Austin kept a
grocery many years. He, however, sold the eastern part of the
lot to Mr. Lum; the next owner was Seymour Bradley, and the
next and present owner is Mrs. Emily Dwight, daughter of
Giles Mansfield. The lot and store occupied by Benjamin
Beecher, is still the property of Eli B. Austin's widow.

The long wooden building reaching from Mrs. Dwight's
brick store to the gangway leading to Brockett's stable, is the
property of the descendants of John Miles. This is the identical estate purchased by John Miles of Timothy Bonticou, in
1766, so that the property has remained in the family nearly
one hundred years. On this place, and as I suppose in this
very building, John Miles kept tavern at the time of the Revolutionary war. And, in after years, Mrs. Miles used to tell her
children how, when the war was over, officers of the army, returning from active service, used to assemble at this house, and
how, as they took final leave of each other, to seek their various homes, those browned, scarred, war-worn veterans would
fall on each other's necks and weep like women. Mr. Miles
was a tailor by trade, and had his shop in the western half of
the present building. Isaac and Kneeland Townsend learned
their trade of him. He denounced the sharp pointed shoe of
his day, made for either foot, and long before rights and lefts
were known, insisted with prescient wisdom that the sole of a
shoe should be cut by the shape of the foot. He was a comical
character, something of an original, and passed under the
soubriquet of " host Miles." He had a son, Mark, who kept
tavern here after his father's death. About 1818, the old house
again became a public house, and was known as Buck's tav-

ern, and so continued until 1833. The timbers of the old floor
may still be seen in Mr. Pease's bookstore, two or three feet
above the present floor. This is the tavern where a certain
man, well known, came so often for his favorite drink, that he
wore a hole through the floor on the spot where he rested his
cane.

The lot east of the gangway, occupied by the store of
Charles Winship, had passed to Thaddeus Beecher, probably
from the hands of Timothy Bonticou. Thaddeus was succeeded by his nephew, John Beecher; and from the last
named Beecher it descended to the late John D. Beecher,
whose widow now ownes it. The lot next east of Charles
Winship's store, also became Thaddeus Beecher's, from whom
it descended to his nephew, Jacob Brown, who sold it to John
S. Graves, the present proprietor.

This completes the circuit, bringing us to the western wall
of Henry N. Whittlesey's store, the eastern boundary of Governor Gilbert's lot.

PIONEERS IN POMOLOGY IN NEW HAVEN.

By NATHANIEL A. BACON, Esq.

READ JANUARY, 1865.

BENJAMIN DOUGLASS, by profession a lawyer, is the first man in New Haven whom the writer learns of as a propagator of choice fruits. In the year 1775, he planted an orchard of sixty-four cherry trees, just out of the New Haven town limits, near East Rock, all of grafted trees, and died (of erysipelas) within one week thereafter. Among them were White Ox Heart, Black Ox Heart, Honey Heart and May Duke. His successor and son-in-law, Wm. G. Hubbard, now deceased, left memoranda that he had gathered and sold bushels of May Duke cherries from these trees as early in the season as the 10th of June, some two weeks earlier than at present.

Jonah Hotchkiss, by trade a house joiner, when a soldier in the Revolutionary Army, brought from Red Hook, Long Island, N. Y., soon after the year 1780, grafts from the Delancey pear, also grafts from a tree bearing large red sweet apples. These grafts were distributed, and the true name of the pear being then unknown, it took the local name of Jonah, from its introducer, which it retains to this day. The tree bearing the original graft is now standing on a lot on the north side of Chapel street, between High and York streets, and produces fruit annually. The apple is still in existence, but without a specific name. He died in 1811.

Nathan Beers, Senior, was killed at New Haven, by the British, in 1779. He was a nurseryman, and cultivated the finest of fruits. He introduced the Catharine, Jargonelle, Warden, St. Michaels, Bergamot, and many other varieties of pears. He introduced choice varieties of apples, and was a successful cultivator of the foreign grape.

Nathan Beers, Junior, followed the occupation of his father, and disseminated many new and choice varieties of fruit. He died in 1849, aged 97 years.

Timothy Dwight, D. D., President of Yale College, cultivated the largest garden in the city with his own hands, and produced the best culinary plants and the finest fruits in the city. He introduced the Chili strawberry, and was the first to successfully cultivate the strawberry as a garden fruit in New Haven. His peaches are said to have been of the choicest kinds, and very abundant—so abundant that they were removed from his grounds by the cart load. He died in 1817.

Daniel Punderson, a nurseryman, cultivated the strawberry for market, and among many seedling pears raised by him was the "Punderson," said to be a seedling from the Jonah. He died in 1829.

James Hillhouse, by profession a lawyer, cultivated extensively the apple, the pear, and the peach. A quantity of apple and pear scions from the King's garden, in France, having been received by him, and finding no person to cultivate them, he, with the assistance of a friend, in one evening by candle light, set one hundred and fifty scions into small stocks. This collection contained about forty varieties of pears. Among his peaches were the Early Ann, Nutmeg, Red Rareripe, Yellow Rareripe, and White and Red Clingstone. His assortment was so arranged as to have ripe fruit from the beginning to the end of the season. To him the public are indebted for the beautiful elms which adorn our streets. He died in 1832.

Eli Whitney, the inventor of the cotton gin, was a cultivator of the choicest varieties of apples. He died in 1825.

Henry W. Edwards, by profession a lawyer, at one time Governor of Connecticut, commenced planting pear seeds in the years 1817 and 1818. He succeeded in introducing some sixty new varieties of pears, some of them of decided merit. Among them were the Button Ball, Edwards, Citron, Frances,

John, Henrietta, William, Emily, Elizabeth, Calhoun, Dallas, Van Buren, Jackson, Black Hawk, Spice, Humbug, Clay, Meadow and Cluster. He also raised quinces and apples from the seed. He died in 1847.

Noyes Darling, educated as a clergyman, was a successful cultivator of choice fruits in all their varieties, and furnished strawberries and other fruits for market. He paid much attention to the formation and habits of the various insects, so destructive to fruits and vegetables. The result of his researches, in part, is embodied in an address delivered by him before the New Haven Horticultural Society in October, 1845. He died in 1846.

Virgil M. Dow, M. D., was an enthusiastic cultivator of new and choice varieties of fruit, devoting much time and attention thereto. This community is indebted to him for many varieties not before known to them. He died in 1851.

Eli Ives, M. D., probably paid more attention to the production of new varieties of many kinds of fruit, and to the cultivation of those that were known, than any other of our citizens. He paid much attention to the grape; raised from the seed raspberries, strawberries, among them the Ives seedling, and pears in great numbers, including the Yale, Dow and Ives Bergamot. He died in 1861.

At a meeting of fruit growers in New Haven, held October 21st, 1844, "The Pomological Society" was formed, and the following officers chosen, viz. :

HENRY W. EDWARDS, *President.*
ELI IVES, *Vice President.*
VIRGIL M. DOW, *Secretary.*
CHARLES NICOLL, *Treasurer.*

The members admitted into the Society have been:

In 1844.—Henry W. Edwards, (since dead.) Eli Ives, (since dead,) Virgil M. Dow, (since dead.) Charles Nicoll, James T. Gerry, (lost at sea,) Noyes Darling, (since dead,) Charles B. Lines, James Goodrich, (since dead.) Philos Blake, John Augustus Totten, (since dead.) Henry Whitney, (since dead,) Aaron N. Skinner, (since dead,) Alfred S. Monson.

In 1845.—Ezra C. Read, George Gabriel, Nathaniel F. Thompson, Abraham C. Baldwin, Eleazar T. Fitch, James Harrison, (since dead,) Stephen D. Pardee.

In 1846.—Silas I. Baldwin, Charles Robinson, Ebenezer H. Bishop.

In 1847.—John Bromham, (since dead,) Nathan B. Ives, Benjamin Silliman, Jr.

In 1848.—Thomas R. Dutton.

In 1849.—John P. Norton, (since dead,) Creighton Whitmore, (since dead,) Elizur E. Clarke.

In 1850.—William Wadsworth, (since dead,) William Johnson, John J. Walter, (since dead.)

In 1851.—William S. Charnley, Oliver F. Winchester, Charles W. Elliott, Charles L. Chaplain, Nathaniel A. Bacon.

In 1852.—Thomas H. Totten, Charles Beers, Jonathan Stoddard, (since dead,) John C. Hollister.

In 1853.—Charles Dickerman.

In 1854.—Alfred P. Monson, Harmanus M. Welch, John E. Wylie, John Peck.

In 1855.—Worthington Hooker, Samuel Peck, Samuel E. Foote, (since dead,) Solomon Mead, Pierrepont B. Foster, Nelson Hotchkiss.

In 1856.—Henry Austin, Oliver E. Maltby, Caleb S Maltby, Isaac Anderson, Nathan F. Hall, Samuel Rowland.

In 1857.—Theodore Newell, Frederick J. Betts.

In 1858.—John A. Blake.

In 1859.—John S. Beach, William I. Beers.

In 1860.—Randolph Linsley, (Meriden.)

In 1863.—William Parmelee, Henry A. Warner.

In 1864.—William W. Winchester.

In 1865.—Charles P. Augur, (Hamden.)

The Officers of the Society chosen in October, 1864, are:

SILAS I. BALDWIN, *President.*
NELSON HOTCHKISS, *Vice President.*
NATHANIEL A. BACON, *Secretary and Treasurer.*

CORRESPONDENCE

PRESIDENT JEFFERSON AND ABRAHAM BISHOP,

COLLECTOR OF THE PORT OF NEW HAVEN.

From original papers in the possession of the New Haven Colony Historical Society.

———◆◆◆———

WASHINGTON Nov. 13. 08.

Sir

Not knowing whether Col⁰. Humphreys would be at present at or in the neighborhood of New Haven, or in Boston, I take the liberty of addressing a request to yourself. Homespun is become the spirit of the times : I think it an useful one and therefore that it is a duty to encourage it by example. The best fine cloth made in the U. S. is, I am told, at the manufacture of Col⁰. Humphreys in your neighborhood. Could I get the favor of you to procure me there as much of his best as would make me a coat? I should prefer a deep blue, but, if not to be had, then a black. Some person coming on in the stage can perhaps be found who would do me the favor of taking charge of it. The amount shall be remitted you the moment you shall be so kind as to notify it to me, or paid to any member of the legislature here ; whom yourself or Colonel Humphrey's agent shall indicate. Having so little acquaintance in or near New-Haven I hope you will pardon the liberty I take in proposing this trouble to you, towards which the general motive will perhaps avail something. I salute you with esteem and respect.

TH: JEFFERSON

Mr ABRAHAM BISHOP

NEW HAVEN Nov. 30. 1808.

Sir,

Since the receipt of your favor of 13. inst, I have waited for the return of Col. Humphreys from Philadelphia, upon the suggestion of his agent, that the Col. would be ambitious to select, personally, such cloth, as might do justice to his factory and your expectations.

The colonel returned this evening and says that four weeks at least will be necessary for furnishing a piece of superior quality, which is in hand.

As soon as it shall be received I will have the satisfaction of forwarding it according to your request.

I have the honor to be,
With the greatest respect
Sir, yr. obt Servt
ABRM BISHOP

PRESIDENT JEFFERSON

———

WASHINGTON, Dec. 8. 08.

Sir

Your favor of Nov. 30. is duly received, & I thank you for your kind attention to the little commission respecting the cloth. I shall be glad to receive it whenever it can come, but a great desideratum will be lost if not received in time to be made up for our new year's day exhibition when we expect every one will endeavor to be in homespun, and I should be sorry to be marked as being in default. I would sacrifice much in the quality to this circumstance of time: however I leave it to the kindness of Colo. Humphreys and yourself. I presume that if put into a very light box, no larger than to hold the cloth closely pressed in & addressed to me it may come safely by the stage or even by the mail, if that be necessary, to save our distance. Accept my salutation & assurances of esteem and respect.

TH: JEFFERSON

Mr. Bishop.

———

N. H. 14. Dec. 1808

Sir,

accordg to yr request, under date of 8 inst you will receive by the mail which conveys this, 5½ yds narrow superf. cloth, from Col. Humphreys factory, being of ⅞th merino wool, price 4.50 per yard. Mr E. Bacon of the house of rep. will do me the favor to receive from you the amt. expressed in the inclosed receipt.

The Col. laments that it is not in his power to furnish you at this time, with cloth of a superior quality,

I have the honor to be
With gt resp.
Sir
Y. mo. ob Serv.
ABRM BISHOP

Pre, Jefferson

———

Washington, Jan. 20. 09.

Sir

This is the first moment I have been able to make the acknowledgment of the receipt of the cloth you were so kind as to procure me in good condition. The cost was paid to mr. Bacon according to your permission, and I pray you to accept my thanks for the trouble of this commission, with the assurances of my esteem and respect.

THO JEFFERSON

Mr. Bishop.

" J. Humphreys Jr. Rec^t for President Jefferson's cloth
p^d 1808 "

President Jefferson D^r
To 5½ yds cloth Bot of
Col Humphreys at $4-50 $24-75

Rec^d payment in full of Abraham Bishop Esqr for
Col Humphreys

JOHN HUMPHREYS Junr

NEW HAVEN Dec 26th 1808.

BISHOP BERKELEY'S GIFTS TO YALE COLLEGE;

A COLLECTION OF

DOCUMENTS ILLUSTRATIVE OF "THE DEAN'S BOUNTY."

By DANIEL C. GILMAN,

LIBRARIAN OF YALE COLLEGE.

PRESENTED TO THE SOCIETY, MARCH, 1865.

—————♦♦♦—————

I. INTRODUCTORY.   OUTLINE OF BERKELEY'S LIFE.

THE name of Bishop BERKELEY will always be held in grateful remembrance by the graduates and friends of Yale College, as that of one of the earliest, wisest and most distinguished benefactors of the institution.

An extended memoir of this eminent philosopher and prelate is still to be desired. The announcement that such a biography is already in preparation under favorable auspices, has led to the collection and publication of the documents which follow. They all pertain more or less directly to his successive donations to Yale College, and they help to illustrate one of the most interesting chapters of his life,—the American episode.

Before presenting these papers, we shall give, for convenience of reference, a brief sketch of the Bishop's life.

GEORGE BERKELEY, D. D., Dean of Derry, and afterward Bishop of Cloyne, in Ireland, was born at Kilcrin, near Thomastown, Kilkenny County, Ireland, March 12th, 1684, and died in Oxford, England, January 14th, 1753.

After having been educated at Trinity College, Dublin, he became a Fellow in that College, June 9th, 1707. In 1713 he accompanied the Earl of Peterborough on his Embassy to the King of Sicily and the Italian states. He soon afterwards made a second visit to the Continent. In 1724 he was made Dean of Derry, and about the same time formed a plan for establishing a College in the Bermudas for the purpose of educating the aboriginal Americans, and of training ministers of the Church of England for labor in the new world. Having obtained a charter for the proposed institution and the promise of a grant of £20,000, for an endowment, Berkeley set sail from the old world, September 17th, 1728, and arrived in Newport, Rhode Island, January 23d, 1729. The latter place he had chosen as a convenient centre for correspondence and inquiry while he was waiting to receive the promised grant. Here he purchased a farm which he called "Whitehall," erected upon it a small house, preached often in Newport, composed his "Alciphron or the Minute Philosopher," and made acquaintances among the clergymen and other prominent men of New England.

At length, persuaded that his expectations of an endowment were doomed to disappointment, Berkeley returned to England, embarking at Boston in September, 1731. He soon sent over to Yale College a fine collection of books, and also a deed of his Newport Farm. It is to perpetuate the grateful remembrance of these benefactions, that the following illustrative documents have been brought together.

In 1734, Dr. BERKELEY was appointed Bishop of Cloyne, and in 1745, the See of Clogher was offered to him and declined. In 1752, his health having become impaired, he removed with his family to Oxford, (intending to superintend the education of his son,) and there soon afterward he died.

The various philosophical writings of Bishop Berkeley are so well known, and the dignity and excellence of his character have been so frequently referred to, not only by his cotemporaries but by more recent writers, that there seems to be no occasion here to dwell upon the theme. Nearly all that follows has, till recently, been hidden in manuscript.

II. HOW THE DEAN'S BOUNTY WAS SECURED.

When Dean BERKELEY determined to return to England, he is said to have divided his private library between Harvard College and Yale College. Soon after reaching home he sent over to Yale College a much more extensive collection of books, selected for the College Library, and also a deed of the "Whitehall" Farm, near Newport, on which he had resided.

The following extract from the manuscript autobiography of Rev. Dr. Samuel Johnson, narrates the circumstances which led to this special interest in Yale College. The Society is indebted to the Rev. Dr. Beardsley for this transcript.

Dr. Johnson, it will be remembered, graduated at Yale College in 1714, and was afterwards a Tutor from 1716 to 1719. He subsequently received Episcopal ordination, and became a Missionary of the Church of England, stationed at Stratford, Connecticut.

"In the year 1729, in February, came that very extraordinary genius, Bishop Berkeley, then Dean of Derry, into America, and resided two years and a half at Rhode Island. He was a gentleman of vast learning and equal benevolence, and came hither with the most extensively benevolent intention of promoting both religion and learning throughout America, among the heathen as well as Christians. The sale of the land in St. Christophers, which belonged to England by the peace after Queen Anne's wars, amounted to 80,000 pounds, and had been designed by her to be a fund for the support of four bishops in America; but that design being neglected in the two following reigns, Dean Berkeley, by dint of his importunity and his mighty eloquence, and in spite of Sir Robert Walpole's reluctance, (who was then Chief Minister,) procured a grant of £20,000 of that money towards establishing a college at Bermuda, in prosecution of his noble design, and a patent for the presidency of it, and he came over to Rhode Island with a view at settling a correspondence there for supplying his college with provisions. Bermuda lies in a spot surrounded with the whole continent of English America; the Dean was therefore

11

made to believe that the most suitable place to answer his intention with regard to the whole, but in this he was misled, as he was soon convinced when he came to Rhode Island. He therefore wrote to his friends to do their utmost to get the patent altered for some place (which probably would have been New York) on the continent, but they could never gain the point. Sir Robert told them any such attempt would be taken for a forfeiture, and indeed they had other uses for their money, said he, than building colleges in America. So the good Dean was obliged to return *re infecta*, and to make some atonement for his great trouble and disappointment he was soon after made Bishop of Cloyne in Ireland, and the whole £80,000 was made a complement of to the Princess Anne upon her marriage to the Prince of Orange.

"Mr. Johnson had read his Principles of Human Knowledge, from which he had conceived a great opinion of him, and it was not long before he made him a visit, that he might converse with so extraordinary a genius and so great a scholar. He was introduced by his friend, Mr. Honeyman, (with whom he corresponded,) the worthy minister of that church, and received by the Dean with much kindness and condescension, and gladly put himself under his instruction. He was admitted to converse freely on the subject of his philosophical works, and presented with the rest which he had not seen, and to an Epistolary Correspondence upon them and any other parts of learning. In consequence of which he wrote many letters, which were very kindly answered, and made him several visits, and on each, spent as much time with him at his house as could possibly be spared from home. This was of vast use to Mr. Johnson and cleared up many difficulties in his mind, both philosophical and theological, as he found the Dean's way of thinking and explaining things utterly precluded skepticism and left no room for endless doubts and uncertainties. His denying matter at first seemed shocking, but it was only for want of giving a thorough attention to his meaning. It was only the unintelligible scholastic notion of matter he disputed, and not anything either sensible, imaginable or intelligible; and it was attended with this vast advantage, that it not only gave new incontestible proofs of a Deity, but moreover the most striking apprehensions of His constant presence with us and inspection over us and of our entire dependence on Him and infinite obligations to His most wise and Almighty Benevolence. On these

accounts, (as well as to inure one to a close and each way of thinking.) Mr. Johnson wished his works might be thoroughly studied
and well considered, especially his wonderfully ingenious Theories
of Vision, as well as his Principles and Dialogues, in which he has
plainly outdone both Mr. Locke and Sir Isaac in some particulars.
While the Dean was at Rhode Island he composed his Minute
Philosopher, wherein he elegantly and powerfully confutes the
infidels in every shape, under feigned names, in several beautiful
and genteel dialogues after the manner of Plato. He had, as he
told Mr. Johnson, been several times in their clubs in quality of
a learner, and so perfectly knew their manner; and he was thereby
the better qualified to write such an admirable confutation of
them On one of those occasions (as he told Mr. Johnson) he
heard Collins declare that he had found a demonstration against
the Being of a God, which he soon after published, in a pretended
demonstration that all is Fate and Necessity, which among other
things is here briefly but excellently confuted, as it had been more
largely by Clarke and Jackson.

"The Dean being about to leave America, Mr Johnson made him
his last visit, on which occasion he expressed a real friendship and
gave him many very valuable books, and they parted very affec-
tionately, and he consented to hold a kind correspondence as long
as he lived. He left Boston in September, 1731. Mr. Johnson had
retained a great kindness for Yale College, the place of his education, and was frequently there, and to all appearance was respectfully treated by Mr. Williams, then Rector, though he knew him
to be a zealous dissenter, a great enemy to the church and of a
very insidious temper. But out of his affection to the college he
had bespoke the Dean's regard to it, not having any further view
than to hope he might perhaps send it some good books. But
Bishop Berkeley, assisted by several gentlemen who had been
liberal subscribers to his own intended college, sent a noble collection of books to the value of (I think) about 500 pounds sterling
for Yale College, and transmitted to Mr. Johnson a deed in which
he gives a farm he had at Rhode Island of about a 100 acres of land,
worth a 100 pounds sterling, the annual income of which was to
be divided between three of those who upon examination by
the Rector with a minister of the Church of England should be
found the best classic scholars in Latin and Greek, towards their
support at college during the three years between their Bache-

lor's and Master's Degrees, in the further prosecution of their studies; and the forfeitures to be divided in premiums of books to be given to those that performed the best exercises. This was indeed a noble donation, but the Trustees, though they made an apppearance of much thankfulness, were almost afraid to accept of it. But behold the gratitude of dissenters! Mr. Williams at the very next Commencement (as appeared afterwards) contrived with the Hampshire ministers, (his father at the head of them,) in a letter to the Bishop of London, through Dr. Coleman's hands, full of abusive and groundless complaints, to get all the people of the church here, of which there were now five, six or seven congregations, deprived of their ministers, and they of their salaries. They were desired by the Society to produce evidence of their accusations, which they attempted to do but could make nothing of it. This was about the year 1734."

President Stiles, in his Diary, gives the following slightly different account of the Dean's donation to Yale College. In paying a tribute to the memory of Dr. Johnson, he remarks as follows:

Dr. Johnson "was an excellent classical scholar, even a good critic, in Latin, Greek and Hebrew. In 1729 to 1732 he was occasionally acquainted with Dean Berkeley, then living on Rhode Island. He persuaded the Dean to believe that Yale College would soon become Episcopal, and that they had received his immaterial philosophy. This or some other motive influenced the Dean to make a donation of his Rhode Island Farm, ninety-six acres, with a library of about a thousand volumes, to Yale College, in 1733. This donation was certainly procured very much through the instrumentality of Rev. Dr. Jared Eliot and Rev. Dr. Johnson. The latter, in conversation with me, 1753, when I made a funeral oration on Bishop Berkeley, told me he himself procured it; he assumed the whole glory to himself. Col. Updike, of New York, an Episcopalian, intimately acquainted with the transaction, told me the Bishop's motive was the greater prospect that Yale College would become Episcopal than Harvard."

It has often been surmised that Berkeley had peculiarly good opportunities for personal observations in this country. This inference has been made from the sermon which he preached before the Society for the Propagation of the Gospel,—but a curious contradiction of this inference appears in a pamphlet of that day.

Rev. Noah Hobart, Pastor of a Church of Christ in Fairfield, makes the following statement respecting Bishop BERKE- LEY's acquaintance in New England. See his "Second Address to the Members of the Episcopal Separation," &c. Boston, 1751, p. 145.

"'Tis likewise true that 'Bishop Barkley, a member of that venerable Body, resided in New England for some time;' and that 'upon his Return he preached the annual Sermon, and gave an account of the religious State of the Country:' But whether he was 'personally acquainted with' any number of 'the most eminent of our Ministers,' I confess I do not know. In the general it is well enough known, that 'this great and good man,' as Mr. Beach very justly stiles him, partly thro' Indisposition, and partly thro' a close application to his beloved Studies, lived a very retired Life while in this Country. He saw very little of New England, was hardly ever off Rhode Island; never in Connecticut; nor at Boston till he went thither to take Passage for London. Accordingly the Bishop confines the account in his Sermon almost wholly to Rhode Island, and I think he describes it very justly. He does indeed say that some Part of his Description may possibly be found to extend to other Colonies; but which Part, or what other Colonies he does not say; and that, I suppose, because he was sensible he had not a sufficient acquaintance with the other Colonies to describe them particularly: And it is not to be wondered at, if he thought them more like Rhode Island in Point of Religion, than they really are. And further, he supposes the Society informed of the State and Progress of Religion in this Part of the World, by their Correspondencies with the Clergy upon their Mission."

III. CONVEYANCE OF THE WHITEHALL FARM TO YALE COLLEGE.

In the archives of Yale College two instruments are preserved conveying the Dean's Farm to the College. Some slight changes in the prescribed terms, mutually agreed upon, led to the repetition of the deed. The second deed is here given, dated August 17th, 1733. The earlier deed was dated July 26, 1732.

"This Indenture made the seventeenth day of August in the Seventh year of the Reign of our Sovereign Lord George the Second, by the Grace of God King of Great Britain, France and Ireland, Defender of the Faith, and in the year of our Lord One Thousand Seven Hundred Thirty Three, between George Berkeley, Doctor of Divinity, Dean of Derry in the Kingdom of Ireland, on the one part, and the Reverend Mr. Elisha Williams, President or Rector with the rest of the Corporation or incorporate Society of Yale College in New Haven in the Province of Connecticut, on the other, witnesseth that for and in consideration of the sum of Five Shillings of Lawful Money of Great Britain to the said George Berkeley by the said Corporation, in hand paid at or before the ensealing and delivery of these presents, the receipt whereof is hereby acknowledged, and for divers other good causes and considerations, he the said George Berkeley hath granted, bargained, sold, and by these presents doth grant, bargain and sell unto the said Corporation and their successors, all that messuage tenement or dwelling house, stable and crib, and a certain tract of land to the same adjoining and belonging, containing about Ninety Six Acres (be the same more or less) and consisting of one orchard and the rest arable pasture, meadow and wood land, situate, lying and being in Newport, in the Colony of Rhode Island and Providence Plantations, and bounded northerly partly on land now or late of James Barker, and partly on School lands, easterly by a highway, and partly by a small piece of land of about half a quarter of an acre with a house thereon, southerly by a highway, and westerly by land now or late in the possession of the Widow Turner, together with all rights, profits, privileges and appurtenances thereunto belonging or appertaining, and the reversion and reversions, remainder and remainders thereof, and all the estate, right, title, property, claim and demand whatsoever of him the said George Berkeley of in and unto the said premises and every part and parcell thereof.

"To have and to hold the said dwelling-house, stable, tract of land, and premises hereby granted, bargained and sold, with their and every of their appurtenances, unto the said corporation or incorporate society and their successors, for ever, under, and subject to the conditions, provisoes and powers, and under the rules and orders hereinafter mentioned, expressed and declared of and concerning the same ;—that is to say, that they the said corpora-

tion or incorporate society, and their successors do and shall, forever hereafter, pay and apply the clear yearly rents and profits of
the said premises from time to time, as the same shall become due
and payable, and as they shall receive the same, (they the said
corporation or incorporate society, and their successors respectively, first deducting thereout, all such reasonable costs and charges
as they, or any of them shall, from time to time, and at any time
hereafter incur, sustain. or be put unto, in the execution of the
trust hereby in them reposed) to three students of the said college, towards their maintenance and subsistence during the time
between their first and second degree; such students being to be
called scholars of the house, and, during that space of time, being
hereby obliged to reside, at least three quarters of each year, between their first and second degree, in the said college: and that the
said students or scholars of the house, be elected on the sixth day
of May, (if not on a Sunday) but if it shall happen on a Sunday,
then the election to be on the day following, such election to be
performed by the President or head of the college, for the time
being, jointly with the senior episcopal missionary of that colony
or province of Connecticut, for the time being, that is to say, he
who hath been longest upon the mission in the said colony, the
candidates to be publicly examined by the said President or Rector and senior missionary, two hours in the morning, in Greek,
and in the afternoon, two hours in Latin, on the day of election,—
all persons having free access to hear the said examination:—and it
is hereby declared and intended, and it is the true intent and meaning of the said George Berkeley, that those who appear to be the
best scholars on said examination, be, without favour or affection,
elected;—and in case of a division of sentiment in the electors, the
election to be determined by lot:—and if the senior episcopal clergyman shall not attend, then any other episcopal clergyman of said
colony be intituled to elect, in course of seniority:—and if none of
the episcopal clergy shall attend, then, and in such case, the election to be performed by the President or Rector of the said college for the time being:—Provided always, that whatever surplus
of money shall arise during the vacancies of the said scholarships,
the same to be laid out for Greek and Latin books, to be disposed
of by the said electors on the said day of election to such of the
undergraduate students as shall shew themselves most deserving

by their compositions in the Latin tongue on a moral subject or theme proposed by the electors.

"Provided also that if at any time or times hereafter any difficulty, dispute or difference shall happen to arise concerning the due Election of the said three Scholars of the House, or any of them in manner aforesaid, that then and in every such case the power of explaining such difficulty, dispute or difference is hereby referred to the said George Berkeley: Provided always, and it is hereby declared to be the true intent and meaning of these presents and the parties thereto, that in case the said rules and orders concerning the said election and the application of the rents and profits of the said premisses be not from time observed, that then and in that case the grant of the said premisses to the said Corporation of Yale College hereby made shall cease, determine and be void.

"GEORGE BERKELEY.

"Signed, Sealed and Delivered (being first duly Stampt) the day and Year above written, the words (or Rector) being first interlin'd in the 25th and 30th Lines, in the presence of us,

"ISAAC BROWNE,
JOHN PIERSON,
HENRY NEWMAN."

IV. RECIPIENTS OF "THE DEAN'S BOUNTY."

The Yale Literary Magazine for 1852, presents a list of the "Scholars of the House," with an explanatory note, from which an extract is here made:

"The subjoined list of those who have been 'Scholars of the House,' under the 'Dean's Bounty,' may serve to show how far the result of this beneficence has fulfilled the design of the pious founder; and it is a fact of no slight significance, taken in connection with the original purpose of Bishop Berkeley, that of this list nearly one hundred are marked as ministers of the gospel, foremost among whom is President WHEELOCK, who founded an Indian school, the germ of Dartmouth College; while hundreds more of the same calling, not here enumerated, have been recipients of this bounty, in the shape of the smaller premiums, among whom may be named DAVID BRAINERD, the 'Apostle to the Indians.'

"This list is believed to be complete from 1733 to 1795. President Stiles's diary affords a complete list during his presidency, to 1795. During the period of President Dwight's administration, from 1795 to 1817, the list is imperfect. We depend here upon the statement of the 'scholars' themselves, or upon the recollections of others acquainted with facts, verified by cotemporaneous written evidence Very extensive inquiry has been made in regard to the 'scholars' of this period, both of the instructors and members of the respective classes; and it is believed that the list is nearly complete. Where there was no examination, we have so stated. In the years marked interrogatively (?) it might safely be affirmed, perhaps, that there were no examinations, as that is the result of our inquiries; but we leave the matter open, to elicit further information."

The list from 1818 is made up from the college records.

LIST OF THE BERKELEIAN "SCHOLARS OF THE HOUSE."

1733. Rev. Benjamin Pomeroy, D. D.
Rev. Eleazer Wheelock, D. D.,
    Pres. Dart. Coll.
1734. Benjamin Nicoll.
William Wolcott, Tutor Yale Col.
1735. Rev. Aaron Burr, Pres. College
    of New Jersey.
Rev. James Lockwood, Tutor Y.C.
Elisha Williams.
Samuel Williams.
1736. Rev. Nathan Birdseye.
Rev. Silas Leonard.
1737. Rev. Mark Leavenworth.
Rev. Gideon Mills.
1738. Hon. Phineas Lyman, Tut. Y. C.
Rev. Chauncey Whittelsey, Tut. Y.
    Coll.
1739. Solomon Welles.
William Williams.
1740. Rev. Jacob Johnson.
Hon. John Worthington, LL. D.,
    Tutor Yale Coll.
1741. Rev. Richard Mansfield, D. D.
Rev. Noah Welles, D.D., Tut. Y.C.
1742. Jared Ingersoll.
1743. Rev. Thomas Arthur.
1744. Hon. Wm. Sam'l Johnson, LL. D.,
    Judge Sup. Ct. of Conn., Rep.

and Sen. U. S. Cong., Pres. Col-
    Coll.
1745. Rev. Warham Williams, Tut. Y.C.
Rev. Jonathan Colton.
1746. Pelatiah Webster.
1747. Rev. Aaron Hutchinson.
1748. Rev. Napthali Daggett, D.D.,Pres.
    Yale Coll.
Rev. William Johnson.
1749. Hon. James A. Hillhouse, Tutor
    Yale Coll.
1750. Elihu Tudor, M. D.
1751. Rev. Judah Champion.
1752. Henry Babcock.
Gurdon Saltonstall.
1753. Rev. Seth Pomeroy, Tut. Yale C.
Jacob Usher.
1754. Rev. John Devotion.
Rev. Justus Forward.
1755. Rev. Luke Babcock.
Moses Bliss.
Rev. Nehemiah Strong, Tutor and
    Prof. Yale Coll.
1756. Robert Breck.
Hon. Simeon Strong, LL.D., Judge
    Sup. Ct., Mass.
1757. Hon. Edmund Fanning, LL. D.,
    Gov. Pr. Edw. Is.

1757. Hon. Titus Hosmer, *Rep. U. S. Cong.*
 Rev. Noah Williston.
1758. Rev. Benjamin Boardman, *Tutor Yale Coll.*
 Hon. Silas Deane, *Rep. U.S. Cong. Minister to France.*
 Rev. Roger Viets.
1759. Rev. Enoch Huntington.
 Alexander King.
 Jesse Leavenworth.
 Rev. Matthew Merriam.
1760. Rev. Levi Hart, D. D.
 Woodbridge Little.
 Rev. Ebenezer Russell White, *Tutor Yale Coll.*
1761. Hadlock Marcy.
1762. Rev. Theodore Hinsdale.
 Rev. Jos. Huntington, D. D.
 William Jones.
1763. Rev. Ebenezer Baldwin, *Tut. Y.C.*
 Amos Botsford. *Tutor Yale Coll.*
 Hon. Stephen Mix Mitchell, LL.D. *Tut. Y. C., Rep. and Sen. U. S. Cong., Ch. Judge Sup. Court of Conn.*
1764. Rev. Samuel Camp.
 Rev. Diodate Johnson, *Tut. Y. C.*
 Chauncey Whittelsey.
1765. Roswell Grant.
 Rev. Joseph Howe, *Tutor Y. C.*
1766. Hon. Jonathan Ingersoll, LL. D., *Judge Sup. Court and Lt. Gov. of Conn.*
1767. Rev. Joseph Lyman, D. D.
 Hon. John Treadwell, LL. D., *Gov. of Conn.*
 Hon. John Trumbull, LL. D., *Tut. Y. C., Judge Sup. Court, Conn.*
 Rev. Samuel Wales, D. D., *Tutor and Prof. Yale Coll.*
1768. Rev. Amzi Lewis.
 Josiah Norton.
 Rev. Elijah Parsons.
 Rev. Seth Sage.
 Buckingham St. John, *Tutor Y. C.*
1769. Rev. Timothy Dwight, D. D., LL. D., *Tutor, Prof. and Pres. Y. C.*

1769. Rev. John Keep.
 Rev. William Seward.
1770. Rev. Joseph Buckminister, D. D., *Tutor Yale Coll.*
 Hon. John Davenport, *Tutor Yale Coll., Rep. U. S. Cong.*
 Rev. Solomon Williams, *Tut. Y.C.*
1771. John Hart.
 Sylvester Muirson.
 Joseph Woodbridge.
1772. Hon. Abraham Baldwin, *Tut. Y.C., Pres. Univ. Geo., Rep. and Sen. U. S. Cong.*
 Thomas Canfield.
 Rev. Joseph Strong, D. D.
1773. Roger Alden.
 Rev. William Robinson, *Tut. Yale Coll.*
 Rev. Ezra Sampson.
1774. Amos Benedict.
 Jared Bostwick.
 Rev. Reuben Holcomb.
1775. Hon. Samuel Whittlesey Dana, *Rep. and Sen. U. S. Cong.*
 Rev. Solomon Reed.
 Benjamin Welles.
1776. Hon. Chauncey Goodrich, *Tutor Yale Coll., Rep. and Sen. U. S. Cong., Lt. Gov. of Conn.*
 Daniel Lyman.
 William Andrew Russell.
1777. William Hillhouse.
1778. Abraham Bishop.
 Ebenezer Daggett.
 Rev. Frederick William Hotchkiss.
1779. Hon. Jeremiah Gates Brainard, *Judge Sup. Ct. of Conn.*
 Hon. Elizur Goodrich, LL. D., *Tutor and Prof. Yale Coll., Rep. U. S. Cong.*
 Rev. Zebulon Ely, *Tutor Yale C.*
1780. Oliver Lewis.
 Rev. John Robinson.
1781. Rev. Henry Channing, *Tut. Y. C.*
 Enoch Perkins, *Tutor Yale Coll.*
1782.* (None.)
1783.† Rev. Samuel Austin, D. D., *Pres. Univ., Vt.*

---

 * "May 6, 1782. The day of beginning of vacation, and also of Dean's examination, but no candidates offered. The only instance of omission since the foundation in 1733."—PREST. STILES'S MS. Diary.

 † It is obvious that if the term of residence had been complied with, in every instance, there could have been but a single scholar for each class: but in consequence of frequent failures in this respect, the accumulated fund was still available. Hence in many years we find several scholars, who were allowed the emolument, in case of residence, sometimes in the order of merit, sometimes by lot, so far as the funds were sufficient. See PRESIDENT STILES'S MS. Diary. "May 6, 1783. Dean's examination. Four senior sophisters offered themselves and were publicly examined. They were so nearly equal that I directed them to decide by lots. The lots fell in the following order, Austin, Holmes, Fuller, White."

1783. Rev. Jonathan Fuller.
Rev. Abiel Holmes, D. D., *Tutor*
Yale Coll.
Charles White.
1784. Ralph Isaacs.
1785. Enoch Huntington.
Hon. Barnabas Bidwell, LL. D.,
Tutor.
Enos Cook.
Roger Newton, *Tutor.*
Samuel Perkins.
1786. Rev. John Elliott, D. D.
Hon. Thomas Ruggles Gold, *Rep.
U. S. Cong.*
Hon. Stanley Griswold, *Senator
U. S. Cong.*
Rev. Reuben Hitchcock.
Rev. William Stone.
1787. Roswell Judson.
1788. Zachariah Tomlinson.
Hon. John Woodworth, L L. D.,
Judge Sup. Ct. of New York.
1789. Rev. Dan Bradley.
Rev. William Brown.
Jona. Walter Edwards, *Tut. Y. C.*
1790. Thomas Mumford.
1791. Barzillai Slosson.
Hon. Josiah Stebbins, *Tut. Y. Col.*
1792. Rev. Timothy Mather Cooley,D.D.
Rev. Isaac Jones.
Nathaniel King.
1793. Rev. Jeremiah Atwater, D. D.,
Tut. Y.C., Pres. Mid. & Dick. C.
1794. Stephen Mix Mitchell.
1795. Ebenezer Grant Marsh, *Tut. and
Hebr. Inst. Y. C.*
1796. (*None.*)
1797. Rev. Ira Hart.
Rev. James Murdock. D. D., *Prof.
Univ. Vt. & And. Theol. Sem.*
1798. James Burret.
Daniel Fuller.
1799. Benjamin Woolsey Dwight.
Rev. Ezekiel J. Chapman.
1800. Samuel Gray Huntington.
Abiram Stoddard.
Chauncey Whittelsey.
1801. Isaac Baldwin *alias* Evelyn Hart.
1802. Hon. Jesup Nash Couch, *Judge
Sup. Ct. Ohio.*
Rev. William Lightbourn Strong.
1803. Rev. Sereno Edwards Dwight, D.
D., *Tut. Y. C., Pres. Ham. Coll.*
Rev. Noah Porter, D. D.
Rev. Henry Sherman.
Rev. Hosea Beckley.
1804. Rev. John Marsh. D. D.
1805. Ziba Foot.
1806. Alfred Hennen.

1806. Hon. Henry Strong, LL. D., *Tut.
Y. C.*
Rev. Hezekiah Gold Ufford.
1807. (*None.*)
1808. "
1809. "
1810. "
1811. "
1812. "
1813. Rev. William Theodore Dwight,
D. D., *Tut. Yale C.*
1814. Rev. John Dickson.
Rev. Joshua Leavitt, D. D.
1815. (*None.*)
1816. George Hill.
Charles Olcott.
Rev. James A. Fox.
Charles John Johnson.
1817. Hon. Joel Jones, LL. D., *Pres.
Gir. Coll.*
David Nevins Lord.
1818. Hon. Francis Hiram Cone, *Judge
Sup. Ct. Geo.*
Horatio Hubbell.
Hon. Thomas Clap Perkins.
1819. Jonathan Humphrey Bissell.
Hon. Asahel Huntington.
1820. Horace Foote.
Alexander Catlin Twining, *Tutor
Y. C., Prof. Mid. Coll.*
John Payson Williston.
1821. Henry White, *Tut. Yale C.*
1822. Rev. Edward Beecher. D. D., *Tut.
Y. Coll., Pres. Ill. Coll.*
Rev. Henry Herrick.
1823. Rev. Norman Pinney, *Prof. Trin.
Coll.*
1824. William Moseley Holland, *Tut. Y.
C., Prof. Trin. Coll.*
Hon. Ashbel Smith, M. D.
1825. Josiah Barnes, M. D.
Hon. Thomas Slidell, *Judge Sup.
Ct. of La.*
1826. Rev. John Phelps Cowles.
1827. Sidney Law Johnson, *Tut. Y. C.*
1828. (*None.*)
1829. George Champlin Tenney.
1830. Hon. Edmund Smith Rhett.
Henry Rogers Winthrop.
1831. (*None.*)
1832. "
1833. "
1834. Hon. Henry William Ellsworth.
Henry Coit Kingsley, *Treas. Y. C.*
1835. Charles Alonzo Gager, *Tut. Y. C.*
1836. (*None.*)
1837. Rev. William Russell.
1838. (*None.*)
1839. Charles Astor Bristed.

1839. Augustus Rodney MacDonough.	1852. William A. Reynolds.
1840. (*None.*)	Fisk P. Brewer, *Tutor Yale Coll.*
1841. "	1853. Rev. Thomas F. Davies.
1842. William Davison Hennen.	1854. Samuel Walker.
1843. Rev. Cyrus Huntington.	1855. William Wheeler.
Lucius Franklin Robinson.	N. Willis Bumstead.
Franklin Taylor.	1856. James L. Whitney.
1844. William Few Smith.	1857. Levi Holbrook.
1845. William Gustine Conner.	1858. Rev. Daniel A. Miles.
Robert Rankin.	Robert C. Haskell.
1846. (*None.*)	1859. Eugene Schuyler, Ph. Dr.
1847. Henry Hamilton Hadley, *Tutor.*	1860. William H. Hale, Ph. Dr.
Prof. Y. C.	Othniel C. Marsh.
Francis Lewis Hodges, *Tut. Y. C.*	1861. Simeon E. Baldwin.
1848. Rev. Henry Martyn Colton.	1862. Arthur Goodenough.
1849. Rev. Benjamin Talbot.	1863. (*None.*)
1850. Clinton Camp.	1864. Charles G. Rockwood.
1851. William Woolsey Winthrop.	1865. Robert P. Keep.

V. BERKELEY'S IMPROVEMENTS ON THE FARM AT NEWPORT.

In the Gentleman's Magazine for 1775, (Vol. 45,) a curious notice of Berkeley may be found. The writer is remarking on a book just published, entitled "Travels through the Middle Settlements in North America in the years 1759 and 1760. By Andrew Burnaby, M. A., Vicar of Greenwich." 4°. pp. 106.

From this book the following extract is given:

"At Newport, about three miles from town, is an indifferent wooden house, built by Dean Berkeley, when he was in these parts. The situation is low, but commands a fine view of the ocean, and of some wild rugged rocks that are on the left hand of it. They relate here several strange stories of the Dean, which, as they are characteristic of that extraordinary man, deserve to be taken notice of. One, in particular, I must beg the reader's indulgence to allow me to repeat to him. The Dean had formed the plan of building a town upon the rocks which I have just now taken notice of, and of cutting a road through a sandy beach, which lies a little below it, (the rocks,) in order that ships might come up and be sheltered in bad weather. He was so full of this project, as one day to say to one Smibert, a designer, whom he had brought over with him from Europe, on the latter's asking some ludicrous question concerning the future importance of the place, 'Truly, you have very little foresight; for, in fifty years time, every foot of land in this place will be as valuable as the land in Cheapside.' The Dean's house, notwithstanding his prediction, is at present nothing better than a farm-house, and his library is converted into the dairy. When he left America, he gave it to the College at New Haven, in Connecticut, who have let it to a farmer on a long lease. His books he divided between this College and that in Massachusetts. The Dean is said to have written in this place The Minute Philosopher."

The reviewer, who appears to be an intimate acquaintance of Berkeley, and may possibly be his son, makes the following criticisms on this extract :

"Several mistakes in this strange story we have a particular pleasure in being able to correct, in justice to a man who, though extraordinary, was also excellent, and whose zeal, however unsuccessful, in the best of causes, entitles him to much better epithets than wild and chimerical. Far from projecting a town, &c., the building, and the only building, which Dean Berkeley had planned, was a tea-room and a kitchen, not even a bed-chamber. For what he said to his designer, (or rather painter,) Smibert, a painter without imagination, as to the probable value of that ground, there is not the least foundation. Possibly the proprietor of it might conceive that there was some latent scheme in contemplation, which might eventually increase the value ; and certain it is, that, influenced by this notion, he demanded a greater price than the Dean chose to give, and therefore declined the purchase. The prediction not having been made, it is no wonder that what was given to a College as a farm should be used as such. This, indeed, was not only foreseen, but intended ; and surely, such a donation from a Church of England man to a society of Congregationalists, might have been mentioned with some encomium, by a man of a liberal spirit. Had Mr. Burnaby been so disposed, Rhode Island would have furnished him with some traits of Dean Berkeley as a philanthropist, &c., more pleasing and more true."

VI. INVOICE OF THE BOOKS PRESENTED TO YALE COLLEGE.

As the collection of books sent over to Yale College was regarded by Rector Clap as the finest which had then been brought to this country, it is thought that many will be interested in 'the following copy of the original invoice, notwithstanding its obvious bibliographical imperfections. The books were formerly kept by themselves in one part of the library ; but for many years this arrangement has not been practical.

A CATALOGUE OF BOOKS FOR YALE COLLEGE, AT NEW HAVEN, IN CONNECTICUT, NEW ENGLAND, MARKT AS IN THE MARGENT, CONSIGN'D TO MR. ANDREW BELCHER AT BOSTON, BY CAPT. ALDEN, MASTER OF THE DOLPHIN.

II. N.   *Folio.*
No. 1—Philonis Judaei Opera, Paris, 1640.
Josephi Opera. per Hudson. 2 vol.
Cotelerii, Patres Apostolici. 2 vol.
Justin Martyr, Athenagoras, Tatian, Hermias and Theoph. Antioch.
Irenaei Opera, per Grabe.
Clemens Alexandrinus, p. Potter.
Tertullian Pamelii et Rigaltii, 2 vol.
Hippolyti Opera p. Fabricium.
Origenis Commentarii. p. Huetium. 2 vol.
...... Hexapla. p. Montfaucon. 2 vol.
S. Cyprian, p. Fell and Dodwell. Charta Magna.
Gregorius Thaumaturgus, Macarius and Basil Seleuciæ
S. Cyrili Hierosolym. Opera. p. Milles.
Montfaucon Nova Collectio Patrum Græcorum. 2 vol.
Athanasii Opera. 2 vol. Cologn.
S. Hilarii Opera. p. Monachos Benedictinos.
Optati Opera. p. Dupin.
Ephraim Syrus. Greek. Oxon.
Basilii Magni Opera. 2 vol.
Gregorii Nazianzeni Opera. 2vol.
Gregorii Nysseni Opera. 3 vol.
Maximi Opera. p. Combefis. 2 vol.
Ambrosii Opera. 2 vol. Paris, 1569.
Epiphanii Opera. p. Petavium. 2 vol. Paris.
S. Chrysostomi Opera. p. Fronto Ducæum. 10 vols.
S. Hieronymi Opera. 3 vol. Paris, 1609.
S. Augustini Opera. 11 Tomis. 7 vol. Paris, 1637.
Synesii Opera. p. Petavium.

Quarto.
Origen de Oratione, p. Reading.
    "   contra Celsum, Spenceri.

No. 1—Origen contra Marcionitas. Arnobiustis Variorum.

Octavo, &c.
Grabe Spicileg.um Patrum. 2 vol.
Fabricii Codex Veteris and Novi Test 6 vol.
Minucius Felix Davisii.
Novatiani Opera. p. Jackson.
Lactantius. p. Spa ke.
Faustinus adversus Arrianos.
Nectarius. p. Allix.
Prudentius, Heinsii, apud Elzevir.
Sulpicius Severus, Hornii.
Paulus Orosius adversus Paganos.

Folio.
Eusebius et alii Historiæ Ecclesiasticæ Scriptores. p. Valesium. 3 vol.
Nicephori Historia Ecclesiastica. 2 vol   Paris.

No. 2—Amphilochii et Methodii Opera.
Hippocrates Fœsii.
Freind, Opera Medica.
Diemerbroeck, Anatome et alia Opera.
Riverii Opera Medica.
Raii Historia Plantarum. 3 vol.
Johnstoni Historia Naturalis. 2 vol.
Miller's Gardener's Dictionary.

Quarto.
Acta Eruditorum, ab anno 1682, ad annum 1706, cum Supplementis and Indicibus. 30 vol.
Willisii Opera Medica.
Bellini de Urinis et Pulsibus.
    "   Opuscula.
Baglivi Opera.
Tournefort Institutiones Rei Herbariæ. 3 vol.
Shaw's Abridgement of Boyle. 3 vol.
Lowthorp and Mottes Abridgement. 5 vol.

No. 2—Pomett's History of Drugs.

Octavo.

Celsus. p. Almeloveen. 2 vol.
Sydenhami Opera.
Mortoni Opera.
Harris, Dissertationes Medicæ.
   "   de Morbis Infantum.
Arbuthnot on Aliments.
Cheyne on Health.
Cheyne on English Malady.
Quincy's Sanctorius.
   "   Di-pensatory.
Robinson's Animal Oeconomy.
Hale's Vegetable Staticks.
Mortimer's Husbandry.
Shaw's Practice of Physick. 2 vol.
Wiseman's Surgery. 2 vol.
Dionis's Surgery.
Turner's Surgery. 2 vol.
Drake's Anatomy. 2 vol.

Folio, &c
No. 3—Harduini Collectio Conciliorum. 12 vol.
Erasmi Opera. 11 vol.
Corpus Juris Civilis. 2 vol. Elzevir.
Grotius de Jure Belli. 2 vol. 8°.

No. 4—Baronii Annals. 12 vol.
Vossii Opera. 6 vol.
Grotii Opera. 4 vol.
Puffendorff de Natura Gentium. 4°.
Cumberland de Legibus. 8°.

No 5—6. Horace. ⎫
6. Virgil.   ⎪
6. Terence.   ⎪
6. Ovid Metam.   ⎬ Delphini.
6. Juvenal.   ⎪
6. Martial.   ⎭
6. Virgil.
6. Terence.
6. Juvenal.
6. Martial.
6. Tully de Oratore.
12. "   Select Orations.
12. "   de Officiis.
12. Sallust.
12. Cæsar.
12. Q. Curtius.
12. Livii Orationes.
6. Cole's Latin Dictionary.
Quintus Curtius, Delph.
Suetonius, Oxon.
Florus Delph.

No. 5—Quintilian.
C. Nepos. Delph.
Sallust, Delph.
V. Paterculus varior.
Dictis Cretensis, Delph.
V. Maximus, varior.
Eutropius, varior.
Augustæ Scriptores, var.
Tacitus, var. 2 vol.
Pliny. 5 vol. var.
Aulus Gellius, var.
Seneca, var. 2 vol.
Justin Delph.
Clark's Cæsar.
Ben. Jonson. 6 vol.
Shakespear. 9 vol.
Steele's Plays.
Rowe's Plays. 2 vol.
Dryden's Virgil. 3 vol.
   "   Fables.
   "   Juvenal.
Pope's Homer's Iliad. 6 vol.
   "   Miscellanies. 2 vol.
   "   Dunciad.
Gay's Fable.
   "   Miscellanies. 2 vol.
Pemberton's Newton.
Paradise Lost and Regain'd. 2 vol.
Addison's Works. 2 vol.
Blackmore's Creation.
Cowley. 2 vol.
Creech's Horace.
Desham.
Hudibras.
Steele's Miscellanies.
Waller.
Lord Lansdown.
Oldham. 2 vol.
Garth's Ovid and Dispensary. 3 vol.
Bp. Williams,   ⎫
Bp. Gastrell,   ⎪
Bp. Blockhall,   ⎪ Sermons at
S. Clark,   ⎬ Boyle's
Whiston,   ⎪ Lecture.
Derham, 2 vol.   ⎪
Bp. Leng,   ⎭
Bp. Chandler against Collins. 2 vol.
Bp. Sherlock's Prophecys. Tracts. 2 vol.
Rapin's Critical Works. 2 vol.
Clarendon. 6 vol.
Burnet's Theory. 2 vol.
Whiston's Theory.
Puffendorf's Introduct.
Builder's Dictionary.
Plutarch's Lives—Morals. 13 vol.

No. 5—Prideaux's Connect. 4 vol.—and
    Life Mahomet.
    Spectator . 8 vol.
    Guardians. 2 vol.
    Christian Hero.
    Daniel's History of France. 5 vol
    Newton's Opticks ; Optical Lec-
      tures.
    Newton's Algebra.
    Prin. Philos. 2 vol.
    Newton's Systemate de Mundi.
    Gravesand's Introduct. 2 vol.
    Ozanam's Mathem. 5 vol.
    Petty's Arithmetick.
    Davenant's Tracts. 6 vol.
    Dialogues Dead, by Bp Cambray.
    Fontanell's Dialogues.
    Bruyere. 2 vol.
    Bp. Gibson's Pastoral Letters.
    Ditton's Fluxions.
    Keil's Astronomy.
    Religious Philosopher. 3 vol.
    Well's Mathem. 3 vol.
    Plautus, var.
    Phædrus, var.
    Apuleius.
    Minute Philosopher. 2 vol.
    Wycherley.

No. 6—6. Horace
    6. Ovid Metam.
    12. Florus.
    Corpus Poetar. 2 vol.
    Ammianus Marcellinus.
    Aurelius Victor.
    Cicero. 2 vol.
    Livy.
    Otway. 1 vol.
    Rowe's Lucan. 2 vol.
    Pope's Odysse. 5 vol.
    Spencer. 6 vol.
    Swift's Miscellanies. 4 vol.
    Don Quixote. 4 vol.
    Prior. 2 vol.
    Bp. Sherlock's Sermons.
    Montfaucon. 7 vol.
    Kennet's History of England. 3
      vol.
    Burnet's Reform. 3 vol.
    Bacon's Works. 4 vol.
    Raleigh.
    Burnet's Archæol.
    Locke. 3 vol.
    Temple. 2 vol.
    Spotswood.
    Malebranche.
    Basnage.
    Tatlers. 4 vol.
    Machiavel.

No. 6—Dechales—Euclid.
    Barrow's Appollonius.
    Stone on Math. Instruments.
    Palladio.
    Religion of Nature.
    Camden's Britannia. 2 vol.
    Grant's Tracts.
    Telemachus. 2 vol.
    Kersey's Algebra.
    Wallis's Algebra.
    Hayes's Fluxions.
    Desaguliers Experiments.
    Collection of Voyages.
    Plato. Ficinus.
    Demosthenes.

No. 7-8—Biblia Polyglotta et Castelli
    Lexicon. 8 vol. fol.
    6. Homeri Ilias. 8°.
    6. Hederici Lexicon. 4°.
    Danet's Dictionary. 4°.
    Holyoake's Dictionary. fol.
    Cooperi Thesaurus. fol.
    General Atlas.
    Wells' Mapps Sewed.
    Collier's Dictionary. fol.
    6. Bennet's Hebr. Grammar.
    4. Buxtorfi Lexicon.
    Grabii Septuagint 8°.
    Test. Græcum Millii. p. Kuster.
    Kettlewell's Works. fol.
    More's Works. 3 vol. fol.
    Cudworth's Intellectual System.
      fol.
    Cave's Prim. Christianity. 8°.
    12 Test. Græ. Millii. 12°.
    Hebraica Biblia. Atthias. 8°.
    Leusdeni Clavis Hebr. 4°.
      "   Heb. Psalter. 12°.
    Critici Sacri. 9 vol. fol.
    Patrick's Comment. 2 vol. fol.
    Hammond on New Testamt. fol.
    Whitby on do. fol.
    Bulli Opera.
    Episcopii Inst. Theo. fol.
    Scott's Works. 2 vol. fol.
    Wilkins' Natural Religion.
    Hooker's Polity.
    Chillingsworth's Works. fol.
    Barrow's Works. fol.
    Tillotson's do. 8°.
    Spratt's Sermons. 8°.
    Smallbridge's do. fol.
    Saunderson's do. fol.
    South's do. 6 vol. fol.
    Atterbury's do. 2 vol. fol.
    Sharp's do. 4 vol. fol.
    Clark's Sermons. 10 vol. 8vo.
    Dupin's Ecclesl. Canons.

No. 7-8—Duty of man's Works. fol.
Jackson's Works. fol.
Bramhall's do. fol.
Heylin's Cosmography. fol.
  " History of the Refor-
    mation.
Stillingfleet's Works. 6 vol. fol.
Rycaut's History of the Turks
  3 vol. fol.
Stillingfleet's Works. 6 vol. fol.
Thorndike's de Controv. fol.
  " Epilogue. fol.
  " of Religious Assem-
    blies.
  " Just Weights and
    Measures
Homerus Schrivelii et Dydimi.
Poetæ Minores.
Musæus, Moschus and Bion.
Theocritus. 8°.
Orpheus. Greek and Latin. Es-
  chenbach.
Palæphatus Antoninus. p. Gale.
Æsopi Fabulæ.
Phalaridis Epistolæ. p. Boyle.
Pindar. fol. Oxon.
Sophocles. H. Steph. 4°.
Euripides p. Barnes. fol.
Aristophanes Biseti.
Herodotus Greek and Latin. fol.
  do. Gron. cum Cebet. Tab. 8°.
Thucydides. p. Hudson.
Decem Oratores Attici. Heb.
  fol.
Isocrates. p. Battie.
Demosthenes. Gr. and Lat. fol.
Plato Ficini. fol. Gr. Lat.
Xenophon apud H. Steph. fol.
Aristoteles. Du Val. Gr. Lat. fol.
Callin achus Fabri.
Athenæus. Casauboni. 2 vol. fol.
Epig: Græc. p. Brodæum.

No. 7-9—Polybius Variorum. 3 vol. 8vo.
Diodorus Siculus. fol. apud H.
  Steph.
Dion. Halicar. p. Sylbergium.
  fol.
Gataker's Antoninus. 4°.
Maximus Tyrius Davisii.
Plotinus. p. Ficinum. fol.
Alcinous. Gr. Lat.
Alexander Aphrodis. Gr. and
  Lat. 12°.
Porphyrius and Arrianus. 8°.
Aristides Canteri. 2 vol 8°.
Longinus. p. Pearce.
Demetrius. p. Gale.
Julius Pollux. 2 vol. fol.
Suidæ Lexicon Gr. Aldus.
Hesychii do. 4°.
Philostratus Olearii. fol.
Strabonis Geograph. fol.
Geog. Vet. Scrip. Min. 4 vol. 8°.
Dion. Chrysostomi Orat. Gr. et
  Lat.
Dion. Cas-ius.
Plutarchi Opera. 2 vol. fol.
Appian. 2 vol. 8vo.
Ptolomæi Greg.
Pausanias. p. Kuhnium. fol.
Sextus Empiricus. p. Fabricium.
Diogenes Laertius. 2 vol. 4°.
Oppian. 8°.
Ælianus Penzhonii. 2 vol. 8°.
Jamblicus. p. Gales. fol.
Eusebii Chronicon. fol.
Zosimi Hist. Gr. and Lat.
Herodian. 8°. Gr. and Lat.
Heliozorus. p. Bourdelet.
Stabæi Opera fol.
Photii Biblioth. Gr. Lat. fol.
35 vol. of Respub. Elz.
Lucian. p. Bourdelet. fol.
6 Leedes, Lucian.

Shipp'd 30th of May, 1733, by order of the Rev. Mr. Dean Berkeley, at
London.

(Signed,)   HENRY NEWMAN.

VII.—BISHOP BERKELEY'S LETTERS TO RECTOR CLAP.

Two autograph letters from Bishop Berkeley are preserved
in the archives of Yale College. They are believed to be the
only examples of his handwriting in possession of the college,
with the exception of the two signatures to the deeds. Both
letters are addressed to Rector Clap.

The first is as follows:

Rev. Sir,

Mr. Bourk, a passenger from New Haven hath lately put into my hands the letter you favored me with, and at the same time, the agreeable specimens of learning which it enclosed, for which you have my sincere thanks. By them I find a considerable progress made in astronomy and other academical studies in your college in the welfare and prosperity whereof, I sincerely interest myself, and recommending you to God's good providence, I conclude with my prayers and best wishes for your society.

Rev. Sir,
Your faithful humble servant,

July 17. 1750.   G. CLOYNE.

The specimens of learning here mentioned, as evincing "a considerable progress made in astronomy," are supposed to be certain calculations by Berkeleian scholars, which Rector Clap sent to the Bishop ;—"one, of the comet at the time of the flood, which appeared 1680, having a periodical revolution of $575\frac{1}{2}$ years, which Mr. Whiston supposes to have been the cause of the deluge; and another, of the remarkable eclipse of the sun in the 10th year of Jehoiakim, mentioned in Herodotus, Lib. 1, cap. 74, and in Usher's Annals."

The second letter is as follows :—

Cloyne, July 25, 1751.

Reverend Sir:

The daily increase of learning and religion in your seminary of Yale College give me very sensible pleasure, and an ample recompense for my poor endeavors to further those good ends.

May God's Providence continue to prosper and cherish the rudiments of good education which have hitherto taken root and thrive so well under your auspicious care and government.

I snatch this opportunity given me by Mr. Hall to acknowledge the receipt of your letter which he put into my hands,—together with the learned specimens that accompanied it and to assure you that I am

Very sincerely, Rev. Sir,
Your faithful well wisher and humble
servant,   G. CLOYNE.

P. S.—The letter which you mention as written two months before your last never came to my hand.

Some of Berkeley's letters to Dr. Johnson are given at the close of Chandler's Life of Johnson. It seems highly probable that other letters of the Bishop pertaining to his American residence and possibly to his gifts to Yale College, are still in existence. If so, their publication will be of great interest.

VIII.—CORRESPONDENCE OF THE WIDOW AND SON OF BISHOP BERKE-
LEY WITH THE FAMILY OF DR. JOHNSON.

In the archives of Yale College are preserved several letters addressed by the widow and son of Bishop Berkeley to members of the family of Dr. Johnson. Mrs. Berkeley's letters accompany very voluminous extracts from the writings of Fenelon, Mad. Guyon, Mr. Tooke, and others with whose religious opinions she seems to have been in sympathy. We append as an example of the familiar tone of the correspondence, a letter from Rev. George Berkeley, the son of the Bishop, to Rev. Dr. Samuel Johnson.

CHRIST CHURCH, OXFORD,
Thursday 25th May 1756.

DEAR AND MUCH RESPECTED SIR.

I return you many thanks for introducing me to the acquaintance of your excellent Son and his Companion, whose stay at this University I endeavoured to render as agreable as I could.

I am sorry to find from Mr. Johnson that you had not received (when he left America) a Packet containing some New Pamphlets on Theological Subjects, wch I sent thro' the Hands of Dr. Bearcroft on ye 7th of April 1755.

As to the establishment of the Xtian Church in America there is little hope at present. The ABp. of Canterbury being much in the Interest of Schismatics and having lately preferred two notorious *Arians*—or as an Apostle calleth them—*Atheists*. The Ld Chancellor is also apprehended to be strongly attached to the schismatical Interest and I grieve that I can say little very little in praise of ye present Sett of Bishops on This Head: The Bishops of London, Oxford, Exeter, Corke, & Cloyne excepted.

Many of my friends who have had the pleasure of conversing with
Mr. Johnson & Co. join with me in lamenting that Mr. Harrison
&c. were not empowered to receive Benefactions for y⁻ Infant
Seminary. If ever any person shall be so empowered I shall (w^th
many more friends to the Xtian Church in this place) use our
utmost endeavours to forward so excellent, so GODlike a Work.

heartily rejoyce to hear that Mr. Hutchinson's invaluable
writings are read in America, and do fervently pray to GOD our
Saviour for his Blessing on your endeavours to make them well
understood in y⁻ College. These Books are held in high esteem
by every truely good Divine in this University, except three or
four who do not understand much of Hebrew. The opposition made
to them is from two sorts of people; 1ˢᵗ, Those who hold not y⁻ Faith
once delivered to the Saints—2ᵈˡʸ Those who have rebelled against
the Great Bishop of our Souls, by tearing asunder the Episcopal
Church—out of wch he hath not promised Salvation. The latter
are very bitter against the readers of Mr. Hutchinson because of
their attachment (wch in Oxford is universal) to the Interest of
the Xtian Church. I am heartily afflicted to find that the So-
cinian & Erastian writings of Tillotson have prevailed much even
amongst serious persons in America—But I hope that the
like Book of remarks on Dr. Birchs' life of that Deluded, Deluding, Traytor to Xtianity, will open their eyes. This Dr. Birch *was*
a quaker (as I am well informed) & I know him to be a rank
Hodleian *at present.*

The prospect of our Church is so very gloomy that I cannot bear to dwell on it; but I humbly trust that the prayers
of her *true* sons, offered up in the Name of the GODman will prevail for her preservation still longer. I propose offering myself a
Candidate for the Holy Order of Deacons at the next Ordination
at our Church on Trinity Sunday; & I beg your Prayers, D⁻. S⁻.
that I may be a Faithfull and Zealous servant to our Redeeming
God. My Mother has been settled wth my Brother & Sister for a
year & half past in Dublin, where I paid them a visit of about 3
months last Summer and intend, GOD willing, to spend half a
year with them as soon as I have kept next Term. My poor
Sister has been for above a year in a very bad State of Health, &
subject to violent fitts wch have reduced her much & made my
Mothers life very unpleasant, that is as unpleasant as outward cir-

cumstances can render the life of a Sincere Xtian, w⁰ʰ I Bless GOD She is.

I have deferred writing to you till this Evening & really am so affected at having taken leave of my new tho' dear friends that I am much more unfit for writing than I was aware of. But tho' I should never have the Happiness of seeing them again in this World yet I humbly trust that [through] yᵉ attonement w⁰ʰ GOD hath made for [us (by] hisDeath) we may all meet never to part.

My Dear Sir, be assured that you or yours [will] never be forgot in the prayers of

Yʳ most respectfull & affectionate
friend in Jesus Xst.

GEO. BERKELEY.

IX.—HONORS TO BISHOP BERKELEY'S MEMORY.

In the extract from Dr. Johnson's memoirs, quoted above, it is intimated that the college did not appreciate the generosity of Berkeley,—but this statement is not authorized. On the contrary, the Corporation records, during the Bishop's lifetime, contain repeated and hearty expressions of thanks for his liberality. When the news of his death was received, one of the Tutors, Mr. Ezra Stiles, afterwards President of the College, was appointed to deliver a Latin oration on his life and character in the presence of the assembled college. A copy of this address is preserved among his papers. At a later day one of the college buildings occupied by the students' chambers was denominated Berkeley Hall. The announcement of the themes for Latin compositions, to be offered for the Berkeley prize, has, until recently, been formally made each year in a Latin notice posted on the college bulletin, and the books which have been bestowed as prizes have borne appropriate inscriptions in Latin indicating the origin of the gift.

The generous donations of the learned Bishop are not likely to be forgotten so long as Yale College lives, and their special value in promoting the study of the Greek and Latin tongues deserves the lasting recognition of the friends of classical culture.

The college is fortunate in the possession of an oil painting by Smybert, the companion of Berkeley on his voyage to this country, representing the Bishop, his wife and child, and several persons who came with them on their American visit.

A

HISTORICAL ACCOUNT

OF

CONNECTICUT CURRENCY, CONTINENTAL MONEY,

AND THE

FINANCES OF THE REVOLUTION.

BY HENRY BRONSON, M. D.

Read November 30th, 1863, and afterward.

PREFACE.

I undertook to write a history of the currency of Connecticut. As introductory to my main design, it seemed necessary to take a general view of the early currency of New England, and particularly of Massachusetts. When I reached the period of the Revolution, my subject became so interwoven with the continental paper money policy, and the financial measures of the war, that I was tempted to enlarge my plan, and for the sake of completeness, to embrace these latter topics. That the historical truths presented might be duly appreciated, I have occasionally paused to set forth some of the principles of financial science—to explain briefly the nature and uses of money, and to show the bearing of the facts stated. This has been done for the benefit of those unaccustomed to inquiries of this kind. History has no significance except so far as it establishes or illustrates useful principles, and furnishes rules for the guidance of human conduct.

My task has been a difficult one. The public must judge of the manner in which the work has been accomplished. At the least, I flatter myself that I have gathered materials which will be useful to some one who shall undertake to write a worthy and durable history of this State.

I have received favors from those connected with the Library of Yale College, and from the officers having in charge the state archives in Hartford, which I desire here to acknowledge. I am particularly indebted to Mr. Charles J. Hoadley, State Librarian, who has given me the benefit of his familiarity with the colonial and state records, and put into my hands copious extracts which he had made for his own use. At my request, he has looked over these sheets as they were passing through the press, and suggested such improvements and corrections as occurred to him.

CONTENTS.

CONNECTICUT CURRENCY, ETC.

———◆◆◆———

CHAPTER I.

PRINCIPLES STATED—EARLY CURRENCY OF NEW ENGLAND.

TRADE, or the exchange of commodities and labor, is necessary to the well being of every community. No matter how
destitute of the arts of civilization a people may be, they find
it convenient to establish commercial relations, each one exchanging, so far as he can, that which he needs less for something he wants more. The love of trade is indeed almost an
instinct, and boys just entering upon existence find pleasure or
advantage in exchanging toys. Older boys swap jack-knives
and jackets, the sharper sort, it is said, with a profit on both
sides!

To facilitate the operations of trade, even rude people have
devised some medium of exchange—have adopted some commodity or thing as a standard or measure of value. With this
standard commodity, which is the product of labor, and is supposed, on that account, to have a definite and certain value, all
other commodities are compared—measured as with a yard stick.
Into this, if it is a good medium, they may be converted with
little loss. This conversion once made, the trader is in possession of a commodity or thing which may be exchanged, at
pleasure, for any other which is offered for sale. Thus a man
who has gathered a bushel of nuts, by giving which he would
obtain something else, first converts the nuts into the accepted

1

medium, and then with this purchases that which he desires, being careful in each transaction, to get as much in labor's worth as he gives. This middle commodity, (which differs not from other commodities except in the singular use that is made of it,) which acts as the medium in the exchange of products, and as a measure of value, is called *currency* or *money.*

Different nations, and the same nation in different ages, have used different articles as currency. And the progress of a people, in its civil and political life, may be, to a certain extent, measured by the perfection it has attained in its circulating medium, and its adaptation to the wants of commerce. Sometimes a people is better than its currency, sometimes worse ; but notwithstanding this there is a very interesting relation between the two. A community must suffer in its material interests when a good currency is exchanged for a poor one. And when men thus suffer, they must deteriorate— go backward—in all that distinguishes civilized life.

In the case of barter, the reason why one commodity exchanges for another, a coat for a violin, for instance, or a pair of shoes for a hat, is to be found in the fact that the things exchanged represent an equal amount of labor. They are commercial equivalents. And the principle is the same when one of the commodities has been adopted as a currency. It is still a product of labor, and the cost of production governs its exchangeable value. If it requires as much labor to raise and bring to market a bushel of wheat, as it does to produce and bring to the same market an ounce of silver, one will exchange for the other. In other words, a coin weighing one ounce will be the price of a bushel of wheat. In truth every exchange of commodities is but the exchange of equivalents ; and it matters not though one of these be desired as a means of obtaining something else, and is called money.

These remarks apply to those articles which may be increased to an equal extent by equal additions of labor, but do not apply, except with qualification, to monopolies. Nor do I forget that profit is a constituent of price in all those things which require capital for their production. Strictly speaking, to the wages of labor must be added the profits of capital before we can know the natural exchangeable value of a commodity. But as a general rule, profit is only a small item in the cost of products, and to simplify the matter, I have left it out of the account. I shall hereafter adopt this course, unless some error of principle is involved in the omission.

The early colonists of this country, coming from England, would naturally use the English currency. Values were reckoned and accounts kept in pounds, shillings and pence. Whatever substance was employed, as a medium of exchange and substitute for coin, its intrinsic value in English money was ascertained before it could itself be used as a standard and measure of value.

In the time of William the Conqueror, a pound of silver, Troy weight, of standard fineness, was coined into twenty shillings, so that a pound in English money contained a pound of the metal. But by successive reductions of the weight of the coins, and the assiduous practice of king-craft, a pound of silver came at last to be represented by sixty-two shillings. In other words, the shilling which in 1066 weighed two hundred and eighty-eight grains, standard silver, had so shrunk in 1600 that it weighed scarcely ninety-three grains. During the period which followed and down to the present time, with a slight exception, the standard of weight and fineness has not been changed.

At the time of the settlement of New England by the English, there was a currency in use among the aboriginal population called wampum, wampum-peage, or peage. The primitive wampum consisted of small spiral shells, a quarter or an eighth of an inch in length, which were perforated in their longest diameter and arranged upon strings, or woven into various forms. By the disposition of different colors, curious and highly ornamental articles were produced, which were worn as belts and bracelets.

Roger Williams, writing of the Indian currency, thus describes it, (I quote from Felt's Massachusetts Currency):—

Their own [money] is of two sorts, one white, which they make of the stem or stock of the periwinkle, when all the shell is broken off; and of this sort, six of their small beads, which they make with holes to string their bracelets, are current with the English for a penny. The second is black, inclining to blue, which is made of the shell of a fish, which some English call hens-poquahock; and of this sort, three make an English penny. One fathom of this, their stringed money, is worth five shillings.

The different colonial governments recognized the shell currency, so called, in their dealings with the Indians, and adopted it, to a certain extent, among themselves. From time to time, as the supply varied, they endeavored to fix its exchangeable value. In September, 1640, the General Court of Connecticut repealed its "late order consarneing wampum at sixe a penny," and established the former rate of "fower a penny." Five years later, it was ordered in the New Haven colony, "that Indian wampom shall passe, the white at 6 a penny, and the blacke at 3 a penny. And some men being at present loath to receive the blacke, it is ordered that in any payment vnder 20s. halfe white and halfe blacke shall be accounted current pay, only if a question arise about the goodness of the wampō, whether white or blacke, Mr. Goodyeare, if the parties repaire to him, is intreated to judge therein."[*] But at length, the English demand for wampum brought upon the market a counterfeit or inferior article. The Indians, according to the record, "abused the English," and supplied them with dyed peage, or peage "made of stone or other vnalowed mater." They also offered it in an unfinished state, or untastefully arranged. The Commissioners of the United Colonies[†] took action upon the subject, and recommended to the separate governments to attempt a reform. In accordance with the suggestion, the General Court of Connecticut, in 1648, ordered " that no peage, white or black, bee paid or received, but what is strung, and in some measure strung sutably, and not small and great vncomely and disorderly mixt, as formerly it hath beene." The Massachusetts Colony passed a similar order.

Wampum was employed by the colonists for many years as a part of their currency. As late as 1704, (and probably later,) the strung beads were in common use for small change.

A new settlement, far removed from the old civilizations and the centers of wealth, is almost necessarily poor—poor in

---

[*] N. H. Col. Records, I. 211.   [†] Hazard, II. 124.

labor, as compared with the work to be done, and poor in capital, which is the support of labor. Houses are to be built, lands to be cleared and subdued, and the soil to be cultivated ; while a sufficient stock of clothing, husbandry and other tools, provisions, and certain domestic animals for draft or burden, must be supplied. However well the original settlers might have been provided with these things, in the commencement, they were sure to be, in a little time, comparatively destitute. In such a country as New England, with a soil that requires a large outlay to give it productive energy, it would be impossible for a single generation to furnish the surplus labor and capital required for an advanced civilization. Consequently, the early colonists were, for a long time, behind hand in their worldly affairs, and generally poor. The utmost they could do was to lay the foundations for a better order of things. They toiled laboriously and husbanded their resources, for the benefit of their children. So far as they could, they economized capital (which is but *hoarded* labor) in all its applications. They exchanged their surplus products with each other in the way of barter, and contrived in this way to save (as they supposed) the expense of a circulating medium. To remove some of the inconveniences of barter and to facilitate trade, they selected certain of the products of their own industry, and endowed these, by legal enactment, with some of the properties of money. The articles chosen for this purpose, and which they judged best fitted for the office, were beaver skins, wheat, rye, oats, Indian corn, peas, flax, wool, beef, pork, live stock, bullets, codfish, &c. The prices of these were fixed, from time to time, by the general courts ; and colonial, town and society taxes, as well as private debts, were paid in them. These prices were considerably higher than the money prices, perhaps one-half. Store-houses were maintained in which the tax-gatherers deposited the public prop·erty till it should be wanted, or could be sold or exchanged. The colonial government of Connecticut continued to receive taxes in farm products, till bills of credit were emitted, and occasionally, in way of experiment, afterwards. The towns continued the practice much longer, and the ecclesiastical societies longer still. The highway tax was, in the country towns, collected in labor when the writer was a young man; and he has himself, for himself, "worked out" the tax—as boys are wont to work. The minister was expected to take anything for pay which his people had for disposal. Were a house to be furnished him, they provided the materials, and built it with their own hands. They supplied him with rye, corn, meat, butter, flax, fuel, hay for his horse, and homespun for his family. They planted and gathered the crops which grew on the parsonage, and their contributions were credited to them on the minister's rate. About "New Year's," when sledding was good, they gave him a grand "wood-spell," and had " a donation party " at his house, in the evening, making the rafters ring with good cheer. I suppose the annual wood-spell is still an institution in many of our old agricultural towns.

Sometimes the towns were taxed by a demand on them to furnish each certain articles in a given quantity, without express reference to the price. In May, 1637, the General Court at Hartford declared " offensive war " against the Pequots, and "ordered that Windsor shall prvide 60 bushels of corne, 50 pieces of pork, 30 lb. rice, [!] 4 cheeses; Hartford, 84 bushells of corn, 2 firkins of Butter, 3 firkins of suet, 4 bushells of oatemeale, 2 bushells of pease, 2 bushells of salt, 500 fish; Wethersfield, 36 bushells of corne, 1 bushell of Indian beanes."*

The colonial government, from time to time, prescribed the terms on which men might have dealings with each other, and named the articles with which debts might be discharged, sometimes without a due respect for the obligation of contracts. In June? 1641, the General Court of New Haven ordered that "all comodityes bought and sold among the planters, and all work, wages and labor (henceforward, till some other course be settled by order) to be payd for either in corne, as the price goeth in the plantatiõ, or in worke, as [at?] the rates settled by the Court, or in cattell of any sort as they shall be

---

* Printed Colonial Records.

indifferently prized, or in good march'able bever according to the goodness."* In November of the same year, the General Court of Connecticut repealed a regulation of the preceding year, providing that debts thereafter made might be paid in merchantable Indian corn at three and four pence a bushel, and ordered, in consequence of the scarcity of money, and the " very cheap rats" at which goods taken on execution had been sold, that " whatsoever execution shall be granted vpon any debts made after the publishing of this order, the creditor shall make choyse of one p'ty, the debtor of a second, and the Court of a third, who shall pryse the goods so taken vpon execution aforesaid and deliver the to the creditor." A similar law had been passed in Massachusetts, the previous year, which was retrospective in its operation. The officer was to " take land, houses, corn, cattle, fish, or other commodities, and deliver the same in full satisfaction to the creditor," the same to be appraised, as in the other case.† Connecticut was always imitating Massachusetts in her enactments, " trotting after the Bay-horse," as some one says ; but in questionable legislation she usually stopped short, or kept a long way in the rear, as we shall see more fully, by-and-by. I can find nothing in her early records, nor in those of the New Haven Colony before the Union, which impaired previous contracts.

Of all the articles—the products of the country—which our fathers used as currency, that which was most available and convenient was the skin of the beaver. Furs were in demand in Europe, and could always, without much loss, be converted into coin or its equivalent.

The early colonists were not in advance of the countries they left in a true knowledge of civil government, or in just ideas of civil liberty, to say nothing of the rights of conscience. Nothing better illustrates this than their laws intended to control industry, commercial intercourse, and the prices of commodities. The general courts were absolute,

---

* N. H. Colonial Record, I. 55–6.

† An Historical Account of Massachusetts Currency. By Joseph B. Felt. Boston: 1839. Page 23.

and they attempted to order and regulate nearly everything relating to human conduct. For instance, the Court at Hartford, in February 1640, conceiving "that much ground w^{th}in these libertyes may be well improved" for raising hemp and flax, and that they "myght in tyme haue [a] supply of lynnen cloth;" therefore, they ordered, for the more speedy procuring of hemp seed, "that every p^rticular family w^{th}in these Plantations shall p^rcure and plant this p^rsent yeare at lest on spoonfull of English hempseed, in some frutfull soyle, at lest a foote distant betwixt eu^r seed, and the same so planted shall p^rsearue and keep in [a] husbandly manner for [the] supply of seed for another year." In the second year, every family that kept a team of two or three draft cattle was to sow at least a rood of hemp or flax. Every person that kept cows, heifers or steers, was to sow twenty perches, and every family having no cattle was to sow ten perches. The tending was in all cases to be of a husbandly sort, and whoever was in default was to undergo the censure of the Court. The government of New Haven established a tariff of prices for "wares and worke," in June, 1641. Seven hours, diligently improved, were to be accounted a day's work of a team; and nine pence a day was to be paid for a steer, twelve pence for a grown ox or bull, sixteen pence for a horse or mare, and six pence for a cart, furniture and man. Master carpenters, plasterers, bricklayers, mowers, thatchers, rivers of clapboards, shingles, lathes, &c., were to have two shillings in summer and twenty pence in winter. Those not "allowed master workmen" got but eighteen pence for summer and fourteen pence for winter. If men sawed by the day, the top man, who was supposed to guide the work and find the tools, was to be paid as a master workman, the pit man as those not master workmen; but if their skill were equal, they received, each, twenty-two pence in summer and eighteen pence in winter. "Dyett" for a laboring man with lodging and washing was fixed at four and six pence a week. Fat venison might be sold for not over two and a half pence per pound, lean, for two pence, and so on. These prices were to be paid in corne, work, cattle, beaver, &c. In May, 1676, the Con-

necticut Court ordered that the prices of provisions should be
set at each session of the General Court, "according to true
intelligence from Boston;" and to prevent "oppression," merchants or traders were forbidden to take more than two pence
in the shilling for "profit, charge and venture" for goods
bought with "ready money" in Boston, or other like market, the
penalty being treble the amount of the oppressive exaction.*
At the same session it was ordered, "that what person soever
shall wear gold or siluer lace, or gold or siluer buttons, silk
ribbons, or other costly or superfluous trimmings, or any bone
lace aboue three shillings per yard, or silk scarfes," the person
so offending was to be assessed and put in the list at one
hundred and fifty pounds for the indulgence; but the law was
not to extend to a magistrate or a like public officer, or to his
wife or children, or to "such whose quality and estate haue
been aboue the ordinary degree, though now decayed." And
no person was allowed to "make, ware or buy any apparell
exceeding the quality and condition of their persons and
estate, or beyond the necessary end of apparell for covering or
comelyness," on penalty of ten shillings for each offense.
This law is similar to one which was enacted twenty-five
years earlier in Massachusetts, the General Court declaring its
"utter detestation and dislike that men or women of mean
condition should take upon them the garb of gentlemen, by
wearing gold or silver lace or buttons, or points at their knees,
or to walk in great boots, ['leather being so scarce,'] or
women of the same rank to wear silk hoods or scarfs, which,
though allowable to persons of greater estates, or more liberal
education, we judge intolerable in persons of such like condition," &c.† These specimens, taken almost at random, exhibit
but confused notions of the proper objects and ends of legislation, or of the methods of procedure when reforms are to be
introduced.

The attempt of our forefathers to get along without the cur-

* Manuscript copy of the laws in Yale College Library. A like copy will be
found in the State Library, in Hartford. The act quoted from above is not in
the printed records.
† Massachusetts Record, Vol. IV., Part 1, p. 60. (Printed.)

rency of the old world, was unwise and unprofitable. The un-wieldy and inconvenient substitutes they adopted were prac-tically expensive, costing more, there is reason to believe, than good hard money. By fixing the prices of the selected com-modities very much above the specie rates, they made them, as far as could be done by legislation, the exclusive currency, threw out of use the coin in the country, destroyed the market for it among themselves, and drove it to other lands. Gold and silver, like other articles, go where there is a demand for them, shunning the places where they are not in request, or are undervalued. If it is alleged that the people were poor and had no surplus products to give in exchange for the pre-cious metals, it may be replied that, in that case, they did not require a currency. They were poor, indeed; their surplus earnings were small; but they had a surplus, neverthe-less; hence their need of money. They had, all along, a trade (quite limited for the first few years) with En-gland, Manhadoes (New York,) and the West Indies. At first they shipped peltry, fish and lumber; and afterwards, pipe-staves, hoops, beef, pork, peas, fat cattle, horses, &c.; and brought back manufactured goods, sugar, molasses, cotton wool, bills of exchange, silver and rum.* They would have brought more silver and less rum and other merchandise, had the first been in greater request at home. Merchants import those articles for which there is an active demand, and refuse those which are out of use. Had the colonists withheld oppo-sing legislation, and rejected substitutes, commerce would have supplied them with all the coin they needed, (which was but little,) in spite of themselves. It is true, the precious metals absorb capital, but so do those commodities which were used in their stead. It requires as much capital to effect the exchanges of a country, when Indian corn is the medium employed, as when silver or gold is used; while there is the greatest difference in the ease and perfection with which the work is done. At this day, no competent person doubts that

* Trumbull's History of Connecticut, I. 478. Palfrey's History of New England, I. 383.

the costly metals make the best currency yet discovered. They are not only more convenient, but more economical than any other, and the remark applies to every people, rich or poor. The fact that the early colonists were in straitened circumstances is the very reason why they should have preferred them as a circulating medium.

Having removed coin from its rightful place by bad laws, and thus secured its expulsion from the country, our fathers complained, absurdly enough, that foreign traders gathered it all up and carried it to other lands. Thus the people were left destitute of a currency, and were compelled to resort to clumsy expedients. And this is the account which historians, past and present, give of the matter. Not one of them, which I have consulted, seems to comprehend the difficulty.

It is a mistake to suppose that the efficiency or sufficiency of a circulating medium depends on its quantity. One ounce of silver, provided it cost as much—provided it represent the same amount of labor—will go as far as ten or one hundred ounces. Its adequacy to perform a certain amount of service is determined by its exchangeable value, which again is determined by the labor it contains, and not by its weight. Gold is more efficient than an equal quantity of silver, or silver than an equal quantity of copper, because it costs more and represents more.

You may remove any proportion of the coin of a country, one-half, three-fourths, or nine-tenths, at the same time increasing, in an equal ratio, the difficulty and expense of restoring the loss, and the remainder will perform the business of exchanging commodities quite as well as the whole did before. It will do this, because the exchangeable value of the currency has not been diminished. I will go further. Had seven-eighths of the specie which our ancestors brought with them in considerable quantities from Europe, been returned within a year, and could no more have been obtained at any cost, the remaining portion would have sufficed for all their needs till it was worn out. In that case, specie would have borne a monopoly price. The exchangeable value of a given quantity would have been augmented in proportion as it became scarce.

When, then, our fathers complained of their destitution in regard to money, it is to be understood that it was not money they lacked, but capital. They confounded the two, as nine-tenths of the world do at the present day. If the currency was bad, it was because they made it so by injudicious inter-ference. They needed capital distressingly; they needed wis-dom; and they did *not* need so frequent sessions of the Gene-ral Court. With capital, they could have had whatever is desirable. Without it, and without the power of exchange, the gold product of California would not have enriched them. The wealth of a people is never increased by the money it keeps, but by the goods or services which it gets in parting with it.

In a new country, not itself a producer of the precious met-als, the money price of home products must be low, or, in other words, a little money will buy much goods and labor. This arises not so much from the poverty of the people, as from the fact that the exchange of surplus exportable commod-ities is made at great expense. Agricultural products, which are the first which a new settlement has to spare, are heavy or bulky, and of costly transportation. These must bear their own charge to market, and the coin received for them must represent the accumulated expense, such as land-carriage, freight, insurance, port charges, custom-house duties, commis-sions, &c., together with the profits of capital. Thus the money, by the time it comes into the possession of the new settlers, will represent much labor. Its entire content in toil and sweat will be manifest in its high exchangeable value, and in the low prices of the home-produced commodities which are bought with it. The same causes will affect the prices of im-ported goods. They will be high because obtained at great cost. But it will make no difference with a people what their money may cost them. That is, it is not material whether an English shilling is the representative of a day's or a week's work: for the higher the cost, the higher will be its exchangeable value, and the greater its exchangeable value, the less of it will be required. From our present point of view, all that is neces-sary in a product used as a medium of exchange, is that it should contain the requisite amount of labor, and have a cost value equal to the work to be performed, and to the commodities for which it is to be exchanged. In an old country, with an industrious population, and abounding in light exportable goods, money will be cheap and agricultural products high.

<hr>

CHAPTER II.

THE MASSACHUSETTS COINAGE OF 1652, AND THE CHANGES WHICH IT WROUGHT. FIRST BILLS OF CREDIT.

THE money which the early colonists brought with them from Europe constituted the first metallic currency of this country. The English coins then in use were crowns, valued at five shillings sterling each, half crowns, shillings, sixpences and smaller pieces, all in silver. There were also copper coins, pennies, half pennies and farthings. Gold, which by a law of England was a legal tender till 1664, and again after 1717, was usually undervalued, and did not circulate. This small stock of specie, to which additions were made, from time to time, by the new-comers, came at length, by means of trade, to be much diminished. In the absence of an active home demand for it, and for the want of surplus exportable commodities, it was sent to Europe in payment for imported goods. Returning immigrants, also, took it away with them. To stop the last of these leaks, the magistrates of Massachusetts, in 1632, forbade any planter, going to England, to take away either coin or beaver, under pain of forfeiture.* Ere long, a trade sprung up with the Dutch plantation on Manhattan Island, which was, at length, after many discouragements, ex-

---

* Felt, 16.

tended to the West Indies and the "Wine Islands."* Along with this trade, several foreign coins were introduced. The most common of these were the duccatoon of Holland, valued at three guilders; the rix dollar, at two and a half guilders; and the "ryal-of-eight." These, the Massachusetts Court made lawful money, in 1642, the first to pass at six shillings, the last two at five shillings each.† Connecticut, in 1643, made the same regulation regarding "good rialls of ⅝ and reix dollars;" except they were to be lawful money only for debts contracted after the order.‡ A portion of the bullion which the buccaneers, or pirates of that day, took from the Spaniards, also found its way to New England. In consequence of this influx of silver, and the circulation of "light Spanish coyne, whereby many people were consened," Massachusetts undertook to have a mint of her own. By coining their own money, they thought they should foil the European merchants, keep the silver in the country, and thus get rich. They were encouraged in this undertaking by the confusion into which affairs had fallen in England. They respected the prerogative of Cromwell's government about as much as he did that of Charles. Their course having been determined, the necessary legislation was soon forthcoming. May 31st, 1652, a "mint howse" was "appointed" in Boston, and all persons had liberty to bring to it "all bullyon, plate or Spanish coyne, there to be melted and brought to the allay of sterling silver by John Hull, master of the said mint, and his sworn officers, and by him to be coyned into twelve penny, six penny and three penny peeces, which shall be for forme, flatt and square on the sides, and stamped on the one side with N. E., and on the other side, with the figure XII, VI, and III, according to the valew of each peece, together with a privy marke," &c. The new money was to be according to the English standard in fineness; the mint master "for valew to stampe two pence in a shilling of less valew than the present English coyne," &c., "every shilling to weigh three penny

* The History of Massachusetts, by Thomas Hutchinson, Esq., 1. 90, 3d ed.
† Felt, p. 26.   ‡ Col. Record, 1. 86.

Troy weight, and lesser pieces proportionably."* "For their paynes and labour, the mint-master, for himselfe and officers," was allowed to take one shilling out of every twenty, or five per cent. (The United States Mint, I believe, charges one half of one per cent. for coinage.) The products of the mint, together with English money, were "appointed" as the only lawful currency of the Commonwealth after the ensuing first day of September (1652.) In the following October, it was found that the excessive plainness of the coin exposed it to washing and clipping. For the prevention of the same, it was ordered that " henceforth all peices of money cojned as aforesajd shall have a double ring on either side, with this inscription, Massachusetts, and a tree in the center on the one side, and New England and the yeere of our Lord on the other side, according to this draught heere in the margent."† The tree on these coins having a fancied resemblance to the pine tree, has given them the name of the pine tree currency. In 1662, two penny pieces were struck off by authority of the Court. These all had the date of that year. The others, throughout the whole period the mint was in operation, nearly thirty-four years, bore the date of 1652. One penny pieces were also authorized, but it is believed that none was ever minted.‡ The coins of that day were all hammered, and shaped by the eye. Consequently, they were irregular in form, and much exposed to clipping. The most perfect of the shilling pieces now in existence weigh from sixty-four to seventy-one grains.

John Hull, mint-master, did his work faithfully. His " mint-drops " were fully up to the required standard, nine hundred and twenty-five thousandths fine. But the weight of the coins, as ordered by the General Court, was shamefully deficient. The discreditable practice, which had been abandoned in England, of degrading the standard, and issuing light pieces, was resorted to, and this without the poor apology of

---

* Felt, 31.

† Mass. Col. Record, p. 104. A rough draught is given in the margin, with a tree in the centre.

‡ Dickeson's Numismatic Manual.

state necessity.* The new shilling was to weigh three penny-weights, or seventy-two grains, twenty-two and a half per cent., or twenty one grains less than the English shilling. Thus the standard of all values was altered, arbitrarily. Creditors and salaried men were defrauded out of that which was their own, to the extent of nearly one-quarter. Those who had agreed to pay ninety-three grains of silver were, by law, discharged by the payment of seventy-two. And yet, that law, so flagrantly unjust, has not, on that account, received the censure of any historian that I have consulted. Even Hutchinson, usually sound on currency questions, has no word of condemnation.

There has been some misunderstanding about the time and manner of introduction of the "New England currency," so called. Its origin may be clearly traced to the action of Massachusetts, in 1652. It was that action which gave a new meaning to the terms, pounds, shillings and pence—which made New England money worth but three quarters as much as sterling money. It was that which made the piece-of-eight and the Spanish dollar equal to six shillings, instead of four and six pence, and the £ equal to three dollars and thirty-three hundredths, instead of four dollars and forty-four hundredths. The issue of paper money, thirty-eight years later, had nothing to do with this change of currency and the altered standard of value, loose statements to the contrary notwithstanding.

John Hull, mint-master, it seems, got fat on his contract, as he well might. The General Court, finding it too lucrative, offered him a sum of money as an inducement to relinquish it. He very naturally refused. The consequence was, he became very rich, as contractors are wont to do. He gave, it is said, thirty thousand pounds, in his own shillings, to his only daughter, as her marriage portion, and left, at his death, one of the largest estates of the Colony.†

---

* I do not understand Mr. Bancroft when he says in his History of the United States, (Vol. III., p. 104.) that "the *necessities* of the Colonies had led them to depreciate their currency." So far as the act of Massachusetts, in making light coins, is concerned, there is no foundation for the statement.

† Hutchinson, I. 165. The story about the £30,000 has been doubted

The Massachusetts people established their mint for their own benefit. It was for them a great institution—the philosopher's stone, which was destined to make them all rich. Like the rest of mankind, they were benighted as to the nature of money, and supposed that a community was rich in proportion to its gold and silver. Having these, they considered themselves in the possession of everything desirable. To increase the supply was the prime object of statesmanship. They thought that the wild scramble among the nations of that day for the specie of the world was a struggle for the substance and concentrated essence of good. Though their legislation drove away the precious metals, this they refused to understand. Impressed with the popular idea, the General Court took measures to confine the products of their mint to the Commonwealth. With about as much wisdom as was current with the governments of that day, an order was passed in May, 1662, forbidding any person, " by sea or land," to take the colony coin out of the country, in any sum exceeding twenty shillings for necessary expenses. Searchers were appointed in the different towns, whose duty it was to see that no part of the precious treasure escaped. The portmanteaus, bags, cloaks and pockets of persons " departing the jurisdiction on horseback " were overhauled, at the place of starting. If a man was caught violating the law, the money was seized, and " all his visible estate confiscated."* These prohibitory measures were of course ineffectual. The pine-tree coins reached Connecticut, and became the common currency of New England, beyond which they did not circulate as money. They were taken to foreign countries, and made their appearance in England, but only as bullion, worth seventy-five per cent. of their face.†

---

* Printed Statutes, edition of 1672.

† The English shilling weighed 93 grs. nearly ; but to show its true value, the charge for coining it, or seigniorage, must be added. This amounted to about 3¼ per centum, which added to the weight would make the piece the equivalent of about 96 grs. of standard silver. The Massachusetts shilling. arriving in England, ceased to be money. Its value as merchandise, as compared with the English coin of the same name, was in the proportion of 72 to 96, or 3 to 4. To convert the money of one country into that of another, involves the expense of

The lightness of a coin will not prevent its exportation, in the way of trade, after the heavier and more valuable pieces, having the same nominal value, have disappeared, or have come to bear a premium. In 1672, the Massachusetts Court, finding that pieces-of-eight were "of more value to carry out of the country than they will yield to mint into coyne," ordered that those of full weight should pass for six shillings each. This measure failing to prevent exportation, their legal value was again raised, in 1682, from six shillings to six and eight pence, provided the piece should weigh one ounce, Troy.* But this law overvalued the coin, and in 1697, the previous regulation was restored.†

The Boston mint was condemned by the friends of the English government. No American colony had before ventured to coin money. None had presumed so much on the forbearance of their masters. And yet, no notice was taken of the unauthorized institution either by Cromwell or Parliament. They had too much on their hands to be looking after the short comings of an obscure people three thousand miles from home. After the death of Cromwell, the enemies of the colonists multiplied. The good natured Charles, who was crowned in 1660, was offended because his royal prerogative had been invaded. The offenders were called traitorous and disloyal; were charged with seeking independence. A commission was sent over to look into their affairs. They gave the colonial government some wholesome advice, and, among other things, required them to stop coining money. They did not stop; but, desirous to appease the wrath of Charles, and save their

---

two coinages, a domestic and a foreign. The Boston shilling, for home circulation, was worth, say, 72 grains of standard silver, *plus* the five per cent. paid John Hull for minting. For exportation to England, it was worth, when of full weight, 72 grains, *minus* the 3¼ per cent. demanded by John Bull for a similar service.

There has been no seigniorage on the coinage of gold in England since 1666. See M'Culloch's Commercial Dictionary, Article, *Coins.*

* The piece-of-eight was estimated, in 1704, at the English mint, to weigh four hundred and twenty grains, sixty grains less than one ounce.

† Felt, 41, 44, 55.

charter, they sent to London, in 1666, at great expense, "two very large masts," for his majesty's navy, and soon after, a ship load of smaller spars. Still later, they plied him with "tenn barrels of cranberryes, two hogsheads of special good sampe, and three thousand codfish."* Last of all, they tendered twenty or thirty beaver skins, "as an annual acknowledgment of allegiance and humble thankfullness for his majesty's gracious clemency," but with no effect. The king remained obdurate, and the charter was vacated early in 1685. The coining of money was only one of the alleged reasons of this procedure, and Hutchinson says no great stress was laid upon it; but it is evident that it had considerable influence. The mint continued its operations a few months after the charter had expired, when it too died, much to the grief of Massachusetts. Its coinage was in circulation down to the Revolution of 1776.

It is uncertain at what time the "Bay shillings" became a common currency, and the standard of value in Connecticut. But as there was considerable trade with Boston, the supplies of foreign goods being purchased there, the new money must have been known in the Colony at an early period. It appears, however, not to have been formally recognized for several years. I find, on examining the inventories on record in the Probate Office in New Haven, that in 1668 "plate" was valued at five shilling per ounce, indicating that the English coin was then the standard. In "March, 167⅘," and in "February, 1677," I notice instances in which the same article was appraised at six shillings per ounce, this fact showing that a change of custom had, to a certain extent, taken place. In 1681, I observe that certain silver spoons are set down at their value in "New England money." The General Court allowed Massachusetts shillings to circulate, but in pursuance of their habitually cautious policy, declined to give them their official sanction long after they had become, practically, the standard of value. This circumstance is not the less remarkable from the fact that they did not neglect, for so long a period, to

---

* Dickeson's Numismatic Manual.

establish the value of foreign coins, on the pine-tree basis. In May, 1683, the Court, "being willing to encourage the bringing in money and the increase of trade," ordered "that for the future, all peices of eight, Mexicoe, pillor and Civill peices," should pass at six shillings each, and "all good peices of Perue are to pass at five shillings, in lieu of New England money,"* fractional coins in proportion. In October of the next year, however, this law was repealed; but a similar and more comprehensive one was afterwards enacted, which recognized an existing fact, and made the coins named, lawful money. It is found in the code of 1702, and reads as follows:

Whereas, for many years past, the money coined in the late Massachusetts Colony hath passed currant at the rate or value it was stampt for; and good Sevil pillar, or Mexico pieces-of-eight, of full seventeen penny weight, have also passed currant at six shillings per piece, and half pieces of proportionable weight, at three shillings per piece, quarter pieces of the same coynes, at sixteen pence per piece, and reals of the same coyne at eight pence per piece—

Be it therefore enacted, * * * That all and every the coynes before mentioned, shall still be and continue currant money within this Colony, and shall be accepted, taken and received at the respective values aforesaid, according as hath hitherto been accustomed—*Provided always*, That such of the said coynes as pass by tale, be not diminished by washing, clipping, rounding, filing or scaling.†

This law, it will be observed, makes each of the foreign coins named, weighing seventeen pennyweights, the equivalent of six Massachusetts shillings, which should have weighed eighteen pennyweights. Doubtless, the size of the latter had been gradually reduced by wear and roguery, (chiefly the latter,) so that their real did not exceed their estimated value. Had they been worth more than the estimate, they would have been withdrawn from circulation to be hoarded, melted or exported. In truth, both the domestic and foreign coins current in the country, in the last years of the seventeenth century, were much reduced in weight by washing, filing, paring with shears, &c. The Spanish eight-real-pieces, which, in the middle of the century, passed in trade for five shillings sterling, were, at a little later period, only equal to four and six pence

---

* Printed Col. Records.

† I have failed to ascertain when this act was passed, but it was probably soon after October, 1697; for, at that date, Massachusetts enacted a similar law.

sterling, each, or six New England shillings.* The pieces gradually got lighter and lighter, so that about 1700, they had lost ten, fifteen, twenty, or twenty-five per cent.† Those which were known as "heavy pieces-of-eight" were withdrawn from circulation as fast as they appeared, while the light ones were used as money and for the payment of debts. To arrest the evil, the aid of legislation was invoked. Connecticut enacted the law which has just been recited, which required that those coins which passed by tale at their former rate, should " not be diminished by washing," &c. Statutes, however, were ineffectual, and the evil went on increasing. In recognition of an existing fact, the General Court of Massachusetts enacted, in 1705, that light money and plate of sterling alloy should pass and be good in payments at seven shillings the ounce.‡ " During the next year, the courts of judicature [of the same Province] chancered [cut down] silver to eight shillings per ounce, in satisfaction of debts, which was nearly at the rate of six shillings to a light piece-of-eight, as current at the time."§ The value of the metallic currency which was in general use at this time, or, say, in the first part of the eighteenth century, was worth about eight shillings per ounce.‖ It passed at this rate in the way of trade. But as

---

* I am not sure that, in the mean time, the Spanish coins in question had not been degraded by lowering the mint standard.

† Merchants' Magazine, Vol. XVI., p. 345, (1847.) The merchants of New York, in a petition to Lord Cornbury, about February, 170⅘, complained as follows:—"The people of Boston, publickly and avowedly, have practiced to clipp and file all the small current money along the continent to 25 per cent. loss, which practice and the unlawfull proffit comeing thareby, did encourage enough to make it their business to carry it [the coin] thither and return it againe to us and our neighbours, where it passed for the same value as formerly; which is now so apparent that, many times, sixteen rials doe not weigh seaventeen penny weight." Documentary Hist. N. Y., IV., 1134.

‡ Felt, p. 60, note.

§ See " A chapter on Colonial Currency" in the Merchants' Magazine for April, 1847.

‖ In 1727, the General Court of Massachusetts passed a law which established a rule for the equitable adjustment of debts contracted in paper money. It enacted that all obligations entered into, before 1712, might be discharged in bills of credit at the rate of eight shillings for an ounce of silver. (Felt, 83.) Said bills, says Hutchinson, were as good as silver till after 1710.

the real value could not be known from the denomination, it was customary to weigh the pieces in order to obtain a correct notion. "Money scales" is an item often met with in the inventories of deceased persons of that day.

The washing and paring of coins was carried on in England, on a large scale, in the latter part of the seventeenth century. The irregular shape of the pieces, and the low state of the art of coinage, rendered these operations comparatively easy. Many of those in circulation, in consequence of the depredations of the clippers, were reduced to two-thirds, sometimes one-half their proper weight. In Macaulay's brilliant pages (see his History of England) will be found a graphic description of the miseries brought upon England by this degradation of the currency. At last, the government, in 1696, was obliged to call in the old coinage, and to substitute a better, which was protected against mutilation by what is called milling. The change cost one million two hundred thousand pounds.

Notwithstanding the large amount of the New England coinage, country pay continued to be received for public taxes at fixed prices. The custom was continued in Massachusetts till 1694, when it was abolished, bills of credit having been introduced.* It was followed some fifteen years longer in Connecticut. As the consequence of this practice, several currencies were in existence, and the prices of commodities were graded according to the particular currency which was offered in payment. To illustrate this point, I will quote a passage from "The private Journal kept by Madam Knight, on a journey from Boston to New York, in the year 1704," first published in New York in 1825, from the original manuscript. Madam Knight was a literary lady, and on her journey, (which was made on horseback,) passed several weeks in New Haven. During this stay she wrote as follows :—

They [the people] give the title of merchant to every trader who rate their goods according to the time and specie [kind] they pay in, viz: pay, money, pay as money, and trusting. [That is, they have a *pay* price, a *money* price, a *pay as money* price, and a *trusting* price.] *Pay* is grain, pork, beef, &c., at the prices

---

* Felt, 54.

set by the General Court that year. *Money* is pieces of eight ryals, or Boston or Bay shillings, (as they call them,) or good hard money, as sometimes silver coin is termed by them; also wampum, (viz., Indian beads,) which serves for change. *Pay as money*, is provisions as aforesaid, one-third cheaper than as the Assembly in General Court sets it; and *trust*, as they and the merchant agree for time. Now when the buyer comes to ask for a commodity, sometimes before the merchant answers that he has it, he says, "is your pay *ready?*" Perhaps the chap replies, yes. "What do you pay in?" says the merchant. The buyer having answered, the price is set; as suppose he wants a six penny knife; in pay, it is twelve pence; in pay as money, eight pence, and in hard money, its own price [value], six pence. It seems a very intricate way of trade, [&c.]

This, it will be observed, is a description of the currency of Connecticut, and not of Massachusetts; consequently nothing is said of bills of credit, to be mentioned by and by. It is possible, however, that Madam Knight may have been mistaken in one particular. So far as my inquiries have extended, pay as money and money (which then meant specie) were not two things but one. The General Court, annually, and whenever it laid a tax, fixed the prices of the commodities which were to be received in payment. They fixed them at one-half or fifty per cent. higher than the money price. The commodities thus selected were accepted by the people at the established prices as a common currency. They were called "country pay," not because they were products of the farm, but because they were received by the Colony or government in payment of rates. I have examined the inventories of estates in New Haven, for the ten years following 1700, for the purpose of ascertaining the currency in which property was appraised. The valuations are usually in country pay, the fact, in most cases, being so stated. If money (coin) or plate is entered, one half is added to convert it into pay. Items like the following are common :—"Plate in pay, £10 " (170⅔ ;) "money, £4 : 16 : 1, in pay, £7 : 4 : 1½" (170⅔ ;) "Cash, £8 : 17 : 0, in pay, £13 : 5 : 6 " (1706 ;) "Cash, 30s. which is in pay, £2 : 5 : 0," (170⅔.) In 1702, is this entry : " £200 money in England, valued in pay at £375." Here twenty-five per cent. is added to convert sterling into New England (pine-tree) currency, and fifty per cent. to the sum of these two to convert the latter into pay. Occasionally other standards are employed. In 1702,

I find an instance in which plate is carried out at (about) nine shillings an ounce; in 1704, another, of silver at seven shillings the ounce; in 170⁴⁄₁₀, another, of plate* at eight shillings per ounce, &c. These examples show some instability of practice, and the confusion growing out of the many currencies in use.

To get a correct notion of the prices, stated in pounds, shillings and pence, which prevailed in the period about which I am writing, it will be necessary to understand the facts which have been mentioned, and the peculiar condition of the currency. This will be specially important, if we would compare the prices of this period with those of others. Suppose the price of a commodity be stated at six shillings, without explanation: it will be safe to assume that country pay is intended, and that one-third must be deducted. The price will then stand at four shillings, in money; but as the current coins were of light weight, being worth only at the rate of eight shillings per ounce, when they should have been equal to six and ten pence the ounce, another deduction of six pence must be made. After this operation, the price reckoned in good Bay shillings, or heavy pieces-of-eight, will stand at about three and six pence. To convert the last sum into sterling money, twenty-five per cent. more must be taken off. In this way alone can an intelligible comparison be made.

The pieces of money which are named in the Connecticut statute of 1702, made up the common metallic currency of New England, for more than a century, beginning with the time an active trade was opened with the West India Islands. When the Massachusetts shillings were introduced, these became the measure of value, changed the imperial standard, degraded it twenty-five per cent., and increased the nominal prices of commodities in proportion. By a well known law, they drove the more valuable English coins that remained in the country out of circulation, the latter seeking a foreign market, where their current value equaled the cost of producing them. The English pound, or pound sterling, as a

---

* "Plate" is understood to have been of the fineness of sterling money.

money of account, gave place to the New England pound, containing only three-quarters as much silver. The several Spanish coins known as Mexican, Peru, Seville and pillar pieces-of-eight (eight reals,) each weighing, in 1704, four hundred and twenty grains, and worth, intrinsically, about four and six pence sterling, were equal, singly, to six Bay shillings. This is on the supposition that all the pieces were of full weight. The Spanish milled dollar, too, which ultimately took the place of the eight-real piece, though a trifle lighter, was considered as good for six shillings. It was in this way that the dollar of New England came to contain six shillings, the half dollar three shillings, the quarter one and six pence, the eighth nine pence, the sixteenth four pence halfpenny—a way of reckoning which is not yet quite obsolete. In the other colonies different customs prevailed, the same coin having a different nominal value. The Spanish dollar in New York and North Carolina represented eight shillings; in New Jersey, Pennsylvania and Maryland, seven and six pence; in South Carolina, four and eight pence; in Virginia, the same as in New Eng".ad.* This diversity of custom was a great inconvenience—an embarrassment to commerce and to all intercourse.

The Board of Trade and Plantations, (established in 1696,) which had a general oversight of colonial affairs in America, had often complained of the different and unstable currencies of the colonies. It proposed, not to restore the English basis, but to fix the standard of value of the coins in use, and thus to prevent its further degradation. By a judicious regulation of this matter, it was thought to " make most of the money center in England." In execution of the plan, the Queen, in June, 1704, issued her proclamation establishing the value of the several foreign coins in common use in the plantations, according to their intrinsic worth, and in conformity to a table prepared by the " master-worker of the mint," Sir Isaac Newton, which is as follows :—

---

* Gouge's History of Paper Money, &c., p. 6.

Weight and intrinsic value of the several species.			Rate of said pieces in proportion to the limitation made by said proclamation.	
	Pwt. Gr.	Value.	To be taken for in the Plantations.	
Seville pieces of eight, old plate,	17 12	4s. 6d.	6s.	This to be enforced from the first of January next, 1704-5.
" " " new "	14	3s. 7¼d.	4s.9¼d.	
Mexico pieces of eight,	17 12	4s. 6d.	6s.	
Pillar pieces of eight,	17 12	4s. 6⅔d.	6s.	
Peru pieces of eight,	17 12	4s. 5d.	5s.10½d.	
Cross Dollars,	18	4s. 4⅔d.	5s.10¼d.	
Ducatoons of Flanders,	20 21	5s. 6d.	7s.4d.	
Ecus of France, or silver Lewis,	17 12	4s. 6d.	6s.	
Crusados of Portugal,	11 4	2s.10½d.	3s.9¼d.	
Three Guilder Pieces of Holland,	20 7	5s. 2¼d.	6s.11d.	
Old Rix dollars of the Empire,	18 10	4s. 6d.	6s.	

All halves, quarters and less pieces, are allowed to pass in proportion to the above rates.

In regulating the value of foreign coins, the Proclamation of Queen Anne seems to have followed the custom of New England, making the pine-tree shilling the standard. It is true, the last named piece is not mentioned, but this is doubtless because it was an unauthorized coin. The royal order was promptly enjoined by the American governors; but for various reasons it proved of no effect except in Barbados.* No formal action was required on the part of the governments of Massachusetts and Connecticut, the prescribed regulations being in harmony with colonial laws. The custom of trade, however, as I have already stated, was not in accordance with existing legislation.

In 1707, the Act of the sixth of Queen Anne, so called, was passed by Parliament. It recites the Proclamation, and enacts that any person in the colonies who shall, after May first, 1709, receive or pay out any of the coins named at a greater or higher rate than is allowed by the Proclamation, shall suffer six months imprisonment and forfeit ten pounds.† The purpose seems to have been to stop legislative tampering with the coin, to prevent the degradation of the standard of value, and to secure uniformity of custom. "Proclamation money," or, more briefly, "proc. money," of which we hear so much

---

* A short History of Paper Money and Banking. By William M. Gouge. p. 6. See also Felt, pp. 59, 60, Doc. Hist. N. Y., Vol. IV.
† See English Statutes at Large.

half a century later, after the paper money system had exploded, derives its name from Queen Anne's order.

The year 1690 is memorable; for then was inaugurated the reign of paper money in America—a reign not yet ended. It began in Massachusetts, the ancient mother of currency heresies. Many years before, the question of setting up a bank had agitated the Colony. The mint did not make money fast enough or cheap enough. Spite the pine-tree shillings, three-quarters weight, the people were much straitened in their means. So soon as their coinage had ceased, the bank project was revived. It appears from a rare tract quoted by Felt, page forty-seven, that a partnership was formed which circulated notes based on land-security. Little more is known of it. Its operations must have been very limited, and its influence upon history inconsiderable. But now a new opportunity occurred of carrying out some paper money scheme, under favorable auspices. Massachusetts, it seems, in concert with Connecticut and New York, had sent an expedition against Canada. It proved a failure, and the troops returned, unexpectedly, to Boston. The government was unprepared to meet the charges, having trusted to the success of the enterprise, and the plunder which success would secure. The soldiers clamored for their wages, and, not receiving them, were, it is said, on the point of mutiny. There was not time to collect a tax, and it was doubtless difficult to borrow. In this emergency, the General Court, "desirous," as they say, "to approve themselves just and honest," and considering withal the "scarcity of money and the want of an adequate measure of commerce," established a "provincial bank," and authorized a committee to issue, forthwith, in the name of the Colony, seven thousand pounds, in bills of credit, from two shillings to five pounds each. One of these bills, which I find copied in Drake's History and Antiquities of Boston, page four hundred and ninety-one, the original being five and three-quarter inches from top to bottom, and five inches from side to side, reads as follows:

No. (916.)   20 s.

This indented Bill of Twenty Shillings due from the Massachusetts Colony to the Possessor shall be in value equal to money, and shall be accordingly accepted by the Treasurer and Receivers subordinate to him in all Public pay^ts, and for any stock at any time in the Treasury. Boston, in New England, February the third, 1690. By order of the General Court.

                                    ELISHA HUTCHINSON, ⎫
[L. S.]   JOHN WALLEY,   ⎬ Comitee.
                                    TIM THORNTON,   ⎭

These bills were, in fact, treasury notes, secured by a tax, and receivable for treasury dues, the phrase "shall be in value equal to money," meaning nothing. They were not favorably received, and would not command money, or goods at money prices. The soldiers lost heavily, not being able to sell their paper notes for more than twelve or fourteen shillings in the pound.* Afterward, in 1692, an order was passed declaring "that all bills of public credit, issued forth by order of ye Generall Court of ye late Colony of ye Massachusetts Bay, shall pass current within this Province in all payments equivalent to money, and in public payments at 5 per cent. advance." Thus they were made lawful tender, for their face, in private transactions, and were received, by the Treasurer, in whatever payment, at five per cent. premium. They were to be redeemed in twelve months. These provisions were designed to prevent depreciation. Felt thinks they had the intended effect for twenty years. The demand for the bills, when the tax became due, made them, for the moment, because of the five per cent. bonus, better than hard money. But the order which had been previously passed, that no more than forty thousand pounds should be emitted was not regarded. The "scarcity of money" was still complained of, and each issue whetted the appetite for more. The whole amount of the emissions, including the reëmissions, up to 1702, Mr. Felt thinks, must have exceeded one hundred and ten thousand pounds. At this period, says Governor Hutchinson, they were as good as silver. (silver, I suppose, at eight shillings per ounce;) and not till after 1710 did they suffer any great depreciation.

---

* Hutchinson, I., 357.

Those issued before the arrival of the new Charter, (granted by William and Mary, in 1691,) were called old charter bills.

I believe the paper money of Massachusetts, emitted before Connecticut had bills of her own, did not circulate in the latter Colony. I think so, because I have been unable to find any trace of them. And this view is confirmed by the neglect of Madam Knight, in the passage already quoted, to mention them, in her enumeration of the different currencies in use. Indeed, while at or near the specie point, they were too valuable to be employed as money, or at least to pay debts with, so long as country pay, representing two-thirds as much labor, was allowed. Had any been received, in the way of trade, they would, like coin, have borne a premium over the common currency, which fact would have been evidence that they had come to the wrong market. Those wishing to buy goods in Boston would have picked them up as a profitable remittance.

The example of Massachusetts, in her perilous paper money experiment, was not lost upon the other English Colonies. With the exception of Nova Scotia, says Hutchinson, they all, sooner or later, adopted her system. Mr. Bancroft makes Virginia* the exception.

CHAPTER III.

CONNECTICUT BILLS OF CREDIT—OLD TENOR EMISSIONS.

THE first bills of credit of Connecticut, like those of the Massachusetts Bay, were issued in a time of financial embarrassment. The colonists, then in the midst of the war with

---

* Mr. C. J. Hoadley, State librarian, of Hartford, has in his possession a Virginia bill bearing the date of 1757. Others are in existence. See Hening's Statutes of Virg., VI., 467. Nova Scotia, too, had issued bills in 1755.

France and its Indian allies, called Queen Anne's war, had
been heavily taxed, the colony tax alone amounting, in some
years, says Dr. Trumbull, to seven pence or eight pence in
the pound, on the whole list, equal, in the latter case, to three
and a third per cent. on taxable polls and estate. But it
must be remembered that the lists were made up very differently then and now, as I shall explain in another place. The
General Court met, by adjournment, in New Haven, in
June, 1709, apparently to devise means to carry on the war.
During a three days' session, they passed the following law.
I copy from the printed statutes:

Forasmuch, as by reason of the great scarcity of money, the payment of the
public debts, and charges of this government, especially in the intended expedition to Canada, is made almost impracticable. For remedy whereof:

Be it enacted [&c.] that there be forthwith imprinted a certain number
of Bills of Credit on this Colony, in suitable sums from two shillings to five
pounds, which in the whole shall amount to the sum of eight thousand pounds
and no more: which bills shall be indented and stamped with such stamps as the
Governor and Council shall direct, and be signed by a Committee appointed by
this Court—they or any three of them, and of the tenor following. That is to say:

No. (——)   20 s.

This indented Bill of Twenty shillings, due from the Colony of Connecticut,
in New England, to the possessor thereof, shall be in value equal to money, and
shall be accordingly accepted by the Treasurer and Receivers subordinate to
him, in all public payments, and for any stock at any time in the Treasury.
Hartford, July the 12th, Anno Domini, 1709. By order of the Generall Court.

J. C. ⎫
J. H. ⎬ *Committee.*
J. E. ⎭

And so mutatis mutandis for a greater or lesser sum.

This form is copied, verbatim, from the Massachusetts note,
the necessary changes of date, &c., having been made. In
printing the bills, the words, "in all public payments," were
omitted, as they were in the next and subsequent issues, which
omission, though "not so material," was provided for by
special act, in May, 1710. The form, date and all, was preserved in all the subsequent emissions, for many years. The
additional date of "May, 1713," however, was afterwards
added, to distinguish the more recent issues. The law pre-
scribing and limiting the denominations of the notes was not

changed. They were signed by a committee of the General
Court, and appear to have been printed, (some of the earlier
ones, at least,) in Boston, under the charge of Mr. Dummer.*

Of the eight thousand pounds in bills first ordered, four
thousand were to be signed and delivered to the Treasurer for
disbursement, the other four to be retained, unsigned, in the
hands of the Committee, till the further order of the Court.
Like the Massachusetts issues, they were to be paid out as
"equivalent to money," and to be received "in all public
payments [on account of taxes only] at the advance of twelve
pence on the pound more," or at the rate of five per cent.
premium. The premium was allowed as often as they were
paid in, though many times in the course of the year. The
effect would naturally be to make them worth more than other
par funds as the time approached for the payment of taxes.
"In all other payments," (other than public payments,) says
Dr. Trumbull, "they were to be received as money."† If, by
this language, Dr. Trumbull meant to say that they were
made a tender for private debts, he is mistaken. Mr. Bancroft, in his History of the United States, speaking of the
legal tender feature as common to the early colonial credit
bills, makes no exception in favor of Connecticut.‡ The law
of this Colony, at that period, said nothing of private obligations.
Probably, both of the historians named have been misled by
the phrase in the form of the bills "shall be in value equal to
money," which, as I understand it, bound no party except the
Treasurer of the State. The legislation of Massachusetts was
different, as has been mentioned.

By the same act which authorized the emission of public bills,
the General Court, " as a fund and security for the repayment
and drawing in of the said bills to the Treasury again, and for
defraying any further charge of the Colony," " granted a rate of
ten pence on the pound in money, one moiety thereof to be
levied according to the next list of heads and estates," and
payable, on the first day of May, 1710; the other half to be

---

* See Journal of the Council.
† History of Connecticut, Vol. 1., p. 474.   ‡ Vol. III., p. 388.

levied on the list of 1710, and payable May 1st, 1711. And liberty was granted " for any person to pay his rate either in bills of credit, silver money, or in pork at fifty shillings per barrel, or beef at thirty shillings per barrel, winter wheat at four shillings per bushel, rye at two shillings and four pence per bushel, and Indian corn at two shillings per bushel. * * * * And no person shall have liberty to pay above two-thirds of his rate in rye and Indian corn," these commodities being less desirable " stock " than some other.

The expedition against Canada failed, and in October of the same year, again, on account " of the great scarcity of money," eleven thousand pounds in bills of public credit were ordered to be issued, and for their redemption, with the five per cent. advance, and for other purposes, a tax of twelve thousand pounds was laid, payable " within the term of six years, * * * * and so much thereof in each of the six years" as should be ordered.* The tax payers were allowed the same option as to the ways of payment as by the act of the preceding May. At the same session, a law was passed requiring that when any salaries of public officers, or the wages of officers and soldiers, or posts, or other persons, were made payable by law, " in country pay," the debt on account of said salaries, &c., should be discharged by the Treasurer, with bills of credit for two-thirds the amount. This act was designed to reduce " pay " to current money, three of the former being only equal to two of the latter.†

In May of the next year (1710,) it was found that the " Colony in general, as well as particular persons," was suffering for the " want of a due circulation of the bills of public credit." " For remedy and prevention thereof" the General Court enacted that " all rates hereafter to be made, pursuant to " preceding acts for drawing in said bills, should be paid either in bullion at eight shillings the ounce, Troy, or in the bills of the Colony. But it was found, doubtless, that the law rating silver

---

* At the next session, the time was fixed for June, 1715.

† It was in this year, (1709,) according to the Merchants' Magazine, (Vol XVI. p. 344,) that New York and New Jersey made their first issues of bills of credit. Rhode Island followed in the next year, (1710.)

at eight shillings per ounce* contravened the act of Parliament and the Proclamation of Queen Anne. Consequently, after three months, it was repealed, and another enacted, providing that the before mentioned rates and taxes should be paid either in money (money at that time meant coin,) "as it shall generally pass in New England," or in the bills of the Colony. Thus country pay was excluded from the Treasury, and a decisive blow given to a most inconvenient currency.

In October, 1710, £5,000 in bills of credit were ordered, and a tax levied of £5,250, payable on or before the last day of August, 1718. £4,000 more were authorized in May, 1711, and a tax laid of £4,500, to be paid before the first day of June, 1720. £6,000 were also ordered in June, 1711, and £6,300 levied by a tax due on or before August thirty-first, 1723. In May, 1712, and in June, 1712, there were *reissued*, in the one case £3,000, and in the other £1,500, the same being bills which had been paid into the Treasury by the rates of 1711 and 1712. A tax was laid in each instance payable in 1720. After this period, it was customary for the General Court to authorize, at stated periods, the reissue of any bills received into the Treasury which were found in a suitable condition for circulation.

From June, 1709, to May, 1713, there had been emitted (or authorized) in all, £34,000 in colonial credit bills, a little more than Dr. Trumbull's estimate at a later period.† Of this sum, £3,500 paid into the Treasury, had been reissued, and there were outstanding, at the last date, £20,000, or, according to a subsequent statement, £23,636 : 11 : 4.

Rogues always prosper when large additions are being made to the currency. Too often they get the start of honest men, and pocket the gains which flow from a more active business. They manipulated the bills of credit, and introduced certain emendations and improvements. Judged by the higher standard of our day, their work was done in a bungling manner ;

---

* Silver was intrinsically worth, in the currency established by the Proclamation, about 6s. 10¼d., but in sterling money, or English coin, only 6s. 8d. (approximately.)

† History of Connecticut, Vol. I., 474.

but they succeeded in converting the smaller into larger notes, " by which means divers persons suffered considerable damages." For the prevention of which evil practices and wrong, the General Court, in May, 1713, enacted that bills of credit not exceeding £20,000, having the additional date of May, 1713, should be forthwith printed, which the Treasurer was authorized at any time, within eighteen months, to exchange for the bills then outstanding. And the people were to be warned by proclamation, to bring in their bills and have them exchanged, " on penalty of having their demands upon the Treasury refused." In October, 1714, the time was extended to June first, 1715. But the bills did not come in as desired. In the meantime, new "cheats and forgeries" had appeared. The notes had "been imitated by several false and counterfeit bills, * * * by false plates and otherwise," and the General Court, October, 1717, again extended the time, and authorized the Treasurer to exchange the bills " of the date of July twelfth, 1709, only," for those having the additional date of May, 1713, till " the fifteenth of May [then] next, and no longer." At the same time, it was enacted " that from and after the said fifteenth day of May, no creditor" should " be obliged to receive in payment the said bills of credit bearing the date of July twelfth, 1709, only." Of course, the government had no intention, at that time, of repudiating any of its true bills; and I suppose it was well understood that no creditor was under obligation to receive them, and that they circulated by consent only. The fifteenth day of May, 1718, soon came round, and many of the old bills were still outstanding. Whereupon, the period was again extended, first to May twenty-fifth, 1719, (when " several thousand pounds" of the old bills were still in circulation,) then to November first, 1719, then again to June first, 1720, and still again to June first, 1721.

But the business of counterfeiting and altering the colony bills went on. In fact, the crime became so common and so dangerous, that the General Court, in May, 1724, felt constrained to increase the penalty from six months' imprisonment, or " standing in the pillory three several lecture dayes," to branding in the forehead with the letter C, cutting off the right ear, confinement to work in the work-house, under a master, till the day of death, and forfeiture of estate. Besides all this, the offender was to be "forever debarred of any trade or dealing within this Colony in any wise, upon penalty of being severely whipped,"—an unnecessary cruelty to a man shut up for life in a work house.

The facts mentioned in regard to counterfeiting, show that Dr. Trumbull is not quite correct when he says that this business was not begun till "about the year 1735," when "there arose a set of villains," &c. The villains had been up and doing long before that.

There is a history connected with the £20,000 in bills, authorized in May, 1713. They were to be placed in the hands of the Treasurer to be exchanged for the old issues. He was "not to give or dispose of them to any other use or end whatsoever, without the order of this Assembly." With the exception of £1,000, emitted for ordinary expenses, in October of the same year, no additional issues were authorized for several years. Instead of this, the General Court would order the Treasurer, from time to time, to apply certain portions of the £20,000 fund "towards the payment of the public debts, * * * and the further necessary charge thereof." This operation began with the act that created the fund, and was continued, year after year, till May, 1719, when £12,952 : 12 : 6 had been thus appropriated, and the issue was exhausted. At this time, "divers persons" bringing "divers sums" in old bills to the Treasury for exchange, had been turned away on the plea of "no funds." Prompt to meet the emergency, the General Court enacted that £4,000, in bills of credit, in all respects like the £20,000, should "be forthwith imprinted," to be placed in the hands of the Treasurer as an exchange fund. £1,290 : 2 : 6 of this money were used to pay "public debts, * * * and the further necessary charges thereof," at the next session of the Court in October.

In October, 1722, it was found that the "torn and defaced" bills, ("unfit to pass,") then in circulation, required attention, and £4,000 were ordered to "be forthwith imprinted," to take their place by exchange. But at the next session of the Court, in May, 1723, £346 : 12 : 6 of the same were wanted and employed to discharge the debts of the Colony, the re-

mainder to be reserved for the purpose for which they were
designed. £2,640 more of the same sort went in the same way
before October, 1724, when the "torn and defaced" bills
needed renewed attention. £4,000 were to be printed without
delay, and £2,000 of the same set apart to liquidate the debts
of the colonial government. Up to October, 1728, £16,000
in all had been struck off or authorized professedly on account of bills "torn, defaced and unfit to pass," the Treasurer,
in the several acts, being directed to make the exchange.
Out of this fund, I find that £9,942 : 17 : 0 were taken for the
payment of the public debts, and the charges of the government.

The bills which have been mentioned, together with those
brought in by taxes and reissued, seem to have been sufficient
for the disbursements till May, 1729, when a new occasion was
embraced for a new emission. It appears that, owing to the
scarcity of small change, the colony bills had been halved and
quartered, and the fragments passed in payments at a propor-
tionate value, as was done by the issuers of notes, at a very recent date, (1862.) To discourage the evil, a law was enacted
in May, 1726, forbidding the Treasurer to receive quartered
bills. To get quit of those in circulation, which are described
in the preamble as "bills of credit * * * torn in pieces"
which "do usually pass from man to man," an act was passed
in May, 1729, requiring £6,000 in new bills to "be forthwith
imprinted," to be exchanged for said notes, and for "all other
outstanding bills of this Colony that are not printed on the
backs." At a later period, the counterfeiters quartered and
halved their bills, in imitation of the genuine, rendering detec-
tion doubly difficult, so that more legislation was demanded in
May, 1736. In the mean time, however, £2,500 of the "exchange bills," so called, were employed for the expenses of government, there not being, at the time, (October, 1732,) "a sufficiency of money" in the Treasury "to defray the charges of
this Assembly." Of the £47,000 authorized emissions from
May, 1713, to October, 1732, both inclusive, all, with the exception of £1,000 in October, 1713, were for the ostensible purpose
of taking up earlier impressions which had been counterfeited,

or removing from circulation torn and defaced, or halved and quartered bills. And yet, £29,885 : 12 : 0, if there is no mistake in my figures, out of the £46,000 net, were appropriated, from time to time, by law, for the payment of colony debts, &c. The wants of the Treasury seem to have been supplied, to a large extent, from the new notes set apart, in the first instance, as an exchange fund.

In the earlier legislation of Connecticut, the same law which authorized the emission of bills of credit, levied a tax payable within a certain period, to sink the whole issue, together with the five per cent. advance. At first, this period was one and two years, then six years, then eight, nine, twelve, and again eight years. After the close of the war, in 1713, the time was frequently shortened. I discover no instance in which this tax was neglected. The same principle of providing by taxation for all bills put in circulation, was observed, so far as can be ascertained, with regard to the reissues—the reissues, I mean, of notes brought in by any sinking fund tax. The idea seems to have been to have all the outstanding notes, for the time being, with the advance, made secure by outstanding taxes, so that the latter, when collected, should sink the former. I know not whether these taxes were all gathered in accordance with the original intention. As they were levied in gross sums, and required additional legislation for their apportionment, according to lists, very possibly they were not. But I have met with no law, till after the Revolution, for their postponement, in the manner which was common in Massachusetts.*

After 1710, the rates of the General Court could not be satisfied with country pay. They must be discharged with bills of credit, or coin at current rates, as has been mentioned. In October, 1719, however, a new practice was introduced, recognizing the bills of other colonies, which now formed a part of the common currency. The regular tax of that session might be paid " in bills of credit of this Colony, with the usual advance, or in the true bills with four signers of the Province of the Massachusetts Bay, [the larger bills had four signers,] or in the true bills of New York, Rhode Island, or New

---

* Felt, 63.

Hampshire, without any advance upon them," &c. There was, at this time, much complaint of the want of a "medium of exchange," though paper money was so abundant that it took twelve shillings to buy an ounce of silver. For the purpose, probably, of mitigating the evil, the General Court made the customary tax levied in October, 1720,* payable either in the currencies allowed the year before, or in "grain at the following prices, viz: wheat at four shillings and six pence per bushel, rye at two shillings and nine pence, Indian corn at two shillings and three pence, all to be good and merchantable." The same latitude was permitted in the two or three years that followed, when "country pay" once more fell into discredit. The paper money of the neighboring colonies was still received, to a greater or less extent, always, however, without the five per cent. premium. The bills of New Hampshire and Rhode Island were the first to be discredited at the public Treasury.

I have said that, at first, there was no law making the colonial credit bills a legal tender for private debts. Doubtless,

---

* It was at about this time that the "South Sea Scheme" in England, and the "Mississippi Bubble," including John Law's bank in France, exploded. The financial troubles in Europe may have wrought disorder in the colonies. Law's bank was at first a private institution, chartered in 1716. Considered with reference to its avowed objects, it was not calculated to excite apprehension. It was authorized to discount bills of exchange, to keep accounts with merchants, and issue notes payable to bearer in coin " of the weight and denomination of that day," (date of the charter.) For a time, it was immensely successful. But in January, 1719, it was taken into the hands of the government, then much involved in debt, and became the Royal Bank, with Law for chief director. A year later, according to the general plan of its founder, it was united with the "India Company," under the same management. This company grew out of Law's scheme to develop the wealth of Louisiana and the Mississippi valley, and aimed to control a large proportion of the foreign trade of France. The bank was to provide the money for the greatest and grandest enterprise of that day. Not long after the union, the bubble burst.

John Law was a gamester, libertine, speculator and enthusiast, but still a man of genius. He understood the laws of finance better, perhaps, than any man of that age; but he labored under the fatal delusion that money is wealth, the source of all wealth—a delusion from which the popular mind has not yet escaped. See "The Mississippi Bubble: A Memoir of John Law." By A. Thiers. Translated, and published in New York, in 1859.

the government questioned its authority to pass such a law. It is true, the authority had been often exercised, rightfully or wrongfully, in the Massachusetts Bay; but Massachusetts had lost her charter. Connecticut had a more precious one which she wished to save. Though never more delighted than when "trotting after the Bay horse," yet, she was not now prepared for such a break-neck adventure. Her legislators had long acted on the belief that discretion was a wise and remunerative, if not valiant, virtue. And yet they wanted all the supposed benefits of their favorite currency, without the embarrassments which "evil disposed persons" sometimes placed in its way. The question was how, in the legitimate exercise of their authority, they could make their bills of credit not a lawful but an accepted tender—how they could constrain men to receive them voluntarily, by simply withholding law. The following act, passed October, 1718, shows how ingenuously they could solve the problem. It is entitled "An Act for the further encouraging the currency of the bills of public credit, and for preventing the oppression of debtors," and reads as follows:

Whereas by reason of the great scarcity of money, and other adequate media for * * * carrying on the affairs of the government, the government did, several years since, project and order the making and emitting of bills of public credit, to be accepted and received in all public payments equivalent to money, with the advance of five pounds per cent. thereon, upon good and sufficient funds granted for the calling in and answering of the same, which bills have likewise obtained a universal currency throughout the government in all private trade and dealing, and are found beneficial and serviceable for facilitating of the same, the whole course of trade from the year 1709 having been generally managed and regulated thereby, and all debts since made and contracted where there has been no special agreement and contract otherwise) generally understood to be contracted for the said bills,—

Now, that encouragement may be given to the said bills in the way of private commerce and dealings, and to prevent oppression by the rigorous exaction of money (which cannot be procured but with great difficulty) for debts contracted with the real intent both of debtor and creditor, to be paid in said bills, though not expressly mentioned:

Be it therefore enacted [&c.] that from and after the first day of November now next ensuing, no debtor for any debt made and contracted since the twelfth day of July, 1709, or that shall be made and contracted before the the twelfth day of July, * * 1727, (express contracts in writing for current silver money, or some speciality always excepted,) that shall tender satisfaction and payment of his full debt in good and lawful bills of credit of this Colony, shall be liable to have execution served and levied upon his estate or person, or be imprisoned upon any recovery of judgment to be granted against him for such debt, any law, usage or custom to the contray notwithstanding.

I presume this law was effectual, and all "rigorous exaction" and "oppression" prevented. It worked so well that the time limited for its operation was afterward extended from 1727 to 1735.

There are many circumstances to excuse, if not justify, Connecticut in her course when first she issued bills of credit. She with the other Colonies was engaged in a bloody and expensive war with the French and Indians, requiring her utmost exertions and all her resources. She saw Massachusetts moving along pleasantly, embarked on a sea of paper money, paying her expenses, in large measure, by promises only. Perhaps her people were beginning to use the bills of their neighbor, and she thought it better to occupy the field herself, and reap the benefits. She showed, too, commendable prudence in her early issues, taxing herself without stint to redeem the whole at no very distant period. If she had stopped her emissions, at the close of the war in 1713, or at any time before 1733, and left the laws then in operation to take their course, comparatively little harm would have been done, so far as her own action was concerned. But the temporary relief which she had undeniably experienced was too fresh in the memory to allow her to stop here. The first effects of a paper inflation are peculiarly exhilarating, and no instance has yet been known of a people once intoxicated recovering their senses in time to save themselves from signal disasters. The sense of public justice is too much weakened for present reform. Those who knew the peril, and would counsel prudence and honesty, are stilled by the din of popular clamor. They who are likely to suffer most are old fashioned, incredulous people, who are without lucrative or influential positions, and have no access to the public trumpet. They find themselves stranded, as it were, on the river's bank, and see the unbelieving throng moving by, pointing the finger and wagging the head at them.

Throughout this business of making paper money, those who

administered the government seem to have been aware that they were standing on ticklish if not dangerous ground. They appeared desirous, in certain cases, that their motives should not be too apparent and their acts too public. They well knew that their course was regarded with disfavor in the mother country, and that the eyes of the authorities were upon them. The Proclamation of Queen Anne, in 1704, and the Act of Parliament which followed it, in 1707, were proofs of the jealousy with which experiments on the currency were regarded. In 1720, the colonial governors in America were instructed to allow of no paper issues which were not necessary to meet the charges of government. In Massachusetts, there was a struggle between the Governor and Council on the one side, and the House of Representatives on the other, one opposing and the other favoring the emissions of bills of credit. Wearied out by his fruitless endeavors to stem the torrent, Gov. Shute returned to England, leaving Lt. Gov. Dummer to encounter the same difficulties. To settle the controversy, Gov. Burnet, in 1728, was directed not to " assent to or pass any act, * * * * whereby bills of credit may be struck or issued in lieu of money, without a clause be inserted in such act, declaring that the same shall not take effect until * * approved by the English government."* Under these circumstances, Connecticut, having much at stake, was naturally cautious. She doubtless thought that emissions of notes to be exchanged for an old impression were least likely to give offense ; and while supplying bills for so good a purpose, could see no wrong in printing a few, at her own cost, for treasury expenses. But the time at last came when a change of plan seemed expedient. The torn and counterfeit bill-system had worked well for a season, but something new was demanded. Connecticut, thought the " progressionists " of that day, was behind the age, and too timid to win laurels in the race of civilization. There was an urgent demand for paper money, and her authorities could find no acceptable way of supplying it. Massachusetts was more inventive—more fruitful of methods—and who could doubt her finan-

---

* Felt's Mass. Currency, p. 85.

cial ability? In 1714, her government, after a severe contest between the advocates of hard money and paper money, and partly for the purpose of heading off a scheme for a private bank of issue, emitted £50,000 in province bills which were to be loaned, on mortgage security, at five per cent. interest, the principal to be paid in five equal annual installments. In 1716, she issued and loaned £100,000, the yearly interest of which was to help support the government. Rhode Island adopted a similar system in 1715. After a bitter controversy, which distracted communities and even divided families, she issued and loaned £40,000. Thus was established the "first bank" of Rhode Island, so called. The "second bank," which was like unto the first, was established in 1721, and the "third bank," of £40,000, in 1728.* Others followed, and the "ninth bank" was born before the race became extinct, their designations reminding us, strangely enough, of certain model institutions of our day, and proving that history but repeats itself.

In May, 1726, the Massachusetts plan found earnest advocates in the General Court of Connecticut, the Lower House favoring and the Upper House opposing it. Two years later, or in May, 1728, a scheme was embraced in the Lower House and a bill passed to emit and loan £50,000 for ten years; but it was rejected by the Council. The friends, however, of a more liberal provision of paper money were not discouraged. They were persons of decayed fortunes and large obligations, who found that the more depreciated the currency, the easier debts were discharged. Men of this class having a personal and selfish object in view, were more persevering than those that opposed them on public grounds.†

In 1730, an association was formed in New London for commercial operations.‡ It embraced many of the leading

---

* Arnold's History of Rhode Island, II., pp. 53, 56, 59, 95.

† "All our paper money making assemblies," writes Dr. William Douglass, of Massachusetts, "have been legislatures of debtors, the representatives of people who for incogitancy, idleness and profuseness have been under the necessity of mortgaging their lands." Summary History of North America, I., 310.

‡ Miss Caulkins' History of New London, second edition, p. 213. I think Miss C. is mistaken when she says that "loans were obtained [by the asso-

men of the Colony, and was able to command a large political influence. Through this influence, it is said, a most extra-ordinary charter was obtained from the General Assembly, in May, 1732. Thomas Seymour, John Curtiss, John Bissel, Solomon Coit, and fifty-seven others were incorporated with the name of the "New London Society united for Trade and Commerce." Soon the society began to issue bills of credit, in the likeness of the colony bills, in imitation of what had been done, in defiance of the General Court, several years before, in Boston.[*] The notes bore the date of October, 25th, 1732,[†] were to run twelve years, and were "put off and sold * * as a medium of trade current, and equal in value to silver at sixteen shillings per ounce," &c. According to Miss Caulkins, they "were hailed by the business part of the community with delight." Some others regarded them with sus-picion, and there was a great commotion in the land. The authorities were alarmed, and Gov. Talcott, appreciating the emergency, convened the Legislature in special session. It met in February, 173⅔, inquired into the circumstances and proceedings of the society, and repealed its charter. At the same time, a law was passed making those who should emit bills of credit, based on any individual or society fund, "sub-ject to the same pains and penalties as those guilty of forging or counterfeiting," &c. This legislation, added to misfortunes in trade, killed off the society. And for the relief of those who had come into possession of its nearly worthless bills, the following action was had. I copy it as a specimen.

"The question was put, whether it be not expedient (*sic stan-tibus circumstantiis*) to emit" £30,000 in bills, "part thereof to be tendered to such persons as this Assembly shall appoint, and shall give security for the drawing in of the bills lately emitted by the New London Society, and the other part of the

---

ciation] from the public Treasury;" for I do not find that the government made any loans except to those who, at the time of its failure, were members of the company, had mortgaged their lands to it, and been made liable for its bills.

[*] Felt's Mass. Currency, p. 71.

[†] So says Miss Caulkins; but there is one of the bills in the possession of the Conn. Hist. Society which has the date of August, 1732.

said sum to be let out for the benefit of the government, all to be on such security, and for such a time or times, and for such interest and with such distinction from other bills in such form as this Assembly shall order and appoint. * * * Resolved in the affirmative."

" Whereas this Assembly hath ordered that £30,000 in bills of credit on this colony shall be emitted, it is now further Resolved, that his Honor the Governor and Nathaniel Stanley, Esq., be desired to procure some meet person to stamp the said bills as soon as may be."*

At the next session of the Assembly, in May, 1733, it was ordered that £15,000 out of the £30,000 should be loaned, £3,000 in each of the five counties, on mortgage security of double value, in sums of not under fifty or over one hundred pounds, payable May first, 1741, or earlier at the pleasure of the borrower, at six per cent. annual interest, bonds to be given for interest, and each town to have of the money in some measure in proportion to its list of polls and estate. At the same session it was enacted that £20,000 in bills should be stamped, " to be done on the new plate, of the tenor of our former bills," the same to be ready by the next session in October.

The legislation is exceedingly brief concerning the last £20,000, and in striking contrast with that which was usual on such occasions. The Assembly does not condescend to give any reason, or announce any purpose or end which is to be subserved. Nor do I find anything to throw light upon the subject on the subsequent pages of the record. From the silence which is observed, it would be natural to infer that the contemplated issue had never been made. Almost as much may be said of the £30,000 authorized in the preceding February. There is an absence of the customary details of legislation, by which the inquirer is much perplexed. And what is particularly worthy of notice, in this connection, is the fact that neither of the laws providing for these large emissions of bills was printed with the other laws in conformity with the uniform practice up to that time. The act ordering the printing of the £30,000

---

was the concluding part of the act repealing the charter of the New London Society; and yet, the first part was printed and the last suppressed. Thenceforward, all the laws ordering paper issues were overlooked when the statutes came to be published.

Several years later, the fact came out, in answer to certain inquiries of the English Board of Trade, that the bills provided for by the acts of Feb., 173$\frac{2}{3}$, and May, 1733, amounting in the whole to £50,000, were, with a trifling exception, all loaned after the manner of the £15,000, either to those bringing in the notes of the New London Society, or to others. On examining the record of deeds of New Haven, I find that £2,250 were loaned, on mortgage, (in one instance five hundred pounds to one individual,) in New Haven, between September seventh, 1733, and May seventh, 1734. It appears from the same record that the notes given for the money were redeemable, some on the first day of May, 1741, others on the first day of May, 1742, and were to be paid, in some cases, in silver at twenty shillings per ounce, or in new bills of public credit; in other cases, in silver at twenty shillings, or gold equivalent, or colony bills, &c.

There are conceivable motives for this blind and summary way of doing up the public business which related to currency matters, and good reasons why the Assembly should not seek unnecessary publicity. They consulted their own convenience, preferred to manage their own affairs, and like others, did not wish to have their favorite plans interfered with. They had an advantage over Massachusetts, New York, and other colonies, in not having, in their government, a representative of the King to report their misdoings. And naturally enough, they were not themselves anxious to declare what would not benefit them if known.

I should not be willing to say that the evil deeds of the New London Society and the condition of its suffering creditors were the mere pretext, and not the true reason for establishing a government land bank, so called. And yet, the occasion seems to have been eagerly embraced, to supply the urgent demand for a "medium of exchange." There was a strong outside pressure upon the Assembly. The people were infatuated, made so by paper money, and thought their temporal salvation depended on their having a more liberal supply of bills of credit. And perhaps the government felt constrained either to issue notes itself, or to consent to its being done by some New London or other irresponsible company.

In October, 1735, the counterfeiters, notwithstanding the severity of the law against them, had been again at work. The bills outstanding of five pounds, two pounds, ten shillings and two shillings had been counterfeited, and the Assembly ordered the emission of £25,000 to be stamped on the new plates, with the date of 1735 "in some proper place," the new impression to be exchanged for the old. A part of these were used as those previously printed for a similar purpose had been. They were found convenient for the ever recurring wants of government.

From October, 1735, to May, 1740, no new issues were authorized. But during this period, opinion seems to have been undergoing a change, running in favor of some new plan to prevent depreciation. In October, 1739, when silver had come to be worth, in currency, twenty-nine shillings per ounce, a bill was introduced into the Assembly ordering a new emission of £10,000. They were to be "legal tenders," as I infer; the form given for the note declaring that it "should pass current in the Colony of Connecticut." The bill passed the Upper House, but the Lower House dissented, perhaps because the sum was too small.

In October, 1739, England declared war against Spain, the assistance of the colonies was demanded, and Connecticut was involved in heavy expenses. In May, 1740, £4,000 in bills were ordered to be struck off, from the new plate, in value from ten shillings to five pounds, and bearing the date of the Assembly then in session. They were to be paid out, in the language of the record, as "premia" for volunteers in the expedition against the Spanish West Indies. In July following, £15,000, in all respects similar, were authorized, £10,000 for general expenses, and £5,000 to be exchanged for the notes issued before 1733, and for torn and defaced bills. At the same time, a tax of £10,500, to call in the £10,000 at the advance, was laid, payable August 31st, 1750, colony bills or current money to be received in payment. These emissions were the last of those called *old tenor*, unless the £3,000 issued in May, 1746, from the *"old* plate," were of this kind. Including the last sum, the whole amount of the old tenor bills was £178,000. A portion of these, however, including considerable sums of exchange bills, were never issued.

I here transfer what purports to be an "account of the several yearly emissions of paper bills, * * * and what has been yearly drawn in again," showing the outstanding balances from year to year. The paper is signed by Gov. Talcott:

To the Right Honble Lords Commissioners for the Board of Trade and Plantations.

May it please your Lordships—In pursuance of your Lordships desire by a letter from Whitehall, dated the 5th of July last past, I herewith send the account of the several yearly emissions of paper bills that has from time to time been paid out by this Colony, and what has been yearly drawn in again, and the sum total in bills of credit that are now outstanding. And as this Colony is a place of but small trade, compared with the Province of the Massachusetts Bay, I must beg leave to refer your lordships to the account you shall receive from that Province for the value of gold and silver yearly as compared with our paper currency, that Province governing in the affair of exchange between us and England, and our paper bills always passing at an equal value with the bills of that Province.

The account is as follows, viz. :

The first emission was in the year 1710* for defraying the charges that had arisen on the expedition to Canada,	£18,941 : 0 : 6		Drawn into the Treasury by a tax on the inhabitants in the Colony, clear of all charges,	£5,202 : 0 : 9
			Remains outstanding,	13,738 : 19 : 9
				18,941 : 0 : 6
What remained outstanding last year,	13,738 : 19 : 9		Drawn in by a tax,	5,298 : 8 : 8
And the Colony emitted, 1711,	10,246 : 9 : 6		Remains outstanding,	18,687 : 0 : 7
	23,985 : 9 : 3			23,985 : 9 : 3
Remained outstanding last year,	18,687 : 0 : 7		Drawn in by a tax,	4,362 : 19 : 3
And the Colony emitted, 1712,	9,312 : 10 : 0		Remains outstanding,	23,636 : 11 : 4
	27,999 : 10 : 7			27,999 : 10 : 7
Remained outstanding last year,	23,636 : 11 : 4		Drawn in by a tax,	3,459 : 0 : 0
Emitted by the Colony, 1713,	4,000 : 0 : 0		Remains outstanding,	24,177 : 11 : 4
	27,636 : 11 : 4			27,636 : 11 : 4

* The first bills were authorized in June, 1709, but were not, it seems, printed and put in circulation till the following year.

Remained outstanding last year,	£24,177 : 11 : 4		Drawn in by a tax.	£2,301 : 18 : 0	
Emitted by the Colony, 1714,	1,000 : — : –		Remains outstanding,	22,875 : 13 : 4	
	25,177 : 11 : 4			25 177 : 11 : 4	
Remained outstanding last year,	22,875 : 13 : 4		Drawn in by a tax,	2.385 : 13 : 4	
Emitted by the Colony, 1715,	2,000 : 0 : 0		Remains outstanding,	22,490 : 0 : 0	
	24,875 : 13 : 4			24,875 13 : 4	
Remained outstanding last year,	22,490 : 0 : 0		Drawn in by a tax,	3,808 : 10 : 1	
Emitted by the Colony, 1716,	5,000 : 0 : 0		Remains outstanding,	23,681 : 9 : 11	
	27,490 : 0 : 0			27,490 : 0 : 0	
Remained outstanding last year,	23,681 : 9 : 11		Drawn in by a tax,	4,027 : 10 : 5	
Emitted by the Colony, 1717,	789 : 7 : 6		Remains outstanding,	20,433 : 7 : 0	
	24,470 : 17 : 5			24,460 : 17 : 5	
Remained outstanding last year,	20,433 : 7 : 0		Drawn in by a tax,	2,853 : 1 : 10	
Emitted by the Colony, 1718,	2,500 : 0 : 0		Remains outstanding,	20,080 : 5 : 2	
	22,933 : 7 : 0			22,933 : 7 : 0	
Remained outstanding last year,	20,080 : 5 : 2		Drawn in by a tax,	2,909 : 10 : 8	
Emitted by the Colony, 1719,	2,651 : 0 : 6		Remains outstanding,	19,821 : 15 : 0	
	22,731 : 5 : 8			22,731 : 5 : 8	
Remained outstanding last year,	19,821 : 15 : 0		Drawn in by a tax,	6,401 : 14 : 1	
Emitted by the Colony, 1720, at two emissions,	4,407 : 18 : 3		Remains outstanding,	17,827 : 19 : 2	
	24,229 : 13 : 3			24,229 : 13 : 3	
Remained outstanding last year,	17,827 : 19 : 2		Drawn in by a tax,	3,183 : 5 : 9	
Emitted by the Colony, 1721,	2,842 : 13 : 4		Remains outstanding,	17,487 : 6 : 9	
	20,670 : 12 : 6			20,670 : 12 : 6	
Remained outstanding last year,	17,487 : 6 : 9		Drawn in by a tax,	3,488 : 11 : 4	
Emitted by the Colony, 1722,	3,500 : 0 : 0		Remains outstanding,	17,498 : 15 : 5	
	20,987 : 6 : 9			20,987 : 6 : 9	
Remained outstanding last year,	17,498 : 15 : 5		Drawn in by a tax,	5,506 : 0 : 7	
Emitted by the Colony, 1723,	4,839 : 3 : 9		Remains outstanding,	16,831 : 18 : 7	
	22,337 : 19 : 2			22,337 : 19 : 2	
Remained outstanding last year,	16,831 : 18 : 7		Drawn in by a tax.	6,168 : 14 : 5	
Emitted by the Colony, 1724,	4,000 : 0 : 0		Remains outstanding,	14,663 : 4 : 2	
	20,831 : 18 : 7			20,831 : 18 : 7	
Remained outstanding last year,	14,663 : 4 : 2		Drawn in by a tax,	4,088 : 18 : 11	
Emitted by the Colony, 1725,	1,624 : 2 : 6		Remains outstanding,	12,198 : 7 : 9	
	16,287 : 6 : 8			16,287 : 6 : 8	
Remained outstanding last year	12,198 : 7 : 9		Drawn in by a tax,	6,299 : 13 : 10	
Emitted by the Colony, 1726,	2,076 : 1 : 1		Remains outstanding,	7,974 : 15 : 10	
	14,274 : 8 : 10			14,274 : 8 : 10	

Remained outstanding last year,	£7,974 : 15 : 0	Drawn in by a tax,	£4,284 : 5 : 5
Emitted by the Colony, 1727,	6,583 : 12 : 1	Remains outstanding,	10,274 : 1 : 8
	14,558 : 7 : 1		14,558 : 7 : 1
Remained outstanding last year,	10,274 : 1 : 8	Drawn in by a tax,	4,559 : 19 : 2
Emitted by the Colony, 1728,	3,505 : 16 : 9	Remains outstanding,	9,219 : 19 : 13
	13,779 : 18 : 5		13,779 : 18 : 5
Remained outstanding last year,	9,219 : 19 : 3	Drawn in by a tax,	4,800 : 0 : 0
Emitted by the Colony, 1729,	2,318 : 3 : 7	Remains outstanding,	6,738 : 2 : 10
	11,538 : 2 : 10		11,538 : 2 : 10
Remained outstanding last year,	6,738 : 2 : 10	Drawn in by a tax,	4,889 : 3 : 3
Emitted by the Colony, 1730,	2,531 : 16 : 8	Remains outstanding,	4,380 : 15 : 10
	9,269 : 19 : 1		9,269 : 19 : 1
Remained outstanding last year,	4,380 : 15 : 10	Drawn in by a tax,	5,021 : 18 : 3
Emitted by the Colony, 1731,	5,307 : 15 : 11	Remains outstanding,	4,666 : 13 : 6
	9,688 : 11 : 9		9,688 : 11 : 9
Remained outstanding last year,	4,666 : 13 : 6	Drawn in by a tax,	5,404 : 6 : 3
Emitted by the Colony, 1732,	3,291 : 8 : 5	Remains outstanding,	2,553 : 15 : 8
	7,958 : 1 : 11		7,958 : 1 : 11
Remained outstanding last year,	2,553 : 15 : 8	Drawn in by a tax,	4,194 : 3 : 6
Emitted by the Colony, 1733,	3,689 : 2 : 3	Remains outstanding,	2,048 : 14 : 5
	6,242 : 17 : 11		6,242 : 17 : 11
Remained outstanding last year,	2,048 : 14 : 5	Drawn in by a tax,	2,715 : 5 : 4
Emitted by the Colony, 1734,	3,150 : 2 : 6	Remains outstanding,	2,483 : 11 : 7
	5,198 : 16 : 11		5,198 : 16 : 11
Remained outstanding last year,	2,483 : 11 : 7	Drawn in by a tax,	2,820 : 15 : 4
Emitted by the Colony, 1735,	3,161 : 5 : 1	Remains outstanding,	2,824 : 1 : 4
	5,644 : 16 : 8		5,644 : 16 : 8
Remained outstanding last year,	2,824 : 1 : 4	Drawn in by a tax,	3,071 : 0 : 11
Emitted by the Colony, 1736,	1,500 : 0 : 0	Remains outstanding,	1,253 : 0 : 5
	4,324 : 1 : 4		4,324 : 1 : 4
Remained outstanding last year,	1,253 : 0 : 5	Drawn in by a tax,	2,959 : 6 : 6
Emitted by the Colony, 1737,	7,445 : 2 : 10	Remains outstanding,	5,738 : 16 : 9
	8,698 : 3 : 3		8,698 : 3 : 3

And by the foregoing account your Lordships may see that there is, to the year 1737, outstanding bills, emitted for defraying the necessary charges of the Colony, but the sum of £5,738 : 16 : 9, and the Colony has granted two taxes, one for 1738, and the other for 1739, not yet brought into the public accounts, which will near or quite sink the whole of the bills now outstanding. But the Colony has further emitted on loan to the inhabitants as follows, viz. :—

4

In the year 1733, loaned out by the Colony, on interest, the sum of £49,975 : 4 : 0.

Drawn in by Interest,	1734,	£	770 : 18 : 11
Do.	more,	1735,	3,666 : 9 : 2
Do.	more,	1736,	3,070 : 10 : 1
Do.	more,	1737,	2,961 : 18 : 11
Do.	more,	1738,	2,903 : 17 : 0
Do.	more,	1739,	3,007 : 0 : 8
			16,389 : 11 : 9
Remains outstanding of the money loaned out.			33,594 : 9 : 3
			£49,975 : 4 : 0

And also the sum of £33,594 : 9 : 3, in loan money, which, added to the foregoing sum of £5,738 : 16 : 9, makes in the whole bills of credit outstanding in this Colony, the sum of £39,333 : 6. This being the exactest account can be made in the affair saving errors, I hope will be agreeable to your Lordships' request, and in conformity to the address of both Houses of Parliament to his Majesty relating thereunto, which is all at present, with my most dutiful respects to your Lordships, and am,

        Your most obedient humble servant to command,

Dated at Hartford, in the Colony of Connecticut,   J. TALCOTT.[*]
in New England, Jan. 12, 17$\frac{39}{40}$.

This is an interesting paper, but nevertheless incomprehensible in several particulars, and not easily reconciled with certain facts. Its careful perusal suggests several observations.

1. The reader is struck with the smallness of the outstanding balances, from year to year, particularly during the latter part of the time previous to 1733. While the currency was steadily depreciating, the bills outstanding are represented to be diminishing, running down from £24,177 : 11 : 4, at the close of 1713, when it took eight shillings and six pence in paper to buy one ounce of silver, to £2,553 : 15 : 8, at the end of 1732, when twenty shillings in bills would purchase the same amount of silver. In the year last named, the notes still outstanding were not half equal to the amount called in by tax during the year. The addition of fifty per centum to the sinking fund tax, for a single year, would have provided means to redeem the whole. What folly to endure the miseries of a depreciated currency, when the remedy was so easy!

2. I can see no propriety in leaving out of the table the £49,975 : 4 in bills " emitted on loan in 1733," these being as truly "outstanding," and doing as much to swell the currency, as the others.

* MSS. in State Library—Finance and Currency, III., 83.

3. It will be observed that the annual payment on account of taxes, and also for interest on the loaned bills, is deducted from the amount of outstanding bills in order to show the balance still in circulation. This is as it should be, provided the receipts were all in Connecticut notes, and these notes were not again put in circulation. But the payments were made in any money which was current in New England, and the colony bills, whether from taxes or loans, were paid out again to a very large extent. Having been deducted as above, and once more put in circulation, they should have been included in the annual emissions. But were they thus included? The answer will appear from what follows: The whole amount of the authorized emissions down to 1737, inclusive, was £156,000. Deducting from this sum the £49,975 : 4 : 0, in bills which were loaned, and there remains £106,024 : 16 : 0, to be accounted for in the table. But the table shows a total of emissions of £119,214 : 12 : 7. This excess of the actual over the authorized issues, amounting to £13,189 : 16 : 7, must be due to reissues. But is it possible the reissues were no greater? They certainly were, judging from the acts of the Assembly. But may not the discrepancy be accounted for by supposing that a portion of the £106,024 : 16 : 0 in bills was never emitted, thus leaving a larger balance for reëmissions?

Dr. Trumbull, a conscientious and industrious historian, whose mistakes must be due to the disadvantages under which he wrote, describes the period between 1713 and 1739, as a time of much prosperity. No general war scourged the land, and the people were contented and happy. There was a considerable increase of population, and trade was enlarged. The colonial finances, the Doctor thinks, were managed with prudence, and the bills of credit suffered " little or no depreciation."[*] In this last particular the facts are not in accordance with the representation. The currency, during the whole of this period, was, in truth, undergoing a rapid and fatal depreciation. Proofs of this could be gathered from the Doctor's own pages. Evidence, too, might be found in the

course which legislation took—in the rising prices of commodities—in the law to circumvent creditors, and prevent
the "rigorous exaction of money," &c.   But there is more
decisive testimony.   The old families of that day took pride
in silver tankards and other descriptions of plate.   When a
wealthy man died, you might expect to find, in the inventory
of his effects a certain number of ounces of silver ware.   This
was valued at so much per ounce in currency.   Instances of
the kind, in sufficient number, may be gathered from the
Probate records of New Haven.   The following facts have
been obtained from that source.   (Uncoined silver was estimated to be worth, in the depreciated coin of that day, at the rate
of eight shillings per ounce, as has already been mentioned.)

1708, September, one ounce of plate was worth 8s. in currency.
1710, May,   "   bullion   "   8s.   "
1721, May,   "   plate   "   12s.   "
1724, July,   ".   silver   "   16s.   "
1729, July,   "   "   "   18s. 2d.   "
1732, May,   "   "   "   18s.   "
1739, June,   "   "   "   26s.   "
1742, December,   "   "   "   26s. 4d.   "
1742, December,   "   "   "   28s.   "
174$\frac{3}{4}$, February,   "   "   "   28s.   "
1744, December,   "   "   "   32s.   "
174$\frac{4}{5}$, January,   "   "   "   32s.   "

These prices of silver, as measured by the paper money of
Connecticut, correspond so closely with the figures in certain
tables in Felt's Massachusetts Currency, and in Belknap's
History of New Hampshire, as to furnish proof, were any
needed, that the depreciation in these several colonies was
the same, and that, practically, one currency was common to
all.   In other words, the bills of each must have circulated
freely in the others, at a common par value; for it is an axiom of
financial science that two or more currencies of different intrinsic or exchangeable values cannot circulate together at the
same nominal value.   The poorer will drive out the better, and
become the sole medium of exchange, and the accepted standard of value.   This principle, as simple and obvious as it is,
is not yet recognized by the popular mind.   People wondered,

twenty months ago, when they saw "gold going up," as the phrase is. They wondered still more, a few months later, when silver change became scarce. When the "nickels"* disappeared, their astonishment was mingled with indignation. It was somebody's fault, and the avaricious Jews were denounced, in the customary style. The issue of a few million of smaller "shin plasters," of the same proportional value as the larger, cured the difficulty, and the poor Jews were again in good standing.

Our own Assembly, as I have already said, authorized the people, for many years, to pay their county rates in good bills of the other colonies. This would not have been done had these bills been worth, in the market, either more or less than the home currency. So soon as the credit of any of these bills got shaky, as compared with the home standard, they were discarded. All met with a common fate at last.

The current coin, as I have already stated, was worth only eight shillings per ounce. It was by this standard that silver bullion was measured, and with which bills of credit were compared. Reckoned by the accepted standard, bills which were at par in 1710, gradually depreciated till 1714, when it took nine shillings in currency to purchase an ounce of silver. Up to this period and after 1703, it is estimated that Massachusetts had emitted £194,000; while up to the same period Connecticut had emitted (not counting issues in way of exchange, or re-issues,) say, £38,000, Rhode Island £13,300. In 1724, Massachusetts had, (see Felt, page eighty,) out of a total issue of £397,006 : 0 : 1, £201,201 : 10 : 10 in circulation; while, in the beginning of the same year, Connecticut had emitted in all, (leaving out bills exchanged and re-issued,) say, £52,929 : 8 : 6, and had

---

* Since the above was written, I have inquired into the intrinsic value of nickel cents. According to the New American Cyclopedia, they are composed of twelve per cent. nickel and eighty-eight per cent. copper. Supposing the former metal to be worth three dollars per pound, and the latter forty cents, (about their present prices,) the nickel cent is worth, for the metals it contains, about six and two-thirds mills, in currency. According to this, those who withdrew them from circulation were mistaken as to their intrinsic value. As I understand it, the mint is still coining them. (This note was written in January, 1864.)

in circulation, according to a report made to the British government, in 1732, £16,831 : 18 : 7.   Comparing the two colonies, the former had twelve times as many outstanding bills of credit as the latter, while its population was about one half greater.   It is true that the Massachusetts people were richer and of a more commercial character than those of Connecticut, and needed more currency on that account.   But making every proper allowance, it may be safely charged that the depreciation of the circulating medium in 1724, when silver was worth sixteen shillings and six pence per ounce, or more than two for one, and for several years afterwards, was chiefly owing to the reckless imprudence of Massachusetts.   Connecticut was traveling the same dangerous road, trotting after the Bay horse in her modest way, but yet having the good sense to keep far in the rear.   Her position was, doubtless, in part, owing to the agricultural pursuits and traditional habits of her people.   They were free from some of the vices of more commercial and "progressive" populations.   "They were," says Dr. Douglass, "a colony of sagacious, laborious husbandmen," governed "by men of wisdom and probity."*   They did not ride fast horses, knew of no royal road to wealth, and till corrupted by paper money, were not given to speculation.

It is easy to understand how the apparent prosperity, of which Dr. Trumbull speaks, might be favored by a depreciating currency.   Whilst this depreciation is going on, there is an unceasing flow of wealth from the pockets of one class of society to those of another—a transfer of values from the creditor to the debtor interest.   This is done by the magic influence of paper money—a kind of money which has no intrinsic worth, and which represents no labor and no certain value.   If a farmer sell his corn, oats and hay for so many pounds in a currency which will exchange for one hundred ounces of silver, or one hundred days labor, and gets his pay when his pounds will purchase but fifty ounces, equivalent to fifty days labor, he is defrauded of half his crop.   All those who take notes, bonds, mortgages and other securities,

---

* Summary, I. 508.   II. 15, 20.

payable at a future day, in money, as well as those who live on fixed salaries and annuities, are defrauded in a similar manner. Thus property passes out of the hands of those who have obtained it by industry and good management, and is delivered over to enrich, without effort or sacrifice on their part, a very different class. Under these circumstances, the more a man owes for value received, the better he is off. If he can borrow to an adequate extent, and his debts become sufficiently large, he may come out a nabob in wealth. And when borrowers and adventurers become opulent, things begin to move. That country is always outwardly prosperous where debtors are living at the expense of their creditors, or where speculators, by means of depreciated and depreciating notes, can control the earnings and products of the industrious classes. But prosperity of this kind is never real, never durable. Connecticut paid dearly for all the thrift she got out of her paper money. The day of reckoning came at last!

It is when a redundant currency is being reduced, and the people are endeavoring to get back upon a specie basis, that manifest a wide spread distress prevails. It is then that the nominal pound or dollar becomes more and more valuable, representing more and more labor. Money appreciates, or, what amounts to the same thing, everything else depreciates. Paper values melt away, property shrinks in proportion to the currency, goods bought at a high figure must be sold at a sacrifice, and the financial world is threatened with shipwreck. Under these circumstances, everybody wants to sell for cash. The sellers rush into market, each trying to escape loss, and each seeming conscious that the devil takes the hindmost. Of course there are no buyers, and prices go down, down. Confidence is destroyed, those who owe money cannot get it, and many men who fancied themselves rich return to nothingness. During all this time, wealth would flow from the debtor to the creditor class, but the numerous failures stop the current, and the latter are rarely gainers. It is in the bankruptcy, repudiation, and general chaos which wind up a financial crisis that we may best read the true nature of paper money inflations.

CHAPTER IV.

NEW TENOR EMISSIONS. GREAT DEPRECIATION.

In May, 1740, it required twenty-eight shillings in paper to buy an ounce of silver, and Connecticut undertook the work of reform. And it is curious that the same expedient was fallen upon that had been repeatedly tried, without success, by Massachusetts.[*] The remedy was sought in the same direction whence the evil had come, to wit: in novel legislation, and new emissions of paper, on the principle "similia similibus curantur." The public mind had been debauched by a depreciated currency, and there was not, at this stage, virtue or firmness enough for any reform which required self-sacrifice. The authorities preferred to go on in their downward career, enacting impotent laws, and fulminating "bulls against the comet." As the result of their deliberations, the Assembly ordered that £30,000 should be emitted, in value from one shilling to three pounds, giving as a reason the charges of the expedition to the West Indies, &c., and the "great scarcity of a medium of exchange, the same bearing a very small proportion to the extent of the demand therefor." The bill was to read as follows:

No.

    This Bill, by a law of the Colony of Connecticut, shall pass current within the same for twenty shillings, in value equal to silver at eight shillings per ounce, Troy weight, sterling alloy, in all payments, and in the Treasury. Hartford, May 8th, 1740.

A.
B. } *Committee.*
C.

    "Said bills [continues the Act] shall pass current in this Colony in all payments and in the Treasury, equal to the value therein expressed, excepting for the discharge of former con-

---

[*] Felt on Massachusetts Currency, p. 64.

tracts by speciality for silver." £8,000 of the sum were to be employed for discharging the public debts, to be paid out as equivalent to silver at eight shillings per ounce. At the same time, a sinking fund tax of £8,400 was laid, payable within five years, in five equal annual installments, the same to be paid in bills of this issue at one shilling in the pound advance, or in silver money at eight shillings the ounce, or in gold equivalent, or in colony bills of other issues at their value in silver at eight shillings. And to make everything fast without the aid of further legislation, the Treasurer was directed to send forth his warrants, at the proper times, for the collection of the tax. The remaining £22,000 were to be loaned to freeholders of the Colony, in sums of not under twenty-five nor over one hundred pounds, on mortgage security of double value, or on bond with two sureties, at three per cent. annual interest, the principal redeemable half in four and half in eight years, to be paid in the bills of this act, " or in good silver at eight shillings per ounce, or gold equivalent, or in any bills of public credit of this or the neighboring governments passing current in this Colony, according to their current value in silver, at the rate aforesaid, at the time of payment, or in good water rotted hemp, or well wrought canvass or duck raised and manufactured according to * * * a law of this colony, * * at the current market price of such hemp, duck or canvass in silver aforesaid."*

Several months later, a letter dated July fifth, 1740, was received by the government from the Lords Commissioners of Trade and Plantations, requiring the amount and tenor of its bills of credit, asking an opinion as to the best mode of sinking them, and censuring the legal tender provision. At a special session of the Assembly in November, an answer was prepared, which is spread upon the record. It is written in a spirit of loyalty and submission, and is an important document, as will be seen by the quotations:

In obedience to your order of the 20th of May last, an account of bills emitted was sent, to which reference is made. * * * * About £3,000 of loaned

---

* See the mortgages on record in New Haven.

bills were drawn in for interest for the year 1740, and the whole of the said loaned bills will be discharged by 1742, and the bills that were outstanding in 1739, are near or quite sunk by the taxes of 1738 and 1739.   *   *   *

Your Lordships will see, by the laws herewith transmitted, the tenor of the several bills of credit issued in this government, and the amount of the old tenor bills, in money of Great Britain, by the account, we conclude you have received from the Massachusetts, to which we humbly refer your Lordships, as in the aforementioned accounts is expressed; and the amount of the new tenor bills is discovered by the form of the bill.

We do further acquaint your Lordships that the emission of £4,000, old tenor, and £8,000 new tenor bills, in May last, and £10,000 bills of the old tenor in July last were all granted in compliance with his Majesty's instructions to this government respecting the expedition to the Spanish West Indies, and for the necessary defence of this government, without which it was impracticable for this government to answer his Majesty's instructions.   And that the £22,000 new tenor bills which were ordered to be loaned to supply our want of a medium of exchange, is ordered to be paid in, the one half in four, and the other in eight years, and that the bills loaned and to be discharged by the year 1742, and the said £22,000 are the only bills ever loaned by this government.

We also signify to your Lordships, that the most easy and effectual manner of sinking and discharging said bills, according to your Lordships' letter, is, in our opinion, to sink and discharge the same in the manner provided in the several acts passed for the emission thereof, to which we refer your Lordships, by which your Lordships will see that the said bills will be gradually drawn in and sunk; which method we think will be least prejudicial to the inhabitants of this government and interruption to the commerce of the Kingdom.

We do also further acquaint your Lordships that the act of May last for the emission of £30,000 bills of a new tenor, which made it obligatory on all persons to take the said bills in payment of debts, dues, &c., was truly made with an honest and real intent to prevent the said bills from depreciating, which we was the rather induced to by the example of our neighboring government of New York, who, we are informed, by such an act, in a great measure have prevented their bills from discounting, and we were not then in the least apprehensive that the inserting such a clause in that act of May last, was any way inconsistent with or contrary to the act of the sixth year of her late Majesty, Queen Anne, entitled *An act for ascertaining the rates of foreign coin in her Majesty's Plantations in America*, having then had no intimations of his Majesty's intentions, nor of the sense of the House of Commons on that occasion; and as soon as possible after the receipt of your Lordship's letters, we have repealed that clause of the act of May last, which made it obligatory on all persons to take said bills in payment as aforesaid, as your Lordships will see by the act of this Court, passed at the present session for repealing the said clause.

And on the whole, we conclude your Lordships will be of opinion that we have not granted large and frequent emissions of paper currency, and if compared with what some other colonies have done, will appear to be a small proportion, and we do assure your Lordships that we shall take effectual care, as much as in us lies, to pay all due regard to his Majesty's intentions, and to the sense of the House of Commons on this occasion.

While the legal tender clause was repealed, the Assembly was seemingly desirous of withdrawing the new bills from circulation. The Treasurer was directed, as he had opportunity, to exchange old tenor bills of this or the neighboring governments for new tenor, giving in the proportion of two and a half for one. This was to be done during the future sessions of the Assembly. But notwithstanding this apparent eagerness to conform to his " Majesty's intentions," those in authority took good care that the intention of the laws enacted to supply "a medium of exchange" should not be frustrated. The business of putting out on mortgage the £22,000 in loan bills went on as before, as the town records of New Haven prove. By October, 1741, when the exchange above referred to was to begin, a large proportion were probably in circulation. The practice of loaning out again any bills received on account of the old mortgages of 1733, was also continued, as I infer from the same record. From these facts we may conclude that the Assembly had no very earnest desire to get in their loaned bills, or to undo anything that had been done. In confirmation of this view, it may be stated that the payment of the mortgage notes due in 1741, 1742 and 1744 seems to have been postponed.* I do not find, on record, any release deeds from the Colony indicating payment, between May, 1741, and May, 1746. In May, 1743, a committee reported to the Assembly that there were due to the Governor and Company, on the first loan, £36,270 : 16 : 8½, in old tenor, and on the last loan, £6,671 : 4 : 8, in new tenor. In June, 1747, a like report stated that the first loan amounted to £55,886 : 10 : 7, old tenor, and the last to £24,687 : 4 : 7½, new tenor. In September, 1752, the first sum had been reduced to £665 : 10 : 6, and the last to £11,120 : 6 : 2½. The loan mortgages had not all been paid up in February, 1757, and the mortgagors were to be sued.

One fact, well understood now, was not recognized as an important theoretical principle, a century and a quarter ago.

---

* It will be remembered that the Assembly, when inquired of by the Lords of Trade as to the best manner of sinking their bills, replied that they would be most easily and effectually discharged " in the manner provided in the several acts passed for the emission thereof."

Our fathers knew, empirically, that large additions to the currency, somehow, produced a diminished value of the units composing it; but they did not perceive distinctly how the facts were connected—how the observed effect was brought about. They did not comprehend the great truth that the whole currency of a country, for the time being, has a determinate and uniform value, and that this value is not changed by increasing or diminishing its volume. Indeed, neither its volume or value will be altered by adding to or taking from it, so long as the currency represents labor, and foreign commerce is permitted. If, when the foreign exchanges rule at par, which is certain evidence that a country has its just proportion of money, and all that it needs for its business, you pour into the channels of circulation any additional quantity of coin, it will not be absorbed or incorporated with the mass, but will flow outward to find a market in other lands. This truth is well illustrated by the gold movement of California. The domestic wants of the State having been once supplied, the whole of its immense product is shipped abroad like an article of merchandise. Nor can the currency be dangerously inflated by anything which represents a nearly uniform amount of labor. You may convert all the agricultural products in the country into a circulating medium, and make them a legal tender at fixed rates, and there will be no expansion and no rise of prices, unless, indeed, these products are overvalued. The moment they should fail to exchange for all they were worth in a labor-currency, they would cease to be used as money, or as a means of paying debts, and be sent to market as commodities. In this way they could not fail to bring a fair equivalent.

But the fact is different when the currency is made of paper. Paper money has no intrinsic value. It costs nothing and represents no labor. Nevertheless, it may be made to take the place of coin, and, if issued with sufficient freedom, it will drive all the specie out of circulation. At the same time, if no more paper pounds or dollars are emitted than are necessary to displace the gold and silver coins of the same denomination; in other words, if there are the same number of pounds or dollars in circulation as before the substitution, the foreign exchanges will not be affected, and the currency will not be depreciated. The paper pounds, though of no intrinsic worth, will have an exchangeable value equal to the coins which have disappeared. This value, however, cannot be aug-mented. But the volume of a paper currency may be in-creased, indefinitely. Any addition made to it, being worth something as money but nothing for exportation and nothing as a commodity, will not be withdrawn. On the contrary, it will combine with it, swelling the mass in proportion to the quantity. You may double a currency of paper, or ten fold it ; but when this is done, the whole will buy no more, and in this sense will be no more valuable than before. If a million pounds in silver or gold be the exact amount which has been displaced by notes, these notes, whatever their number or denominations, will have a current exchangeable value of one million pounds. This is the law. And in this particular, paper money differs wholly from metallic or other money which is the product of labor; inasmuch as the latter has a value distinct from its uses as a currency, and may always be disposed of as commodity without loss. Thus, a circulating medium which represents a nearly uniform amount of labor cannot be dangerously inflated, nor will it turn to ashes in the hands of its possessor.

When the lawgivers of Connecticut emitted, in 1733, £50,000, and in 1740, £49,000, in bills of credit, they in-creased the volume, but not the value or efficiency of the gen-eral currency. They did not even relieve, except for the moment, the pretended "scarcity of money." They aug-mented the number of pounds, but each pound represented a proportionally smaller amount of coin, and would command an equally smaller amount of the comforts and luxuries of life. They altered, arbitrarily and wickedly, the standard of all values, and, in effect, compelled him who had contracted for one currency to take his pay in another. He who had agreed to give four days' labor discharged the debt with two or three. By a process of legislative juggling, property was transferred from the creditor to the debtor interest—wrested from the productive classes and bestowed, by the foulest injustice, on adventurers and speculators. And what the Colonial Assembly did in 1733 and 1740, the United States Congress repeated in 1862, 1863 and 1864.

The expedient which is at this day adopted in every well ordered government to prevent the depreciation of notes allowed to circulate as money, is to make them convertible, at the will of the holder, into coin. So long as this convertibility is preserved they cannot, theoretically speaking, be issued in excess. The moment the currency becomes redundant, and the notes suffer the slightest depreciation, they return to their issuers to be redeemed in specie, and thus the volume of paper is reduced. But in practice, this system does not prevent important and even disastrous fluctuations; and the problem still is, How may we get the benefits without the evils of a paper circulation?

The threatening attitude of the royal government in 1740, appears to have checked the emissions of paper money for four years. In the meantime, the Assembly felt constrained to do something to better the currency. They saw that all attempts to prevent depreciation had hitherto failed, but were not yet prepared to withdraw their bills from circulation. They consulted the Solons and Lycurguses of Massachusetts, and once more put the colony nag upon the trotting course. Having (they say) been enjoined and commanded by the Lords Justices of the Regency, August 21, 1740, to take effectual care that the act of Queen Anne's reign should be "punctually and *bona fide* observed, and put in execution," in compliance with which act the same was published with the laws of 1740, the "currencies notwithstanding continuing very unstable," they therefore resolved [May, 1742,] that coined silver, sterling alloy, shall pass at six shillings and eight pence per ounce in all business, trade, &c., and shall be lawful money—that after the first of January then ensuing, all bargains, contracts, &c., shall be deemed and taken (unless otherwise expressed,) to be made in money at the value aforesaid—that the courts shall give judgment in lawful money as defined by this act,—and that bills issued or to be issued, shall be regulated by the same standard according. to their current value, this to be declared from time to time by the Assembly.

This law, gotten up in imitation of one passed by Massachusetts, in 1741,[*] seems to have restored, in a modified form, the tender provision, making notes[†] good money at their true value, coin being the standard. Nor did it answer any desired purpose. For this reason, and for others which are referred to as "adverse constructions," and "great inconveniences," the act was repealed in May, 1744. The truth is, probably, it was found to be oppressive to debtors. It not only compelled them to pay in a metallic currency or its equivalent, instead of bills, but it practically raised the standard of silver money. According to the law, an ounce of metal was to be equal to six shillings and eight pence, instead of eight shillings, the old current rate. The measure must have been unpopular—an affliction to the numerous debtor class, and to all those whose thrift was dependent on a depreciated currency.

The war with Spain continued. Early in 1744, France joined in the contest against England, her "natural enemy," and America became the theater of important transactions. New England (Gov. Shirley taking the lead) projected a secret expedition against Louisburg (Cape Breton,) the strongest fortress in America. By a fortunate combination of accidents, it succeeded. The colonies were put to great expense, and in the dilapidated condition of their finances, they had no resort but to paper money. Connecticut emitted, in May, 1744, £4,000 ; in October of the same year, £15,000 ; in March, 1744½, £20,000 ; in July, 1745, £20,000, and in May, 1746, £20,000, all new tenor, the bills ranging from one shilling to three pounds, each emission bearing the date of the Assembly authorizing it, and each secured by a sinking fund tax, payable in from seven to fourteen years, in new tenor bills, at the advance, or in something equivalent.

---

* Hutchinson, I., 361. By the Massachusetts law, the oldest counselors, one from a county, met once a year to ascertain the depreciation of the bills.

† I have occasionally termed bills of credit *notes* of circulation, or notes, in accordance with present custom. This is not in conformity with the practice of our fathers. Till after the Revolution, promises to pay, intended for money, were always called bills of credit. Other promissory engagements were named notes.

At the same date as the last emission, (May, 1746,) £3,000 were ordered to be struck off, in small bills, from two to five shillings, with " the date of this Assembly," from the *old* plate, a tax being laid as before. (I suppose these were old tenor bills.) After this the government printing press was allowed an interval of rest, no other issues being authorized for eight years.

It was expected that these large emissions of colony bills would be tolerated by the British government, in consequence of the greatness of the emergency. And as Louisburg was taken, its capture being the most important success of the war, it was not doubted that Parliament would refund the expense of the expedition, and thus render it unnecessary to collect the heavy taxes which had been levied.

In May, 1747, the Assembly, getting a glimpse of the gulf which was before them, and conceiving that the bills of the neighboring governments, which circulated " promiscuously " with theirs, had the effect to depreciate the colony notes, enacted that thenceforth the bills of this colony only, or gold or silver, should be received for court or jury fees, imposts, duties, excise, &c., into the Treasury. At the same time, all bonds, notes, &c., made payable after the ensuing first day of October, in bills of the adjoining governments, or of New York, were made void. But this last clause in the act was soon repealed.

The war closed in April, 1748; but the enormous issues of paper money growing out of the contest, gave a fatal blow to the currency. Rhode Island is reported to have had in circulation in the beginning of 1744, £440,000.* Massachusetts, says Gov. Hutchinson, emitted during the last years of the war, between two and three million pounds. Connecticut issued in the same period, £82,000, and during the war, £131,000. In the latter sum are included all the new tenor issues, amounting to £109,000.

---

* Felt, p. 115. I think the sum named must be an exaggeration. The Merchants' Magazine, Vol. XX., p. 90, quoting from Sparks, says that Rhode Island had emitted in 1749, not less than £335,300, of which £135,00 were still outstanding, in one form or another. The last sums are probably too small; that relating to emissions certainly is. I have not seen Potter's pamphlet on the currency of Rhode Island.

These last emissions broke the camel's back. The credit of the colonial governments was utterly prostrated. An ounce of silver which, in 1739, could be bought for twenty-eight shillings in paper, and in 1744, thirty-two shillings, cost, in 1749, fifty-five or sixty shillings. Trade was embarrassed, and the utmost confusion prevailed. No safe estimate could be made as to the future, and credit was almost at an end. No man could safely enter into a contract which was to be discharged in money at a subsequent date. Prudence and sagacity in the management of business were without their customary reward. All values, as measured by paper money, were uncertain. The public mind was demoralized, so to say; public and private justice was forgotten. Doubt and suspicion took the place of confidence, and men were afraid to trust one another. If a man had goods to sell, he asked an extra price to cover the risks of the currency. At the same time, bills of credit circulated briskly, giving support to an active cash trade. Those having them, fearing their fingers would be burned, got rid of them speedily.* Desiring more substantial property, they would offer increasing prices till somebody would take them. This impatience of holding always gives poor money a lively circulation; and the poorer it is, so long as it will pass, the quicker it moves.

The new issues, called new tenor, instead of benefiting the currency and preventing depreciation, had a disastrous effect. They damaged the old emissions, produced new complications, introduced more confusion, and sunk rapidly in value. A break-down, through their agency, became necessary. In the expectation, however, that they would fare better in the general wreck, they did not sink so low as the old emissions. They came finally to be worth in the proportion of one to three and a half, one shilling new tenor being equal to three shillings and six pence old tenor. They were never used as the ordinary medium of exchange. Accounts were kept, and payments made, as previously, in old tenor. If new tenor bills

* Hutchinson, II., 391.

5

were employed, in a business transaction, these were converted, by multiplication, into old tenor.

CHAPTER V.

DOWNFALL OF PAPER MONEY. THE SPECIE STANDARD RE-SUMED.

AFTER the war, a plan was proposed by Thomas Hutchinson
of Massachusetts, then Speaker of the House, and an influential member of the hard money party, for redeeming the bills
of that Province. After much opposition, and a final hair-
breadth escape in the House, it was adopted by the Assembly,
and approved by the Governor. The law was passed in January, 1748, and required that the money expected from England to reimburse the Colony for the expenses incurred in the
capture of Louisburg, &c., should be appropriated to such redemption. In September, 1749, the money arrived, consisting
of "653,000 ounces of silver and ten tons of copper," equal,
(says Drake, in his History and Antiquities of Boston, page
622,) to £183,649 : 2 : 7½. According to Felt, the commissioners, in closing their labors, in June, 1751, reported that they had
redeemed, in all, £1,792,236 : 5 : 6—£50,705 : 6 : 8, old tenor bills,
£38,431 : 7 : 0, middle tenor, and £1,703,099 : 11 : 5, new tenor
—" at the rate of about one in specie to ten in paper,"[*] or in
New England money, one to seven and a half. In other
words, one ounce of silver was given for fifty shillings in bills,
or a Spanish dollar for forty-five shillings. Two years later,

---

[*] Felt's Mass. Currency, p. 124. All the above sums seem to be stated in old
tenor, one shilling of the new, or middle tenor, being reckoned as equal to four
shillings, old tenor.

£131,996:3:9, in old tenor, were still in the hands of the people.

And now Connecticut, unwilling to be left behind, began to think of another equestrian performance. She was also desirous of averting threatened and hostile legislation in the British Parliament. In May, 1749, the Assembly passed a law of the following purport:—All allowances of sterling money by the Parliament towards reimbursing the expenses of this Colony in the late expedition to Cape Breton, and such as may be made for expenses in the late intended expedition against Canada, are hereby fully appropriated to the calling in, exchanging, sinking and discharging the now outstanding bills of credit made and issued by the Colony, the bills received to be burned to ashes. One half of the bills of exchange drawn for said allowances was to be sold for bills of public credit, the other half for silver coin. " When the coined silver procured for the sales of said bills of exchange shall be fully paid and lodged in the hands of the Treasurer, he is hereby directed to pay the same out in exchange for the bills of credit, at the same rate that the said silver money is received and accounted for in the sale of said bills of exchange, and such bills of credit brought in and redeemed by such exchange " are to be burned to ashes. To provide for the remainder of the bills, three three penny taxes were levied, payable on the first day of May in the years 1751, 1752, and 1753. The taxes were to be paid in old or new tenor bills—three and six pence of the former being reckoned as equal to one shilling of the latter—or in Spanish milled dollars, or pieces-of-eight, at thirteen shillings and nine pence each, new tenor. Out of the proceeds of each of said taxes, £9,000, new tenor, were to be burned. At the same session, the Governor was requested to write to Eliakim Potter, agent of the Colony at the Court of Great Britain, to inform him of the act which had been passed, and to say that the colonial government had never made large emissions of bills of credit till lately, when it had been done solely on account of his Majesty's service—that the money allowed by Parliament had been fully appropriated for the purpose of calling in said bills, and that this money, together with the taxes which had been levied, would sink all the outstanding bills. And the Governor was to signify to Mr. Potter a grateful sense of his services in his vigorous opposition to the bill " before Parliament relating to paper currencies, which seems to have a threatening aspect on our liberty and privileges granted by charter, especially as it would invest the Governor of the Colony with a power to negative all acts passed by our Assembly "—and at the same time, to desire him to continue to oppose the act, and " endeavor a speedy payment of the money granted to us for the expenses of the late expedition to Cape Breton," &c.

In May, 1750, the Assembly ordered that the bills of exchange on England should not be sold to or drawn in favor of any person not now a settled inhabitant of the Colony, and as a sop to the English merchants, it was further ordered that the purchaser of the bills should buy with them merchandise in Europe. At the same time, the committee in charge of this business was to sell £10,000 in said bills, the buyer to give bonds to pay for the same, one-half in coined silver, at the rate of five shillings and four pence per ounce, or its equivalent in gold, and the other half in outstanding bills, on or before May, 1754, with three per cent. annual interest payable in coin. Thus the time for redeeming the last of the bills was put off for no good reason that is apparent. Doubtless, the government was willing to delay the business as long as possible. Perhaps the intention was to defer it till certain taxes, originally levied for sinking the bills, became due. Beyond this period, the time could not, with any decency, be extended. Thus the costly benefits of a wretched paper money system were continued, and the evils apprehended from a change postponed. The public mind was infatuated, and could not view with composure the contemplated reforms.

As introductory to the proposed change in the currency, the Assembly enacted, in October, 1750, that all fines, fees, penalties, duties, forfeitures, fares, &c., mentioned in any act, should be payable in proclamation money. At the same time, said fines, &c., might be discharged by an equivalent in colony bills, or in bills at their current value, as measured by coin.

As I understand it, £800,000 were appropriated by Parliament, in 1747, to reimburse the colonies for their expenses in the Louisburg expedition.* Of this sum, Connecticut received (according to a note which will be found in Drake's History and Antiquities of Boston, page 622) £28,863 : 19 : 1, supposed to be sterling money. I have not been able to make out this fact from our own records in the state offices in Hartford. Of this amount, £10,000 appear to have been drawn for before the middle of the year 1750, and the draft sold on a three years credit. Bills of exchange for the remainder were afterwards disposed of, and "gold, silver, and bills of this colony" received in payment. It was calculated that on "the first day of the session of the Assembly in May, 1754," the coin produced by these sterling bills would be all paid into the Treasury. The records and papers which have come within my reach do not place the matters under consideration in a very clear light. With regard to the financial affairs of the Colony there is an absence of clear and full statement, which is much to be regretted. Where the data are insecure, I have been cautious in drawing inferences.

The following report of a committee made to the Assembly in October, 1751, will show the amount of outstanding bills, and the condition of the Treasury, at the date mentioned:

"Outstanding bills, in old tenor,...........................£340,218 : 18 : 7
Silver in Treasurer's hands at eight shillings (per oz.,) and gold
    at £5 : 17 : 6,.. 1756 : 19 : 3
Bonds due to the Governor & Co., in old tenor,............... 8,086 : 14 : 4
Bonds due the Governor & Co., in old tenor, or bills of the neigh-
    boring governments,.. 5,856 : 7 : 9
Bonds due in silver, at eight shillings for interest,.............. 1,189 : 7 : 9
    September 6th, 1751."†

In the above report, it will be observed, no new tenor bills are mentioned, these being, doubtless, converted, as was the custom, into old tenor, and thus expressed. The statement relative to the condition of the government, proved that the taxes levied in May, 1749, together with the moneys granted by Par-

---

* See Arnold's Rhode Island, Vol. II., p. 170. He refers for his authority to the "Trumbull Papers," Vol. I., p. 30.

† Finance and Currency, Vol. III., MSS.

liament, were more than sufficient to redeem the notes still in
circulation.   The Assembly therefore ordered that two-thirds
should be abated of the three-penny tax made payable in October, 1751.   The same proportion was afterwards abated of that
payable in October, 1752.

In 1751, the long delayed and much dreaded legislation on
bills of credit, spite the " vigorous opposition " of Mr. Eliakim
Potter, was consummated in the English Parliament.   The law
passed applied to his " Majesty's colonies or plantations of
Rhode Island and Providence Plantations, Connecticut, Massachusetts Bay, and New Hampshire," and declared that after
the twenty-ninth day of September, 1751, it should not be lawful for the governors, lieutenant-governors, &c., of these several
colonies to make or pass, or give assent to the making or passing, any act whereby bills of credit should be created or issued
under any pretense, or whereby said bills should be reissued, or
the time set for their redemption extended—every such act to
be void.   All outstanding bills were to be called in within
the periods named by the acts emitting them, unless said
acts had been altered, &c. ; and in case any borrower of loaned bills should fail, a tax was to be levied for the deficiency.
Acts creating bills for the expenses of the current year, not
to run over two years, were excepted from the operation of this
law.   The law was not to extend to paper bills emitted in extraordinary emergencies, as in the case of invasion, a fund having been established for sinking the same within five years.
Said allowed bills were in no case to be legal tender.   And
should any governor, &c., assent to a law in violation of this
act, he was to be dismissed from office, said assent to be void.*

This legislation, considering the insufficiency of milder measures, was no more stringent than should have been expected,
and no more so, probably, than was necessary to secure the
end.   By acting more directly upon the governors, it seems
designed to save, as much as possible, the pride of the colonists.
So far as Connecticut was concerned, however, the penalty of
removal from office did not apply.   Her governors had no neg-

---

* Statutes at Large, XXIV., Geo. II., Cap. 53.

ative in legislative proceedings, nor was the power conferred till given by the Constitution of 1818.

In May, 1752, the currency had become an intolerable nuisance, and there are signs that many of the people were getting impatient of government delay. The course which Rhode Island pursued was bitterly denounced. While Connecticut was endeavoring to draw in her bills, her enterprising neighbor was making new and large emissions to fill the void. John Ledyard and twenty-five others, merchants and traders of Hartford County, petitioned the Legislature for relief. They uttered words of wisdom and truth, not often heard at that day, when they said:—" As the medium of trade is that whereby our dealings are valued and weighed, we cannot but think it ought to be esteemed of as sacred a nature as any weights and measures whatsoever, and in order to maintain justice must be kept as stable; for as a false weight and a false balance is an abomination to the Lord, we apprehend a false and unstable medium is equally so, as it occasions as much iniquity, and is at least as injurious." They, at the same time, complained of the Rhode Island bills, and prayed " that the medium of trade may be rendered stable for time to come, and that the just value of our now outstanding debts may be secured to us." Chauncey and Elisha Whittlesey and twenty-seven others of New Haven County, also sent in a memorial. They represented themselves as sufferers from a depreciated currency, feared that the trade of the Colony would be ruined, and prayed that the bills of Rhode Island might no longer be tolerated.

The Assembly agreed to support the memorialists, and an act was passed (in May, 1752) putting the notes of Rhode Island under the ban of the government. It applied to those emitted after the twenty-fifth day of December, 1750. These were declared not current, and debts, contracts, &c., could not be discharged with them, except by previous agreement when payment was made within the time specified.

The colony bills brought in by taxes, &c., appear to have been paid out again to meet the wants of the government till May, 1753, when the Assembly directed the Treasurer to do so no longer, " on any occasion;" but, instead, to defray the public charges by the payment of " £1,500, lawful silver money, bought in for the interest on the last emission of loan, and no more." This was an important step in the right direction, and looks as if reform was at least desired.

In September, 1752, as appears from the Treasurer's book, £63,233 : 9 : 1, (reckoned in old tenor and including a small sum in counterfeits,) in bills which had been received from numerous individuals in payment or part payment of bills of exchange sold, were " consumed to ashes."

Connecticut's delay in redeeming her bills of credit, proved to be a source of great embarrassment. Before her arrangements were completed, she and her sister colonies were involved in another war, fierce and destructive, with France. Active hostilities commenced in the beginning of 1755, though no declaration of war was made till May, 1756. In March, 1755, the Assembly met (for the second time in that year) to act upon certain proposals of Governor Shirley touching the war. Extraordinary zeal was manifested, and a vote passed to raise one thousand men. But there was the greatest difficulty in providing for the extraordinary expenses of the government, and a scheme was devised to liberate the coin then in the Treasury which had been appropriated for the redemption of the outstanding bills of credit. Five thousand pounds in gold and silver were to be paid out, while certificates, or interest bearing Treasury notes, were to be issued to the public creditors, according to the following regulations :

Possessors of bills of credit of this Colony, who bring them to a committee appointed by the Assembly, to have for them orders on the Treasury for silver or gold, payable in 1756, 1757 and 1758, one-third in each year, with lawful interest—the form of the orders to be [as follows:]

To the Treasurer of the Colony of Connecticut for the time being—

Pay unto   or his order   ounces   pennyweights and grains of coined silver, Troy weight, sterling alloy, or gold equivalent, on or before the first day of May,   , with the lawful interest from the date hereof until paid.

By order of the Assembly at Hartford, March thirteenth, 1755. Dated the day of   , A. D.

$\left.\begin{array}{c} \\ \\ \end{array}\right\}$ *Committee.*

—The bills so brought in to be burnt. The value of the outstanding bills is to be computed for every fifty-eight shillings and eight pence, old tenor, one ounce of coined silver, and for every forty-two pounds of old tenor, one ounce of coined gold, the new tenor to be computed at the rate of one shilling for three and sixpence of the old tenor. For provision of payment, a tax is laid of four pence on the pound to be paid by the last of December next, in lawful silver money, or in gold at the rate mentioned, or the bills of credit issued in January last, or that may be now emitted by this act,* or in the now outstanding bills of credit of this Colony either of the new tenor at fourteen shillings and seven pence, or in the old tenor at fifty-one shillings, for six shillings [a Spanish dollar] lawful money, or in any of the orders drawn on the Treasurer by the committee appointed to receive the now outstanding bills of credit, or in pork at fifty-one shillings per barrel, beef at thirty shillings per barrel, wheat at three and six pence per bushel, rye at two shillings per bushel, Indian corn at one shilling and nine pence per bushel, flax at four pence per pound, [deducting the expense of carrying] to the nearest place of transportation. [Other like taxes were laid, payable in December, 1756, and December, 1757.]†

The outstanding notes, whose payment was postponed by this act, are understood to have been the last of the old issues. As they were equal to £5,000 in coin, they must have amounted to £44,000, old tenor. I am unable to say with certainty that those previously redeemed were discharged at the same rate as that fixed for the bills which remained. There was an obvious propriety in having an uniform rate ; but a government, in breaking faith with its creditors, is not necessarily governed by the rules of propriety or consistency.

Though accounts at this time, as a general rule, were still kept in old tenor currency, there was a frequent reference to proclamation money as the fixed standard of values. As compared with silver, bills were fluctuating and uncertain. They not only differed at different times, but varied as the place varied, at the same time. By frequently making these comparisons, the people came to understand that it was paper that rose and fell, or fell to rise no more, while specie was stable. The changes were so frequent and sudden, that ecclesiastical societies which had voted their ministers yearly salaries, in current money, sometimes appointed a committee to alter the sums as

---

* These were new issues of notes bearing interest and payable in coin, which will be referred to by and by.

† MSS. Colony Record, Vol. VIII., 265.

the currency altered, and thus secure an uniform compensation.*

In the beginning of 1755, or a little earlier, accounts began to be kept in "lawful money." When an inventory was put upon the probate record, there was usually some remark to show in what currency the items were valued. If it was taken in old tenor, a note like the following was added—" N. B. proc. money is one equal to eleven;" that is, eleven shillings in old tenor bills were worth one shilling in silver, which is at the rate of eighty-eight shillings per ounce. The breaking out of the war with France, and the probable postponement of the day of redemption, doubtless caused this great additional depreciation of bills.† One year later, or early in 1756, "lawful money," or "proc. money," began to make its appearance in the account books of private individuals. Wheat was charged at three shillings and nine pence, or four shillings a bushel, which just before had been set down at forty-five or forty-eight shillings. In October of this year, a resolution of the Assembly informs us that the bills of credit had been reduced to a "small remainder," and that provision had been made "that after the first day of November, 1756, all accounts in this government [would] be kept in lawful money." The Governor (Fitch) was desired to advise the governors of New

---

* History of Waterbury, p. 284.

† The following table, taken from Felt's volume, shows the depreciation of the currency from 1710 to 1752, in Massachusetts. It answers equally well for Connecticut, and the other New England colonies. The amount in bills required to purchase an ounce of silver, was in

Year	Value		Year	Value		Year	Value
1710, 1711,	8s.		1724, 1725, 1726, 1727,	17s.		1738, 1739, 1740, 1741,	28s. to 29s.
1712, 1713,	8s. 6d.		1728,	16s. 6d. to 18s.		1742, 1743, 1744,	28s.
1714, 1715,	9s.		1729,	19s. to 22s.		1745,	35s. to 37s.
1716, 1717,	10s.		1730,	21s. to 19s.		1746, 1747, 1748,	37s. to 40s.
1718,	11s.		1731,	18s. 6d. to 19s.		1749, 1750, 1751, 1752,	60s.
1719, 1720,	12s.		1732,	19s. 6d. to 20s. 6d.			
1721,	13s.		1733,	21s. to 23s.			
1722,	14s.		1734,	24s. to 27s.			
1723,	15s.		1735,	27s. 6d.			
			1736,	37s. to 26s. 6d			
			1737,	26s. 6d. to 27s.			

Hampshire and Rhode Island of these facts, and to inform them that there were in the hands of the inhabitants of this Colony considerable sums of the bills of their respective colonies for which it was hoped "a just and equitable provision" would be made, notwithstanding "the fixed periods for the payments of said bills are supposed to be past." Thus "disputes and difficulties betwixt the governments would be prevented," and "the affection and good harmony now subsisting" perpetuated, &c.*

Connecticut, then, in redeeming her bills of credit, gave one ounce of silver for fifty-eight shillings and eight pence in paper, or at the rate of one shilling for eight shillings and ten pence. In other words, she paid about one-ninth, and repudiated the remainder, thus falling considerably below the standard of her oracle and pattern, Massachusetts. Her design seems to have been to redeem her bills at the market price. She measured her duty by her credit, her obligations by her own poor performances. There was no well meant endeavor to keep faith with the public creditors; no attempt, at any period, to improve the value of paper money by withdrawing a part from circulation. So far as it was a simple question of resources, the Colony might, by a system of taxation, have called in her bills, and thus have restored the currency and discharged the whole debt. In this way, the accepted medium of exchange would not (till wholly withdrawn) have been altered, but only its credit reëstablished. The amount of the outstanding bills in October, 1751, reckoned in old tenor, was £340,218 : 18 : 7. By far the greater part of this sum was in new tenor bills, but the exact proportion I have been unable to ascertain. Taking the report of the Committee, in 1739, and the subsequent issues, in old tenor, as the ground for an estimate, there were not, probably, more than £30,000† of this

---

* Colony Records, Vol. VII., 322. MSS.

† Of the large amount of loan bills of 173⅗ and 1733, equaling £50,000, there appear to have been outstanding, in 1752, but £665 : 10 : 6, (see ante, p. 52.) Out of so much of the last amount as had been ordered to the end of 1739, including the £25,000 of 1735, and including all emissions before 173⅗, there remained in circulation, at the first named date, (end of 1739,) only £5,738 : 16 : 9, (see ante.

description, in circulation, in 1751. But suppose there were £40,000, in old notes, there would then remain £300,219. To show the amount of bills which this remainder represented, it must be reduced to new tenor, or, in other words, divided by three and a half. We thus get £85,777. This sum, representing the new tenor bills, added to £40,000 old tenor, makes £125,777, as the total of outstanding bills. The annual tax required to redeem this sum by successive installments, paid in depreciated currency, would at first bear very lightly. Estimated in lawful money, it probably would not have been on an average, from first to last, more than equal to half the sum nominally paid. The whole required amount might have been, say, £62,888. The grand list of the Colony, in 1753, (including the "additions," £15,969, and excluding the "fourfold assessments," £10,300,) was about £1,231,613,* property being valued at an arbitrary rate which had been nearly uniform for more than fifty years, and which was fixed when silver was the measure of value.† Taxes, therefore, amount-

---

p. 49.) A portion of the bills once withdrawn, may have been again paid out after 1739; but it will be fair to conclude that, of all the old tenor emissions, there were not more than £30,000 fit for currency in 1751.

* The population of Connecticut, in 1753, may be estimated, in round numbers, at 130,000.

In answer to inquiries by the Board of Trade, a committee stated, in May, 1749, that the population of the Colony was about 70,000, exclusive of 1,000 Blacks and 500 Indians, in all 71,500. This estimate must have been very much below the truth, as it was probably designed to be. The same committee reported that the number of inhabitants had greatly increased in ten years; that there were about 10,000 militia from sixteen to sixty years of age, divided into ten regiments; that the Indians were given to idleness and drink; that the people were generally employed in clearing and tilling, though there were some tradesmen, tanners, shoemakers, tailors, joiners, smiths, carpenters. The trade of the Colony was not large. Horses, lumber, and some provisions were sent to the West Indies and exchanged for sugar, molasses, rum, salt, and bills of exchange. Surplus provisions were usually sent to Boston, New York and Rhode Island, where European goods were purchased. There was no foreign trade, though, before the war, some vessels had visited the Mediterranean. The revenue of the government amounted to about £9,000, in bills of credit, of which sum £2,000 were for the support of schools. See MSS. entitled Trade and Maritime Affairs, For. Correspondence, Vol. I., Doc. 165.

† By the code of 1750, the polls of persons "from sixteen years old to seventy," with certain exceptions, went into the list at eighteen pounds; an ox, at

ing in the whole to about five and one-tenth per cent. (reckoned in silver) would have sunk the last of the outstanding bills of credit, and thus have saved (in the mercantile sense) the honor of the government. But if we deduct the money which was received from England, and which was used as a redemption fund, amounting to £28,863 : 19 : 1, sterling, or £38,485 : 5 : 3⅓, New England currency, taxes equal to less than two per cent. would have been sufficient. But there were objections to this course—obstacles in the way of redeeming the colony bills so long as they were the recognized currency of the people. The government doubtless did not know the extent of the difficulty; but they had a correct appreciation of the practical consequences of the several possible methods of proceeding. The debtor class, which had of late governed legislation, could distinguish right from wrong when it came their turn to suffer. For once, they had sound argument on their side, and reasons which might well prove decisive.

In the first place, those of the creditor class who had been wronged by the progressive depreciation of bills, their substance having been transferred by installments and without consideration to the debtor class, would not, as a general rule, have been made whole by a reversal of the process, and a restoration of bills to their original credit and value. A very large proportion of those who had suffered were dead. Of the living, very many must have been so effectually stripped that their interests no longer lay with the creditor class. Indeed, numbers had doubtless been driven over to the debtor ranks, and were ready to be again robbed when a contraction of the currency should take place.

When money is appreciating they that suffer are the debtors. They are wronged in the same way that creditors are when the currency is depreciating. They are obliged to pay in a medi-

four pounds; a cow, three pounds; a horse or mare, three pounds; house lots of three acres, twenty shillings per acre; upland pasture, eight shillings per acre; meadow lands in Hartford county, fifteen shillings per acre; do. in the other four counties, seven shillings and six pence per acre; boggy meadows, five shillings per acre, &c. It was estimated by a committee, in 1764, that a tax of one penny on the pound would raise about five thousand pounds.

um which is becoming daily more valuable; when the yard-
stick which measures their goods is growing longer and longer.
Borrowing when paper is worth twenty or forty cents on a
dollar, they must satisfy the debt when it is equal to sixty or
a hundred.   In other words, a contract which, when made,
could be discharged for three or six days' work, must be met
by the labor of eight or twelve days.   Thus men are condemned
to toil without reward.   Thus values are transferred, and the
debtor class is cruelly wronged.   In the mean time, creditors
reap a golden harvest ; their gains, so long as they get their
pay, equaling the losses of the other party.   They not only receive what they loaned, what they contracted for, or what in
justice belongs to them, but they obtain an additional sum,
perhaps twice or thrice as much, in a better currency.   He
who parted with two days' labor gets, in return, three or five,
and interest.   Thus is treasure heaped up at the expense of
debtors.   Thus men became rich without toil or sacrifice of
any kind.   But their gains have a limit.   Debtors are crippled
and finally ruined by a restricted money market.   One after
another goes to the wall, till wide spread bankruptcy prevails.
Then gains are made by nobody.

Practically, a greatly depreciated currency can never be restored.   And the difficulty, in common cases, does not arise
from the magnitude of the debt, but from the ruin wrought by
a prolonged and increasing money pressure.   Nothing so effectually kills off business and cripples industry as a contracted and
still contracting currency.   The more active and enterprising
of the people, those who conduct the exchanges of a country,
and are usually more or less in debt, give up in despair.   Prices
go down, the bottom falls out, and panic ensues.   The loss of
confidence and the apprehension of disaster make matters
worse.   Though the contraction proceed after an uniform rule,
the effect will be irregular and spasmodic.   No government is
wise enough to manage a currency which is being forcibly and
very largely reduced.   Nor is it strong enough to control the discontents and revolutionary outbreaks which must surely arise.
This is especially so, when it is seen to be itself the cause of all
the mischief, remotely in its reckless issues, and immediately

in its ruthless measures of contraction. Those who are injured by a pinched money market, and a continued appreciation of the currency, including the whole debtor class, are always a large majority of the people. If they cannot coerce their rulers by their votes, they will find some other way of controlling them.

A large currency debt is the most unmanageable and inconvenient form of indebtedness which can afflict a country. It cannot be increased or diminished without robbing a very large class of the people. It cannot be withdrawn, with the intention of restoring its value, without bringing on a tetanic spasm, and destroying the very sources of wealth. And the danger to the public interests is greatly increased if the government happens to owe a large interest-bearing debt—a debt which was possibly contracted at the highest point of inflation, and at enormous sacrifice. Let the policy of restriction prevail, and the yearly interest will become more and more burdensome. Let what will come, this must or should be paid, in good solid money, now more valuable than ever; and at a time, too, when incomes have nearly disappeared, and when two or four days' work, two or four bushels of corn, are required to pay for one. Heavy taxes, at such times, to apply, perhaps, on the "dead horse" account, and coming as they do out of capital, not profits, are borne with impatience; and if any relief, within easy reach, is to be had, the tax paying debtors, should they happen to be voters, will discover it.

Governments are apt in finding out costly ways of raising money; but they did not discover the most expensive one till paper money was invented. And a more dishonest and dishonorable method it is difficult to conceive. The wealth of a country is made the sport of those in authority. Fortunes are transferred by bits of pictured paper. Thousands are made rich, and as many impoverished, and a nation is ruined by a few revolutions of the printing press. The people are swindled by a false measure of value as truly as they would be by deceptive weights or india-rubber yard sticks. Rulers may talk in *ad captandum* style about the interest which is saved by notes of circulation; but they know little whereof they speak, and nothing of true economy. To save a few thousands, they break the most solemn contracts, change the ownership of property, and cause the sacrifice of millions. And I here say nothing of the increased cost of government resulting from an inflated currency and augmented prices. Paper money, I am tempted to say, is the most dangerous invention of modern times. Popular, insinuating and insidious, it proves, at last, to be an " infernal machine" which no engineer, guided only by his discretion, can run safely. No government is sufficiently pure or wise to use it without abusing it. It is a power that had better be prohibited. If allowed, barriers should be erected and the limits fixed by the fundamental law—a law which will not yield to (so called) " state necessity."

Connecticut, in discarding the currency she had herself established, and repudiating her obligations, pursued a practical and practicable course. She could not compensate the class which had lost by her faithless and nearly worthless promises. The attempt to restore her bills to good credit would have injured, for nobody's good, still another class, and brought untold calamities upon the whole community. Surrounded by difficulties, pressed by Parliament, unable to go forward, unwilling to go backward, discouraged and disgraced, she lay down in the furrow and declared she could not pay. It was easier, and, under the circumstances, wiser, to wipe out and begin anew. The plighted public faith, so called, was no obstacle to this course. The sponge was applied to a convenient extent, and a new system inaugurated. Thenceforth, honesty became the rule of action, false measures were discarded, and hard money, the product of hard labor, again became the standard of value. The practical bankruptcy of the government and people made the change comparatively easy. There can be no shock when nobody pays. It is the persistent effort to pay in the usual currency when its volume, as compared with the demand, is largely reduced—to pay in a pinched money market, when the circulating medium is becoming every day more valuable—which intensifies the pressure, and brings on a crisis. A general bankruptcy, by greatly diminishing the number of borrowers, affords relief—relief, I mean, to the money market. Nor can there be any stringency when an old currency is repudiated, and a new one takes its place. There may be vast suffering; estates may be lost and won; but the change may take place quietly, and without financial embarrassment.

Before the plan for redeeming the colony bills had been consummated, another war with France broke out, as has already been mentioned. Troops were to be raised and equipped, and money must be had. The Assembly met in January, 1755. "To provide for the extraordinary emergencies of government, occasioned by the invasion of his Majesty's dominions in North America by the French and Indians," they voted to issue Treasury notes, of a new description, to the amount of £7,500. The system of "borrowing without interest" having exploded, these notes bore interest, and were payable at a fixed date. The denominations varied from nine pence to forty shillings. Here is the prescribed form :

No. (   )   20s.
  The Possessor of this Bill shall be paid by the Treasurer of the Colony of Connecticut, Twenty shillings, lawful money, with interest at five per cent. per annum, by the eighth day of May, 1758. By order of the Assembly at New Haven, January eighth, 1755.

By the same act, a tax of two pence on the pound, sufficient to sink the bills, was laid, payable in the new issue, or in lawful money, on the last day of August, 1757.

In March, (1755,) an issue of £12,500, in notes of the same tenor and denominations, was ordered, payable May eighth, 1759, a tax at the same time being levied of three and a half pence on the pound, to be paid in lawful money or the recent issues, on the last day of December, 1758. The notes were to be paid out to the public creditors "*as their value should be at the time.*" In August following, £30,000 of the same sort were authorized, and in October, £12,000. Then there was an interval lasting till March, 1758, when £30,000 were ordered, the same to be paid "out with interest computed." Other amounts were afterwards added; £70,000 in 1759; £70,000 in 1760; £45,000 in 1761; £65,000 in 1762; £10,000 in 1763, and £7,000 in 1764. The last sum was on

6

account of the Indian war which followed that with France, the latter closing early in 1763. The entire issues since January, 1755, amounted to £359,000. The notes were of the same tenor throughout, and, with a single slight exception, of the same denominations. They bore five per cent. annual interest, were payable in from two to five years, in lawful money, and were put forth in strict conformity to the Act of Parliament. The usual sinking fund taxes, which, in the year that completed the conquest of Canada, (1760,) amounted to two shillings and one penny on the pound, were not forgotten.

These interest bearing notes, it will be remembered, were not a legal tender. According to the record, they were " paid out as their value should be at the time of putting off the same," or according to their market price. At a later period, when probably no sacrifice was deemed necessary to make them acceptable to the public creditors, the Treasurer was to compute the interest and add this to the face of the note. Strictly speaking, they do not appear to have constituted a part of the currency, though debts were discharged with them, by consent. Undoubtedly, they were designed to act as money, as is apparent from the small denominations which were issued. But as they bore different dates, and carried different amounts of interest, and were consequently of unequal value, they could not well circulate together, or act as the common currency. The interest does not seem to have been paid during the whole period the notes had to run. There is no indorsement on them, and when they finally reached the Treasury, simple interest was added, the result, perhaps, of several years accumulation. Under these circumstances, they would naturally be held for the gains they had made, or were expected to make. If parted with, they would be sold like a private note of hand, below or above par, according to the confidence reposed in the signer, the rate of interest, the amount accrued, and the time the note had to run. In this state of things they could not act as money, and were not a measure of value. On the contrary, they were themselves measured, money being required for this purpose. During all this period, coin was the standard of value. Contracts were made and debts paid in it, or its equivalent. Government bills, like ordinary commodities, were converted into it before their value could be stated. They are understood, however, to have been worth something like their face and accrued interest, spite the late breach of colony faith. I find instances in which they were credited on book account at an advance, the latter probably being for interest.

By means of taxes and the considerable sums of money received from England on account of the war, (£26,000 sterling, in specie,* in August, 1756, and larger sums afterwards,) the notes seem to have been all paid at maturity or before. I find no evidence that those which had once reached the Treasury were ever reissued. They may have been, however, when brought in by taxes, which were designed to meet the ordinary expenses of the government. It appears from a report made to the Lords Commissioners of Trade and Plantations, in May, 1764, that only about £82,000, in bills, were outstanding, at that time. These had been emitted, some small sums in 1761, the remainder at later periods. All the older issues had been called in and burned. At the date of the report, £192,000, in Treasury notes, had been authorized which had not yet become due, they being payable in 1765, 1766, 1767 and 1768. £110,-000, therefore, out of the £192,000, had been redeemed in anticipation of the time fixed for payment. Under the circumstances, it is not surprising that the government credit was preserved, and the par value of its paper maintained. The experiment proved how much better, more profitable and more honorable it was to raise money, in the ordinary way, paying what it was worth, than to attempt it by the fraudulent, interest-saving method previously resorted to. During the war, the Colony borrowed considerable sums of money at six per cent. per annum. It had of Gov. Shirley, in 1756, a loan of £10,000, sterling, for two and three years.

The last of the notes issued (those of March, 1764,) became due in March, 1768. No others were authorized till May,

---

* See Coll. Con. Hist. Society, I. 285. The cost of importation, including freight, insurance, commissions, and all other charges, amounted to £1,171 : 9 : 11, or more than four and a quarter per cent.

1770, at which period the Colony must have been out of debt. At the last named date, £10,000 were emitted, bearing two and a half per cent. interest, the denominations ranging from two shillings and six pence to forty shillings. The notes were payable in lawful money, became due May tenth, 1772, and were secured by two taxes of two pence each, payable, one, December thirty-first, 1770, and the other, December thirty-first, 1771, in lawful money or bills of credit. In October, 1771, £12,000 were authorized; in May, 1773, £12,000; in October, 1774, £15,000; all of "suitable denominations," and all to run two years, *without interest*, seasonable and sufficient taxes being provided for the redemption of each issue. These last sums, amounting to £39,000, bearing no interest, were of course designed solely for currency. Twenty-five years had elapsed since bills of the kind had been emitted. They introduced a new paper money era; but as they did not exceed the sum required for the trade of the Colony, and were not interfered with by the notes of the adjoining governments, they did not depreciate. The population, now about one hundred and ninety thousand, had, probably, nearly doubled since 1746, while wealth and commerce had much increased. The desire, however, " to borrow without interest," or below the market rate, was not a favorable omen. It led to fresh disasters.

CHAPTER VI.

PAPER MONEY OF THE REVOLUTION. CONNECTICUT AND CONTINENTAL EMISSIONS.

THE war of the Revolution was opened with the skirmish at Lexington, April nineteenth, 1775. A blaze of excitement spread through the land. The Connecticut Assembly met, in special session, on the twenty-sixth of the same month, to provide for the war. They organized the militia, directed Commissary Trumbull and the other commissaries to purchase military stores, including one hogshead of New England rum, and to meet expenses, passed an act to emit, forthwith, £50,000 in bills of credit, payable in two years, in lawful money or bills of this issue. In May, £50,000, dated June first, were ordered, and in July, £50,000 more, dated July first, making in the whole £150,000 for the year 1775. These notes were in all important particulars like those of the preceding years. Their redemption, which was promised in two, three and four and a half years, was secured by three seven-penny taxes. The time of payment, in the two last instances, was extended beyond the limit prescribed by the parliamentary act of 1751, unless, indeed, the emergency was an "extraordinary" one, and the case one of "invasion," such as the act contemplated.

In May, 1776, the Assembly authorized the issue of £60,000, dated June seventh, and payable January first, 1781, and in June, £50,000, dated June nineteenth, and payable January first, 1782, the bills ranging, in the first instance, from one to twenty shillings, and in the last, from six pence to forty shillings. The taxes, which were levied as usual, might be paid in colony or continental bills, (the latter soon to be issued,) or in lawful money. In the particulars not referred to, the notes were like those of the preceding year. They were the last previous to 1780, except £5,250 of the same tenor, emitted, because of the scarcity of small change, in October, 1777, in two penny, three penny, four penny, five penny and seven penny notes, sixty thousand of each denomination, redeemable in October, 1782. John Chester and twelve others were appointed a signing committee for the last issue, each bill to have one signature. The duty being somewhat burdensome, twelve others were afterwards added to the committee, all to work without fee or reward. I do not find that any special tax was laid to redeem this issue, and I believe it is the only instance of the like neglect on record.

Owing to causes which will be hereafter explained, Connecticut authorized no more bills till January and May, 1780, when £190,000, in all, (which may be called *new* tenor,) were ordered. I shall speak of the circumstances by and by. That the reader may have before him, in one view, the important facts relative to the paper money issues of Connecticut, I here print a list of all the authorized emissions, from the beginning, giving the amount and tenor of the notes, the dates of the assemblies ordering the same, denominations, dates of the bills, times of redemption, &c. (The emissions to be exchanged for older issues are included.)

Session.	Amt. and tenor.	Denomination.	Date.	When redeemable.
May, 1709,	£ 8,000, O. T.	2s to £5,	July 12, 1709,	{ May, 1710. } { May, 1711. }
Oct. 1709,	11,000, O. T.	2s. to £5,	July 12, 1709,	Within 6 yrs.
Oct. 1710,	5,000, O. T.	2s. to £5,	July 12, 1709,	Aug. 1, 1718.
May, 1711,	4,000, O. T.	2s. to £5,	July 12, 1709,	May 31,1720.
June, 1711,	6,000, O. T.	2s. to £5,	July 12, 1709,	Aug 31,1723.
May, 1713,	20,000, O. T.	2s. to £5,	{ July 12, 1709, and May 1713, }	Sundry times
Oct. 1713,	1,000, O. T.	2s. to £5,	same.	May 31,1721.
May, 1719,	4,000, O. T.	2s. to £5,	same.	
Oct. 1722,	4,000, O. T.	2s. to £5,	same.	
Oct. 1724,	4,000, O. T.	2s. to £5,	same.	
Oct. 1727,	4,000, O. T.	2s. to £5,	same.	
Oct. 1728,	4,000, O. T.	2s. to £5,	same.	
May, 1729,	6,000, O. T.	2s. to £5,	same.	
Feb. 1733,	30,000, O. T.	2s. to £5 ?		
May, 1733,	20,000, O. T.	2s. to £5,		
Oct. 1735,	25,000, O. T.	2s- to £5 ?		
May, 1740,	4,000, O. T.	10s. to £5,	May, 1740,	
May, 1740,	30,000, N. T.	1s. to £3,	May 8, 1740,	
July, 1740,	15,000, O. T.	10s. to £5,		
May, 1744,	4,000, N. T.	10s. to £5,	{ May 8, 1740, May 10, 1744, }	
Oct. 1744,	15,000, N. T.	10s. to £5,	Oct. 11, 1744,	May 31,1755.
March, 1744⅘,	20,000, N. T.	10s. to £5,	Mar. 14, 1744⅘.	
July, 1745,	20,000, N. T.	10s. to £5,		
May, 1746,	20,000, N. T.	10s. to £5,	Date of As'bly	
May, 1746,	3,000, O. T. ?	2s. to £5,		
Jan. 1755,	7,500,	9d. to 40s.	Jan. 8, 1755,	May 8, 1758.
March, 1755,	12,500,	9d. to 40s.	Mar. 13, 1755,	May 8, 1759.
Aug. 1755,	30,000.	9d. to 40s.		Aug. 1760.
Oct. 1755,	12,000,	9d. to 40s.		Apr. 1,1760,
March, 1758,	30,000,	9d. to 40s.		Mar. 4, 1762,
Feb. 1759,	20,000,	9d. to 40s.		May 1, 1763,
March, 1759,	40,000,	9d. to 40s.		Mar. 1, 1764,
May, 1759,	10,000,			May 1, 1763,
March, 1760,	70,000,	9d. to 40s.		Mar. 1, 1765,
March, 1761,	45,000,	9d. to 40s.	Mar. 26, 1761,	Mar. 26,1766,
March, 1762,	65,000,	9d. to 40s.	Mar. 4, 1762,	Mar. 4,1767,
May, 1763,	10,000,	5s. to 40s.	May 12, 1763,	May 1, 1765,
March, 1764,	7,000,	9d. to 40s.	Mar. 8, 1764,	Mar. 8, 1768.
May, 1770,	10,000,	2s. 6d. to 40s.	May 10, 1770,	May 10,'72, 2½ p.c.

(right margin, rotated:) Receivable into the Treasury at 5 per cent. advance.

(lower right margin, rotated:) At 5 per cent. annual interest.

Session.	Amt. and tenor.	Denomination.	Date.	When redeemable.	
Oct. 1771,	£ 12,000,	2s. 6d. to 40s.	Oct. 10, 1771,	Oct.10, 1775,	
May, 1773,	12,000,	2s. 6d. to 40s.	June 1, 1773,	June 1, 1775,	
Oct. 1774,	15,000,	2s. 6d. to 40s.	Jan. 2, 1775,	Jan. 2, 1777,	
April, 1775,	50,000,	2s. 6d. to 40s.	May 1, 1775,	May 10, 1777,	Without interest.
May, 1775,	50,000,	2s. 6d. to 40s.	June 1, 1775,	June 1, 1778,	
July, 1775,	50,000,	2s. to 40s.	July 1, 1775,	Dec. 31, 1779,	
May, 1776,	60,000,	1s. to 20s.	June 7, 1776,	Jan. 1, 1781,	
June, 1776,	50,000,	6d. to 40s.	June 19, 1776,	Jan. 1, 1782,	
Oct. 1777,	5,250,	2d. 3d. 4d. 5d. 7d.	Oct. 11, 1777,	Oct. 10, 1782,	
Jan. 1780,	40,000,	9d. to 40s.	Mar. 1, 1780,	March, 1784,	
May, 1780,	100,000,	9d. to 40s.	July 1, 1780,	Mar. 1, 1785,	5 p. c.
May, 1780,	50,000,	9d. to 40s.	June 1, 1780,	Mar. 1, 1784,	

The delegates of the "United Colonies" to the Continental Congress, assembled in Philadelphia, May tenth, 1775. To provide means to carry on the war, they resolved, June twenty-second, 1775, five days after the battle of Bunker Hill, to emit "two millions of Spanish milled dollars,* in bills of credit," the "twelve confederated Colonies" to be pledged for their redemption. The form prescribed was the following: "This bill entitles the bearer to receive —— Spanish milled dollars, or the value thereof in gold or silver, according to the resolutions of Congress, held at Philadelphia, on the tenth day of May, 1775." The date here mentioned was not that of the resolution authorizing the emission, as several writers have assumed, but that of the meeting of Congress. The bills were to range from one to twenty dollars. On the twenty-fifth day of July, an additional one million was ordered in bills of thirty dollars each, a committee of twenty-eight to sign the same, each bill to have two signatures. Four days later, it was resolved that the twelve colonies, then represented, should redeem the $3,000,000 in bills ordered, in four equal annual payments, beginning November thirtieth,

* The Spanish milled dollar, or the piece-of-eight, with a new name, was universally known and in general use. It was adopted as the unit of continental money, doubtless, because the currencies of the different colonies were conflicting. The pound and its parts meant different things in different places. In New England and Virginia, 6s., in New York, 8s., and in Pennsylvania, 7s. 6d. made a dollar. The accounts of Congress were kept in dollars, ninetieths and eighths. A Pennsylvania penny (the delegates were sitting in Philadelphia) was equal to the ninetieth part of a dollar, and the eighth of a penny to half a farthing. Whether there were current coins to represent these fractions, I cannot say.

1779. The proportion of "each Colony to be determined according to the number of inhabitants of all ages, including negroes and mulattoes," was estimated (till "the list of each Colony is obtained ") as follows :—

Virginia,	$496,278
Massachusetts Bay,	484,244
Pennsylvania,	372,208½
Maryland,	310,174½
Connecticut,	248,139
New York,	248,139
North Carolina,	248,139
South Carolina,	248,139
New Jersey,	161,290½
New Hampshire,	124,069½
Rhode Island,	71,959½
Delaware,	37,219½
	$3,000,000

In this manner was inaugurated a system which was to furnish (what proved to be) a "national currency." Thus was conferred the boon of a circulating medium having, in the language of a distinguished modern financier, an uniform value throughout the country !

The paper emitted by Congress was to be received for the taxes levied for its redemption ; while the gold and silver paid in were to be exchanged for bills. The latter, however collected, were to be "cut by a circular punch an inch in diameter," and afterwards burned. The business of obtaining the paper, engraving the plates, printing, signing, &c., occupied several weeks, so that these first installments of paper money did not make their appearance till early in August.* According to the Journal of Congress, the authorized emissions, in the year 1775, amounted, in all, to $6,000,000. At the close of 1776, they figured up $25,500,000 ; at the end of 1777, $38,500,000 ; at the end of 1778, $102,000,300. They, finally, near the close of 1779, reached the enormous sum of $242,052,-780, bearing no interest. They were of different denomina-

---

* Political Essays on the nature and operation of Money, Public Finances, and other subjects. By Pelatiah Webster, A. M. Philadelphia: 1791.

tions, varying from one-sixth* of a dollar to eighty dollars. It is said, however, that not more than $200,000,000 were in circulation at any one time. This sum was largely increased by the colony and state emissions which, however, had no general currency.

The circulating medium of Connecticut was made up in part of its own, and in part of continental bills, the former, doubtless, constituting the largest portion during the first years of the war, but the latter preponderating at a later period. The two circulated in the Colony at a common par value, and were popular. For several months their credit did not suffer, and prices were not affected. There was only a "flush" money market. Long established habits, in such cases, do not give way at once, and the evidences of inflation fail to appear till after a considerable interval. Early in the year 1776, men began to hesitate, and to inquire whither they were drifting. They probably had not forgotten certain notable passages in their own history. First, small change grew scarce, then all silver money disappeared. Some persons refused to take the bills. At this juncture, patriotic individuals in certain of the colonies stepped forward and offered to give coin for continental paper. Considerable sums, sometimes as much as a thousand pounds at a time, were thus exchanged.† Congress took action on the subject. January eleventh, 1776, they resolved that if any person should be "so lost to all virtue and regard for his country" as to refuse the bills, or discourage the circulation thereof, and should be convicted by a "committee of safety," such person should be published and treated as a public enemy, and precluded from all trade and intercourse, &c.‡ —that is, he was to be outlawed.

The colonial governments did what they could, by legislation, to support the waning confidence in paper money. Mas-

---

* In the resolution of Congress of November 2d, 1776, $500,000 were "to be speedily issued in small bills of two-thirds, one-third, one-sixth, and one-*ninth* of a dollar." I do not find that any of the last denomination were ever emitted.

† Historical sketch of Continental Paper Money, by Samuel Breck. Philadelphia: 1863.—A pamphlet of 33 pages.

‡ Printed Journal of Congress.

sachusetts, as early as May, 1775, made its own notes a legal tender. Connecticut, more cautious, waited till after the Declaration of Independence, which declaration, by the way, her authorities seemed in no hurry to ratify. At the regular October session of the Assembly, 1776, the revolutionary proceedings of Congress were approved, while a resolution declaring "that this Colony is, and of right ought to be, a Free and Independent State," was adopted.

The first act after this was one punishing high treason; the second required an oath of fidelity; the third was one to support the credit and currency of the bills of the Continental Congress, and of this State; the order of the acts showing, perhaps, their supposed relative importance. The law last named made the bills referred to "a legal tender as money, in all payments within this State." And as certain evil minded persons, inimical to the liberties of the states, had endeavored to depreciate said bills, it was provided that any one who should so depreciate or undervalue them by offering, demanding or receiving them at a rate below their nominal value, in exchange for coin; or who should, directly or indirectly, offer, demand or receive a greater sum in said bills for any houses, lands or goods than the same could be purchased for in gold or silver, &c.;—every person so offending should forfeit the full value of the money so exchanged, or the houses, lands and goods so sold or offered for sale, one half to go to the person who should prosecute to effect.

But this somewhat stringent act was not sufficient, and more legislation was called for. "The necessaries and conveniences of life" rose rapidly, and exorbitant prices were demanded. This was attributed to "monopolizers, the great pest of society." To circumvent them, a law was passed in November, (1776,) regulating prices. "Labor, in the farming way, in the summer season," was not to exceed in price three shillings per day, wheat six shillings per bushel, rye three shillings and six pence, Indian corn three shillings, good wool two shillings per pound, the best grass fed beef twenty-four shillings per hundred, good West India rum six shillings per gallon, (by the hogshead,) best New England rum, three shillings and six pence, &c., &c. ; "all other necessary articles to be in a reasonable accustomed proportion to the above." Whoever violated this act was to "suffer the pains and penalties of the laws of this State against oppression."

In the following month, (December,) in accordance with the recommendation of the "committees of the several states of New England," a more detailed and stringent bill was passed on the same subject. The maximum price of several articles was raised, and the profits of wholesale and retail dealers prescribed. The penalty of transgression was the price of the article sold, but in no case was it to be less than twenty shillings. As the volume of the currency was increased, and commodities got dearer, new regulations became necessary. This policy, of course, proved ineffectual. A convention of delegates from the New England States and New York assembled in Springfield, July thirtieth, 1777, " for the purpose of holding a conference respecting the state of the paper currency, and the expediency of calling in the same by taxes or otherwise :" to consult together as to the means of preventing depreciation, and to take into consideration the "acts lately made to prevent monopoly and oppression," &c.* According to Hildreth, they advised the levying of taxes for the support of the war, the redemption of bills of credit issued by state authority, the repeal of laws limiting prices, and the enactment of others against forestalling and engrossing.† Connecticut acted in accordance with the advice. In August, she repealed her laws against " excessive and unreasonable prices," and in October,‡ (1777,) passed " An act to encourage fair dealing, and to restrain and punish sharpers and oppressors." By this last act, no person could buy or sell (except in small quantities for his own consumption) certain enumerated articles—rum, sugar, molasses, wine, tea, coffee, salt, woolen, linen or tow cloth, stockings, shoes, hides, leather, wool, flax, cotton,

---

* Revolutionary War, VII., Doc. 390: MSS. State Library, Hartford.

† History of the United States, Vol. III., p. 227, (first series.)

‡ In speaking of legislative acts, I have always assigned to them the date of the month in which the Assembly came together, without inquiring whether the acts referred to were, in fact, passed in that month or the next following.

butter, cheese, wheat, rye, beef, pork, cider, tobacco, &c., &c.,
till he had become known as the friend of freedom, obtained a
license, and taken the oath of fidelity. A breach of the act
(which was to continue in force one year) was to be punished
by forfeiture of double the value of the goods bought or sold.
Congress observed with apprehension the effects of a redundant
currency. She would fain check the rise of prices, and recommended conventions of the states. One was appointed to meet
in New Haven on the fifteenth day of January, 1778, commissioners of all the northern states, Delaware included, to be
present. Roger Sherman, William Hillhouse and Benjamin
Huntington, were chosen by the Assembly of this State. It
was to carry out the views of this convention that the Legislature attempted once more to regulate prices, and passed the
law of February, 1778. It was more stringent and more comprehensive than any which had preceded it. It established the
price of every important article, and made provision for those
which were not enumerated. Labor of whatever kind was not
to be more than seventy-five per cent. higher than before the
war. Importers might (with certain exceptions) charge one
continental dollar for each shilling sterling paid for his goods
in Europe. Retailers of foreign goods were permitted to make
a profit of twenty-five per cent. Inn-keepers might advance
fifty per cent. on the wholesale cost of their liquors, &c., &c.
The particulars of the law are too numerous to be mentioned
here. Among other things, it declared that any person who
should be convicted under it should pay a fine of not less than
forty shillings, and be forever disqualified from holding office
in this State, "or of prosecuting or maintaining any suit at
law, or of taking out any execution." And no person whatever could "commence or maintain any suit, either in law or
equity, in any court," till he had sworn "by the ever living
God," that he had not been guilty of a breach of this act.

This was indeed sorry legislation, a disgrace to any people.
It gives one an unsatisfactory opinion of the wisdom, not to say
intelligence, of our revolutionary fathers. Men in the government, state and continental—good and great men, as we have
been accustomed to think—altered the standard of values, and

then enacted that values should not be changed. They shortened the yard-stick—cut off twelve or twenty inches—and then decreed that it was still a yard-stick of full length, which should give to the purchaser an undiminished amount of cloth. In other words, they endeavored to compel the people to part with their labor or goods without an equivalent—to exchange two days' work for one, or for nothing. To carry out their schemes, stores were broken open by committees, the goods seized and sold at the established prices, and those who owned them branded as speculators, Tories, and the like.* The action of Congress was calculated to destroy all confidence in the government. The state of things brought about by paper money and their own violent proceedings, was the apology which was offered for every oppressive measure. The army was in great need of woolen cloths, blankets, stockings, shoes, hats, &c., and they urged upon the states the necessity of seizing any of these things kept for sale—of seizing all stock and provisions required for the army, which had been "purchased up or engrossed by any person with a view of selling the same," giving receipts to the owner. And as there were certain persons who, "instigated by the lust of avarice, were assiduously endeavoring, by every means of oppression, sharping and extortion, to accumulate enormous gains," they advised that the retailers of goods should be licensed, and their number limited; that no one should purchase clothing or provision required for the army (except for his own use) without a "certificate under the seal and sign manual of the supreme executive authority" of some state, and that "such punishment should be inflicted upon all atrocious offenders, as shall brand them with indelible infamy," &c. These were harsh measures, "but (unhappy the case of America!) laws unworthy the character of infant republics are become necessary to supply the defect of public virtue, and to correct the vices of some of her sons."† It pains me to say that the soundest men of the time—such men as John Jay, and the illustrious Washington—shared, on this sub-

---

* Pelatiah Webster's Essays, p. 11.
† Journal of Congress, December 20, 1777.

ject, the senseless prejudices of the day. To Reed, President of Pennsylvania, the latter wrote, December twelfth, 1778, as follows: "It gives me very sincere pleasure to find, * * * that the Assembly is so well disposed to second your endeavors in bringing those murderers of our cause, the monopolizers, forestallers and engrossers, to condign punishment. It is much to be lamented that each state, long ere this, has not hunted them down as pests to society, and the greatest enemies we have to the happiness of America. I would to God that some one of the more atrocious in each state was hung in gibbets upon a gallows five times as high as the one prepared by Haman." A matter which so turned the wisest heads of the country, might be expected to excite the multitude. Nor were the complaints against the speculators, &c., wholly groundless. The blame, however, did not rest on them so much as on those who, by the continued emissions of paper money, tempted to speculation, guaranteed its success, and made it profitable. The "pestilent" race was called into life by bills of credit, and had these been stopped in season, they would have "hung" themselves.

The speculation which is the inevitable effect of excessive paper issues, is not without some collateral advantages. So far as it is carried on by means of cash, it multiplies the uses for money, creates a demand for it, and tends to make it scarce. In this way, the natural consequences of a cheap currency are, in a measure, counteracted. Depreciation is, to some extent, prevented or retarded. Speculation, then, as a secondary effect, establishes lower prices than would otherwise prevail. Similar results follow monopolizing, or "engrossing." When goods are withheld from market consumption is prevented, and future comparative abundance secured. This abundance will show itself in correspondingly reduced prices, when the hoarded articles are again thrown upon the market. These remarks are intended not to justify, but to explain.

To prevent the downward course of continental bills, Congress, January fourteenth, 1777, after resolving that said bills ought to pass current, and be deemed equal to gold and silver, and that any person giving or taking them at less than their par value, was an enemy to liberty, and should forfeit the money or property exchanged, recommended to the several states to make them (as had already been done in several instances) a lawful tender, at their par value, in all payments, a refusal to take them to extinguish the debt.* The advice was heeded. And as certain disaffected persons, doubtful of the result of the war, had ventured to show a preference for the old colonial bills, (those emitted before the war,) thinking, not unreasonably, that these were more likely to be redeemed than those issued at a later date, Congress declared such conduct "calculated to sap the confidence of the public in the continental bills," &c., and advised the states, December third, 1777, to call them in, giving for them new money, continental or state; those not presented for redemption within a limited time, to be refused payment. But all these measures, including embargo laws of the most harassing description, were of no avail. Goods and coin went up, and bills went down. You cannot make paper dollars, costing nothing, representing nothing, having no intrinsic value, and, when issued in excess, no certain exchangeable value, equal to gold and silver, or to anything else which is the product of labor. The experiment has often been tried, and always with one result; and the sooner politicians and (so called) statesmen find out their mistake, the better for the country. Penal acts, tender laws, "committees of inspection," mob violence, and military force, may frighten people, but they can never change the decrees of nature, or make irredeemable and depreciated paper money anything but a nuisance. Thus discourses our friend, Pelatiah Webster:

"It is not more absurd to attempt to impel faith into the heart of an unbeliever by fire and faggot, or to whip love into your mistress by a cowskin, than to force value or credit into your money by penal laws." * * * *

"The fatal error that the credit and currency of the continental money could be kept up and supported by acts of compulsion, entered so deep into the mind of Congress and all departments of administration through the states, that no considerations of justice, religion, or policy, or even experience of its utter inefficiency, could eradicate it; it seemed to be a kind

---

* Journal of Congress.

of obstinate delirium, totally deaf to every argument drawn from justice and right, from its natural tendency and mischief, from common sense, and even common safety."

" This ruinous principle was continued in practice for five successive years, and appeared in all shapes and forms, i. e., in tender acts, in limitations of prices, in awful and threatening declarations, in penal laws with dreadful and ruinous punishments, and in every other way that could be devised, and al. executed with a relentless severity, by the highest authorities then in being, viz., by Congress, by assemblies and conventions of the states, by committees of inspection, (whose powers in those days were nearly sovereign,) and even by military force; and though men of all descriptions stood trembling before this monster of force, without daring to lift a hand against it, during all this period, yet its unrestrained energy ever proved ineffectual to its purposes, but in every instance increased the evils it was designed to remedy, and destroyed the benefits it was intended to promote; at best, its utmost effect was like that of water sprinkled on a blacksmith's forge, which indeed deadens the flame for a moment, but never fails to increase the heat and force of the internal fire. Many thousand families of full and easy fortune were ruined by these fatal measures, and lie in ruins to this day, without the least benefit to the country, or to the great and noble cause in which we were then engaged."*

---

* Essays, pp. 129, 132.

Mr. Webster was a native of Connecticut, but *not* an uncle of the late Noah Webster, as stated by Gouge, in his History of Paper Money. He was graduated at Yale College in the class of 1746, studied for the ministry, and was afterward ordained. At a later period, he became a merchant of Philadelphia, and, at the breaking out of the war, met with considerable losses. He was in the habit of familiar intercourse with the delegates to Congress, and his house was the common resort of the members from Connecticut. His Essays, twenty-five in number, were printed at irregular intervals, mostly in pamphlet form, between 1776 and 1790. In 1791, they were gathered, by the author, into a volume of 504 pages, and copious notes added. They contain views far in advance of those most generally entertained at that day. The first essay, published in the Penn. Evening Post, October 5, 1776, suggests the law which limits and controls the value of a paper currency. " I conceive," (he says,) " the value of the currency of any state has a limit, a *ne plus ultra*, beyond which it cannot go, and if the nominal sum is extended beyond that limit, the value will not follow." In the same paper, he

The popular clamor against monopolizers, engrossers and speculators, though known to be misdirected, was doubtless regarded with complaisance, if not favor. Men who were the guides of public opinion, feeling that the credit of the continental money must be upheld and confidence maintained, were quite willing to see the evils produced by it attributed to other causes. There was, to some extent, an endeavor to keep the masses in ignorance of the sources of their misery; or at any rate to permit a misconception when the states could profit by it. In 1778, some members of Congress proposed to pay a soldiers' bounty, one-half in coin. Washington objected to it. The measure, said he, in a letter to Gouverneur Morris, " would have a tendency to depreciate our paper money, which is already of little value, and give rise to infinite difficulties and irremovable inconveniences. Nothing after this would do but gold and silver. All would demand it, and none would consider the impracticability of its being furnished. The soldiers seeing the manifest difference in the value between that and paper, and that the former would procure at least five or six fold as much as the latter, would become dissatisfied. They would reason upon the subject," &c.*

Congress was slow to learn or reluctant to acknowledge the necessary laws which govern currency and trade. They began with a wrong system and, turning away from the lessons of experience, obstinately clung to it. So late as November 19th, 1779, they earnestly recommended to the several states to prevent "engrossing and withholding" by the strictest legislation, and " forthwith to enact laws for a general limitation of prices, to commence from the first day of February next," on the basis of twenty in paper for one in specie.† When the

---

advocates the calling in of bills of credit, to an extent " equal to the excess of the currency," by effectual taxation. I do not find evidence that Mr. Webster had ever read Adam Smith's Wealth of Nations, which made its appearance in the early part of 1776. Had he been acquainted with that immortal work, his expressions, which are often infelicitous and unscientific, would, I think, have shown it. His death took place according to the Triennial of Yale College, in 1795.

* Washington's Writings, Vol. VI., p. 55.
† Journal of Congress.

recommendation was made, currency was worth at the rate of thirty-eight for one; when the new prices were to commence, forty-seven for one.*

Practically, the attempt, by forcible means, to make paper dollars the equivalent of hard money or hard labor, increased the "real" price of every description of goods. A man will not work unless his industry can be rewarded; nor will he bring his commodities to market unless he can obtain for them a fair equivalent. If his corn, his cattle and his cloth, are wrested from him by atrocious laws and sold at half their value, he will stop production, and soon have nothing to sell. Or if he continues to labor, he must be paid for the risk he runs. If there is danger of being robbed, he who furnishes the goods must charge for insurance. So much was production diminished and the cost of articles increased by the violent measures taken to cheapen them, that early in 1780, "even hard money would buy little more than half so much country produce as before the war."†

It is a common error, even of those who, to some extent, shape public opinion, that a currency ought not to depreciate so long as the issuer is solvent. The "promises to pay" of a government which represents and controls the entire wealth of a country surely must be "good," so long as its obligations are not beyond its resources. If a sovereign state cannot make a good note, who can? But this line of argument overlooks certain important facts. What is a currency note, made a legal tender, with the unlimited power of issue? It promises to pay to the bearer, say, one dollar.‡ But what is a dollar under the operation of a tender law, with no restriction on the manu-

---

* P. Webster, 123, note.

† P. Webster, p. 107. These enhanced prices may have been, at this period, partly owing to the influx of specie and its temporary depreciation—a fact which will be referred to by and by.

‡ The continental bills promised "Spanish milled dollars;" but as the resolutions authorizing the issues called the bills themselves Spanish milled dollars, and designated no time for their redemption, the remarks in the text are not inappropriate. The treasury notes for currency of 1864 promise "dollars" to the bearer, without naming the time for payment.

facture? The term has no certain meaning. It signifies one thing to-day, another thing to-morrow. In the eye of the law, the rectangular bit of paper inscribed with the promise, is itself a dollar. So considered, it is possessed of no fixed value, and of course cannot measure anything which has value. It represents nothing solid or stable. Though to a man who would discharge a debt, (due perhaps in coin,) it is as good as a silver dollar or a day's labor, to the receiver, it may not be worth the tenth part of that amount. A hundred like it might not enable one to purchase a breakfast. Did it promise to pay, on demand, or in sixty days, so many pounds or ounces of shingle nails, or so many dozen of solid-headed pins, the case would be different. It would then have something like a definite value, provided there were confidence in its prompt re-demption. But an agreement to pay in dollars, ("Spanish milled," if you please,) when the law has declared that agreement is payment—that the promise of a dollar is itself a dollar—that fragments of pictured paper printed without limit on government presses are the solid coin—is without significance. It secures nothing; it pledges nothing. In effect, it promises nothing. No matter what may be the wealth of a government, such an agreement does not make over to the holder of its paper any known part of that wealth. The contract may be fulfilled without anything of a determinate value passing from debtor to creditor. The pledge may be redeemed by returning to the person demanding payment the identical picture which he had offered for redemption. The solvency of a nation has not necessarily anything to do with the value of its notes of circulation. A bankrupt state—one that nobody will trust for a farthing—having the authority to enforce its decrees, can make as good a currency as any other, even that of " the best government on earth." Neither can do more than furnish a circulating medium which, when accepted as such, and issued in excess, will decline in value in proportion to its abundance. The only reason that it is worth anything is the fact that it performs the functions of a currency, and is the recognized medium of exchange. It is true, it may have a speculative value depending on the opinions entertained as to what the government may, from choice, finally do with it. If it is the expectation that it will, at last, be redeemed in something better than unmeaning promises, this circumstance will give it a distinct value—a value in addition, perhaps, to its currency-value. In the last case, currency-notes would cease to be currency. They would be withdrawn from circulation and held for investment.

The amplest provision of funds to secure the redemption of bills of credit at maturity will not prevent their depreciation. This truth is sufficiently illustrated by the history of the colonial currencies before the war. Still, the fact seems never to have been understood. Legislatures persisted in thinking that when a tax had been granted, payable in bills, in three, five, or ten years, sufficient to sink the whole, due precautions had been taken to secure a sound currency. This error was so firmly planted that the experience of the Revolution could not uproot it. "The evil of depreciation," wrote Gov. Trumbull, in his celebrated letter to Capellan, dated August, 1779, "had its rise in, and owes all its rapid increase to, the single cause of our not having provided, at a sufficiently early period, for its reduction and payment by taxes."[*] Men appeared unable to comprehend the principle, already commented on, (nor do they yet fully understand it,) that a currency issued in excess, whatever the circumstances, must, so long as it is used as currency, decline in value in proportion to that excess. It is true, the certainty of redemption, in *coin*, at a fixed time, will present a limit to depreciation ; but this effect is brought about by the withdrawal of bills from circulation. When paper money has become so cheap, or has so declined in value, that it is worth more to hold for redemption than to pay out as money, it will be laid aside. Those seeking investments and wishing the highest rate of interest will file it away with their promissory notes. Thus the currency is contracted and its value sustained. As compared with coin, it cannot fall below a certain limit, this limit being determined by the time the bill has to run, the current rate of interest, and the confidence with which prompt

---

* See Stuart's Life of J. Trumbull, Sen., p. 462.

payment is expected.   The same principles apply to a currency note bearing interest.   The interest will not prevent its depreciation, even though regularly paid, unless it be sufficiently high to tempt some one to stop its circulation, and hold it for final redemption.   There is, in fact, no method possible by which the value and credit of a redundant currency can be preserved which does not, in some way, reduce its volume. Legal tender acts can reverse no law of nature.   Restrictions on prices, a perfect system of taxation, hopeful financial prospects and solid wealth can have no effect, so long as the quantity of money is the same.*   Would that self-styled statesmen understood this truth !

---

* I have just received (November, 1864) the "Speech of Henry G. Stebbins of New York City," delivered in Congress, March 4, 1864. A considerable part of his remarks are much in the strain of the memorable "circular letter" of Congress of September 13, 1779. He argues, strenuously, in favor of the ability of the government to pay all its debts. He shows by incontestable figures how rich we are, (or were,) and for proof refers to the census tables of 1860. He speaks of our coal, iron, silver, and lead mines, and dwells with pride on the "prolific sides," and the "huge volumes of treasure" of the Rocky Mountains. He cannot doubt the financial ability of the country, for "westward the star of empire takes its way." In view of the security offered, he is unable to understand why the $400,000,000 of government legal tender notes "should sell at from thirty-three and a third to forty per cent. discount." Now I would like to ask Mr. Stebbins what the "security" which he speaks of has to do with the worth of the notes ? They pledge to the holder not coal, or iron, or gold, or western lands, or the smallest item of wealth, but only "legal tender." The dollars which they agree to pay have no outside existence—no existence save in the ink of the printer. What bearing, then, has the wealth of a nation on the value of its tender notes ? Were our means of payment increased a thousand fold, these notes would be worth no more. Nor would the depreciation of the currency be prevented though all the real property of the country were mortgaged for its redemption, so long as its quantity was undiminished—so long as no one was tempted to convert notes into real property. The "assignats" of France, first issued in 1789, were "secured" by the crown lands, and the confiscated estates of the church, of the monasteries and the emigrants, amounting, it is said, to half the territory of the nation. Into these lands, they might be converted at the pleasure of the holder. Their circulation was enforced by the severest laws. Any person who refused to receive them in payment for debt was condemned to twenty years' confinement in irons, while "forestalling" was declared to be a capital offense. (See Alison's History of Europe, I., 315, Harper's Ed.) The depreciation was but three per cent. for the first twelve months, and but moderate for the first two years. At the fall of Robespierre, in July, 1794, the issues amounted to nearly $1,500,000,000,

In countries in which depreciated paper is the common currency, the precious metals have lost their peculiar functions. They are no longer money; they are simply commodities. But as they are the product of labor, and represent a nearly uniform amount of it, they may still be used to measure values. They maintain the same relation to other things that they did before, and are given, in the way of exchange, in the same proportions. They may be employed as the measure of paper money as of other things. Known to every people, generally recognized as the medium of trade, largely used to pay off international balances, promptly indicating disturbances in the commercial world, they have peculiar advantages when thus employed. The price of gold or silver, considered as a commodity, does not govern the price of paper—does not cause its depreciation—a fact which some men in high positions cannot or will not understand. Gold and silver might be struck out of existence without a change in the value of paper money— of paper money as measured by any fixed standard. Nor do these metals govern the exchangeable price of industrial products. A bushel of wheat would have exchanged for two bushels of Indian corn, or for a pair of shoes, or for a definite number of depreciated paper dollars, though "hard money" had never been known. Gold and silver indicate, with considerable certainty, the fluctuations of other things, but control nothing into which they do not themselves enter. They are of little importance to a country which has proscribed them as a currency. They supply no fundamental want, and their absence would only deprive a people of certain articles of plate, jewelry, &c. Though convenient for export and for paying off international balances, foreign trade could be carried on very well without them.

The relations of commodities, one to another, as it regards

---

and finally to some $1,750,000,000, (or, according to a French Encyclopedia published in 1857, to 45,578,000,000 francs,) all "secured" by the pledge of public property. A dinner, in 1795, cost, in assignats, ten thousand francs! The end was, of course, repudiation and national bankruptcy. The catastrophe was hastened, it is true, by a doubt about the security, and a well grounded apprehension that the revolutionary government and its acts might come to an untimely end.

price, are not affected by depreciated paper money. These cannot be altered so long as the labor required to produce them is unchanged. If the products of industry, including the precious metals and labor itself, are measured by a fluctuating paper standard, their prices will vary, but vary alike, and in one direction. They will move up or down together, as the currency is expanded or contracted, without losing the established relations existing among themselves. To speak correctly, the alteration which they seem to undergo is but seeming. The change is in the money which measures, and not in the things which are measured.

CHAPTER VII.

METHODS ADOPTED BY CONGRESS TO SUPPLY THE TREASURY AND REPAIR THE FINANCES.

AFTER the public credit had been shaken by large issues of paper money, Congress attempted, October third, 1776, to raise money by loan, and committed the grave mistake of offering for it less than the market price. They resolved to borrow immediately "five million of continental dollars," at four per cent. annual interest, in sums of not less than three hundred dollars, and recommended that a loan-office should be established in each state, a commissioner for the same to be appointed by said state. The Connecticut Assembly, December, 1776, chose John Lawrence of Hartford, (State Treasurer,) to fill the office, and pledged the State to deliver United States three years loan-office certificates, (or treasury notes,) bearing four per cent. interest, to all subscribers. The scheme of course failed. Afterward, February twenty-sixth, 1777, the rate of interest on money borrowed, or to be borrowed, was raised to six per cent. Other certificates were put upon the market, though those already offered had not been disposed of. To make them more saleable, the interest was made payable, not in depreciated bills, but in drafts, "at thirty days sight," on the United States commissioners in Paris, five livres being reckoned as equal to one dollar. (The livre was overvalued about six per cent.) Foreign drafts were often resorted to by Congress when they got out of money, and wished to gain time. There were frequently no funds to meet them, and they came back protested. From the loan-office certificates, some assistance, *in currency*, was secured.

Congress endeavored to obtain an additional supply of money by a lottery. A resolution in favor of one "for defraying the expenses of the next campaign," was adopted November first, 1776. A scheme was reported and forthwith approved. The object was not to obtain a profit, but to procure a loan. As I understand it, the prizes amounted to $5,000,000, less fifteen per cent., ten of the fifteen to go to the managers. These prizes were to be paid in "treasury bank notes," or loan-office certificates, to run five years at four per cent. annual interest. The tickets were to be paid for in "ready money," and to be drawn in four classes, "the first to begin at Philadelphia on the first of March, 1777." The tickets sold but slowly, and the drawing was postponed, from time to time, till May first, 1778. Before the third class was drawn, which was not till March first, 1780, the interest on the loan-office certificates for prizes was raised to six per cent., while the unsold tickets were to "be the property and at the risk of the United States." The drawing of the fourth class was appointed for the first Monday of April, 1781. On the twenty-first day of December, 1782, Congress resolved that lottery tickets which had drawn prizes should be received and certified as claims against the United States, "at the rate of one dollar in specie for forty of such prizes."

There were many disaffected people in the country—loyalists and enemies to liberty. They were numerous in Connecticut. It was thought that some money or means might be obtained from them—and why should not they be made to pay? September twenty-seventh, 1777, Congress resolved that the Board of War be directed to coöperate with General Washington in "effectual measures for supplying the army with fire-arms, shoes, blankets, stockings, provisions, and other necessaries; and that, in executing this business, these collections be confined, as much as circumstances will permit, to persons of disaffected and equivocal characters." Soon after, the several states were "earnestly recommended, as soon as may be, to confiscate and make sale of all the real and personal estate of persons who have forfeited the same, and the right to the protection of their respective states, and to invest the money in loan-office certificates," &c. The advice was not unheeded. In most of the states that had not already acted, laws were passed proscribing all wealthy absentees by name, and putting their property into the hands of trustees. As a financial expedient, however, "this procedure proved a complete failure; but it gratified party hatred, and served to enrich some speculators."*

In addition to these measures to secure the means required for the war, Congress, urged by the critical condition of affairs, but without any rightful authority, clothed General Washington, late in December, 1776, with the power "to take, wherever he may be, whatever he may want for the use of the army, if the inhabitants will not sell it, allowing a reasonable price for the same; and to arrest and confine persons who refuse to take the continental currency, or are otherwise disaffected to the American cause." Other powers were given which made Washington dictator "for and during the term of six months"—powers, wrote Robert Morris, that Congress "durst not have trusted to any other man." He did not abuse the trust.

Congress had no financial system during the early years of the Revolution. Fearing the war would become unpopular, they proposed no taxes for two years and a half—a nearly fatal blunder. They valued liberty, but were opposed to the burdens necesary to maintain it. At last, they were driven into a

---

* Hildreth, III., p. 229, (first series.)

different policy, and proposed, November twenty-second, 1777,
to raise "in the course of the year, 1778, commencing January first, by quarterly payments, $5,000,000, by a tax on the
states. The proportion assigned to Connecticut, until the
accounts could be finally adjusted, was $600,000, or nearly
one-eighth of the whole ;* to provide for which the Assembly
promptly laid two rates of twelve pence each, both payable
within the year 1778. At the same time, Congress proposed
an important measure to the states, one which had been recommended by the Springfield Convention, and which was urged
by the General Assembly of Connecticut. While continental
paper money, payable in "Spanish milled dollars," was worth
but thirty-three and a third per cent. they "earnestly recommended the several states to refrain from further emissions of
bills of credit, and * * * forthwith to call in by loans or
taxes, and to cancel the paper money, small bills for change
under a dollar excepted, which such state has already emitted ;
and, for the future, to provide for the exigencies of war, and
the support of government by taxes," &c. Connecticut, un-
wearied in her endeavors to promote the common cause, was
ready for the change. In February, 1778, she enacted that no
more bills should be issued for currency by her authority ; that
those in circulation should be taken up and canceled by loans,
and that the charges of the government should be met by
taxes. It was also enacted that none of the bills of this State,
except those under one dollar, should "be current in any payment, trade or dealing after the twentieth of March next,"
though they might be received into the Treasury for taxes till
the first day of July. The last named period was afterwards
extended to March 1st, 1779. While the state bills were, in
this way, proscribed as money, holders of them were permitted, till the said twentieth day of March, 1778, to exchange
them for the Treasurer's promissory notes, "or bills emitted
on the credit of the United States." The said Treasurer's notes

---

* Journal of Congress. Connecticut, at this period, had a population of
about two hundred thousand, or one-fourteenth of all the states. She afterwards
complained that her proportion of the money-requisitions was too large.

were to carry interest at six per cent., and to run one year. None was to be for a less sum than ten pounds, and the whole were not to exceed £235,000,* the estimated amount, probably, of the outstanding bills of one dollar and over. In April, 1779, the said bills, which were "not yet brought in," were still to be taken by the Treasurer, and continental money given in exchange for them till the ensuing September. By these measures the state issues of the higher denominations were withdrawn from circulation, and no more is heard of them as a part of the currency. The small remnant which remained, though forfeited by the neglect of holders, was presented and allowed as a claim against the United States government, under the Constitution, forty for one.

In May, 1777, the Treasurer of the State was ordered to borrow not exceeding £72,000, " in continental bills or bills of this State," and to issue his notes, payable in one year, with interest at six per cent., said notes to be for sums of not less than thirty pounds. In May, 1778, the Treasurer was instructed to borrow £100,000, also at six per cent., payable in two years. At the same session, it was ordered that the holders of the ten pound notes which were authorized to the extent of £60,000 to be paid as premiums to enlisted soldiers, in December, 1776, redeemable in three years, should, after June 1, 1778, receive six per cent. per annum instead of four, as stipulated. One year later, (May, 1779,) a committee was directed to obtain a further loan of £45,000, at six per cent.

December sixteenth, 1778, Congress resolved to raise in the ensuing year, $15,000,000, by taxes. In addition to this, the states were called on, December thirty-first, "to pay their quotas of $6,000,000, annually, for eighteen years, commencing with the year 1780, as a fund for sinking the loans and emissions of these United States to the thirty-first day of December, 1778, inclusive." The bills emitted prior to 1780, and no others, were to be taken on these quotas. Those received, when

---

* December 15th, 1788, the state auditors burned £311,140, in notes given "in 1777, &c., for bills of the old emissions," for which notes new ones had been issued for their specie value and interest, dated February 1st, 1781. See Finance and Currency, Vol. V., Doc. 281, 275, 276.

not wanted for the payment of the interest or principal of
loans, were, " together with the $15,000,000 for the year ensu-
ing, not to be reissued, but burned or destroyed." Having
thus provided (on paper) for the past, Congress proposed to
make sure of the future by a grand demonstration in the way
of paper money. They ordered (" the faith of the thirteen
United States " being pledged) $50,000,400, on the fourteenth
day of January, and other smaller sums in February, April
and early in May. At length, they became frightened at their
own temerity. Bills were worth but twenty-two for one in
specie, when the states were required, by a resolution dated
May nineteenth, 1779, to pay their respective proportions of
forty-five millions before the first day of the following January,
Connecticut's quota being $5,100,000, Massachusetts' but
$6,000,000. Notwithstanding " the present ease of paying,"
(I use the language of Congress,) the states did not respond.
The amount of taxes paid to the continental government, during the war, up to September thirteenth, 1779, was but
$3,027,56, (in currency, I suppose;) while the whole sum con-
tributed by the American people, in any shape, (in taxes and
loans,) was no more than $36,761,666. Of the loans $7,545,197
were borrowed before the first day of March, 1778, the interest
on which was payable in France ; and $26,188,909, since the
said first of March, the interest payable here. Besides these
sums, there was " money due abroad, not exactly known, supposed to be about $4,000,000," for which values had been re-
ceived. The other funds for the support of the war had been
obtained by bills of credit which, at this period, amounted to
nearly $160,000,000. The " Board of Treasury " had declared
in May previous that it was " impracticable to carry on the
war by paper emissions, at the present enormous expenses of
the commissary-general's, quartermaster-general's, and medical
departments." Congress made known, in June, (1779,) its
" intention not only to avoid further emissions, but to diminish the quantity in circulation ;" and yet, the flow of paper
money continued. The flood rose higher and higher, and the
currency got worse and worse. Over $100,000,000 were issued
in the first eight months of 1779. Under these circumstances,

the most desperate efforts to bolster up the tottering fabric of public credit were vain. Congress appealed to the country again and again, and the appeals were read in the churches. They begged, cajoled and threatened; talked of the resources of the country; of immutable justice and plighted faith; of the ruin and disgrace of repudiation ; and then went off in a rapture at the excellencies of a paper currency. " Let it be remembered," they exclaimed, " that paper money is the only kind of money which cannot 'make to itself wings and fly away.' It remains with us; it will not forsake us ; it is always ready and at hand for the purpose of commerce or taxes, and every industrious man can find it." And this wretched sophistry, intended to blind the people, received the unanimous approval of a body of chosen statesmen, including such men as John Jay !* And what is not a little remarkable, the "circular letter," in which is found this choice specimen of rhetoric, makes the following admission :—" The moment the sum in circulation exceeded what was necessary as a medium in commerce, it began and continued to depreciate in proportion as the amount of the surplus increased." As early as the twenty-second day of November, 1777, a resolution of Congress announced the law which governs a superabundant currency. This is its language :—" No truth is more evident than that where the quantity of money of any denomination exceeds what is useful as a medium of commerce, its comparative value must be proportionately reduced." Though the true principle was, in this manner, occasionally acknowledged, it was not recognized as a living, practical truth—was not allowed to have its legitimate influence on the legislation of the country.

I do not here forget the well understood fact that the amount

---

* It appears from the Life and Writings of Mr. Jay, Vol. I., p. 88, that this somewhat celebrated letter, addressed by Congress to the people, (see the Journal of Congress, September 13th, 1779,) and so " distinguished for perspicuity, eloquence and patriotism," was drawn up by that distinguished and able statesman. Congress, of which he was then president, took the unusual course of requesting of him this service. To appreciate the effort, it should be mentioned that Adam Smith's celebrated " Wealth of Nations," which sets forth clearly the nature and functions of money, had then been before the world three years and a half !

of money, technically so called, does not alone govern the prices of commodities.   There are, among commercial peoples, in
the advanced periods of society, certain money-saving expedients which are made use of to facilitate exchanges.   These, to
the extent that they are employed, diminish the amount of
money required for the business of the country.   Most of the
large payments, in the great commercial centres, are, at the
present day, made by means of deposits in bank, or ledger
credits.   The average deposits of the associated city banks of
New York, at this time, (October, 1864,) are about $146,000,000,
while the circulation is only some $4,130,000.   These two sums
represent, approximately, the amount which those doing business with these institutions must keep on hand for making payments.   Each answers a similar purpose.   Both serve to transfer values.   As a general rule, deposits (controlled by means of
checks or drafts) are employed for the larger, and notes of circulation (or specie where this is in use) for the smaller transactions.   The proportion between the two, required for the
business of a people, depends on several circumstances which
cannot be determined with certainty.   Where the population
is sparse, and a retail trade only is carried on, exchanges are
made, almost wholly, by currency.   This condition of things
exists in the earlier agricultural stages of society.   In the first
and middle periods of the Revolution, there were no banks, and
trade (barter being left out of the account) was carried on by
means of money.   In a place like New York, at this day,
probably ninety-five or ninety-seven per cent. of the exchanges
are effected by means of bank deposits.   The " clearings " of
the associated banks, at the clearing-house, show the magnitude
of the business done by checks and drafts.   They amount, at
this time, (October, 1864,) to about $500,000,000 per week ;
while the " balances " which are paid in money, or some substitute for it, equal only some $16,000,000, or but a little over
three per cent. of the gross amount.   If we embrace in one
view both city and country, or, say, all the states of the Union,
the currency used in trade and commerce would probably equal
the deposits.   According to the finance report of the Secretary of the Treasury, made in 1863, the aggregate circulation

of all the banks was, in the year next before the present war, $202,005,767, and the deposits $257,229,562. But to the former amount must be added the specie then in the hands of the people, in order to show the proportion of currency to deposits. Were this addition made, the lesser might be converted into the larger sum. There are, however, many circumstances to be taken in the account in determining this proportion.

Does any one doubt whether deposits do in fact perform the functions of money, and thus save currency? That they do is shown by the obvious fact that all payments might be made by checks and drafts. Thus what is called a circulating medium might be dispensed with entirely. It would be inconvenient, however, both to individuals and to banks, to manage a retail business in this way. So goods might be exchanged directly, and of course without the intervention of a medium of any kind, as in the case of barter. This is done, to a large extent, in every farming community. Under the pressure of necessity, it might be done so as nearly or wholly to exclude the use of money. The quantity of money of a country, then, need not bear any absolute ratio to its business transactions, or to the prices of commodities. To get at this ratio, we must take an account of exchanges made by means of checks and drafts, and in the way of barter. Could we make an estimate of the money required for every description of trade, and then assume that the transfer of money concluded every commercial act, and discharged every obligation, we could tell the effect which would be produced (I mean the permanent effect) by any addition to the money of a country. If one hundred millions were demanded and used as currency, and fifty millions were added to the sum, the prices of all goods, and of everything produced or controlled by labor, would be raised fifty per cent. This would be the effect, as deduced from inevitable law. Speculation and other temporary influences might modify the result, but these could not annul, or suspend, or delay (except for the moment) the operation of the law.

The time at last came when restrictive legislation, backed by poor declamation, would not satisfy the people. Congress felt constrained, in view of the bottomless pit into which the coun-

try was sinking, to promise some limit to their own action—
some limitation of paper issues. These issues which were in
circulation on the first day of September, 1779, amounted to
$159,948,800. At that date, Congress resolved that they would
"on no account whatever, emit more bills of credit than to
make the whole amount of such bills $200,000,000." Nor
would they increase the sum beyond its present limit, unless
"absolutely necessary." Four days after the date of the "circular letter" announcing these excellent resolutions, and before,
probably, it had been printed and put in circulation, $15,000,260
in bills of credit, "on the faith of the United States," were
authorized. As Congress sat with closed doors, the members
being pledged to the strictest secrecy,* the public, doubtless,
did not know of this speedy renewal of paper issues.

On the twenty-ninth day of November, 1779, the whole of
the deficiency, equaling $40,051,120, was made up. Then,
when continental money had lost thirty-nine fortieths of its
value, the promise "to stop the press" was redeemed. Only
ten days before the last of the paper emissions was resolved
on, Congress attempted, once more, to put in operation the restrictive policy. It "earnestly recommended to the several
states forthwith to enact laws for establishing and carrying into
execution a general limitation of prices," on the basis of
twenty in paper for one in specie. It also proposed "strict
laws against engrossing and withholding." A stringent "act
to prevent sharping and engrossing" had already been passed
by Connecticut, while a modified law to regulate prices was
enacted the succeeding January.

Though it is affirmed that the bills in circulation did not, at
any one time, exceed $200,000,000, yet, the whole amount
issued was largely in excess of that sum. The authorized emissions, with the date, as I have been able to glean them from
the printed Journal of Congress, poorly indexed, amounting
to $242,052,780, were in accordance with the following table.

---

* See Journal of Congress, May 11, 1775, and April 30, 1783. Notwithstanding
the pledges of members, the British government was promptly apprised of all the
important proceedings of Congress.

The issue of $10,000, however, which was ordered January fifth, 1776, " for the purpose of exchanging ragged and torn bills," is not included. I have also omitted the $10,000,000, less five dollars, authorized January fourteenth and May seventh, 1779, which were designed to take the place of the counterfeited emissions of May twentieth, 1777, and April eleventh, 1778.

1775. June 22,.............	$ 2,000,000	
July 25,.....	1,000,000	
November 29,.............	3,000,000	
		$ 6,000,000
1776. February 17,.............	4,000,000	
May 9 and 22,.............	5,000,000	
July 22 and August 13,.......	5,000,000	
November 2,................	500,000	
November 2 and December 28,	5,000,000	
		19,500,000
1777. February 26,.............	5,000,000	
May 20,.....................	5,000,000	
August 1 and 15,............	1,000,000	
November 7,............ ...	1,000,000	
December 3,............ ...	1,000,000	
		13,000,000
1778. January 8,................	1,000,000	
January 22,................	2,000,000	
February 16,....	2,000,000	
March 5,...................	2,000,000	
April 4,...................	1,000,000	
April 11,.................	5,000,000	
April 18,...................	500,000	
May 22,.....................	5,000,000	
June 20,....................	5,000,000	
July 39,....................	5,000,000	
September 5,............	5,000,000	
September 26, ...	10,000,100	
November 4,......	10,000,100	
December 14,...............	10,000,100	
		63,500,300
1779. January 14,................	50,000,400	
February 3,................	5,000,160	
February 19,...............	5,000,160	
April 1,....................	5,000,160	
May 5,.....................	10,000,100	
June 4,...................	10,000,100	
July 17,....................	5,000,180	

8

```
1779. July 17,................ ..........$10,000,100
      September 17,..............    5,000,180
      September 17,.............. ..... 10,000,080
      October 14,.....................   5,000,180
      November 17,...............    5,000,040
      November 17,.................  ....... 5,050,500
      November 29,................... 10,000,140
                                   ——————  140,052,480

                                     $242,052,780
```

I also give an account of the dates and denominations of the
bills, prepared from the private collection of a friend and from
the Journal of Congress:

1775. May 10th, $1, 2, 3, 4, 5, 6, 7, 8. 20, 30.
1775. November 29th, $1, 2, 3, 4, 5, 6, 7, 8.
1776. February 17th, $⅙, ⅓, ½, ⅔, 1, 2, 3, 4, 5, 6, 7, 8.
1776. May 9th, $1, 2, 3, 4, 5, 6, 7, 8.
1776. July 22d, $2, 3, 4, 5, 6, 7, 8, 30.
1776. November 2d, $2, 3, 4, 5, 6, 7, 8, 30.
1777. February 26th, $2, 3, 4, 5, 6, 7, 8, 30.
1777. May 20th, $2, 3, 4, 5, 6, 7, 8, 30.
1778. April 11th, $4, 5, 6, 7, 8, 20, 30, 40.
1778. September 26th, $5, 7, 8, 20, 30, 40, 50, 60.
1779. January 14th, $1, 2, 3, 4, 5, 20, 30, 35, 40, 45, 50, 55, 60, 65, 70, 80.

In a report made to Congress by the Register of the Treasury, January twenty-fourth, 1828, and printed in the American State Papers, Finance, volume fifth, page 764, the authorized issue of $500,000, November second, 1776, in bills
of two-thirds, one-third, one-sixth and one-ninth of a dollar,
is overlooked. No bills of the last denomination are known
to antiquarians, and it is believed that none was ever emitted.
And from the fact that no fractional notes, bearing the date
of November second, 1776, have been discovered, it has been
inferred that the entire issue was suppressed. But this inference is not fairly drawn. It was not customary to give a
new date to each emission, as will be seen by an inspection of
the preceding tables. Old plates would naturally be employed
so long as they were fit for use; and when new ones were engraved, old dates often seem to have been preserved. I have
been unable to find any proof that the bills of November
second, 1776, which were of the same denominations as those

authorized the seventeenth of February preceding, were *not* issued.

Breck, in his Sketch of Continental Paper Money, page eighteen, makes a great mistake when he says that the continental emissions, during the war, were " about $300,000,000." The table which Gouge gives, (taken from the American Almanac,) in his History of Paper Money, page ten, which makes the old issues $357,476,541, represents, if I understand it, not the original emissions merely, but the entire disbursements of the Treasury, in continental money, from the beginning to the close of the war.

After Congress had ceased to issue more bills, the Treasury continued to pay out those which were received. About $83,000,000, old tenor, were disbursed in 1780, and over $11,400,000 in 1781. The specie value of the whole must have been less than $2,000,000.

The pride of France had been deeply wounded by the treaty of 1763, and she rejoiced to see England in the way of being humbled. At an early period, a disposition was shown to help the revolted American Colonies. Arthur Lee, the agent of the secret committee of Congress, in London, in the spring of 1776, entered into negotiation with Beaumarchais, an eccentric French courtier and dramatist, and the confidential agent of the French ministry. Lee, according to his own statement, was promised assistance, in the way of gift, to the extent of two hundred thousand louis-d'or, nearly $1,000,000, in arms, ammunition and specie; but the affair was to be managed in the most secret manner possible, to avoid a rupture with England. To turn aside suspicion, it was arranged that the business should be done through a commercial house bearing the fictitious name of Roderique, Hortales and Co., of which Beaumarchais was the responsible head. His receipt shows that he received from the court of France, June tenth, 1776, (before the declaration of independence,) one million livres. August eleventh, of the same year, a like amount was put into his hands, contributed, at the solicitation of the French King, by the Spanish government. In May, June and July of the next year, France made other advancements to the extent of 1,074,496 livres.* These several sums amount to $569,437.

Beaumarchais, entering enthusiastically into the scheme of the French ministry, became a great Spanish merchant and "rebel sympathizer." He hired "an immense house" in Paris, installed himself in it with his officers and clerks, borrowed "from the different state arsenals two hundred cannons, mortars, shell, cannon balls; twenty-five thousand guns, two hundred and ninety thousand pounds of powder, and clothing and tents for twenty-five thousand men." His first three ships, escaping the English cruisers, "arrived at the commencement of the campaign of 1777, in the roads of Portsmouth."† Other vessels, with their cargoes, arrived at a later period. In the mean time, the French court, pressed by the English embassador, denied (notwithstanding what had occurred) having any knowledge of the transactions of their secret agent. Beaumarchais ingeniously took advantage of his position. Though "M. de Vergennes, the minister, and his secretary had repeatedly assured" Arthur Lee "that no return was to be expected for these cargoes, or for what M. de Beaumarchais furnished us," the latter, alledging that the shipments had been made on his own private account, presented a claim against Congress for advances—a claim for "divers invoices and cargoes shipped"—amounting, according to the Journal of Congress of June fifth, 1779, to 4,547,593 livres, nearly £200,000 sterling. This demand, after the assurances of Lee, was indeed a surprise. But Beaumarchais, who had become deeply involved in debt, was importunate, and the sum above named was, at length, paid, one million livres (which were known, at the time, to have been furnished by France, for the benefit of the United States, to *some one*) having been first deducted. This course appears to have been taken to prevent the exposure of cabinet secrets. Beaumarchais was not satisfied with the deduction, and continued his suit for the

---

* For several of these facts I am indebted to a curious volume, translated from the French, entitled "Beaumarchais and his Times," by Louis de Loménie, published by Harper & Brothers, 1857. See Chapters XVIII, XIX, XX.

† *Ibid.* pp. 289, 291.

balance. His renewed application, strangely enough, was favored by the court of France. At length, after the overthrow of the French monarchy, when reasons for concealment no longer existed, the name of the person to whom was paid the one million livres advanced, June tenth, 1776, was produced. Old suspicions were confirmed, the receipt being signed by *Beaumarchais.* The latter, notwithstanding, persisted in his claim, and after his death, in 1799, his heirs continued to press it. On this claim, Congress, wearied with importunity, allowed, in 1835, eight hundred thousand francs.

In the first volume (chapter tenth) of Pitkin's Political and Civil History of the United States, may be found a good and apparently truthful account of this mysterious affair. Pitkin, however, relies on the declarations of Arthur Lee to prove the original intentions of the French court. The author of " Beaumarchais and his Times" controverts the statements of Lee, and accuses him of "falsehood," &c. The truth is the French minister prevaricated and shuffled. He took effectual measures to help the Americans, and then, wishing to escape the charge of bad faith, denied what he had done. During the progress of the negotiations for peace, he declared to the British minister, in the presence of Dr. Franklin, that " independence was declared by the Americans *long before* they received the least encouragement from France, and he defied the world to give the smallest proof to the contrary."*

Beside the assistance which the United States received through Beaumarchais, the French government paid directly to the American commissioners, previous to the treaty of February, 1778, and as a gratuity, two million livres.† In addition to this amount, one million livres were loaned by the farmers-general of France.

---

* Franklin's Works, Vol. IX., p. 274, Spark's edition.

† In the articles of settlement between Franklin and the French minister, dated February 25th, 1783, which will be found in the Appendix to the last volume of the Journal of Congress, "the aids granted by the King to the United States" are recapitulated. In the third class are comprehended "the aids and subsidies furnished to the Congress, under the title of gratuitous assistance from the pure generosity of the king, 3,000,000 of which were granted before the

After the capture of Burgoyne's army, in October, 1777, it became evident that the dismemberment of the British empire might, by timely assistance to the Americans, be made certain. France, therefore, desiring to take an open part in the struggle, sought an alliance with the United States, and signed a treaty, dated February 6th, 1778. Material aid was also rendered in the way of loan—three million livres in the course of the year 1778, one million in 1779, four million in 1780, four million in 1781, and six million in 1782; in all eighteen million livres, or $3,333,333, at five per cent. annual interest. The interest, however, was afterwards remitted till " the date of the treaty of peace" with England—a favor which the minister of Congress acknowledged " to flow from the pure bounty of the King." Beside all this, France, in 1781, furnished in way of subsidy, six million livres, and guaranteed a loan, at four per cent., made in Holland, of five million Dutch florins, equal to ten million French livres. Including all these items, the French government, during the war, assisted the United States to the extent of thirty-seven million livres, nine million by subsidy, (including the one million paid to Beaumarchais in June, 1776,) eighteen million by loan, and ten million by guarantee, the whole equaling $6,851,852. This sum does not include the one million livres from the farmers-general; nor does it comprehend a loan of six million livres, at five per cent. interest, which, in February, 1783, was made " from the funds of the royal Treasury," at the solicitation of Franklin, to " meet urgent and indispensable expenses." Other moneys were obtained from other sources. Mr. Jay, with much difficulty, borrowed $150,000 of Spain, in 1781, at five per cent. interest; while John Adams, in June, 1782, contracted with " certain lenders " in Holland, for a loan, at a similar interest, of five million guilders, or ten million French livres, on which contract $671,200 had been paid, April twenty-ninth, 1783.

The above were all the sums which the agents of Congress

---

treaty of February, 1778." To make the three million livres, it will be necessary to include the 1,000,000 paid to Beaumarchais, June 10th, 1776, and to exclude the other sums furnished him, 1,074,496 by France, and 1,000,000 by Spain.

were able, by the greatest efforts, to beg or borrow from the courts and capitalists of Europe till after the close of the war. In the aggregate, they amounted to \$8,639,348, counting only so much of the last Dutch loan as had been received at the last mentioned date. They were quite disproportionate to the need of the states; but were, nevertheless, a great help. The alliance with France was an important event, happening at a most interesting period of the war. It made certain a result which was before doubtful; but it did not give the relief which was expected. Above all, it did not rescue the perishing credit of the continental government, so recklessly sacrificed by paper money and bad management.

The depreciation of the currency, and the embarrassment which it introduced, gave great encouragement to the British government. The adherents of the latter openly declared that they had but to wait a little to see America become its own conqueror. This subject gave Washington the greatest anxiety. Speaking of the difficulty growing out of paper money, he declared it "the only hope, the last resource of the enemy." Said he, in another place, we are laboring under two of the greatest evils, a reduced army and the "want of money, or rather a redundancy of it, by which it is become of no value." " A wagon load of money," he remarked, on still another occasion, " will hardly purchase a wagon load of provisions."* To increase the confusion, the issues of May twentieth, 1777, and of April eleventh, 1778, were extensively counterfeited by the Tories of New York, so that Congress was constrained, by a resolution bearing date January second, 1779, to call them in to be exchanged. The soldiers complained of the worthless character of the money they received, and some corps declined to accept it. The two regiments of the Connecticut line that mutinied in May, 1779, were impelled by poor pay and scanty food. The depreciation of the currency in which their wages were paid was afterwards made good to them.

---

* Writings, Vol. VI., p. 229.

CHAPTER VIII.

MORE PAPER MONEY, AND THE FINAL OVERTHROW OF THE SYS-
TEM.   HOW CONNECTICUT SUPPORTED THE WAR.

IN the beginning of 1780, all seemed to be satisfied that the
credit of the currency was irrecoverably gone—that broken promises could not be made as good as gold and silver.   At this
juncture, when existing facts could no longer be ignored, the Assembly of the State undertook to do justice (on paper) to certain of its creditors, and thus declared its intentions :—" It be-
hooves every government to render justice, as far as possible,
to every member belonging thereto, and in a most especial
manner to those who have placed a particular confidence in
their equity."   Therefore it was enacted, (in January, 1780,)
" that the notes executed and issued by the Treasurer of this
State, by virtue of an act passed in December, 1776, and the
bills of credit which have been loaned to this State in consequence of an act passed in May, 1777, and in consequence of
another act passed in February, 1778, and also the bills of public credit which have been loaned as aforesaid in consequence
of an act passed in May, 1778, shall be paid for, together with
the interest, to the respective lenders, in gold or silver, or in
bills of credit of this State, according to the full value of the
said bills or notes when they were loaned or issued as aforesaid."

By the same act, three taxes were granted, each of twelve
shillings on the pound, payable in April, June and November,
(1780,) in continental money, or at the option of the tax payer,
in gold and silver, or the bills emitted by the present or future
assemblies, one in coin or the new bills being reckoned as
equal to thirty in continental money.*   The two first of these

---

* These taxes, amounting to thirty-six shillings on the pound, did not prove so
burdensome as was to be apprehended, owing to the continued depreciation of the

taxes—those payable in April and June—were intended to meet state expenses and the demands of Congress. The last was to remain in the Treasury till otherwise ordered. "For the relief of the indigent," abatements were permitted in each town to the extent of one-twentieth part of the taxes. As a further measure to meet the requisitions of Congress, authority was given to borrow one million pounds in "bills of the common currency of the United States, already issued," on the following conditions:—Every one who shall deposit with the Treasurer for the use of the State any sum in said bills, not less than one hundred and eighty pounds, shall receive therefor one-thirtieth part of the amount in silver or gold within six years from the date of deposit, with six per cent. annual interest, the interest payable in coin, or in state bills having not more than seven years to run, and bearing not less than four per cent. annual interest. The Treasurer's notes which were to be issued for this loan were called bank notes, and were to be paid "to the possessors." Owing probably to the continued depreciation of bills, this law was repealed in May following.

Another part of this act authorized the emission of £40,000, "lawful money, in bills of public credit, computing every six shillings to be equal to one Spanish milled dollar," redeemable March first, 1784, with interest from date, (March first, 1780,) at five per cent. per annum. They were issued on the plan of those emitted with so much success at the breaking out of the French war, in 1755; and it was expected, without considering the difference of circumstances, that they would be received with similar favor. For their payment, a six penny tax, becoming due January first, 1784, was laid, and the Treasurer was to issue his warrant for its collection, &c. And as the bills emitted in virtue of this act were "founded upon the most indubitable principles of public credit, and ought to be regarded

currency. In April and June, bills were worth, in Philadelphia, sixty for one, in November, eighty for one. At the last rate, a tax of twelve shillings would have amounted to less than two pence, in specie. It should, however, be remembered that the depreciation was somewhat less in Connecticut and New England than in Philadelphia, and some other places.

accordingly," the Assembly ordered that they should be "received in payment of all salaries, fees and rewards for services within this State." It also enacted that if any quartermaster or commissary, using this money, should "knowingly give more for any purchase, hire or service, than the same might have been obtained for in coin," he should forfeit the amount of the sums so expended, and pay a fine of one hundred pounds in the bills of this act. And as there were "villains and traitors" about, "who, under the mask of friendship, and by dark, insidious and detestable conduct, endeavored to defeat every public measure, by offering exorbitant prices," &c., it was further provided that if any person should offer or give "excessive or unnecessary prices for any article or service," either in coin or bills of this act, or should, by his conduct, "afford a reasonable proof" of a design or intention to injure the public credit, he should pay such fine as the court should judge reasonable, and be imprisoned for a term of not more than three years. The act of February, 1778, regulating prices, had been, soon after its passage, and at the instance of Congress, first suspended and then repealed; and the present law was enacted in consequence, apparently, of a desire which Congress had expressed (November nineteenth, 1779) to try once more the restrictive policy. The plan proposed required that paper should pass at one-twentieth part of its nominal value, and Connecticut did not, in this instance, come quite up to the requirment. She was not often delinquent.

At the same session, (January, 1780,) the statute of October, 1776, making continental and state bills a legal tender, was so changed as to make them a tender "according to their current value," [as measured by specie,] at the time of the contract, &c.; but creditors living in other states which should not "make similar laws to promote equal justice" were not entitled to the benefits of the new law. This alteration was made, notwithstanding Congress had just refused to reccommend to the states a similar measure.

In February, 1781, the modified tender act of January, 1780, was, in anticipation of any action on the part of the general government, repealed, "the longer continuance of said act being of no public use or benefit." Thus ended the legal tender iniquity in Connecticut.

One month later, Congress showed signs of repentance. March sixteenth, she proposed to the states to amend their tender laws, and two months afterwards, (May twenty-second, 1781,) advised their unconditional repeal, " experience having evinced the inefficiency of all attempts to support the credit of paper money by compulsory acts." This experience, though frightfully expensive, was supposed, till a recent period, to have been worth all it cost.

In the year last mentioned, at its May session, the Connecticut Assembly repealed so much of the law of January, 1780, as made the bills then authorized receivable for all [public] salaries, fees, rewards, &c.

The legislation of Connecticut, during the trying period of the revolutionary war, and on the exciting questions of the time, was sufficiently reprehensible; but as compared with that of the other states, it was moderate and conservative. Her leading statesmen were, after the standard of that day, shrewd, considerate and wise. Throughout her colonial existence, she was distinguished for the comparative mildness of her laws. In illustration of this fact, it may be stated that her government was the only one from New Hampshire to Georgia which did not make death the penalty of counterfeiting.

Congress was disappointed at the failure of all their schemes to establish the public credit. The supports on which they relied had given way—their most cherished plans had come to naught. It seemed as if the war could no longer be maintained either by borrowing, begging, printing, taxing or impressing; and patriotic resolves were useless. Good intentions on the part of those who governed could not save a rebel population. The country had been nearly destroyed by bad legislation, and the reckless, senseless use of paper money. The army, greatly reduced in numbers, was perishing from privation. The people had lost confidence in their rulers, and a deep gloom settled down upon the land. But something must be done. With small prospect of relief, Congress renewed its efforts to raise money on loan-office certificates, and made a show of a still more vigorous taxation. October sixth, 1779, " deeply concerned that the sums required were so great," they made a requisition on the states for $15,000 000, monthly, for nine months, beginning with the first day of February, 1780. (This was in addition to all former requisitions.) Fearing that this measure would not sufficiently reduce prices, they once more advised the states (as already mentioned) to pass limitation-acts, and to enforce "strict laws against engrossing and withholding"!

The fund of continental bills was exhausted. The requisitions payable in continental money had produced little and promised still less. It seemed doubtful whether the army could much longer be kept together with paper money, even though the taxes were collected. In this state of things, when the British trooops were overrunning the southern country, and the people were well nigh disheartened, Congress resolved, February twenty-fifth, 1780, to call on the states for "specific supplies"—beef, flour, Indian corn, hay, salt, tobacco, rum, rice—those articles most needed for the use of the army. These things were apportioned among the states, at stated prices, according to the natural advantages of each. New England was to furnish most of the rum; and what is not a little remarkable, about four gallons of this popular beverage were required for each barrel of flour. (The Indian corn appears to have been wanted for forage.) On the fourth day of November, Congress again called for army supplies and money, equal in value to $6,000,000, in silver. Georgia, now a loyal state, made so by British bayonets, was not embraced in the call. Other requisitions, made during the year, produced little but disappointment, as proved by the fact that the entire disbursements of the Treasury, for 1780, including eighty-three million of continental money, were but $3,000,000, specie value. The scheme of supplying the army by taxes payable in "specifics" proved to be excessively burdensome and expensive, and was abandoned.

Driven to the wall, but not yet ready to abandon its paper delusions, or to give up the war, Congress hit upon a new expedient which it hoped might replenish the Treasury. As it was pledged to issue no more continental bills, a little ingenuity was necessary. The new scheme was adopted and recommended, March eighteenth, 1780, and required the states to levy a tax of fifteen million dollars, monthly, for thirteen months, (instead of for nine months, as required by a former resolution,) payable in continental bills, or in specie at the rate of one for forty. Connecticut's quota was $1,700,000 monthly, $22,100,000, in all, or more than one-ninth part. Of this amount, she appears to have paid into the continental Treasury, first and last, $9,151,484$\frac{40}{90}$ in bills, or $228,787$\frac{12}{90}$, specie value.* This requisition on the states, amounting in the whole to $195,000,000, was designed to call in all the paper money of Congress then afloat. In lieu of the bills withdrawn, the resolution provided that others should be issued to the extent of one-twentieth part of those retired. The new bills would amount to about ten million dollars, which is Mr. P. Webster's estimate of the currency which the country naturally required. They were to be issued by the individual states, in exchange for the old notes, and in proportion to their several quotas, and guaranteed by the United States. They were to be paid in Spanish milled dollars, were to bear five per cent. (Hildreth incorrectly says six per cent.) annual interest, and to run six years, funds (i. e., taxes) to be provided to sink one-sixth part each year. Of these bills, the states issuing them were to receive, for their own use, six-tenths, and the general government four-tenths.

The new scheme for reforming the currency, restoring the government credit, and controlling prices, was a conspicuous failure. The taxes recommended by Congress were but partially collected ; the old tenor nuisance was not abated, and the new tenor bills did not secure the confidence of the public. Of the latter, there were issued, according to Mr. Hildreth, $4,400,000, this sum taking the place of $88,000,000, old tenor, paid into the state treasuries and destroyed.† Mr. Hildreth may be correct in this matter, but a statement which I find in

---

* American State Papers, Finance, I., 58. When the Constitution went into operation, all the states had paid in, under the resolution of March 18, 1780, $119,498,566.

† History of the United States, Vol. III., p. 446, first series.

the American State Papers* represents that the general government "appropriated" of the new issues, received from all the states, $1,592,222$\frac{44}{90}$, two-thirds of the amount emitted by Massachusetts and Pennsylvania. As the sum to be paid into the United States Treasury was four-tenths of the whole, the issues of bills under the resolution of March, 1780, must have been $3,980,556; while the old bills called in to make room for them must have equaled $79,611,126. The new currency rapidly declined in value. The agents of Congress paid it out at different rates, but by average at three for one of specie, no account being taken of the accrued interest.† At length, it became worth, in the general market, no more than five or six for one, and Congress advised that the states should stop the supply. Connecticut (and I might add Delaware, North and South Carolina and Georgia) emitted none of the new bills, though she took up enough of the old paper to entitle her to a large issue. Mr. Hildreth improperly classes her with those states that wholly failed to meet the requisitions of Congress, and leaves us to infer that she emitted nothing because this failure precluded her from the right of doing otherwise.‡ The true reason why the state did not avail herself of her right will be mentioned in another place.

The Assembly of Connecticut, in April, (1780,) approved the resolution of Congress of March eighteenth. They thought their quota of continental bills disproportionally large, but engaged to sink the amount assigned to the State as fast as circumstances would permit. At the same time, they resolved to issue the new bills reccommended by Congress, and as a fund for their redemption, laid a tax of seven pence on the pound, " lawful money," for each of six successive years, payable December thirty-first, 1781, and afterward, in bills issued in

---

* Finance, I., 53.

† See Journal of Congress, April 4th, 1781.

‡ From a document in the State Library, dated Pay-table office, May 17, 1787, and signed Oliver Wolcott, Jr., it appears that the continental bills received from J. Law, Esq., and destroyed by the commissioner of accounts of Connecticut from January, 1780, to August, 1783, amounted to $8,102,424$\frac{5}{9}$, nominal money, in sundry emissions from May 10, 1775, to January 14, 1779.

accordance with this act, or in like bills emitted by other states. A tax of twelve shillings on the pound was also granted, payable "in the common currency of the United States," September first then next, the bills when collected to be destroyed. At the next session, in May, the new bills which were to be provided by Congress were "not prepared." There was a great pressure on the Treasury, and a law was enacted that £100,000, in lawful money, should be emitted, on the faith of the State, bearing five per cent. annual interest, and payable March first, 1785, in specie. These bills, bearing date July first, 1780, were to be in lieu of those reccommended by Congress. The act was not in accordance with the plan. At the same time, two taxes were laid, one of four pence on the pound, payable on the first day of the ensuing August, and one of six pence, payable the succeeding first day of January. Specie only, or bills emitted since February, 1780, or yet to be emitted, were to be received for these taxes. The notes thus collected were not to be reissued except by order of the Assembly.* At the same session, another issue of £50,000 was ordered, the bills to be dated June 1, 1780, and payable March first, 1784. They were of the same tenor as those of the last emission, and were not to be reissued. To redeem them, a tax of seven pence was laid, to be paid in the new bills or hard money, on or before January first, 1784.

The three emissions of January and May, 1780, amounting to £190,000, bearing five per cent. interest, were the last of the paper money of Connecticut.

In October, 1780, an important law was passed by the Assembly. It was entitled "An Act to ascertain the current value of continental bills," &c., and enacted "that all contracts made on or before the first day of September, 1777, for lawful money, or bills of credit of this State, or continental bills of credit, shall be deemed equal to the same nominal sum in gold or silver; that all contracts made between the first day of September, 1777, and the eighteenth day of March, 1780, un-

---

* In October, 1780, it was ordered that £33,000 and no more of the bills of the July emission should be reissued.

derstood or expressed to be for the common currency of the United States or of this State, shall be rated in Spanish milled dollars, or other coins equivalent, agreeable to the following table, which shows the value of one hundred Spanish milled dollars, in continental bills of credit, at the several times therein expressed," &c. The table referred to was in accordance with a scale of depreciation adopted by Congress, (see the abstract near the end of this chapter,) in conformity with which loan office and commissary certificates were to be liquidated.* For political reasons, perhaps, it did not represent truly the facts. The depreciation was usually much greater than is stated. For instance, on the first day of September, 1777, when the table commences, paper is put down at par, when, in fact, it was worth in Philadelphia but thirty-three and a third per cent. of its face. On the eighteenth of March, 1780, paper was valued at the rate of forty for one of specie, when it could not be exchanged at a better rate than sixty for one.† The State was a considerable loser and its creditors gainers, by this over-valuation of continental money. The scale as adopted by the State and made the "rule in all courts of law," the calculation being made for the first and fifteenth of each month, is printed in the several editions of the "Statutes" down to 1808. By a later act passed in October, 1782, "all actions

---

* "*Resolved*, That the principal of all loans that have been made to these United States shall finally be discharged, by paying the full current value of the bills when loaned, which payments shall be made in Spanish milled dollars, or the current exchange thereof, in other money, at the time of payment." Journal of Congress, June 8th, 1780.

The assumed value of the bills when loaned may be ascertained by reference to the table above referred to. The latter will be found at length in the fifth volume of American State Papers, p. 766, the calculation being made for every day of the period which it covers. The rule thus laid down was observed by this State. Other states adopted scales of their own.

† This rate was not uniform throughout the country, but varied with the expenditures of the government, the activity of business, &c. As a general rule, the depreciation was first perceived, and was also greatest, in the centers of commerce and population. In New England, it was usually less than in Philadelphia. The difference in "exchange" led, at one time, to extensive speculation. Men called sharpers, in Philadelphia, exchanged their goods for bills, and with the latter, went to Boston, and swept the market of similar goods, pocketing a large profit.

brought before any of the Superior or County courts for the recovery of any debt due by bond, note, or book account, contracted before or on the seventh day of January, 1782," for the discharge of which continental bills had been tendered and refused, were to be decided "according to the rules of equity."

In November, 1780, the holders of the ten pound notes of 1777, [issued in exchange for the bills of credit of the old emission,] or of any notes given for Connecticut money, or for moneys loaned to the State, were invited to exchange them, principal and interest, for new notes, the latter being reduced in accordance with the scale of depreciation adopted in October previous. The new promises, dated February first, 1781, were redeemable, in gold and silver, one year after the war, and bore six per cent. interest, payable annually.

When once satisfied that the war could not be carried on by paper money of any kind, and that heavier taxes must be laid, Connecticut bent her neck to the yoke, and acted with promptness and efficiency. Indeed, she had never been backward in the imposition of taxes. Washington singled her out, in a letter to Edmund Pendleton, in November, 1779, for her policy in this regard, and placed her in opposition to "the other states." Her last issues of notes for currency were not in accordance with the recommendation of Congress. But these were designed for a temporary purpose only, and measures were taken to call them in speedily. In October, 1780, a tax was granted of five pence on the pound, payable October first, 1781, in silver or gold or the bills of the July emission, (£33,000 of which had been reissued,) and another of twelve pence on the pound, payable December thirty-first, 1780. The last was for the purpose of sinking "the residue of bills emitted since January first last," and for bounties to soldiers. Payment was to be made in specie, or in state money emitted since the preceding January, or in new continental bills issued under the authority of the State, or in old continental paper at the rate of forty for one. To meet, in part, the requisition of Congress, and to clear the way for the issue of the new continental money, a tax was

9

also laid of four dollars on a pound, to be paid at the same date in old continental currency, or in new state bills at the rate of one for forty, or in gold and silver at the same rate. To show how the Connecticut people were taxed at this period, I will refer to an advertisement which I find in the " Hartford Cour. ant" for January fifteenth, 1781. Israel Williams, collector, of Hartland, gives notice that he has received from the Treasurer of the State ten warrants to collect rates, as follows:— twelve shillings on the pound, due July first, [1780,] payable "in old continental [money]"; four pence on the pound, due August first in [new] state money; twelve shillings on the pound, due September first, in old continental; two pence on the pound, due October first, in state money; twelve shillings on the pound, due November first, in old continental; twenty-four shillings on the pound, due December twenty-ninth, in old continental; one shilling on the pound, due December twenty-ninth, in state money; six pence on the pound, due January first, [1781,] in state money; one shilling on the pound, due February first, in state money; two and a half pence on the pound, due March first, in silver or gold. All these rates were on the list of 1779. The advertiser also states that he has three other warrants for taxes on the list of 1780:—one of twenty-four shillings on the pound, [due March first, 1781,] in old continental; one of one penny, [due March first, 1781,] in silver; one of two pence, [due May first, 1781,] in silver. Here are in all thirteen different taxes, amounting, in the aggregate, to eighty-seven shillings five pence half-penny, on the pound, all becoming due in the space of ten months. Of this amount, eighty-four shillings on the pound were payable in old continental bills, worth, at the time of the collector's notice, one hundred for one; three shillings on the pound in [new] state money, and five and a half pence on the pound, payable in specie. And the taxes were not much lighter at other periods of the war. In 1777, when bills were worth about one-third their face, they amounted to twenty-eight pence on the pound; in 1778, to fifty-five pence on the pound, bills being equal to one-fifth their nominal value; in 1779, to thirty-one shillings,* equal, say, to fifteen pence on the pound, in specie, or six per cent. on the list of polls and estates.

But it should be remembered that the lists, at that period, did not represent truly the property, real and personal, of the State. Dwelling houses, for instance, until May, 1780, did not go into the list; but house lots of three acres were rated at twenty shillings per acre, one-third higher than the other best lands. Till January, 1779, the polls of all male persons between sixteen and seventy years of age, were set in the list at eighteen pounds; but at that time the law was changed, and those between sixteen and twenty-one years were put down at nine pounds. Even after the change, about two-fifths of the amount of the taxable lists were derived from polls, representing no property. By the revised laws of 1784, which, in regard to the principles and most of the details of taxation, were not different from those which, for long periods, had been and continued to be in force, dwelling houses went into the list " at fifteen shillings for each fire-place therein," proper deductions being made if the buildings were old and decayed. Horned cattle and " horse-kind " were set down at from one to four pounds each; the best meadow lands, (which were in Hartford County,) at fifteen shillings per acre; meadow lands, salt and fresh, in the other counties, (Middlesex and Tolland were not incorporated,) seven and six pence; plowed lands, in the years of bearing crops, ten shillings per acre; cleared pasture lands, eight shillings; bush pasture, two shillings; uninclosed lands, from two shillings to six pence per acre; coaches, twenty-five pounds each; phaetons, fifteen pounds; chaises, five pounds; gold watches, five pounds; money on interest, at six per cent. of its amount; plate, at six per cent. of its value. These are specimens. Lawyers were assessed at fifty pounds and upwards; physicians and surgeons, at ten pounds and upwards; tavern-keepers, at fifteen pounds and upwards; persons following " any mechanical art or mystery," five pounds and upwards; the best corn-mills, eighty

---

* See MSS. Finance and Currency, Vol. V., for a report of a committee giving a list of the taxes during the war.

pounds, &c., &c. On the gross sum of all these items, taxes
were levied, one penny on a pound raising, in 1783, after abatements, about six thousand two hundred and fifty pounds.
What proportion the lists made up in the manner described,
bore to the entire property of the State, real and personal, it is
difficult to say. The first may have been to the last as one to
twenty-five.

The Assembly resorted to other methods to sink their quota
of the old continental money. They authorized the Treasurer
to exchange, to the extent of £50,000, old for new continental
bills, the latter to be issued by this State, in pursuance of the
Act of Congress of March eighteenth, the exchange to take
place at the established rate of forty for one. And as a large
part of the State's quota of old bills was still outstanding, a
resolution was passed, November, 1780, that, for the speedy
calling in of three million, a public lottery be authorized, the
same to be drawn on or before the twentieth of May [then]
next. The tickets were to be purchased with old bills and to be
drawn out in new bills. The scheme was advertised several
times in the Hartford Courant ; but neither this nor the other
plan which proposed an exchange of the old for the new money
seems to have succeeded. I judge so from the fact that none of
the new currency was ever emitted by this State.* It was not
emitted, because the new bills, as the record says, (May, 1782,)
"could not be issued on a par with gold and silver." The
truth is, the proposed new tenor money was not regarded with
favor. The people, I suppose, could see no advantage in exchanging promises, giving forty for one, with no additional security.

To meet its most pressing engagements, the State also proposed to raise money by loan. In November, 1780, the Governor was authorized to negotiate a loan of £200,000, lawful
money, in Europe or America, to run from seven to twenty
years, with annual interest at not over six per cent.—" funds
to be established." $30,000 were also to be borrowed at six

---

* I find that the act for a lottery was repealed at the February session, 1781,
the money paid for tickets to be refunded.

per cent. interest, the latter payable in gold or silver, redeemable one year after the war, the lender to receive the annual interest one year in advance.

According to the report of the Secretary of the Treasury, May eleventh, 1790, showing the estimated specie value of the moneys paid by the several states to the United States, from the beginning of the war to the above period,* Connecticut was credited with $1,607,259, as follows, omitting fractions :—

On account of specie requisitions, [leaving unpaid $381,869,]   - $210,420
Paid in indents, or certificates for interest on the public debt, [leaving
   $698,091 in indents unpaid,]   -   -   -   -   -   -   111,791
On account of the requisition of March eighteenth, 1780, in continental
   bills at forty for one,   -   -   -   -   -   -   228,787
On account of taxes collected in old emissions on the several requisi-
   tions, specie value,   -   -   .   -   -   -   -   375,996
Continental money credited on the treasury books from the beginning
   of the war to the present time, $251,720. [This sum is omitted in
   the footing. See next item.]
Value in specie of the continental money credited,   -   -   -   172,797
Credits on the books of the quartermaster, commissary, marine, cloth
   ing, and hospital departments, specie value,   -   -   -   507,468

                                                    ――――――
                                                    $1,607,259

This then is the amount paid by Connecticut directly to the general government for the support of the war. In the same

---

* The following are the total amounts debited and credited to each State. See Am. State Papers, I., 54, 55.

	Dr.	Cr.
New Hampshire,................$	440,974	$ 466,555
Massachusetts,...................	1,245,737	3,167,020
Rhode Island,...................	1,028,511	310,395
Connecticut, ...	1,016,273	1,607,259
New York,.......	822,803	1,545,889
New Jersey,.......................	366,730	1,607,259
Pennsylvania,...................	2,087,276	2,629,410
Delaware,......	63,817	208,879
Maryland, ...	609,617	945,537
Virginia,.....................	483,282	1,965,011
North Carolina,.................	795,431	219,839
South Carolina,.................	1,024,743	499,325
Georgia,.......................	687,579	122,744

account there are charges against the State for continental
money advanced, amounting to $1,716,517, equal in specie to
$1,016,273. If this sum is deducted from the other, a balance
will appear in favor of the State of $590,986.

Soon after the act of Congress of March eighteenth, 1780, old
continental bills, then worth sixty for one, began to depreciate
more rapidly than ever. In January, 1781, they were valued one
hundred for one, and about the first of May, two hundred for
one. They still, however, continued to discharge the functions
of a currency. Their circulation was brisk. Anything, even
hard money, might be bought with them, if only a sufficient
sum were offered. At last, " May thirty-first, 1781," says Pelatiah Webster, (page five hundred and two,) " continental
money ceased to pass as currency, but was afterward bought
and sold as an article of speculation, at very uncertain and
desultory prices, from five hundred to one thousand for one."
In the end, the " two hundred million lost all their value, and
were laid aside. The annihilation was so complete that barber-
shops were papered, in jest, with the bills; and the sailors, on
returning from their cruise, being paid off in bundles of this
worthless money, had suits of clothes made of it, and with
characteristic light-heartedness turned their loss into a frolic by
parading through the streets in decayed finery, which, in its
better days, had passed for thousands of dollars."* The outstanding portion of this money, (which, at the close of the war,
amounted, according to Hildreth, to about $70,000,000,) was
finally funded, under the Constitution, one hundred dollars in
paper being exchanged for one dollar in United States stock.†

I here subjoin a table showing the depreciation of old continental bills on the first of each month, made out in accordance
with the rule of Congress.‡ The figures in the last column
showing the depreciation in Philadelphia, (day of the month
not indicated,) is taken from Mr. Webster's volume of Essays:

---

* Breck's Sketch, p. 15.

† See " Act making provision for the debt of the United States," approved
Aug. 4, 1790.

‡ See ante, p. 128, note, and Am. State Papers, Finance, V., 766.

SCALES OF DEPRECIATION OF CONTINENTAL MONEY.

| Year and Month. | Value of 100 continental dollars in specie,—scale of Congress. | | | Number of continental dollars given for one dollar in specie, according to the Merchants Books of Philadelphia. | Year and month. | Value of 100 continental dollars in specie,—scale of Congress. | | | Number of continental dollars given for one dollar in specie, according to the Merchants Books of Philadelphia. |
	Dolls.	90ths.	8ths.			Dolls.	90ths.	8ths.	
1777.					April,	9	05	0,	12¼, 14, 16, 22.
January,				1¼.	May,	8	20	5,	22, 24.
February,				1½.	June,	7	40	6,	22, 20, 18.
March,				2.	July,	6	69	4,	18, 19, 20.
April,				2.	August,	6	12	9,	20.
May,				2½.	September,	5	50	0,	20, 28.
June,				2½.	October,	4	83	2,	30.
July,				3.	November,	4	31	4,	32, 45.
August,				3.	December,	3	77	0,	45, 38.
September,	100	00	0,	3.					
October,	91	12	6,	3.	**1780.**				
November,	82	73	0,	3.	January,	3	36	3,	40, 45.
December,	75	42	6,	4.	February,	3	00	5,	45, 55.
					March,	2	60	7,	60, 65.
1778.					March 18,	2	45	0,	
January,	68	52	0,	4.	April,	2	45	0,	60.
February,	62	27	7,	5.	May,	2	45	0,	60.
March,	57	12	6,	5.	June,	2	45	0,	60.
April,	49	64	2,	6.	July,	2	45	0,	60, 65.
May,	43	40	0,	5.	August,	2	45	0,	65, 75.
June,	37	71	5,	4.	September,	2	45	0,	75.
July,	33	02	5,	4.	October,	2	45	0,	75, 80.
August,	28	66	1,	5.	November,	2	45	0,	80, 100.
September,	25	00	0,	5.	December,	2	45	0,	100.
October,	21	43	0,	5.					
November,	18	32	1,	6.	**1781.**				
December,	15	69	3,	6.	January,	2	45	0,	100.
					February,	2	45	0,	100, 120.
1779.					March,	2	45	0,	120, 135.
January,	13	43	2,	7, 8, 9.	April,	2	45	0,	135, 200.
February,	11	47	0,	10.	May,	2	45	0,	200, 500.
March,	10	00	0,	10, 11.					

The new tenor Connecticut money, (the issues of 1780,) owing to the persevering efforts made to call it in, fared better. It did not, however, maintain the credit to which its projectors thought it entitled. Though declared by state authority to be " founded upon the most indubitable principles," it was worth but ten shillings on the pound in December, 1780; had become " cheap " in July, 1781, when nearly £120,000 were in circulation ;"* and was received for taxes, in January,

---

* See Connecticut Courant for July 17, 1781.

1783, at the rate of two for one. After the war had closed, the bills were bought up on speculation at the same figure. They were then supposed to amount to about £49,000, exclusive of interest. In October, 1788, some £28,000, and in May, 1790, some £22,000 were still in the hands of the people. The accounts of the Treasurer, Mr. Lawrence, had been so loosely kept that it was found impossible to state the precise amount. In some cases, where parcels of bills were burned, the principal and interest included in the amounts were not given separately. John Lawrence, who was Treasurer from 1769 to 1788, nineteen years, became infirm from age and disease before he left office. He was severely censured by the Legislature, in January, 1789, but I do not understand that there was any evidence of a want of integrity.

There were reasons enough why the state bills of 1780 declined in value. They bore too low a rate of interest, and, above all, there was no confidence in their being paid, either principal or interest, at maturity.* At the same time, their credit was respectable, as compared with that obtained by the promises of other states, and of the continental Congress. Though designed for circulation, and of convenient denominations, they did not, in strictness, so far as I can ascertain, form a part of the currency. At any rate, they were not the standard of value. They were distrusted at the outset, and the accruing interest was a hindrance. Throughout the period which followed their emission, accounts appear to have been kept in specie. The items in the inventories of deceased persons, including bills of credit, were valued in hard money. The disbursements on account of the continental army, in 1781, and afterward were made, mostly or wholly, in solid coin. Specie was in fact abundant. It became so in consequence of the expenditures of our French allies, and of the British government in New York, &c. It had, in truth, become so cheap, so depreciated, in 1783, that bills of exchange on Europe were sold at a discount of from twenty to forty per cent.† But though the new bills

---

* Gov. Weare, of New Hampshire, wrote in August, 1781, that " continental bills of the new emission" were refused in payment of goods, in Massachusetts and the neighboring colonies. See " Letters to Washington," by Sparks.

† P. Webster, p. 267, note.

were nowhere the standard of value, they doubtless performed some of the functions of money. A demand was created for them, as well as for the other obligations of the State, by the persistent endeavors made to call them in by taxation. Without question, they were often accepted, at their depreciated market value, in the purchase of commodities and the discharge of debts, as were, doubtless, the other evidences of state indebtedness, as well as the loan-office certificates of the general government. In this way they saved currency. At no time, after the war, were they alone sufficient in amount to answer the ends of a circulating medium. A successful attempt to use them as the exclusive currency of the State, would have quickly brought them to a level with specie. In disposing of them, no account appears to have been taken of the accrued interest, which was not paid till their final redemption. As I understand it, they were never a legal tender in private dealings, either at their nominal or market value. The same session of the Assembly which authorized their emission repealed the old tender law, and the new law which was enacted applied only to "bills of credit heretofore emitted."

Nearly all the Connecticut bills of 1780 were discharged by taxes, payable in kind, the greatest proportion of them, interest included, before they became due.* They were not redeemed "in Spanish milled dollars or other coins equivalent," according to promise. It was the expectation, doubtless, that the pledge would not be made good ; and this was a sufficient cause for their great decline in value. The State took advantage of its fallen credit to call them in, while the tax-payers were benefited to the full extent of the depreciation. Had they been a legal tender, and formed the sole currency of the people, their sudden withdrawal would have caused their equally sudden appreciation. The last taxes levied would have been paid in a medium equivalent to coin, while the last bill-holders would have received the value promised. A government which

---

* Taxes amounting to 17 pence on the pound were laid in May and October, 1780, to sink these bills, all payable between August, 1780, and October, 1781. These should have raised £110,000. See "Finance and Currency," Vol. V., Doc. 193.

damages its credit by neglecting the measures necessary to sustain it—which calls in its depreciated notes by taxes instead of paying them in the manner stipulated—profits by its own delinquency, and in effect repudiates its obligations. It might as well buy up its paper in the open market at ten shillings in the pound. The small balance of the bills which remained, at the date of the federal Constitution, went in as a claim against the general government, at par value, with interest.

CHAPTER IX.

THE CONFEDERATION OF THE STATES GIVES NO FINANCIAL STRENGTH. BANK OF NORTH AMERICA.

At the beginning of the war, the attention of many patriotic individuals was turned to the advantages which would flow from a closer union—a more centralized government. Among the benefits proposed were a better credit, and the improved financial condition of the country. The Congress which assembled at the opening of the contest had no defined powers. The authority which it exercised was assumed, not granted; implied, it may be, but not expressed. It grew out of its relation to the states, and the condition and necessities of the country. The delegates from several of the colonies received no instructions whatever. Connecticut was as usual wary. Her Assembly appointed five delegates, " any three of whom are authorized and empowered to attend said Congress, in behalf of this Colony, to join, consult, and advise with the delegates of other colonies in British America, on proper measures for advancing the best good of the colonies." Afterward, they were " empowered to represent this Colony, to consult, advise, and resolve upon measures necessary to be taken and pursued for the defense, security and preservation of the rights and liberties of the United Colonies, and for their common safety; and of such their proceedings and resolves they do transmit authentic copies, from time to time, to the General Assembly."* The Colony or State, however, when once warmed up, was behind no other in efficient acts and measures of her own.

The necessity of conferring definite and ampler powers on Congress, and of forming "a more perfect union," soon became apparent. On the twelfth day of June, 1776, two days after the resolution declaring independence was passed in committee of the whole, Congress appointed a "committee to prepare and digest the form of a confederation to be entered into between these colonies," consisting of one from each colony, Roger Sherman being the member from Connecticut. On the twentieth day of July a report was made and a plan presented. This was debated, and an amended draft reported August twentieth. Owing to a disagreement about details, and the pressure of business, the discussion was not resumed till April, 1777. It was then continued, with one long interruption, till November, 1777, when the thirteen "Articles of Confederation and perpetual Union" were adopted. This result was not reached till serious differences had been overcome. Forbearance, concession and compromise, at length, won the victory. It was not to go into operation till approved by all the states. A circular letter was drawn up, in which it was recommended "to the immediate and dispassionate attention of the several legislatures," "as the best which could be adapted to the circumstances of all, and as that alone which affords any tolerable prospect of general ratification." The adoption of the plan, it was affirmed, would "confound our foreign enemies, defeat the flagitious practices of the disaffected, strengthen and confirm our friends, support the public credit, restore the value of our money, enable us to maintain our fleets and armies, and add weight and respect to our councils at home and to our treaties abroad."

Connecticut was the first state, after South Carolina, to an-

---

* See Journal of Congress, May 11th, 1775, and January 16th, 1776, &c.

thorize her delegates to sign the Articles. She gave her assent February twelfth, 1778; * but instructed her delegates to move certain amendments. The eighth article required that "all charges of war and all other expenses" should " be defrayed out of a common treasury, which shall be supplied by the several states, in proportion to the value of all land within each state granted to, or surveyed for, any person, as such land and the buildings and improvements thereon shall be estimated according to such mode as the United States, in Congress assembled, shall, from time to time, appoint." Connecticut wanted the expenses, &c. apportioned according to "the number of white inhabitants in each state." She desired, also, to add a proviso to the fifth paragraph of the ninth article, thus—" provided no land army shall be kept up in time of peace, nor any officers or pensioners kept in pay, not in actual service," and not disabled in the military service of the government. The amendments were rejected by Congress, eleven votes to one. Numerous other amendments, proposed by several of the states, shared the same fate. At length, the Articles were ratified by all the states except New Jersey, Delaware and Maryland. These required, among other things, not without a show of reason, that those states claiming western lands should cede them for the benefit of all, as their possession, if finally secured, would be due to the blood and treasure of all. Ere long, however, New Jersey, rather than defeat the union, and in a patriotic spirit, gave her assent. This was November twentieth, 1778.† On the first day of February following, Delaware, trusting for future amendments to "the candor and justice of the several states," yielded her objections. Soon afterward, May twentieth, 1779, the delegates from Virginia laid before Congress certain resolutions of that State (which was largely interested in the western lands) authorizing and requiring its delegates to ratify the Articles of Confederation to the exclusion, if necessary, of those states which refused to sign the same. The next day the delegates from Connecticut presented a resolution of simi-

---

* See Journal of Congress, June 27th, 1778.
† See Journal of Congress, Nov. 25th, 1778.

lar import passed by the General Assembly of their State, and dated April seventh, 1779; but Maryland, by the same resolution, was not to be prevented "from acceding to the Confederation at any time." The acceding states would not consent to a partial union; while some of them having no western lands, hoped to gain advantage from delay.

Maryland persisted, and the states were "at a dead lock." The country was in imminent peril. The enemy rejoiced, while the friends of liberty almost despaired. At this stage, New York revived the hopes of patriots. On the nineteenth day of February, 1780, she authorized her delegates in Congress "to limit and restrict the western parts thereof, by such line or lines, and in such manner and form, as they shall judge expedient," &c.* At the same time, Congress, while urging Maryland to subscribe the Articles, used its utmost endeavors to induce other states to imitate the example of New York, reminding them "how indispensably necessary it is to establish the union on a fixed and permanent basis."† Soon afterward, Connecticut came up to the work, and, for the good of the whole, surrendered her claim to the western territory, reserving, however, a large tract, one hundred and twenty miles from east to west, adjoining Pennsylvania, and afterwards known as the "Connecticut Reserve." On the second day of January, 1781, Virginia, her movements quickened (according to Hildreth) by the terror of Arnold's invasion, authorized her delegates to cede to the United States that magnificent tract of territory lying northwest of the Ohio.‡ So much being accomplished, Maryland reluctantly yielded her objections to the Confederacy; "and from an earnest desire to conciliate the affection of the sister states," and without giving up "any right or interest she hath, with the other United States, to the back country," empowered her delegates to subscribe the Articles.§ This was February second, 1781, and the subscription was made March

---

* See Journal of Congress, March 1, 1781.
† Journal of Congress, September 6, 1780.
‡ See Journal of Congress, March 1, 1784, when the grant was perfected.
§ See Journal of Congress, Feb. 12, 1781.

first, 1781. Thus the Union was perfected, and a load of anxiety lifted from the breasts of a nearly despairing people. This result was secured by the most important and magnanimous sacrifices. The states which had signed with the expectation of cessions of land by their associates in the Confederacy were not disappointed.

The general confidence placed in the Articles of Confederation and Perpetual Union proved to be a delusion and a snare. They did not secure unity, or power, or credit, or respectability. The government which they established was but a compact or league between sovereign states. There was no adequate central authority. Congress could frame laws for the people, but was not able to execute them ; could " recommend " or " resolve," but was not competent to enact ; could make requisitions for money, but had not the legal capacity to collect a farthing. Between it and the people the states were an effectual barrier. The latter alone had the requisite machinery for levying and collecting internal taxes, and duties on foreign commodities; and also for " prohibiting the exportation or importation of any species of goods," &c. They alone had sovereign authority, and were determined to keep it. So long as continental bills retained their power, Congress occupied a position of influence and respectability. It could " order " and " resolve " to some purpose ; but when this resource failed, it was stricken to the dust. Destitute of money, its right arm was broken, its authority contemned, its dignity gone. The officers of the army bullied it ; armed soldiers insulted it, and all distrusted it. For eight long years the Confederacy strugled for an impotent and humiliated life, and then died by the hands of its friends.

The eighth article of the Confederacy—that which apportioned the expenses of the government among the states— may require to be noticed, more particularly, in this connection. It will be remembered that at the beginning of the contest Congress proceeded on a different basis. The three million tax to be levied to redeem the two first issues of bills of credit was distributed according to assumed population of all kinds. In the subsequent requisitions for money, &c.,

the states were called on to pay, not conformably to any expressed rule, but in proportion to their supposed ability
(roughly estimated) at the time, with the proviso "that
the sums assessed shall not be considered as the proportions of the states, but being paid shall be placed to their
credit, respectively, bearing an interest of six per centum per
annum, from the time of payment until the quotas shall be
finally ascertained and adjusted by the Congress, agreeably to
the confederation hereafter to be adopted and ratified."[*]
When the Articles of Confederation were under consideration,
the committee of the whole reported in favor of taxation according to population; but this provison, taxing slaves, was
opposed by the slaveholding states. An amendment was introduced and carried making the value of lands with improvements the rule in distributing the expenses of government, the
four New England states being against, and the four southern-
most states in favor of the measure. After the Articles were
ratified and alterations refused, Congress, embarrassed in the
application of the eighth article, as a rule of taxation, agreed
to a change, and recommended (April first, 1783) that the common Treasury should be "supplied by the several states in
proportion to the whole number of white and other free citizens and inhabitants of every age, sex and condition, including those bound to service for a term of years, and
three-fifths of all other persons not comprehended in the foregoing description, except Indians not paying taxes, in each
state." This proposed change, the result of a compromise
between the free and slave states, and agreed to in Congress
by nine, including all those south of New York, (except Georgia,
which was not represented,) was referred to the several states
for ratification. The "Articles" required that it should be
approved by all. The Assembly of Connecticut, at its next
May session, and Pennsylvania, at a later period, agreed to the
amendment;[†] but I do not find that it was finally adopted.[‡]

---

[*] Journal of Congress, Nov. 22, 1777.

[†] See Journal of Congress, Aug. 28, and Sep 1, 1783.

[‡] Curtis's History of the Constitution of the U. S., I., 213, note; II. 160.
Jour. Cong., Sep. 24, 1786.

At the time it was proposed, however, an estimate was made (in the cases of New Hampshire, Rhode Island, Connecticut and Maryland, from " authorized documents ") of the taxable population of the several states, omitting three-fifths of the slaves, in accordance with the rule of the contemplated amendment. The proposed excise duty was apportioned, provisionally, in conformity with the same rule, as were all the requisitions afterwards made for supplying the confederated Treasury.* Connecticut's quotas were thus considerably reduced. Under the new regulation they were less than one-eleventh of the whole.

The provision which failed to become a law of the Confederation afterwards found a place in the Constitution of 1789, as the rule of *direct* taxation and representation. The expenses of the war and the debts of the confederated government were finally paid in consistency with this constitutional provision; but indirect taxation was the chief source of the revenues thus appropriated.

In February 1781, Congress determined to abandon the system of boards and committees, and to put each of the executive departments of the government under a single head.

---

* In the "Madison Papers," vol. I, p. 431, will be found the "grand committee's" estimate of population above referred to. It is as follows:

New Hampshire,	82,200
Massachusetts,	350,000
Rhode Island,	50,400
Connecticut,	206,000
New York,	200,000
New Jersey,	130,000
Pennsylvania,	320,000
Delaware,	35,000
Maryland,	220,700
Virginia,	400,000
North Carolina,	170,000
South Carolina,	150,000
Georgia,	25,000
	2,339,300

In the report, South Carolina is set down at 170,000, but the figures were reduced, as above.

Robert Morris, a merchant of Philadelphia, was appointed, by an unanimous vote, Superintendent of Finance. He accepted the office on condition, it is said, that all transactions should be in specie. To facilitate the management of his department, he proposed a national bank. A plan was submitted to Congress which was approved, May twenty-sixth, Massachusetts alone voting against it. Its capital of $400,000, (afterward increased to $1,000,000,) divided into shares of four hundred dollars each, was, after considerable delay, subscribed. The general government, however, was obliged to take $254,000 of the amount. The institution was incorporated by Congress, December thirty-first, 1781, by the name of the Bank of North America. It commenced business on the following seventh of January. Thomas Willing was its first president. In the ordinance creating it there was no limit to its circulation, and none to its capital except that it could own in property only "to the amount of 10,000,000 of Spanish silver milled dollars." Its bills, receivable for all public dues, and payable on demand in coin, were the first of the kind issued in America. In the commencement, they were, very naturally, received with distrust; but ere long they obtained a general currency. Connecticut, without delay, gave them the benefit of its laws against counterfeiting paper money, and made them receivable for taxes payable in specie.* "Morris' Bank," so called, was afterwards (April, 1783) chartered by the Assembly of Pennsylvania, grave doubts being entertained whether Congress had the power which it pretended to exercise. Established at a time of great financial embarrassment, it was obliged to resort to sundry artifices to magnify its apparent resources.† It proved at length a successful enterprise, and made large dividends. Considering its

---

* In May, 1788, the Assembly enacted that "none of the notes or paper anticipations, [post notes?] called Morris' notes, shall be received into the Treasury of this State, after the first day of June next, in payment of any tax or arrearage of tax now due," for discharging any requisition of Congress, "but the same shall be paid in money only, and applied to the use of the United States, according to the requisition of Congress and the resolves of the General Assembly," &c.

† Gouge's History of Banking, p. 13.

limited means, the benefits which it conferred on the government and country have, I conceive, been greatly exaggerated. It still exists, as a state institution, with a capital of $1,000,000.

In 1784, the Massachusetts Bank, at Boston, and the Bank of New York, in New York city, were chartered by state authority. No others were established till after the adoption of the federal Constitution.

CHAPTER X.

WAS INDEPENDENCE WON BY PAPER MONEY? ERRORS EXPOSED.

THE issues of paper money, state and continental, during the war of the Revolution, were the result of a short-sighted policy. They produced all the evils, in the most aggravated form, which are known to result from such a policy. They discouraged sober industry, frugality and honest dealing, and encouraged improvidence, extravagance, speculation and peculation. There were "shoddy patriots" in those days who, while they shouted for liberty, cheated the soldiers and plundered the Treasury. Vice and immorality ran riot. The depreciation of the currency wrought the greatest injustice, while the tender laws legalized robbery on the most extended scale. Men well able to pay discharged their debts for twelve pence or six pence in the pound. General Washington himself was a sufferer from this cause. August seventeenth, 1779, he wrote to his business agent at Mount Vernon, Lund Washington, that he was "resolved to receive no more old debts (those which were contracted and ought to have been paid before the war) at the present nominal value of the money, unless compelled to do it, or it is the practice of others to do it." He

did not think it his duty to ruin himself for the benefit of
others, unless the common good required it ; and could not see
how a man of honor and honesty could take advantage of the
times, and propose to discharge an old obligation by paying
one shilling or sixpence in the pound.* Paper money, says
honest Pelatiah Webster, "polluted the equity of our laws,
turned them into engines of oppression and wrong, corrupted
the justice of our public administration, destroyed the fortunes
of thousands who had confidence in it, enervated the trade,
husbandry and manufactures of our country, and went far to
destroy the morality of our people." At last "it expired
without one groan or struggle," unlamented, "aged six years."
Says another, an apologist for paper money: It was "the
bane of society. All classes were infected. It produced a rage
for speculation. The mechanic, the farmer, the lawyer, the
physician, the member of Congress, and even a few of the
clergy, in some places, were contaminated. The morals of the
people were corrupted beyond anything that could have been believed, prior to the event. All ties of honor, blood, gratitude,
humanity and justice were dissolved. Old debts were paid
when the paper money was worth no more than seventy for
one. Brothers defrauded brothers, children parents, and
parents children. Widows, orphans, and others were paid for
money lent in specie with depreciated paper,"† &c. In the
end, all those who had witnessed its effects were, for the time,
satisfied with the experiment. Washington hoped he should
never hear of it again, and in 1786, branded a scheme for introducing it, once more, into Virginia as "a nefarious plan of
speculation."‡ Similar plans in other states he characterized
as "very foolish and wicked."§

We have been accustomed to think that whatever our fathers
did in the Revolution was wise and good. Paper money, it is
said, was a necessity. By its agency, armies were supported,
battles fought, and our independence achieved. "Without it
we should have been subdued." Thus orators have declaimed.
Thus historians have written, and copying from one another

---

* Washington's Writings, VI. 321.   † Breck's Sketch, p. 23.
‡ Writings, IX. 120.   § Ibid. IX. 186.

will, doubtless, continue to write. But the facts have not always been fairly construed nor correctly stated. "The heroes of seventy-six" were not all wise men—were not all statesmen. They did some weak and wicked things, and attempted others that were quite impracticable. Bills of credit they issued at the very outset of the war, and by repeated acts established the paper money policy, without trying to provide means in other ways. They emitted them because they had confidence in them; because they thought other provision unnecessary, and because the lessons of experience had been forgotten. Congress was unwilling to impose burdens on the people. "Do you think," said one of their number, "that I will consent to load my constituents with taxes, when we can send to our printer and get a wagon load of money?"* The truth is, the masses had never been convinced of the folly of the paper money experiments which had been made, on former occasions. In colonial times, they were choked off, prematurely as they thought, by the stern decrees of the British government: this was the feeling in New England. Those who issued bills of credit in 1775 did not do it because every other measure had been tried and failed. They did not continue the issues, in 1776 and 1777, under the pressure of any demonstrated necessity, and as the only alternative. On the contrary, they were governed by false notions of economy, by popular clamor and the debtor interest. They wished to wage a cheap war—one which should provide an economical method of discharging debts. Do not their acts justify this conclusion? They did not try taxation to which they had been accustomed, and which, at first, they were well able to bear. Instead of this, they went plunging on in the road to certain ruin. The first five million tax, Congress did not so much as "recommend" till after the lapse of more than two years and a half. Money might have been obtained by loan, but this was not attempted for eighteen months, nor till $20,000,000 in continental bills had been emitted, and the public credit shaken. And when an effort was made, the proposed rate of interest

---

* P. Webster.

(four per cent.) was too low to tempt lenders. The next thing that was tried (with about equal success) was a lottery.

But Congress, it will be said, had no control over the property of the country—had not the power to levy taxes or borrow money, and by its acts to bind the people. But the states had the needful authority. This, however, they refused to exercise. They pursued the policy of the general government, and (while credit lasted) made their contributions to the common cause, in paper money. As for Congress, it had as much authority in the first as in the third year of the war—as much to levy taxes and make loans as it had to issue bills of credit. It was in the habit of doing things which it had no legal right to do. Besides, its " recommendations," at an early period, when the fever was up, had the force of law; while any power which it lacked, the state authorities might have conferred. If the machinery for the convenient collection of taxes were wanting, this could have been supplied by the states. The latter found no difficulty in making continental bills legal tender, or in doing anything which seemed to cost little. There doubtless would have been found some means to get at the resources of the country had it not been for the misplaced confidence in paper issues. A firmer will, with a greater readiness to make sacrifices, would have opened a way. The paper money plan, after deluding the people and wasting their means, broke down at a critical period of the war. Then, when enthusiasm had nearly died out, and gloomy forebodings had taken its place—when credit was greatly impaired, and the country approaching a state of exhaustion, Congress and the state governments, sensible of their error, resorted to ways and means which should have been adopted at the outset. In the then crippled condition of the country, could anything but failure have been anticipated? The taxes called for were not paid. On the thirtieth day of October, 1781, Congress demanded of the states $8,000,000 for the service of the year 1782. On the thirtieth of January, 1783, but $420,031$\frac{28}{90}$ had been received into the Treasury.* Instead of alledging that

---

* Journal of Congress.

our independence was won with paper money, we might better say that it was gained in spite of it. The subsidies and loans from France were obtained at a most critical juncture. Indeed, it is difficult to see how we could have recovered from the blasting influence of paper money, and continued the struggle, without the active assistance of that nation.

It cannot be denied that bills of credit were, in the beginning of the war, a convenience. They afforded a ready and certain means of raising money at a small apparent cost. Nor would much injury have resulted had the issues been checked seasonably, when the channels of circulation were filled. But it is much easier to open the sluices of paper money than it is to close them. Whoever yet knew the flow to be stopped till disaster had overtaken those in the management? So long as the current is feeble, doing no mischief, it seems unnecessary to restrain it. When it has become a flood, resistance is hopeless.

It is quite true that the general and state governments were, for a time, provided with funds by means of a paper currency. The amount which Congress received from this source was considerable; though, owing to depreciation, the sum was but a fraction of that which it should have been, and for which its obligations were given. So desperate was the situation that a large proportion of this money was put forth when it was worth but ten or five or three cents on the dollar. The loss to the successive bill-holders was of course equal to the sum which the government gained. According to my estimate, taking the Philadelphia table of depreciation as a guide, the $242,052,780 of the authorized continental issues must have brought into the Treasury some $53,000,000, specie value. Hildreth makes the amount much greater, the tax on the country, according to him, equaling, "perhaps" $70,000,000.* But I suspect that Hildreth was governed in his calculations by the rule of depreciation established by Congress, unreliable as it is known to be. Of the $53,000,000, nearly one half was derived from the bills issued, at their par value, in 1775 and ·1776. Beside the amount which came from the old emis-

* History of the U. S., Vol. III., p. 446, (first series.)

sions, the government received about $530,741, specie value, from the new issues of 1780, reckoning these to have been paid out at the rate of three for one of coin. But this sum was not finally lost to the holders of the new bills. The $53,000,000 may be stated as the amount which continental money extracted from the pockets of the bill-holders. The resources of the country were depleted by the operation to this extent. Had notes of circulation not been used, the funds thus obtained would have remained in the hands of the people, to be drawn forth, it may be, in other less objectionable ways. Mere convenience could not excuse the action of Congress. A more enlightened policy and a truer statesmanship, backed by a higher order of patriotism, would have saved much treasure, and wrought out more glorious results.

The loss to continental bill-holders was widely distributed, but fell with most weight on the commercial classes. In this point of view, it may be regarded as a tax on the people very unequal in its operation, but no more so perhaps than the measures which are often resorted to in war-time to obtain money. But there is another aspect to this paper money policy—another effect, already alluded to—which no one can deny or defend. The laws emitting paper money and making it legal tender were iniquitous, (in the language of Washington, "nefarious,") because they broke contracts, robbed creditors for the benefit of debtors, plundered the industrious classes to enrich speculators and gamblers, and bestowed rewards on dishonesty and immorality. The man who had parted with a month's or year's labor, or its worth in cloth or coin, and, as an act of indulgence, had taken a note payable at a future day in dollars, was cruelly and shamefully defrauded. The governments under which this was done, though instituted to administer justice and protect the right, deceptively altered the terms of the note. They, in effect, interpolated a clause making that which was redeemable in one thing payable in another. By juggling legislation, they changed the meaning of the important word dollar, and thus annulled the contract.* What

---

* Thus wrote David Ramsey, in 1789, after having spoken a kindly word for paper money: "Congress attempted to prop its credit by means which wrecked

should we think of a statute which expunged "wheat" from all contracts to deliver that article, and inserted in its place "straw" or "chaff"? Should we regard the enactment as ingenious—or flagitious? Would not the courts set it aside on account of its fundamental wickedness, and for the reason that it broke contracts?—This operation of the tender laws was quite distinct from the losses sustained by the bill-holders. The forced sacrifices from this cause exhausted the resources of the more industrious and thrifty portion of the population, without conferring any benefit on the government. In the end, rulers and the ruled were alike brought to shame.†

It is peculiarly important that the currency should be kept sound during the progress of a great war, when so many disturbing causes are at work. This is required in order that industry may be as little interfered with as possible—that labor receive its just reward—that capital be not unnecessarily sacrificed—that habits of extravagance receive no encouragement, and the fell spirit of speculation no rewards. A paper currency, issued in excess, increases largely (enormously, it may be)

---

private property, and injured the morals of the people, without answering the ends proposed. * * The poor became rich, and the rich became poor. * * The evils of depreciation did not terminate with the war. They extend to the present hour. That the helpless part of the community were legislatively deprived of their property was among the lesser evils, which resulted from the legal tender of the depreciated bills of credit. The iniquity of the laws estranged the minds of many of the citizens from the habits of love and justice. The nature of obligations was so far changed, that he was reckoned the honest man who, from principle, delayed to pay his debts. * * Truth, honor and justice were swept away by the overflowing deluge of legal iniquity. * * Time and industry have already, in a great degree, repaired the losses of property, * * but both have hitherto failed in effacing the taint which was then communicated to their principles, nor can its total ablution be expected till a new generation arises, unpractised in the iniquities of their fathers." Hist. of the Am. Rev., Philadelphia, 1789, II. 133, 135, 136.

† A curious but fair illustration of the changes wrought by paper money on the relations of debtor and creditor may be seen in the following extract from Gordon's History of the American War, IV., 145.—"A merchant of Boston sold a hogshead of rum for £20, cask included. The purchaser did not settle for it till after the seller applied to him for an empty hogshead, for which he was charged £30. When they came to settle, the merchant found, upon examining, that he had to pay a balance of £10 on that very cask, which, with the rum it contained, had been sold for £20."

Dr. Gordon copies largely from P. Webster's Essays, without credit.

the cost of war, while, at the same time, the reservoirs of wealth are dangerously depleted, and the sources which should supply the waste dried up. It increases, too, the sacrifices and the perils which come in the train of peace, as I shall explain in another place.

It may be unnecessary to say here that paper money does not increase the capital of a country—cannot add to its productive means, except so far as it displaces the coin which was before in circulation. The coin thus liberated is added to the list of exportable commodities, and may be used to increase the supply of imported goods or capital. From the gross gains, however, must be deducted the expenditures required to furnish and maintain a paper currency. The charges for paper, engraving, printing, signing, &c.—for renewing defaced and mutilated bills, for catching and punishing counterfeiters, &c.— are much more considerable than is generally supposed, and are greater in proportion as the currency is inflated.* Suppose the $200,000,000 of continental bills which were in the hands of the people in the beginning of 1780, had continued to be the circulating medium of the states:—the annual cost of supporting the system would have been large, and might have exceeded the whole amount saved. The saving, if any, would, of course, have been equal to the interest on the specie naturally required to do the business of the country. This Mr. P. Webster estimated at ten or eleven million dollars.

It is true that an increase of the currency by means of paper money gives activity to business, and, to a certain extent, stimulates industry. Men engaged in the production and exchange of commodities receive more nominal dollars than they did before, and, very innocently, think themselves getting rich. They do not consider the fact that their dollars have a diminished value. The delusion is a most agreeable one, encourages business men, and prompts to more vigorous exertion. As a result, production is, for the time, augmented and wealth in-

---

* The French assignats were, at one time, while still in circulation, scarcely worth the expense of printing alone. See Smith's Wealth of Nations; Supplement by the editor. II. 359. Hartford edition.

creased. But this is only the first effect of a money inflation. Continue to apply the stimulus, and other effects follow—speculation, reckless enterprise, extravagance and fraud. Industry is neglected or despised. At last come paralysis and collapse, when it is seen that far more has been lost than gained.

That is a vulgar error which supposes that, in a time of war, when government must obtain and disburse large sums of money, more currency is needed than at other periods. This mistake comes from assuming that the large financial operations of the government are an addition to the ordinary business transactions of the country. No doubt, many thousand soldiers are to be paid. Military and naval stores are to be purchased, on a large scale. The work of destroying human life cannot go on without much money. But, in the aggregate, no more men are to be provided for, no more wages to be paid, than before the war. Many persons that were previously employed by individual capitalists, have gone into the service of the state. There is a transfer of laborers from peaceful to war-like occupations, but no addition to their number or wages. Nor is the sum total of commodities to be exchanged by the use of money increased. Indeed, there is a rapid and progressive diminution. Laborers in becoming soldiers cease to be producers. Their industry no longer adds to the exchangeable commodities of a country. The uses of a circulating medium, then, instead of being enlarged, are contracted by war. If the operations of government are on a more extended scale, those of individuals are limited in a still greater proportion.*

---

* As an example of the crude notions which prevail in high places on the subject of the text, I would refer to the published opinions of the judges of the Court of Appeals of New York in the famous legal-tender case, September, 1863. It was the right and duty of Congress, says Judge Balcom, to call forth and maintain an army and navy sufficient to put down the rebellion; but this could not be done, he continues, "without adequate pecuniary means, and without the expenditure of vastly more money than could have been borrowed in coin in the entire world." "Could Congress have been justified by the Constitution," exclaims the Judge, "if it had permitted the republic to perish, because enough gold and silver coin could not be borrowed to save it?" The issue of several hundred million of government legal tender paper money was, therefore, justifiable, and within the meaning of the Constitution. This is the reasoning; and

Nor do additions to the currency make it more efficient, or give it increased value, as I have explained in another place. After the revolutionary Congress had put forth two hundred million in bills, the whole were worth no more—had no more exchangeable value—than the money which they had displaced. Nor did this large amount of paper do the business of the country more easily or more perfectly than it would have been done by a contracted and more valuable currency. Indeed, as a matter of fact, the contrary was true.

The idea of making the currency more efficient by increasing its volume, is quite as absurd as it would be for a cloth-dealer to think of facilitating his operations by multiplying his yard-sticks. Two or four yard-sticks, in one man's hands, would measure no more cloth than one. Nor would the process be expedited, though the government should enact that each yard measured by four sticks should be called four yards, and should pass current for four. In the last case, the merchant would, indeed, have a greater number of nominal yards, but no more goods than before. He could in no way be benefited, unless he had old debts to pay in *yards*, which he could discharge in the new measure, one being equal to four. In this way, he would save three-quarters of his cloth, and become rich at the cost of his creditors.

A government which hastily resolves to issue paper money, and thus depreciates the currency, commits a grave offense against honesty and good morals. It does an act which is equivalent to altering the standard of weights and measures, without protecting those under contract to receive or deliver goods, who would be ruined by the new law. It does an act which is no better in principle or effect than dividing or debasing the coin. The kings of Europe used to melt up their money and issue new pieces, one half or one quarter the weight of the old, retaining the names. With the new issues, bearing falsehood on their face, spendthrift princes paid their debts, and

Judge Davies, in his opinion, starting from similar premises, and by an equal display of logical acumen, arrives at the same conclusion. Respect for the highest court of the great State of New York, prevents my saying more.

in this way, contrived to over-reach their masters, the Jews. All creditors were obliged to receive them at their nominal value, getting, say, six pences or three pences when shillings were due. But the trick was apparent, and in process of time it became too disreputable for repetition. As civilization advanced, a more refined and less obvious method of cheating was required. Rulers discovered that the desired objects might be attained by the use of bills of credit, and without shocking, in an equal degree, the half enlightened moral sense. By their agency, men might be swindled, almost without their knowing it. So cunning was the plan that a people might be deprived of their earnings or savings while the hand which robbed them was invisible. But when a person is to be plundered by those whose duty it is to protect him, is the suffering or wrong less because the thing has been done cleverly? Is a pick-pocket a more respectable character than a highwayman? On the contrary, would it not be more manly—more statesmanlike— to throw off disguise, and do what must be done openly and by direct means? A depreciated currency note is no more respectable than a false coin. It claims to be what it is not, and is, therefore, a cheat and a snare. In an important sense, the coin is the better of the two. So long as it contains any of the precious metal, it represents labor and has a substantial value. It will be worth no less next year than it is this. Its purchasing power will remain, though government should continue to make other pieces like it or lighter than itself. But it is not so with paper money. Though valuable to-day, it may be nearly worthless six months hence. Should you lay aside some thousand for a time of need, your store when wanted may have turned to useless rags. Every new emission reduces the reserved fund, and makes all the hoarders of money poorer. Nor will the catastrophe be averted should you put your "legal tenders" in a savings bank, loan them, or buy with them money stocks, or a life annuity.

CHAPTER XI.

CONNECTICUT FINANCES AT THE CLOSE OF THE WAR.

THE state indebtedness, at the close of the war, consisting of certain sums due the " Connecticut line " of the continental army, treasury notes, pay-table orders, and sundry other obligations, I find it difficult to determine with entire certainty. I give below what may be considered an approximate estimate, in May, 1783, which I have derived from document number 180, in the fifth volume on Finance and Currency in the State Library.

Debts contracted since 1775.

Securities due the Connecticut line, exclusive of interest,..............£427,725
Treasury notes payable one year after the war, dated February first,
   1781. [These were originally given partly for moneys borrowed, and
   partly in exchange for bills of credit of the old emission]........... 395,010
Do. given for horses for Col. Sheldon's regiment, dated June 1st, 1781,
   and payable June first, 1783,................................... 5,900
Do. given for beef cattle, payable one year after the war,............ 40,284
Do. for sundry services and supplies estimated at.... 20,000

     Total securities,..£888,920

State bills of 1780, in circulation, exclusive of interest,.............. 49,000
Orders drawn by the committee of pay table, not yet received by the
   Treasurer, April fifteenth, 1783,................................. 72,460

     Total state money debt,...............................£121,460

Committee of pay-table orders in excess of the two and six penny tax,.. 62,183
Unliquidated debt, say,...... 35,000
Other specified items, ... 27,590

                          £124,773

The several sums in this statement amount to £1,135,153. It is the clearest and most complete account which I have been able to find; but it does not always harmonize with apparent facts to be derived from other documents. The latter, however, are more uncertain as to date or in some other particulars, and I have selected from a paper which seemed, on the whole, most reliable. In the document numbered 200, in the same volume, which should apparently bear the date of October, (1783), the whole debt of the State is made out to be £1,097,276, £35,876 less than appears by the other statement. But the truth is, the finances at the close of the war were in great disorder. In the confusion which prevailed, it is doubtless true that only an aproximate estimate of the state indebtedness could then be made.

Connecticut, then, came out of the war with a debt of more than eleven hundred thousand pounds, nearly the whole of it reduced to specie value, and payable in coin; and all, except bills of credit, bearing six per cent. annual interest. In addition, there was a considerable amount of accrued and overdue interest. The aggregate was, indeed, a formidable sum; but when increased by Connecticut's share of the continental debt, reckoned at one-tenth of the whole, it became appalling The population of the State was, at this time, a little over 200,000, and the taxable list of polls and estates nearly £2,000,000. From the last sum there had to be deducted, because of financial embarrassments, a large per centage (twenty-five per cent.) for abatements.* It should, however, be remembered that a considerable part of the state indebtedness had grown out of the fact that the State had made advancements for the common cause beyond her proportion. A large sum had been paid under a misapprehension of the existing acts of Congress. Connecticut had settled with her line of the army up to the first of January, 1782, when Congress resolved that after the first of January, 1780, the army should be paid by the general government. The Assembly, therefore, after recounting the services which it had rendered, by which means, in spite of

---

* At the close of the war, it was ascertained that the abatements of taxes had, throughout its duration, amounted, on an average, to about one quarter. A committee was appointed, in May, 1783, to inquire into the subject. A tax of one penny on the pound, which should have produced more than eight thousand pounds, netted but little over six.

" taxation to the utmost," " an immense local debt " had been incurred, resolved in January, 1784, that his Excellency, the Governor, through our delegates, should make a claim on Congress for certain extraordinary expenditures, among others, for the moneys paid to the Connecticut line, through misapprehension. I cannot find that any special attention was given to this application. Commissioners were, however, afterward appointed to ascertain the claims of the several states against the United States, and to adjust the accounts.* Finally, the whole matter was turned over to the new government.

In May, 1783, the Assembly voted to procure a loan of £609,-572, lawful money, redeemable in from three to ten years, with six per cent. annual interest payable in gold and silver, the avails of which were to be used to pay the principal of the debt then due, or to become due before the first of June, 1784. No notes were to be issued under ten pounds. Takers of the loan might pay for the same in state obligations "as ascertained in hard money." To meet the interest, the tax of two pence on the pound laid in 1781, payable December first, annually, in gold and silver, and set apart for interest, was increased to six pence.

The interest on the state debt was not paid with regularity, if at all, in cash. Usually a settlement was made, for the time being, by an issue of interest-certificates, which were receivable

---

* On the 20th of February, 1782, Congress passed a resolution providing for a commissioner for each state, the same to be nominated by the Superintendent of Finance, and approved by the state for which he may have been designated, with full power to liquidate and settle all accounts between it and the United States, for money, supplies and services provided by said state, the same to be estimated according to the scale of depreciation established June 28th and July 29th, 1780. The purpose was to ascertain the expenses of the war up to January 1, 1782, in order that they might be apportioned equitably among the members of the Confederacy. Annual interest was to be credited or debited to each state which had furnished more or less than its proportion. June 3, 1784, more particular rules were laid down for the guidance of the commissioners. At a still later period, May 7, 1787, an ordinance was passed providing for five commissioners, whose duties were similar to those whose term of service had expired— one for each of the five districts into which the states were divided. A report was to be made in twelve months, and the states were to be allowed six months in which to present their claims.

for certain taxes. No sooner was peace restored than the most serious discontents arose on account of the burden of taxation. The half pay for life granted by Congress to officers of the army was the subject of bitter complaints, and in some towns of the State of riotous demonstrations. To increase the burden of the tax payers, all moneys loaned to the State or the United States, and the polls of non-commissioned officers and soldiers serving in the army were, by law, left out of the list. The public debt, said the Assembly in their application to Congress, already referred to, January, 1784, "imposes such a burden upon the inhabitants that they are endeavoring to avoid the weight of it by emigrating into states where the burden of taxation is much less." The population of Connecticut, at this time, was made up, almost wholly, of small farmers who gained a living by the sweat of the brow, and who earned, in good times, but a small surplus. So limited were their means, and so severe the drain upon their resources, that the Assembly felt constrained, in May, 1784, to suspend for three years the gathering of taxes " not then in collection," excepting the annual December six penny tax for interest, and such other taxes as it might be necessary to grant for the support of civil government. There were then due to the State large arrearages of taxes, the accumulation of several years.* To facilitate the payment of these, it was further enacted that any of the state securities due before March first, 1784, which had been reduced to specie value, should be receivable for all taxes except those granted for sinking the state bills, for the payment of army notes or the state interest, for the support of civil government, and for the use of the United States. The holders of the bills, notes, &c., thus excepted were considered as preferred creditors. Certain taxes had been levied for their special benefit which were payable in the obligations which they themselves held.

---

* In a document dated May 17, 1783, (Finance and Currency, Vol. V., Doc. 194,) will be found a statement of the balances of state taxes then due from the several towns. Those payable in continental currency amounted to £1,446,807; those payable in state money to £17,389; those to be paid in specie to £205,160. The paper is signed by Oliver Wolcott, Jr., and William Moseley, committee.

The taxes granted for the maintenance of government, state and national, could be discharged only in specie, or "Morris' notes," or orders on the civil list. The State was earnest in its endeavvors to discharge its public debt. Excise and import duties were laid which were pledged to the public creditors, and payable in soldiers' (army) notes or interest certificates. The bills of credit of 1780 were to be received at their nominal value for western lands sold, except twenty seven dollars in hard money for each township * As for the requisitions of Congress, Connecticut followed the example of the other states, and delayed or declined payment. In October, 1786, the Governor was to inform the President of Congress, by letter, of the embarrassment of the State by reason of the arrears of taxes, &c., "inducing a non-compliance" with the requisitions of Congress.

In the several ways which have been mentioned, by a most stringent system of taxation—a system once suspended, but never abandoned—the state debt was so diminished that, on the first day of November, 1789, it amounted to only about £608,043.† It was diminished, not by payment in full, in good

---

* 500,000 acres of western lands lying west of Pennsylvania and south of Lake Erie were afterward (May, 1792) granted to sundry persons, inhabitants of certain towns lying on and near the Sound, who had suffered from the depredations of the British during the war. The aggregate of damages sustained, according to the report of a committee, in May, 1791, was £151,606 : 8 : 6.

† In the Am. State Papers, Finance, I., p. 29, will be found a statement by Mr. Pomeroy, (the Comptroller,) of the state debt, at the time mentioned, as follows:

Notes issued to the Connecticut line, payable a part in each year from 1782 to 1789,	£148,561 : 3 : 4¼
Do. dated February, 1781, as per act of Assembly, November, 1780,	153,229 : 8 : 6¼
Do. of various dates, as per act of Assembly, May, 1781,	33,947 : 11 : 8¼
Do. dated June 1, 1781,	1,932 : 8 : 0
Do. of various dates, as per act of May, 1783,	41,841 : 6 : 1¼
Do., as per act of May 1789, for old notes re-loaned,	180,890 : 1 : 0
	560,404 : 18 : 9¼
Notes payable out of civil fund list,	2,856 : 11 : 4
Interest certificates,	19,140 : 3 : 9¼
Balance of state bills of 1780,	24,948 : 9 : 1
Balance of orders payable out of the one shilling tax,	692 : 8 : 10
	£608,042 : 11 : 10

11

faith, and in hard cash, but by first reducing the nominal amount of the debt, and secondly, by a mode of taxation which secured to the State the benefit of its poor credit. By making the taxes which were imposed on account of the public debt, payable in the depreciated evidences of that debt—in soldiers' notes, interest certificates, pay-table orders, bills of credit of 1780, &c.—the government diminished the burdens of the people one half or more. But what the tax-payers gained the public creditors lost. I am not denying that Connecticut did well under the circumstances—as well as she conveniently could, and better than could have been expected: I am only stating what her performance was, and how the parties interested were affected by it.

CHAPTER XII.

COST OF THE WAR. FINANCIAL EMBARRASSMENTS. THE ARTICLES OF CONFEDERATION NEED MENDING.

THE whole expense of the revolutionary war, according to Mr. Hildreth, was about $170,000,000, two-thirds of it borne by the general government, and the balance by the individual states. I do not know whence these figures are obtained, but the gross sum must be too large. The Register of the Treasury, in 1790, estimated the expense at $135,193,703, specie value, inclusive of $21,000,000 (by computation) expended by the several states. The following is his account, copied (slight errors excepted) from the published "Statements of the Receipts and Expenditures of the Public Money during the administration of the Finances by Robert Morris, Esq.," &c. (In the treasury payments, continental bills are reckoned, the old, according to the scale of Congress, the new, at the average rate of about one and nine-tenths for one. See pp. 31, 32.)

GENERAL ABSTRACT OF THE ANNUAL ESTIMATES, AND ABSTRACT STATEMENTS OF THE TOTAL AMOUNT OF THE EXPENDITURES AND ADVANCES AT THE TREASURY OF THE UNITED STATES.

The estimated amount of the expenditures of

			Dolls.	90th.
1775 and 1776, is, in specie,			20,064,666	66
1777,	"	"	24,986,646	85
1778,	"	"	24,289,438	26
1779,	"	"	10,794,620	65
1780,	"	"	3,000,000	00
1781,	"	"	1,942,465	30
1782,	"	"	3,632,745	85
1783,	"	"	3,226,583	15

To Nov. 1, 1784, as per schedule D, and
 subordinate accounts,................ 548,525 63

    Amount total,.............$92,485,692 75

The foregoing estimates, being confined to actual treasury payments, are exclusive of the debts of the United States, which were incurred at various periods and should be taken into view, viz. :

Army debt, upon commissioners' certificates,.......... $11,080,576.01
For supplies furnished by the citizens of the several states, for which certificates were issued by the commissioners,................................... 3.723,625.20
Supplies furnished in the quarter-master, commissary, hospital, clothing and marine departments, exclusive of the foregoing,.............................. 1,159,170.05
Supplies on accounts settled at the Treasury, and for which certificates were issued by the Register,...... 744,638.49

            $16,708,009.75

(The loan office debt formed a part of the Treasury expenditures.)
The foreign expenditures, civil, military, naval and contingencies, amount, by computation, to........... 5,000,000.00
The expenditures of the several states cannot be stated with any certainty, because the accounts thereof remain to be settled. But as the United States have granted certain sums for the relief of the states, to be funded by the general government, therefore estimate the total amount of said assumption....... .... 21,000,000.00

  Estimated expense of the war, in specie,......$135,193,702.60

  The advances made from the Treasury were principally in a paper medium, called continental money, which in a short time depreciated ; the specie value of it is given in the foregoing estimate. The advances made at the Treasury of the

United States, in continental money, old and new emissions, were estimated by the Secretary of War, in 1790, (see "Statements," &c., pp. 26–32,) as follows:

	Old emission.		New emission.		
	Dolls.	90th.	Dolls.	90th.	
In 1776,............	20,064,666	66			These bills are esti-
1777,............	26,426,833	01			mated, in the table of
1778,............	66,965,269	34			treasury payments, the
1779,............	149,703,856	77			old at $82,920,575, and
1780,............	82,908,320	47	891,236	80	the new at $1,089,624,
1781,............	11,408,095	25	1,179,249	23	specie value.
	357,476,541	50	2,070,486	13	

No unpaid interest which accrued after the war appears to enter into the preceding estimate of expenditures, except that which had accumulated on the sums expended by the state governments. The amount assumed for these sums is doubtless small enough, (as appears from the final settlement,) so that no deduction need be made on account of included interest. The Register's whole estimate must be taken as only an approximation to the truth. But as the scale of Congress (which overvalued continental money) was used to ascertain the specie value of the sums paid out of the Treasury, and to liquidate and settle the claims against the government, and the advances made by the several states, the assumed grand total of $135,193,703, it is fair to suppose, very considerably exceeds the actual expenditures. In other words, the war probably cost less in treasure alone than the government paid, or rather agreed to pay.

To meet the expenditures of the war, money had been borrowed as far as possible. A continental debt was thus created which, on the twenty-fourth day of April, 1783, according to the Journal of Congress, amounted to the following sums:

FOREIGN DEBT.

Due to the farmers general of France,.............Livres		1,000,000
Due to individuals in France on unliquidated accounts, estimated,..................................	"	3,000,000
Due to the crown of France, including a loan of 10,000,000 borrowed in Holland, and for which France is guarantee,..................................	"	28,000,000
Due to do., a loan for 1783,.....................	"	6,000,000
	Livres	38,000,000

Or in dollars, at five livres and eight sous each,	$7,037,037
Due to lenders in Holland, received in part of the loan contracted for by Mr. J. Adams, 1,678,000 florins,..	671,200
Borrowed in Spain by Mr. Jay,....................	150,000
One year's interest of Dutch loan of 10,000,000 livres,	26,848
Foreign debt, Jan. 1, 1783,................	$7,885,085

DOMESTIC DEBT.

Due on loan office certificates, reduced to specie value,	11,463,802
Interest unpaid for 1781,....	190,000
Interest unpaid for 1782,..........................	687,828
Credit to sundries in treasury books,.................	638,042
Army debt to Dec. 31, 1782,......................	5,635,618
Unliquidated debt, estimated at...................	8,000,000
Commutation to the army, agreeable to the act of 22d March last,.....................................	5,000,000
Bounty due to privates,...........................	500,000
Deficiencies in 1783, supposed....................	2,000,000
Domestic debt,...........................	$34,115,290
Total debt,...............................	42,000,375

ANNUAL INTEREST OF THE DEBT OF THE UNITED STATES.

On the foreign debt, part at four and part at five per ct.,	369,039
On the domestic debt, at six per cent.,..............	2,046,917
	$2,415,956*

This debt (from which continental bills were excluded—on
the ground apparently that as they were worth nothing, they
constituted no obligation) was increased before the end of the
year, so that it may be stated, at the conclusion of the war, in
round numbers, at $44,000,000. This sum does not, of course,
include the obligations of the individual states† which, accord-

----

* See Journal of Congress, April 29, 1783.

† I have been unable to find any general account of the state debts at the close
of the war. The following statement, made out after the adoption of the Constitution, is taken from the Am. State Papers, Finance, I., 28, 29 :

Massachusetts, principal and interest to Nov. 1, 1789,......	$5,226,801
Connecticut, principal and interest to Nov. 1, 1789,........	1,951,173
New York, principal and interest to Jan. 1, 1790,.........	1,167,575
New Jersey, " principal unredeemed,"..................	788,681
Virginia, principal on domestic debt, an! principal and interest (£40,826) on foreign debt,.....................	3,680,743
South Carolina,.......................................	5,386,232
	$18,201,206

ing to Mr. Hildreth, amounted to twenty five or twenty-six million dollars.) If the aggregate indebtedness were sixty-nine or seventy millions, and the whole expenditures $135,000,-000, the difference should show the amount raised, in different ways, by taxation. In another place, I have assumed the losses sustained by the holders of continental bills of credit to be equal to a tax of $53,000,000. But I have not confidence enough in the figures to proceed further in this direction.

So soon as the war was over, a spirit of speculation made its appearance. This was favored by the new fields which were opened for profitable investments, and the abundance of the precious metals. A period followed lasting till the inauguration of the new government in the spring of 1789, which was distinguished by financial disaster and great privation.

The change from war to peace—from the business of destroying to that of supporting human life—rendered necessary a great change in the industry and capital of the country. A like change, whatever the occasion, can never be abruptly made without enormous losses—losses which cannot long be concealed. At the time the states were so nearly exhausted by herculean military efforts, they were called upon to bear new burdens—to make new sacrifices. The people, seeing no end to their sufferings, naturally became discontented. Specie, for some time plentiful, had, owing to the revival of trade and the excessive importation of goods, become scarce, and the currency, so far as it was made up of coin, underwent a sharp contraction.* Then it was that the pecuniary burdens of the war were

---

Amount brought forward,..............	$18,201,206
New Hampshire, estimated,.........................	300,000
Pennsylvania, estimated,.............................	2,200,000
Maryland, estimated,................................	800,000

$21,501,206

Four of the states, it will be observed, are not mentioned, and those named may have had (as in the case of Connecticut) a larger indebtedness at the close of the war. Guided by the above statement, Mr. Hamilton thought that the whole indebtedness of all the states at that time (Jan., 1790) might amount to about $25,000,000. The state debts generally bore six per cent. interest.

* It appears from the "English custom-house books" that the imports from England in the two first years after peace, (1784 and 1785,) amounted to £5,987,-

justly appreciated. They were felt to be insupportably oppressive.[*] The impatient multitude, struggling for emancipation, cast about for objects on which to vent their rage. They complained of the continental and state governments, of unequal and unjust laws, high public salaries, extravagant court fees, the extortions of lawyers, the oft-repeated requisitions of Congress, the impost and excise taxes, and cruel exactions of every kind. They felt that they were wronged and robbed, and yet toiled on ineffectually. In their desperation, comparing their privations with their better condition during the war, they began to clamor once more for paper money. The debtor class united themselves to speculators, adventurers and gamblers in favoring this movement. The dire calamities and rank injustice which were sure to flow from the desired measure were uncared for. Men had become reckless. The moral sense was blunted, the public conscience seared—the natural effect of war and a depreciating currency. Rhode Island was the only New England State that sought a remedy for the present evils in new paper issues. A party was formed which, thoughtless of consequences, advocated this policy. It was opposed by the mercantile class, and favored, as a general rule, by the farmers. It awakened fierce passion and bitter strife, and ended in mobs and riots. At length, when the new party obtained the control of affairs, a government paper money " bank " of £100,000 was establish-

---

490, sterling, and the exports to £1,642,939, sterling, a difference of £4 341,551 sterling, which could be paid only in specie, or in bills of exchange derived from favorable balances in the trade with other countries. There are no data from which the whole trade of the United States, at that time, can be correctly estimated. See Pitkin's Statistical View of the United States, p. 30, 2d ed.

* The list of polls and estates of this State which, at the end of the war, amounted to about £2,000,000, had, in May, 1785, run down to £1,559,623 : 16 : 8, and in 1788 to £1,462,860 : 10 : 11. (In 1795, it was only £1,715,516.) A part of this great reduction was doubtless owing to the act of May, 1784, which imposed diminished taxes on live-stock ; but a part also must have been due to a pinched money market and high taxes. Industry was discouraged, agriculture contracted. There was little motive to accumulate tax-paying property. Men sold their farms and emigrated to other states. Young men forsook their occupations and took to the seas. Thus the list, as derived from polls and estates, was much reduced, and the rate of taxation correspondingly increased.

ed. the bills to be loaned on pledge of real estate, and to be receivable for continental taxes. This was in May, 1786. "The new system," says Arnold, "was more destructive in its effects upon the peace and prosperity of the State than any that had yet been attempted, and whose baleful influence was to extend far beyond the period when its name and objects had passed away."* A "forcing act" was soon necessary to compel the refractory to take the bills, and a fine of £100 was imposed for refusal. When this act was decided by the highest court to be unconstitutional, a special session of the Assembly was called, and the judges summoned to appear "to assign reasons and grounds" for their decision. Defending themselves with intrepidity, they "gave no satisfactory reason for their judgment," and were discharged. By the course she took in this matter, Rhode Island earned, as she had done before, no little infamy. Her promises soon came to be worth no more than six or eight for one of specie. The other offending states—those which yielded to the paper money pressure—were New York, New Jersey, Pennsylvania and Georgia.

In the stormy and perilous times about which I am writing, in no state did affairs wear a gloomier aspect than in Massachusetts. The unquiet, over-burdened masses, hoping little relief from the established order of things, looked to untried expedients and unauthorized measures. "No desperately indebted people," says some one, "can long endure a regular, sober government." Excited passion, breaking over legal restraints, culminated in a formidable rebellion. It made its first appearance in western Massachusetts, and was headed by one Capt. Daniel Shays. The insurgents called for sundry reforms in the state government, prevented the sessions of the courts and demanded paper money. Four thousand militia soon restored order; but men's minds were powerfully impressed with the dangers with which good government was threatened, and the utter helplessness of the Confederation.

During this critical period† Connecticut was not a disinterested

---

* History of Rhode Island, II., 519.

† In the debate on the assumption of the state debts, in the first Congress un-

spectator. Many of the people, at first a majority, sympathized with the malcontents of Massachusetts and the other states, as has been mentioned. But their "steady habits," their conservative education, their traditionary respect for the state government, taken in connection with the prompt and energetic measures of those in power, prevented any dangerous outbreak.

In the condition of things which has been described, little could be done in the way of paying the public debts. The requisitions of Congress upon the states were little heeded, the less so as they were repeated, and the unpaid interest was allowed to accumulate to a large extent. Of the sums called for from 1782 to 1786, amounting to more than six million of dollars, to meet the interest on the domestic debt, about one million only had been paid on the thirty first day of March, 1787.* The insufficient loans which Congress was able to obtain in Europe were used to pay interest on the foreign debt.† Under these circumstances, the government credit was so poor that liquidated and certified claims against it were worth no more than twelve and a half or fifteen cents on the dollar. At the time the debt was finally funded, (January first, 1791,) there had accumulated of unpaid interest, in the whole, $15,-050,884; $2,020,716 of it on the foreign, and $13,030,168 on the domestic debt. On the latter debt, there had been paid of interest, but $4,944,128‡, and this in indents.

---

der the Constitution, " Mr. Sedgwick declared that the insurrection which had just taken place in Massachusetts, was occasioned by the burden of taxes necessarily imposed on the people of that State, to pay a debt incurred merely for national purposes." The debts of Massachusetts, Connecticut and South Carolina amounted to about one half of those of all the States. See Pitkin's Polit. and Civ. Hist., II., 344, 345. Felt intimates that the debt of Massachusetts, in 1785, was £1,468,554 : 7 : 5. See Mass. Currency, p. 200.

* Pitkin's Polit. and Civ. Hist. of the United States, II., 184–5.

† There were borrowed in Europe, after the war and before the Constitution went into operation, the following sums:

In Holland by contract dated March 9, 1784, at four per cent. 2,000,000 guilders.
Do. do. June 1, 1787, at five per cent.................... 1,000,000   "
Do. do. March 13, 1788, at five per cent................ 1,000,000   "
The whole equaling, say, $1,600,000. See Appendix to the Journal of Congress.

‡ See American State Papers, Finance, Vol. I., 484.

Even before the concluding act of Maryland gave a quasi-vitality to the Confederation, statesmen had seen that, financially considered, it had fatal defects. It needed no prophet to perceive that the public creditors could not be paid—that the interest on the debt could not be discharged—that the faith and honor of the government could not be preserved—so long as Congress had no control over the wealth of the country. Without this control, no fund could be established, no security given as a basis for public credit. This fact was made apparent by the too often fruitless efforts of our commissioners to borrow money in Europe. It was signally illustrated by the peremptory refusal of the King of France, at one period, to make any further pecuniary advances. To remedy the difficulty, Congress, February third, 1781, the day after Maryland had authorized her delegates to subscribe the Articles, "recommended to the several states, as indispensably necessary, that they vest a power in Congress to levy for the use of the United States a duty of five per cent., *ad valorem*, at the time and place of importation, upon all goods, wares and merchandises of foreign growth and manufactures," excepting "articles imported on account of the United States or any of them, and wool-cards and cotton-cards, and wire for making them," &c.; "also a duty of five per cent. on all prizes and prize-goods." The moneys (when collected) were appropriated to the payment of the public debts incurred for the support of the war, and the duties were to continue till said debts were discharged. Connecticut granted the required authority without delay, but limited the operation of the law to three years after the close of the war. This was not satisfactory, and the State was called on to amend its act.* A new grant was made in January, 1782, in which the objectionable clause was removed. A harmless provision was added, intended to quiet apprehension, that no part of the moneys collected should be used " for the payment of any pensions or half-pay to discharged officers, or as a pension, gratuity, or consideration to any person or persons not then in the actual service of the United States."

---

* See Journal of Congress, March 22, 1781.

After the lapse of nearly two years, all the states had adopted the recommendation of Congress except Rhode Island. To hasten her movements, Congress, December sixth, 1782, appointed a "deputation" to visit her " for the purpose of making a just representation of the public affairs of the United States, and of urging the absolute necessity of a compliance with the resolution," &c. But just as the deputation was about to depart, news came that Virginia had withdrawn her consent to the measure. Thus hope was deferred, and good men were " deeply affected." It seemed doubtful whether the states would part with more power—whether they would ever yield up to the Confederation enough of authority to clothe it with respectability, or to prevent its downfall.

When the war at last came to an end, the minds of far-seeing men were turned anxiously to the future. It was perceived that before the young republic could hold up its head among the nations of the earth, its finances must be reformed. Madison had been a member of Congress nearly two years ; and Hamilton, aged twenty six, had recently taken his seat. These master spirits devoted their best energies to the salvation of the country, and the impost scheme was revived. On the twelfth of February, 1783, Congress agreed, by a nearly unanimous vote, to " a proposition reported by the committee of the whole," "that the establishment of permanent and adequate funds on taxes or duties * * are indispensably necessary towards doing complete justice to the public creditors," &c. After much earnest discussion, a resolution was adopted April eighteenth, 1783, asking the states to invest Congress with the power to levy a duty of five per cent., *ad valorem*, on all imported goods, except liquors, wines, teas, pepper, sugar, molasses, cocoa and coffee. The last were to pay a moderate specific duty. The moneys thus obtained were to go to discharge the interest and principal of the debts of the United States, contracted for the support of the war. The resolution also recommended that the states should establish, in the most convenient way, such "substantial and effectual revenues" as might produce, in addition to the above, $1,500,000, annually. A provision required that the collectors should, in both cases, be appointed by the states, but they were to "be amenable to and removable by the United States." This important measure required the assent of all the states, and was to continue in operation twenty five years. Hamilton voted against the resolution as it finally passed, because the plan did not concede enough to the Union; but urged its adoption by New York, partly on the ground that she was a creditor state, the debts due from the United States to her citizens very considerably exceeding the amount the latter would have to pay in taxes.* On this matter, however, a word may be said. If New York was a creditor state, she became so by way of trade or purchase, and not by her contributions for the support of the war. In this last regard she was the great debtor state, which she still continued to be. She justly owes the federal Treasury, on the old account, $1,852,036, and interest since January first, 1790.

These recommendations were sent forth, accompanied by an address to the states, prepared, it is said, by Madison, and written with considerable force. Appended to this paper were several other documents, the famous "Newburgh Addresses," so called, the argumentative letter of Hamilton, intended to answer the objections of Rhode Island to the former revenue scheme, &c.†

This measure, estimated to produce about $2,416,000, and sadly defective in some particulars, did not meet with a very flattering reception. Peace had returned, the outward pressure was gone, and little interest, comparatively, attached to the central government. Congress was thinly attended. Some of the best men had left it, and gone home to look after their respective state sovereignties. There was dissatisfaction with several of its acts, and a jealousy of its power. Under these circircumstances, its plan for raising a revenue gave rise to much opposition and prolonged debate. Connecticut was violently agitated. Though the great influence of Gov. Trumbull and his Council were on the side of Congress, its scheme, at two different sessions of the General Assembly, was rejected, "through

---

* Life of Hamilton, II., 186, 2d edition.
† See Journal of Congress, April 29, 1783.

the votes, principally, of farmers and mechanics," who supposed the burden of the taxes would rest on themselves. The question became mingled with several others hardly less exciting—questions relating to " commutation pay," the powers of Congress, " the order of the Cincinnati," and the system of state taxation. " These matters shook the State, politically, from one end to the other more fiercely than it had ever been shaken before, and the excitement was intense."* The Lower House of the Assembly, in a petition to Congress, remonstrated against the powers exercised, and the policy pursued by that body. At length, however, passion and prejudice were softened, and the storm abated. The arguments, the resolution and influence of Gov. Trumbull and the federal party were able to control events. On the twentieth day of May, 1784, the popular branch of the Assembly, by a vote of ninety-three yeas to forty-two nays, passed an act levying the proposed duty on imports,† but ignoring the "supplementary " tax, designed to raise $132,091, Connecticut's proportion of the $1,500,000. Notwithstanding this law did not grant all that was asked, it was considered, at that time, a great triumph for the Union. But the authorities of the State did not cease to cherish their political privileges. Those constitutional or chartered rights which had been watched over with jealous care for more than a century, and for the permanent security of which an eight years' war had been waged, were not to be yielded up without a struggle.

After waiting impatiently for nearly three years, a committee of Congress reported (February fifteenth, 1786) that two states only, Delaware and North Carolina had agreed to the revenue scheme presented for their consideration, in all its parts; though in the case of the former, the plan was not to go into operation till the other states had made similar grants. Six states, New Hampshire, Massachusetts, Connecticut, New Jersey, Virginia and South Carolina, had passed laws complying with the impost part of the scheme, but not with the other portion. Pennsylvania had done as much, and made a show of doing more, but attached a proviso to the act. Rhode Isl-

---

* Stuart's Life of Jonathan Trumbull, Sen., p. 632. † Ibid. 644.

and had passed a law, but it did not conform to any part of the plan recommended. Maryland, New York and Georgia had enacted nothing "in pursuance of the system of April, 1783." In this gloomy condition of affairs, Congress did its whole duty ; and once more earnestly commended the subject to the attention of the hesitating states, warning them "that the most fatal evils will inevitably flow from a breach of the public faith, pledged by solemn contract," &c.   As there seemed little prospect of securing the adoption of the "supplementary" part of the scheme—that which pledged an internal revenue—they were willing to accept such state action as secured to the government the duties on imports.   The Treasury was empty, and the calls upon it most pressing.   The entire receipts from taxes between November first, 1781, and January first, 1786, amounted but to $2,457,987, a sum insufficient to pay the interest on the public debt for a single year, to say nothing of the ordinary charges of the government.   During the latter portion of the time, there had been received, on the average, only $371,052 per annum, not enough to meet the current expenses.

At length, as it regarded the tax on imports, all the states had so far yielded to the importunity of Congress that the system would go into operation when New York should adopt it. Governed by petty jealousies, and an apprehension that her commercial advantages would be interfered with by the proposed tax, she stubbornly refused her consent.   At last, however, she passed a law on the subject ; but it gave to the State "the sole power of levying and collecting" the duties.   By another act, she ordered the emission of £200,000 in bills of credit, which were expressly declared to be receivable for import duties.   Her legislation was, of course, not satisfactory.   It did not comply with the recommendation of April, 1783.   Under these discouraging circumstances, Congress by resolution, August eleventh, 1786, urged the executive of New York "immediately to convene the Legislature * * for the purpose of granting the system of impost," &c., so that the same might be carried "into immediate effect."   Gov. Clinton, feeling "unhappy to be formally called on by Congress," replied that he had no power "to convene the Legislature before the time fixed by law, except *on extraordinary occasions.*" He, therefore, with " the highest deference and respect," declined.   On the receipt of his letter, Congress renewed its request in the words of the former resolution.   At the next session of the Legislature of New York, in January, 1787, the question again came up for consideration.   Hamilton, who was a member, advocated the measure with great ability ; but, on the final vote, it was rejected by a decisive majority.   This action gave the finishing blow to the Confederation.*   It had only life enough left, after naming its successor, to make arrangements for its funeral.

CHAPTER XIII.

FIRST UNITED STATES COINAGE.   CONNECTICUT COPPERS.

AFTER the war, the country suffered much from the circulation of base coin sent over from Europe, or manufactured at home.   Congress had previously (February twenty-first, 1782) proposed to establish a mint.   The Superintendent of Finance was to prepare a plan ; but nothing was done for several years.   July sixth, 1785, it was resolved " that the money unit of the United States be one dollar," and " that the several pieces shall increase in a decimal ratio."   More than a year later, August eighth, 1786, the denomination, weight and fineness of the several coins of gold, silver and copper were established, in accordance with the previous regulations.   An ordinance for a mint was passed October sixteenth following.   And as " the great quantity of base copper coin daily imported into

---

* Life of Hamilton, II., 448, 2d edition.

.or manufactured within the several states " was highly injurious, &c., it was ordained "that no foreign copper coin whatsoever should, after the first day of September, 1787, be current within the United States, and that no copper coin struck under the authority of a particular state should pass at a greater rate than one federal dollar for two pounds and one quarter, averdupois weight, of such copper coin," or at a higher rate by weight than the United States coin. The next year, April twenty-first, (1787,) the "Board of Treasury" was authorized to contract with James Jarvis for three hundred tons of copper coin, of the federal standard, to be manufactured at his own expense, he " to allow to the United States on the amount of the coin contracted for, not less than fifteen per cent." The devices on this coin, as fixed July sixth, 1787, were as follows : On one side " thirteen circles linked together, a small circle in the middle, with the words ' United States ' round it, and in the centre, the words ' We are one ;—on the other side, a dial with the hours expressed on the face of it, a meridian sun above, on one side of which is to be the word ' fugio,' and on the other, the year in figures, ' 1787 ;' below the dial, the words "Mind your business.' "

These copper "cents" were the first coins manufactured by authority of the United States, and the only ones previously to the date of the federal Constitution. They are supposed to have been struck at the " New Haven mint,"* in a building which stood immediately upon the water's edge, nearly in front, or a little to the west, of the residence of the late Harvey Hoadley, in East Water street, about which, buried in the rubbish, the boys were wont to find coppers, some forty years ago.

In a memorial dated October eighteenth, 1785, Samuel Bishop, James Hillhouse and John Goodrich, of New Haven, and Joseph Hopkins of Waterbury, applied to the Legislature of Connecticut for liberty to establish a mint for coining copper coins or coppers. "There is [they alledged] a great and very prevalent scarcity of small coins in the State," in consequence of which "great inconveniences are severely felt," particularly " by the laboring class who are the stay and staff of any com-

---

* New Am. Cyclopedia, Art. Coins, p. 441.

munity." Our late enemies and our fellow-citizens, they continued, are busy counterfeiting, &c.* The petition was granted at the same session, and the persons named were authorized to make copper coins not exceeding, in value, £10,000, lawful money, each piece to be of the value of the British half penny, and to weigh six pennyweights. They were to have " a man's head on the one side, with a circumscription in the words or letters following, (viz.): AVCTORI: CONNECT: and on the other side, the emblem of liberty, with an olive branch in her hand, with the words and figures following, (viz.): INDE: ET LIB: 1785." The grant was to continue during the pleasure of the Assembly. Of the coins stamped, one twentieth part was to go to the State, and none was to be put in circulation till inspected and approved by a committee, of which Hon. Roger Sherman, James Wadsworth and David Austin, Esquires, and Messrs. Ebenezer Chittenden and Isaac Beers were the members. They were not to be a legal tender except *for change, and for any sum not exceeding three shillings.* At the same session, an act was passed forbidding any person, without the permission of the General Assembly, to manufacture copper coins. The penalty was one hundred pounds, one half to go to the informer.

In January, 1789, Daniel Holbrook and James Wadsworth, Esquires, were appointed a committee to inquire into the conduct of those authorized to manufacture coppers, and to ascertain whether the resolution of the Assembly as to the intrinsic value of the coins, and the proportion to be paid into the Treasury of the State, had been complied with. From their report, made in May, 1789, it appears that the original grantees, November twelfth, 1785, entered into an agreement with Pierpont Edwards, Jonathan Ingersoll, Abel Buell and Elias Shipman, and formed a company by the name of the " Company for Coining Coppers." The business was carried on until about June first, 1786, when the company, unable to procure more stock, was obliged to suspend operations. In September of the same year, a lease of privileges and apparatus was given, for six weeks, to

---

* See " Miscellaneous" papers in the State Library, Vol. III., Doc. 243.

Mark Leavenworth, Esq., (afterwards a proprietor,) Isaac Baldwin and William Leavenworth, all natives and the two last residents of Waterbury. There were frequent changes of ownership. At the date of the report, April ninth, 1789, James Jarvis (who had removed from New York to New Haven) owned nine parts in sixteen, James Hillhouse, Mark Leavenworth and Abel Buell, each two parts, and John Goodrich one part. Up to about June first, 1787, when the coinage ceased, there had been inspected by the committee during the three years the mint was in operation, 28,944 pounds [avoirdupois] of coined coppers. Reckoning eighteen pieces, each weighing one hundred and forty-four grains, as equal to one shilling, (the committee's estimate,) and the whole inspected coinage would amount to £3,908 : 6 : 8. Of this amount, the State should have received 1,447$\frac{1}{8}$ pounds by weight, which "amounts to £192 : 19 : 2." But there had been paid into the Treasury only 1,386$\frac{1}{6}$ pounds, which "amounts to £184 : 16 : 2," leaving a balance due the State of 61$\frac{2}{6}$ pounds, or "£8 : 3 : 0." (There is a small error in each of the quoted sums, made in converting weight into money.)

A large amount of work was accomplished at the New Haven mint in 1787. The coins were extensively circulated. Though the dies were often poorly executed, the blanks were of excellent material.* The market seems to have been largely overstocked, and as the coppers did not contain metal enough to keep up their value as an article of commerce, a depreciation followed. As early as June, 1786, I find a merchant advertising to take them at twenty shillings the pound, or at par, payment to be made half in gold or silver, and half in goods "at lowest cash price." An aged gentleman of New Haven tells me that he remembers when they passed at four for a penny, then six for a penny. In December, 1 90, the Assembly directed that the accumulated stock in the Treasury should be sold for liquidated notes, or securities of the State, provided two shillings per pound (forty-eight pieces and six tenths weighed one pound, nearly) could be obtained. The notes, &c., mentioned had not then probably recovered from their great depres-

---

* Dickeson's Numismatic Manual, 1859, p. 103, and onward.

sion. It may have been partly in consequence of the depreciation of coppers that the manufacture was stopped in 1787.

The committee of investigation appears to have found no sufficient cause of censure in the management of the mint ; and yet the Assembly, after the report had been made, in May, 1789, ordered that those interested in the company should be notified to appear and show cause, if any they had, why the powers granted them should not cease. To give them the opportunity, their privileges were extended from the twentieth of June, 1789, to the rising of the Assembly at the October session. The reason of this procedure is doubtless to be found in the fact that the new Constitution, taking from the states the authority to coin money, had gone into operation.

Abel Buell, the master spirit in this coinage, had, at the time of the committee's report, gone to Europe, ostensibly, it is said, to purchase copper for coining, but really to obtain a knowledge of the machinery used in manufacturing cloth. Before leaving, he had given (the committee say) his son Benjamin liberty to make coppers, which business the latter was then pursuing, having just begun to stamp the coins. Abel Buell was a mechanical genius. He was born in Killingworth, and was apprenticed to Ebenezer Chittenden, a gold and silver smith. At the age of nineteen, he was married. At twenty, he altered, very ingeniously, a five shilling bill of credit to one of five pounds. For this he was, after conviction in March, 1764, punished by branding on the forehead with the letter C., cutting off the right ear, imprisonment in the Norwich jail, (he was sentenced for life,) and confiscation of estate. In view, however, of his youth and other mitigating circumstances, he was soon released on bond,—he to live in and not to leave Killingworth. In October, 1765, he asked the Assembly for liberty " to trade and deal without penalty," and to go where he pleased. His petition was refused, but in October, 1766, it was renewed. He had, he said, discovered a method of grinding and polishing crystals and other stones of great value, " the growth" of this Colony. The petition was now granted on condition that a bond be given of £200 for good behavior.

In October, 1769, Buell again addressed the Legislature. He

stated that he had discovered the art of type-founding, and asked encouragement in the form of a lottery, or in some other way, that he might erect a foundry and prosecute the business. To prove the value of the discovery, and as a specimen of his abilities, his memorial was "impressed with the types of his own manufacture." The Assembly, in accordance with the report of a committee, voted to loan him £100 for seven years, he to "set up and pursue within one year the art of lettter founding in this Colony." After twelve months, £100 more were to be loaned for seven years. Soon, (about 1770,) Mr. Buell removed to New Haven, and employed for his foundry the Sandemanian meeting house in Gregson street, and employed fifteen or twenty boys in making types. Not much came of the undertaking, however, and the business seems soon to have been abandoned. Soon after, he was engaged with Bernard Romans in constructing a map of North America, and visited Pensacola to make a survey of the coast. He was arrested for attempting to break the Governor's seal and to open a letter, but escaped. The map was engraved by Mr. Buell and Amos Doolittle, of New Haven, and published during the war. It is stated, erroneously, to have been the first map engraved and published in this country. In August, 1777, "said Buell having wholly failed to set up and practice the art [of type-founding], and since become insolvent and is absconded," &c., the Assembly voted to accept from Mrs. Aletta Buell, of New Haven, the wife of Abel, the one hundred pounds, "which she had procured with the utmost difficulty," and to discharge the £200 bond held by the State.*

At length, Mr. Buell became connected with the company for coining coppers, as we have seen. He is reported to have invented machinery which turned out one hundred and twenty pieces per minute. He lived in a house on Chapel street, fronting the Green, the land being described in a mortgage deed to Henry Whitney, of Derby, dated August sixteenth,

* See State Archives, "Industry," Vol. II. What I have said concerning Mr. Buell's inventions, and also of his efforts to obtain his liberty, has been derived chiefly from this volume. Most of these documents, with others relating to "early American inventions," are printed in the Patent Office Report for 1850-51.

1784, as running back forty feet—" bounded north by the Green twenty feet, east by highway through the glebe land, west by land leased to Ebenezer Chittenden, south by land leased to the said grantor, which land was leased to the said grantor by Christ's church for ninety-nine years, renewable at pleasure, for eight pence half penny a foot for the forty foot, by the year."* At a later period, there was " a shop or building adjoining the south end of the dwelling house," which, January twenty-first, 1789, Buell deeded to James Jarvis, of New Haven, to secure a note for one hundred and fifty pounds.†

When Mr. Buell returned from England to this country, he brought with him a Scotchman by the name of M'Intosh. They erected a cotton mill in Westville, (New Haven,) one of the first in this country. Afterward, Buell removed to Hartford, thence to Stockbridge, Massachusetts. Finally, about 1825, he returned to New Haven, and soon. after died in the almshouse.‡

In 1785, a mint for coining coppers was established in Rupert, Vermont. In 1787, cents were made in Boston, Massachusetts.

I have hitherto had no convenient opportunity to refer to certain copper coins, of private manufacture, struck in Granby in this State, in 1737. They are known as " Higley's coppers," and are supposed to have been made (from a rude set of dies) by Dr. Samuel Higley, who, a few years before, had attempted to manufacture steel. The copper used was dug in Granby, and is of excellent quality, being much sought by jewelers for mixing with gold. The coins were circulated in Connecticut and New England, but have now nearly disappeared.

---

* Land Records, Vol. XLI., p. 160.

† *Ibid.*, Vol. XLIII., p. 349.

‡ Many of the facts contained in the preceding sketch of Buell's life—those relating to the places of his birth and death, his apprenticeship and marriage, his removals, his concern in the map of North America, and in the cotton mill at Westville, his visit to Pensacola, the place where he made types, and the number of coppers which his machine turned out—have been derived from Barber's Connecticut Historical Collections. (See Killingworth, p. 531.) Mr. Barber states that his information came from Mr. William Storer, watch maker, who died in New Haven a few years ago.

There is one in the cabinet of the Connecticut Historical Society, bearing the date of 1737, with " I am good copper," on one side ; " Value me as you please," on the other.*

CHAPTER XIV.

THE CONSTITUTION AND PAPER MONEY. THE PUBLIC DEBT FUNDED: BANKS CHARTERED.

THE feebleness of the Confederation was very much due to its financial inability. Those who sought a change, desired a government which, by its own authority, could tax the people, and command the wealth of the country. Another object to be secured was protection from the evils of a paper currency. There was, at the time the Convention assembled in Philadelphia in May, 1787, " for the sole and express purpose of revising the Articles of Confederation," a general outcry against the recent legislation of Rhode Island (then called *Rogues*' Island) perpetuating the paper money nuisance. Reflecting the popular feeling, the wits of " The Anarchiad " satirized the State. When her government refused to appoint delegates, and stood aloof from the Convention for the avowed reason that she apprehended some interference with her right to issue bills of credit, the indignation felt was not diminished. In the " Constitution " which was finally (September seventeenth, 1787) adopted, the power "to coin money, emit bills of credit, make anything but gold and silver coin a tender in payment of debts," was wisely taken from the states. At the same time, the general government was authorized " to coin money, regulate the value thereof and of foreign coin, and fix the standard of weights and measures." In the first draft of the

---

* See Phelps' History of Simsbury, p. 118, and Prime's Coins, Medals and Seals, p. 72.

Constitution, the power was granted to emit bills of credit,—
" to borrow money, and emit bills, on the credit of the United
States "—but objections were made, and debate ensued. " Mr.
Ellsworth thought this a favorable moment to shut and bar
the door against paper money." Mr. Madison was " satisfied
that striking out the words would not disable the government
from the use of public notes, as far as they could be safe and
proper, and would only cut off the pretext for a *paper currency,* and particularly for making the bills a tender either for
public or private debts."* In conclusion, the clause authorizing the emission of bills of credit was stricken out, nine states,
to wit: New Hampshire, Massachusetts, Connecticut, Pennsylvania, Delaware, Virginia, North Carolina, South Carolina
and Georgia, voting in favor, and two states, New Jersey and
Maryland, against the motion. Thus to prevent the abuse of
a power which a few members thought might be useful, in
certain emergencies, the proposed grant was withheld altogether. In this manner, " the authority of Congress was confined to borrowing money on the credit of the United States,
which [power] appears to have been intended to include the
issuing of government notes not transferable as currency."†
The original proposition was not objected to on the ground
that it might justify a tender law, for no one appears to
have suspected that such a law could, under any circumstances, grow out of it. To a candid mind, it would seem clear
that the framers of the Constitution *meant*, in the words of
Ellsworth, " to shut and bar the door against [government]
paper money," and particularly, to prevent, in the language of
Madison, " making the bills a tender either for public or private
debts." Until recently, it has been supposed—admitted—that
the Constitution gave us the amplest security against the
mighty evils which flow from a depreciated, legal tender currency. But the safeguards upon which we once relied have
been swept away, and we are now repeating (in a financial
sense) revolutionary history.

* Madison Papers, III., p. 1346, note.
† See Curtis' History of the Constitution, II., pp. 330, 364.

In January, 1790, Hamilton, the first Secretary of the Treasury under the Constitution, presented to Congress his famous plan for funding and paying the public debt. It was by this time largely increased, principally from unpaid interest, and amounted to more than $54,000,000. Provision was made for the whole by act of Congress, August fourth, 1790. By this act, the foreign debt was a preferred claim. It was to be paid in full, principal and interest, and a loan was authorized, not to exceed $12,000,000, for that end. The " domestic debt," so called, consisting of loan office certificates, reduced to specie value in accordance with the scale of Congress, bills of credit at one hundred for one, and sundry other obligations, fared differently. Two-thirds of the principal of the debt thus made up was to bear six per cent. annual interest from and after the first day of January, 1791; the other third, six per cent. from and after the year 1800. The stock issued for arrears of interest was to draw three per cent. from January first, 1791. By the same act, state debts to the extent of $21,500,000 were assumed and apportioned, Connecticut's allowance being $1,600,000.* Some states, however, were not able to present claims equal to their proportions, and the whole stock was not issued for the special purpose for which it was designed. But the amount was swelled by certain

* The following is the apportionment. See Laws of the United States; Act approved, Aug. 4, 1790.

New Hampshire,	$300,000
Massachusetts,	4,000,000
Rhode Island,	200,000
Connecticut,	1,600,000
New York,	1,200,000
New Jersey,	800,000
Pennsylvania,	2,200,000
Delaware,	200,000
Maryland,	800,000
Virginia,	3,500,000
North Carolina,	4,000,000
South Carolina,	2,400,000
Georgia,	300,000

$21,500,000

balances found due to some of the states on a final settlement
of accounts between them and the United States.* On the
score of balances, or advances beyond her proportion, Connecticut had a credit of $619,121. Of the stock issued for
state debts and revolutionary balances, principal and interest,

---

* A board of three commissioners was appointed to adjust these accounts on
"the principles of general equity." They were to debit each state with all advances made by the United States, with interest to the last day of the year
1789; and to credit each for its disbursements and advances with interest to the
same date. This done, they were to strike the balance due to each state, find
the aggregate of the balances, and then apportion the same between the states,
agreeably to that provision of the Constitution which relates to representation
and direct taxes. "The difference between such apportionments and the respective balances shall be carried, [so said the law,] in a new account, to the debit
or credit of the states respectively." Thus certain states became creditors of the
government to the extent in all of $3,517,584, and others debtors to an equal
amount, as appears from the report of the commissioners made in 1793.

The following tables distinguish those states which had advanced more
than their proportions for the support of the war, from those states which had
paid less. It is derived from Pitkin's United States, II., 538.

CREDITOR STATES.

New Hampshire,	$75,055
Massachusetts,	1,248,801
Rhode Island,	299,611
Connecticut,	619,121
New Jersey,	49,030
South Carolina,	1,205,978
Georgia,	19,988
	$3,517,584

DEBTOR STATES.

New York,	$2,074,846
Pennsylvania,	76,709
Delaware,	612,428
Maryland,	151,640
Virginia,	100,879
North Carolina,	501,082
	$3,517,584

The balances found due *to* the United States, with the exception of a small
amount ($222,810) allowed to New York for expenditures on state fortifications
were never paid! When, after several years' delay, a member of Congress proposed to seize the United States stocks held by New York, for payment, the state
Legislature, then in session, ordered their immediate sale!

four-ninths were to bear an interest of six per cent. from the first day of January, 1792, three ninths, of three per cent. from the same date, and two-ninths, of six per cent. from January first, 1800.   According to a statement of the Secretary of the Treasury, Oliver Wolcott, Jr., December twenty-ninth, 1796, "the entire debt of the United States, on the first day of January, 1791, including the assumed debt and the balances due the creditor states, as the same has been settled and funded," exclusive of a balance of $472,301 paid by the new government on account of the old, was as follows. (Continental bills are entered at one hundred for one, and the " new emissions " of the states at specie value :)

Foreign debt, viz:

Due in France, inclusive of $1,922,907 interest,	..$8,190,532	
Due in Holland, (interest paid,)	3,863,000	
Due to Spain, inclusive of $76,371 interest,	250,582	
Due to foreign officers, inclusive of 21,438 interest,	..209,426	
	Total Foreign debt................	$12,513,341
Domestic debt,	....$27,197,490	
Interest on do.,	13,030,168	
		40,227,659
Unliquidated claims, including continental emissions,	....	2,127,514
Assumed debt, (state debts:)		
Principal,	.........$12,181,254	
Interest,	6,090,561	
		18,271,815
State balances :		
Principal,	3,517,584	
Interest,	703,517	.
		4,221,101
	Total Foreign and Domestic debt, Jan first, 1791,...	*$77,361,429

In strictness, the $472,301 paid by the new government on account of the old, ought to be added to this account, while the interest which accrued on the state balances for four

---

* See American State Papers, Finance, Vol. I., p. 483. The general footing of the foreign debt does not correspond with the items. The mistake ($200) I have not corrected.

years after the date of the statement, at four cent. amounting to $362,813. should be deducted. This done, the debt would stand, at the period named, at $77,270,917.

Thus a debt which hung like a millstone around the neck of the Confederacy, as well as of the state governments, threatening anarchy or revolution, was finally disposed of. The foreign creditors were paid off, principal and interest, to the last farthing, by means of the loan of $12,000,000 which the President was authorized to make. The domestic creditors were obliged to compromise their claims, making a large sacrifice. The obligations they held, already reduced to specie value, were again cut down some twenty-five or thirty per cent. by the diminished or delayed interest which the government promised. They received, however, a far better security than they parted with, and were, as they had reason to be, well satisfied with the settlement. Continental certificates which, before the funding system was proposed, were sold for twelve or fifteen cents on a dollar, when converted into United States stock became at once a staunch security. "Our credit," wrote Washington, in June, 1790, (nearly two months before the law funding the debt was passed,) "has got higher than that of any nation in Europe."* A sinking fund was established, the public revenues were ample, and the debt, principal and interest, was all paid in due time. The six per cent interest-paying bonds were sold, February first, 1792, at twenty-seven and a half per cent. premium.

Connecticut was paid by the general government, on account of revolutionary expenditures, in the stocks which have been described, as follows :—

State debt assumed, principal and interest,. $1,600,000
State balance assumed, principal and interest,............$619,121
Add four per cent. annual interest for five years, commencing December 31st, 1789, according to act of Congress,.. 123,824 742,945

$2,342,945

* Writings, X., p. 98. One reason of this relatively high price of American securities will be found in the fact that the governments of Europe were, at that time, more or less involved in the uncertainties connected with the French Revolution.

This sum was sufficient to extinguish the entire indebtedness of the State which, at the time it was assumed and funded, amounted, principal and interest, to a little more than £600,000, or say, $2,002,260.08, leaving a balance in favor of the State of some $340,685.* But the amount thus provided for by the general government, it should be remembered, did not represent the entire war expenditures of Connecticut. Besides the heavy taxes which had been levied and paid during the contest, on account of the State, some £533,000 ($1,777,000) of the principal of the debt had been discharged between 1783 and 1790. In addition to this, 500,000 acres of Western lands, valued at £151,606, were afterward (May, 1792) granted to persons living on and near the Sound, who had suffered from the hostile incursions of British troops.

That part of the United States stock which was issued on account of the "state balance" was placed to the credit of the State on the books of the general government. By law, it was not transferable. In October, 1794, the Assembly authorized the holders of the remaining outstanding debt of Connecticut to bring in their claims for settlement, to wit:—(1) notes of the Treasurer computing interest to January 1st, 1795, on those bearing interest, and reducing to specie value such as are liable to liquidation; (2) Imlay's certificates† acknowledged as evidences of debt by act of October, 1793, computing interest as aforesaid; (3) interest certificates; (4) "orders of the late committee of pay-table and of the several comptrollers of public accounts, subject to liquidation when unliquidated;" (5) bills of credit of 1780, with interest according to their tenor, and bills before 1780, at the rate of forty for one. The holders of these claims were to receive, in satisfaction of the same, United States stocks, whenever Congress should enable the State to make the necessary transfers, which were not to exceed $430,-

---

* Perhaps this sum should be increased some $8,094.31. See MSS. volumes of the Comptrollers' reports in the Comptroller's office; also, Am. State Papers, Finance, I., 483.

† Wm. Imlay was Commissioner of loans of the United States for this State. His certificates were issued for that part of the loan (called the "assumed debt") which was subscribed in excess of the $1,600,000 assigned to the State.

000. The stock was soon made transferable, and, from time to time, the transfers were made. In October, 1798, a law was passed "that all state notes, interest certificates, pay-table orders, and bills of credit of this state," then outstanding, which should not, on or before the fourth day of the following March, be presented to the office of the Comptroller to be discharged by a transfer of stock, (or to be registered in said office, at the option of the holders,) should "be forever after barred and precluded from settlement and allowance," &c. In May, 1799, the time, thus limited, was extended to April first, 1800. In May, 1800, the Assembly resolved that the "holders of state notes, interest certificates, pay-table orders and bills of credit, which have been registered pursuant to the acts of October, 1798, and May, 1799, who shall present the same at the office of the Comptroller" at any time before the first day of April, 1801, shall "receive in specie for principal and interest at the rate of fourteen shillings on the pound;"* but unliquidated notes were to be first liquidated, and the holders of the bills issued before 1780 were to receive at the rate of one shilling for forty. Imlay's certificates, not mentioned by name in the laws of 1798 and 1799, were put on the same footing as state notes. The privileges secured by this resolution were afterward extended, first to June fifth, 1803, and then to June fifth, 1805.

That part of United States stock not required to meet the state indebtedness remained to the credit of the State; but as the principal was being paid off from year to year, the Comptroller was authorized, in May, 1803, to subscribe the money thus received to the several banks of the State, they consenting thereto. Thus Connecticut became an owner of bank stocks which it still continues to hold. They amounted, in 1864, to $406,000, of which $165,000 were in the Hartford Bank,

---

* I presume it was the intention of the Legislature to pay to the state creditors, under the resolution, a sum which would be equivalent, in value, to United States stocks delivered within the time prescribed by the acts of October, 1798, and May, 1799. State notes, &c., it will be observed, carried interest at the rate of six per cent., while a portion of the stocks of the United States paid but three per cent.

$122,000 in the Phœnix Bank, $59,300 in the Middletown Bank, $54,800 in the New Haven Bank, and $4,900 in the Farmers and Mechanics Bank. But they did not all come from the moneys received for United States stock.

I have pointed out the manner in which the Connecticut war debt was finally paid. It was paid not in full, nor according to the original contract. It was first reduced in conformity with the scale of depreciation adopted in October, 1780, and the principles of supposed equity. The specie value of the money or goods or services received, not the nominal and stipulated money value, was the rule of settlement. Soldiers' wages were adjusted by the same rules. The depreciation of the bills in which their wages were paid was made up to them. The state debt thus "liquidated" and adjusted was discharged in the manner stated. It did not fare quite so well as the "domestic debt" of the United States. Five-ninths of the whole, it will be remembered, bore a reduced or deferred interest. The holders of state bills, however, were much better dealt by, first and last, than those who held continental money.

After the expiration of the statute of limitations, (June fifth, 1805,) petitions were frequently presented to the Legislature for the payment of small amounts of the still outstanding public debt, including bills of credit. The sums asked for were so small, and the expense incurred and time consumed so considerable, that the Assembly, at their May session, in 1811, resolved "that the holders of state notes, interest certificates, pay-table orders and bills of credit of this State, may present such evidences of debt at the Comptroller's office, and the Comptroller is hereby directed to register the same, and to draw on the Treasurer for the amount thereof, including the interest up to the period when the statute of limitations took effect, according to the provisions heretofore made for payment of registered debt," &c. Small sums were, from time to time, brought in, and were discharged under this resolution. The Comptroller, in his annual report, continued to make a statement of the nominal public debt till 1842, at which time it amounted to $2,390.76. It had been thus reported for several years, though small amounts had been paid from time to time.

This sum embraced every description of indebtedness of revolutionary origin. The outstanding bills, issued before 1780, were estimated at $1,235.70; those emitted in 1780, at $45.87. The interest on the last named sum, which is computed down to 1805, is set down at $26.27. Judging from the number of bills which are still met with in the hands of antiquarians and others, I conclude that the above estimates are too small. It will be remembered that the amount of bills in circulation (those of 1780) at the close of the war was never ascertained with any certainty. Perhaps the number still remaining in the hands of the people is much swelled by undetected counterfeits. Since the last statement by the Comptroller, some of the bills have been redeemed under the resolution of 1811, which, as I understand it, is still in force. £9 : 10 : 0 ($31.67) in bills emitted before 1780, were registered in favor of C. A. Lay, Williamsburg, N. Y., February eighteenth, 1853. Soon after, (April twenty-eighth, 1853,) one bill of forty shillings, ($6.67,) dated June first, 1775, was registered in the name of J. P. C. Mather, of New London, then Secretary of State. These amounts are understood to have been paid in full, without the authority of law; for the resolution of 1811 required that bills of credit, &c., should be redeemed " according to the provisions heretofore made for the payment of registered debt," &c. The law of 1794 declared that the bills emitted before 1780 should be discharged at the rate of forty for one; while the resolution of 1800 provided that the holders of state notes, interest certificates, pay-table orders, and bills of credit of 1780, should " receive in specie at the rate of fourteen shillings on the pound."

In an elaborate report dated December thirteenth, 1790, Hamilton set forth the advantages of a national bank, and proposed a plan. His project met with a vigorous opposition in the House of Representatives, but was finally adopted. An act to incorporate the Bank of the United States was approved February twenty-fifth, 1791. It was to have an allowed capital of $10,000,000, in shares of $400 each, payable, one-quarter in gold and silver, and three-quarters in six per cent. interest-paying stock of the United States. When $400,000, in specie, had been paid in, it could go into operation. It might own, in property of all kinds, inclusive of its capital, $15,000,000, and might have an indebtedness, exclusive of its deposits, not exceeding $10,000,000. The corporation was forbidden to loan to the United States more than $100,000, or to any individual state more than $50,000. Nor was it permitted to lend to any foreign prince or state. It was designed to be the fiscal agent of the government, and its bills were receivable for all public dues Up to the time of the expiration of its charter, (March fourth, 1811,) and the winding up of its affairs, it was a well managed and prosperous institution.

About the period the United States Bank was incorporated and soon after, several state banks were authorized. At the May session of the Assembly of Connecticut, in 1792, the Hartford Bank was chartered with a capital of $100,000, which might be increased to $500,000, divided into shares of $400 each. No more than three-fourths of the directors, exclusive of the president, were "eligible as directors the next succeeding year." The Bank could "not trade in anything except bills of exchange, gold or silver bullion, or in the sale of goods for money lent." Nor could its "bills or notes," which must be payable on demand, amount to more than fifty per cent. of its capital stock and deposits. The State reserved the right to subscribe, at any time within one year, for thirty shares. The charter was not limited as to time, nor was any restriction imposed as to the rate of interest. At the same session, the Union Bank of New London was incorporated with a capital of $50,000, (which might be augmented to $500,000,) to be divided into one hundred dollar shares. At the next session of the Legislature in October, the New Haven Bank, the third bank in the state, was chartered. Its capital was $100,000, and its shares one hundred dollars each. In the matter of voting, there was, as in the case of the Hartford Bank and the Union Bank of New London, and of others chartered subsequently, a discrimination in favor of the small share-holders. In October, 1795, the Middletown Bank was incorporated, and in May, 1796, the Norwich Bank, each with a proviso that the act creating it might be altered or repealed at the pleasure of the Assembly. These were all the banks which were in existence in this State, at the close of the century.

www.ingramcontent.com/pod-product-compliance
Lightning Source LLC
Chambersburg PA
CBHW030900270326
41929CB00008B/508